# McGraw-Hill's

# SPANISH

-for-

# EDUCATORS

# McGraw-Hill's
# SPANISH
-for-
# EDUCATORS

**José M. Díaz and María F. Nadel**

**McGraw·Hill**

New York   Chicago   San Francisco   Lisbon   London   Madrid   Mexico City
Milan   New Delhi   San Juan   Seoul   Singapore   Sydney   Toronto

**Library of Congress Cataloging-in-Publication Data**

Díaz, José M.
  McGraw-Hill's Spanish for educators / José M. Díaz, María F. Nadel.
      p.    cm.
    ISBN 0-07-146490-5
    1. Spanish language—Conversation and phrase books (for school employees)    I. Title:
Spanish for educators.    II. Nadel, María F.    III. Title.

  PC4120.S34D53    2006
  468.3'421024371201—dc22                                     2006044421

1 2 3 4 5 6 7 8 9 0   FGR/FGR   0 9 8 7 6

ISBN 0-07-146490-5

McGraw-Hill books are available at special quantity discounts to use as premiums and
sales promotions, or for use in corporate training programs. For more information, please
write to the Director of Special Sales, Professional Publishing, McGraw-Hill, Two Penn
Plaza, New York, NY 10121-2298. Or contact your local bookstore.

This book is printed on acid-free paper.

*To Mark Nadel and Sonya Mosco*

# Contents

# 1 Information Parents Need to Enroll Their Children in School 31

## 2 The School Building  65

## 4 The Curriculum  135

# 5 Success in School: Enlisting Parental Support 187

# 6 Health, Medical Problems, and Emergencies 225

# 7 In the Counselor's Office 249

# Preface

*McGraw-Hill's Spanish for Educators* is a comprehensive, easy-to-follow book that offers the essential tools for communicating with Spanish-speaking students, parents, and school personnel. The book focuses on the aspects of school life and education about which you will most likely have to communicate with Spanish-speaking students and their parents.

Communicating in Spanish will help you establish a partnership with parents in the education of their children by demonstrating respect for and appreciation of their language and culture. It will also be a satisfying experience for you, and you can use this book as a point of departure for increasing your knowledge of the Spanish language. As your ability to understand and speak Spanish improves, you can use your knowledge to help your students improve their knowledge of English.

*McGraw-Hill's Spanish for Educators* uses standard Spanish that can be understood by any native speaker of the language. It would be impossible to cover all the regionalisms found in Spanish-speaking countries and in the United States, but once you become familiar with the vocabulary that appears in this book, you will be able to learn more from the Spanish speakers you encounter.

The book begins with an introduction to Spanish pronunciation, greetings, and grammar. Each of the seven chapters that follow includes lists of useful vocabulary and sample sentences that you will be able to start using immediately, plus relevant grammatical explanations and practice exercises.

## How to Use This Book

*McGraw-Hill's Spanish for Educators* emphasizes two main skills: listening and speaking. Although you can set to work on Chapter 1 with very little (or no) preparation, we suggest that you begin by reading the Introduction, which covers basic guidelines for Spanish pronunciation, important "grammar basics," and vocabulary and expressions essential to social interchange.

Beyond the Introduction, you can choose any topic or chapter that interests you or that is pertinent to your school situation, or you can begin with Chapter 1 and proceed through the rest of the book.

How you use this book depends on your particular situation. Are you an administrator? A counselor? A teacher? What grades do you teach? Do many students in your school work after school? Go to college? Have special needs? The answer to these and other questions—that is to say, your needs at any given time—will determine where you begin and which chapters you concentrate on.

Throughout the book, we have incorporated cultural notes, which will help you to understand salient differences between the educational system in the United States and that in many Spanish-speaking countries.

## Vocabulary

Building a large storehouse of words is important for spoken language. *McGraw-Hill's Spanish for Educators* is full of everyday words, phrases, and expressions that are useful in a school environment, and it provides an opportunity to learn words and sentences without worrying about grammar. Each chapter includes lists of useful vocabulary related to the theme of the chapter. We have used the most generic words and expressions wherever possible, since it would be impossible to include all words and expressions found in the Spanish-speaking world. Generally, we have chosen the word that is most commonly used in America. As you read through a section, it is not necessary to learn all the words presented there, but obviously the more you commit to memory, the more confident and fluent your Spanish will be. The following tips will be very helpful.

- Use the knowledge that you already have. For example, take advantage of the fact that English and Spanish share many cognates.
- Create your own personalized vocabulary by listing the words you find most useful and practicing them aloud regularly. Keep separate lists for nouns, adjectives, and verbs, and even sublists such as the following.
  - Nouns—feminine/masculine
  - Verbs—ending in **-ar**, **-er**, or **-ir**, regular verbs, irregular verbs, stem-changing verbs
  Creating such lists will not only help you to remember the words, it will help you to use them.
- Do the practice exercises carefully, check your answers, and learn the vocabulary used in them. The vocabulary practiced in the exercises was chosen for its usefulness in communicating in a school setting.
- Practice with and learn from the Spanish speakers you encounter. They can expand your knowledge and are a great source of regionalisms from their country of origin. Take advantage of their expertise.

Chapter 4 provides an extensive list of school subjects that a typical student encounters, as well as useful vocabulary in each subject area.

The English-Spanish Glossary focuses on the Spanish used in school and school-related activities. Use it for quick reference to answer the question "How do you say that in Spanish?" (**¿Cómo se dice en español?** [KOH-moh seh DEE-seh ehn ehs-pah-NYOHL]).

## Grammar

While the Introduction covers what we consider "grammar basics," other grammar points are gradually introduced as needed in the chapters. When using the grammar sections, be sure to carefully read the examples, which not only illustrate the grammar point but also show you the differences between English and Spanish, differences that don't allow word-for-word translation of sentences. Essential grammar and vocabulary are repeated throughout the book and reinforced in the examples and practice exercises.

In the Appendix, rules for conjugating regular verbs are summarized, and several important stem-changing and irregular verbs are conjugated.

Even though essential grammar points are covered in these pages, *McGraw-Hill's Spanish for Educators* is not a grammar book. It is not necessary to become confident with all the topics discussed in any grammar section before proceeding to another section of the book. It is up to you how thoroughly you want to explore a given topic; you may want to consider using a basic Spanish grammar book to supplement your knowledge.

## Pronunciation

The Introduction begins with basic guidelines for Spanish pronunciation. In addition to knowing the sounds of the letters, authentic pronunciation requires some knowledge of stress—the loudness of a syllable. To make communication easier, *McGraw-Hill's Spanish for Educators* incorporates the phonetic pronunciation of every word and phrase used in it, with the stressed syllable in CAPITAL letters.

Remember that your best source for pronunciation is the Spanish speaker with whom you are communicating. Don't hesitate to ask him or her to pronounce any word or phrase in this book. Spanish speakers are always willing to help those who try to communicate with them in Spanish. Listen to and imitate the sounds they make.

It also helps to listen to spoken Spanish every chance you get. Spanish TV newscasters are excellent models. You may want to tape sections of a program (sports, weather, or soap operas) and listen to the tape over and over. Initially, you may understand only a few words, but don't give up. Limit the time you spend listening at first, then—as you get more comfortable—increase the length of the session. You can also tape-record your own speech, then listen to the tape as a way to check your pronunciation.

In conclusion, the only way to learn a language is to use it. Take every opportunity you are given to practice, practice, and practice some more. If you wait until you can say something perfectly, you will never speak Spanish. Take chances! You will not only learn to communicate in Spanish—you will establish new relationships, cement old ones, and learn more about the world around you, here in the United States and in the Spanish-speaking world.

# Introduction to Spanish Pronunciation, Greetings, and Grammar

1

## Spanish Pronunciation

You will find that Spanish pronunciation is much more uniform than the pronunciation of English. With very few exceptions, Spanish consonants and vowels have one sound and one length. Learning the correct pronunciation of each letter in Spanish will help you to form syllables and, in turn, to form words. If you are not sure of the correct pronunciation, be sure to use body language when you are speaking. This will help you get the message across.

Some basic pronunciation guidelines follow to help you get started.

- Spanish vowel sounds are clipped and short. To help you mimic authentic pronunciation, we have added "h" (not pronounced) after the vowels *a, e,* and *o* ("ah," "eh," "oh"). The vowels *i* and *u* are represented by "ee" and "oo" in the pronunciation.
- Spanish consonants are not pronounced as strongly as English consonants and are never followed by the "h" sound that often follows English consonants.
- Each Spanish word of more than one syllable has a syllable that is stressed. The stressed syllable appears in CAPITALS in the pronunciation.
- Spanish *b* and *v* are both pronounced like a weak English "b."
- Spanish *c* (before *a, o,* or *u*) and *qu* (before *e* or *i*) are pronounced like English "k."
- Spanish *c* (before *e* or *i*) and *z* (in all positions) are pronounced like English "s."
- Spanish *ch* is pronounced like the "ch" in "church."
- Spanish *g* (before *e* or *i*) and *j* (in all positions) are pronounced like a very strong English "h."
- When Spanish *h* appears at the beginning of a syllable, it is silent.
- Spanish *ll* is pronounced like the "y" in "yes."
- Spanish *ñ* is pronounced like the "ny" in "canyon."
- Spanish *rr* and *r* (at the beginning of a word or after *l, n,* or *s*) are strongly trilled.

In this book, Spanish words, expressions, and sentences in text are followed by their pronunciation in square brackets, as shown here: **yo** [yoh].

## Greetings, Introductions, and Leave-Taking Expressions

As you begin to learn Spanish, there are some expressions that are key to greeting, introducing yourself, and getting to know the Spanish-speaking parents, students, and support staff in your school.

While you are studying these expressions, note that Spanish has both a formal and an informal way to address a person. If you are talking to someone older, someone you are meeting for the first time, or someone in a position of leadership, you should use **usted (Ud.)** [oos-TEHD]. After knowing the person for a while, or after they ask you to address them informally, you may use the **tú** [too] form. Keep in mind that in some Spanish-speaking countries, parents and children use **usted** [oos-TEHD] to address each other. In some countries, parents use the **usted** [oos-TEHD] form to make a statement more forceful. When you address a student, you will normally use the **tú** [too] form, but at times—such as to emphasize the serious nature of what you are saying—you may use the **usted** [oos-TEHD] form when addressing him/her.

Practice the following expressions by saying them aloud.

| | |
|---|---|
| Good morning. | **Buenos días.**<br>BWEH-nohs DEE-ahs |
| Good afternoon. | **Buenas tardes.**<br>BWEH-nahs TAHR-dehs |
| Good evening. / Good night. | **Buenas noches.**<br>BWEH-nahs NOH-chehs |
| Hi. / Hello. | **Hola.**<br>OH-lah |

If you want to introduce yourself, there are a couple of ways to do this in Spanish.

| | |
|---|---|
| My name is _____. | **Me llamo _____.**<br>meh YAH-moh |
| I am Mr. _____. | **Soy el señor _____.**<br>SOH-ee ehl seh-NYOHR |
| I am Mrs. _____. | **Soy la señora _____.**<br>SOH-ee lah seh-NYOH-rah |
| I am Miss/Ms. _____. | **Soy la señorita _____.**<br>SOH-ee lah seh-nyoh-REE-tah |
| I am the (English) teacher. (*male*) | **Soy el maestro de (inglés).**<br>SOH-ee ehl mah-EHS-troh deh (een-GLEHS) |
| I am the (Spanish) teacher. (*female*) | **Soy la maestra de (español).**<br>SOH-ee lah mah-EHS-trah deh (ehs-pah-NYOHL) |

If you want to introduce someone in Spanish, you may use the following pattern.

| | |
|---|---|
| This is (Pablo). (*male*) | **Este es (Pablo).**<br>EHS-teh ehs (PAH-bloh) |
| This is (Ana). (*female*) | **Esta es (Ana).**<br>EHS-tah ehs (AH-nah) |
| May I introduce (Pepe). | **Quisiera presentarle a (Pepe).**<br>kee-SYEH-rah preh-sehn-TAHR-leh ah<br>(PEH-peh) |
| | **Le presento a (Pepe).**<br>leh preh-SEHN-toh ah (PEH-peh) |

If you are the person being introduced, you may respond with any of the following expressions.

| | |
|---|---|
| A pleasure. | **Mucho gusto.**<br>MOO-choh GOOS-toh |
| The pleasure is mine. | **El gusto es mío.**<br>ehl GOOS-toh ehs MEE-oh |
| It is a pleasure meeting you (*male*). | **Es un placer conocerlo.**<br>ehs oon plah-SEHR koh-noh-SEHR-loh |
| It is a pleasure meeting you (*female*). | **Es un placer conocerla.**<br>ehs oon plah-SEHR koh-noh-SEHR-lah |

In Spanish, when you are talking *about* a teacher or other person with a title, you use the definite article (**el, la, los, las** [ehl, lah, lohs, lahs]) with the title, for example, **señor** [seh-NYOHR], **profesor** [proh-feh-SOHR], **doctor** [dohk-TOHR], followed by the person's last name.

| | |
|---|---|
| Mr./Mrs. Pérez | **el señor / la señora Pérez**<br>ehl seh-NYOHR / lah seh-NYOH-rah<br>PEH-rehs |
| Doctor Wahl | **el doctor / la doctora Wahl**<br>ehl dohk-TOHR / lah dohk-TOH-rah Wahl |
| Professor Smith | **el profesor / la profesora Smith**<br>ehl proh-feh-SOHR / lah proh-feh-SOH-rah<br>Smith |
| Mrs. Moore is the math teacher. | **La señora Moore es la maestra de matemáticas.**<br>lah seh-NYOH-rah Moore ehs<br>lah mah-EHS-trah deh<br>mah-teh-MAH-tee-kahs |

When you are addressing someone *directly*, do not use the definite article with the title.

| | |
|---|---|
| Mr. Pérez, where is your daughter today? | **Señor Pérez, ¿dónde está su hija hoy?**<br>seh-NYOHR PEH-rehs, DOHN-deh ehs-TAH soo EE-hah OH-ee |

There are several ways to express "good-bye" in Spanish. Here are some of the most common ones.

| | |
|---|---|
| Good-bye. | **Adiós.**<br>ah-DYOHS |
| Have a nice day! | **¡Qué te vaya bien!** (*informal*)<br>keh teh BAH-yah byehn |
| | **¡Qué le vaya bien!** (*formal*)<br>keh leh BAH-yah byehn |
| See you (on) Monday. | **Hasta el lunes.**<br>AHS-tah ehl LOO-nehs |
| See you (on) Tuesday. | **Hasta el martes.**<br>AHS-tah ehl MAHR-tehs |
| See you (on) Wednesday. | **Hasta el miércoles.**<br>AHS-tah ehl MYEHR-koh-lehs |
| See you (on) Thursday. | **Hasta el jueves.**<br>AHS-tah ehl HWEH-behs |
| See you (on) Friday. | **Hasta el viernes.**<br>AHS-tah ehl BYEHR-nehs |
| See you (on) Saturday. | **Hasta el sábado.**<br>AHS-tah ehl SAH-bah-doh |
| See you (on) Sunday. | **Hasta el domingo.**<br>AHS-tah ehl doh-MEEN-goh |

As you can see, you can use **hasta** [AHS-tah], meaning "until," with a time expression to indicate when you will see that person. Here are a few other common expressions.

| | |
|---|---|
| See you later. | **Hasta luego.**<br>AHS-tah LWEH-goh |
| See you soon. | **Hasta pronto.**<br>AHS-tah PROHN-toh |
| See you tomorrow. | **Hasta mañana.**<br>AHS-tah mah-NYAH-nah |

| See you next week. | **Hasta la semana próxima.** |
| | AHS-tah lah seh-MAH-nah |
| | PROHK-see-mah |
| See you next month. | **Hasta el mes próximo.** |
| | AHS-tah ehl mehs PROHK-see-moh |
| See you next year. | **Hasta el año próximo.** |
| | AHS-tah ehl AH-nyoh PROHK-see-moh |

To ask about someone's well-being, you may use the following questions.

| How are you? | **¿Cómo estás tú?** |
| | KOH-moh ehs-TAHS too |
| | **¿Cómo está usted?** |
| | KOH-moh ehs-TAH OOS-TEHD |
| How is it going? | **¿Cómo te va?** |
| | KOH-moh teh bah |

Here are some typical responses.

| I am fine, thanks. And you? | **Estoy bien, gracias. ¿Y tú? /¿Y Ud.?** |
| | ehs-TOH-ee byehn, GRAH-syahs. |
| | ee too / ee OOS-TEHD |
| Very well. | **Muy bien.** |
| | MOO-ee byehn |
| So-so. | **Regular.** |
| | rreh-goo-LAHR |
| | **Así, así.** |
| | ah-SEE, ah-SEE |

**¿Qué tal?** [keh tahl] is a more informal way to find out how someone is doing. It is perhaps equivalent to the English "What's up?" You may respond to it with the expressions you have already learned.

Many Spanish speakers use two last names. The first name is usually followed by the paternal last name, then by the maternal last name, for example, **Diego Orozco Velásquez** [DYEH-goh oh-ROHS-koh beh-LAHS-kehs]. Some women take their husband's last name, but retain their maiden name. In this case they use **de** [deh] before the husband's last name, for example, **Ana Loyola de Rivero** [AH-nah loh-YOH-lah deh rree-BEH-roh]. This custom is beginning to disappear, but it is still common.

## Practice I-1

*Write in Spanish what you would say in each of the following situations.*

1. You have just met the parents of one of your students, and you want them to meet your student teacher. Introduce him/her.

   _____

2. You have met the mother of one of your students. During Parents' Night you are introduced to the father. What do you say?

   _____

3. At the end of Parents' Night, you want to say good-bye to the parents. What do you say?

   _____

4. Introduce yourself to the mother of one of your students.

   _____

5. It is Friday, and one of your students is leaving the classroom. Tell him/her that you will see him/her on Monday.

   _____

6. You have made an appointment with the parents of one of your students. They are supposed to come back next week. Tell them that you will see them then.

   _____

7. Find out how one of your students is doing.

   _____

8. You are not feeling well and one of your students asks you how you are. How do you respond?

   _____

9. While walking down the hall, one of your students says "**¿Qué tal?**" to you. How do you respond?

   _____

10. Tell one of your students to have a nice day.

    _____

## Grammar Basics

### Subject Pronouns

When you hear Spanish being spoken, you will be able to know about whom the person is speaking if you pay attention to the ending of the Spanish verb. You will find that Spanish speakers often leave out the subject pronouns. If you are a beginner, however, you should use the subject pronouns until you become familiar with the different endings. Then if by any chance you make a mistake on a particular verb ending, the listener will know about whom you are talking.

The subject pronouns are as follows.

| | | |
|---|---|---|
| I | **yo** | yoh |
| you (*informal*) | **tú** | too |
| he | **él** | ehl |
| she | **ella** | EH-yah |
| you (*formal*) | **usted (Ud.)** | oos-TEHD |
| we | **nosotros** | noh-SOH-trohs |
| we (*all females*) | **nosotras** | noh-SOH-trahs |
| they | **ellos** | EH-yohs |
| they (*all females*) | **ellas** | EH-yahs |
| you (*plural*) | **ustedes (Uds.)** | oos-TEH-dehs |

In this book we will be using both the **tú** [too] and the **usted (Ud.)** [oos-TEHD] forms, depending on whom you are addressing. When you are talking to more than one person, use the formal **ustedes (Uds.)** [oos-TEH-dehs] form. The plural familiar form (**vosotros/vosotras** [boh-SOH-trohs/boh-SOH-trahs]), is not included here because it is rarely used in Latin America.

### Verbs

Information about the conjugation of present tense verbs is included here to provide familiarity with basic verb forms as you begin your study, as is a short explanation of command forms. Discussion of the different categories of irregular verbs appears throughout the text, with the conjugations of the most common irregular verbs—identified as (*irreg.*) in verb lists—included in the Appendix.

### Present Tense

**Meanings and Uses of the Present Tense**   The present tense in Spanish can have more than one translation in English.

| ENGLISH MEANINGS | SPANISH |
|---|---|
| I walk very little.<br>I am walking very little.<br>I do walk very little. | **Yo camino muy poco.**<br>yoh kah-MEE-noh MOO-ee POH-koh |

It can also be used in the following ways.

- To ask for instructions

  Shall I buy the book?　　　　**¿Compro el libro?**
  　　　　　　　　　　　　　　KOHM-proh ehl LEE-broh

- To refer to what will happen in the near future

  I'll go out tomorrow.　　　　**Salgo mañana.**
  　　　　　　　　　　　　　　SAHL-goh mah-NYAH-nah

  I'm running tomorrow.　　　　**Corro mañana.**
  　　　　　　　　　　　　　　KOH-rroh mah-NYAH-nah

In the set of examples above, the word "tomorrow" (**mañana** [mah-NYAH-nah]) makes it clear that the verb expresses a future action. In Chapter 5, pages 197–198, you will find a list of words and expressions that are useful when talking about the future.

When talking about what you do, are doing, or will do in the near future, use the present tense.

| | |
|---|---|
| We arrive at school early. | **Nosotros llegamos a la escuela temprano.**<br>noh-SOH-trohs yeh-GAH-mohs ah lah ehs-KWEH-lah tehm-PRAH-noh |
| I am reading a novel. | **Yo leo una novela.**<br>yoh LEH-oh OO-nah noh-BEH-lah |
| She will erase the chalkboard later. | **Ella borra la pizarra más tarde.**<br>EH-yah BOH-rrah lah pee-SAH-rrah mahs TAHR-deh |

**Regular Verbs**  English infinitives include the word "to" with the verb. Spanish infinitives have one of three endings: **-ar**, **-er**, or **-ir**. To form the present tense of a regular Spanish verb, drop the infinitive ending (**-ar**, **-er**, **-ir**) and add the following endings to the verb's stem (the part that remains when you remove the infinitive ending).

- Verbs ending in **-ar**

| PRONOUN | VERB ENDING |
|---------|-------------|
| yo | -o |
| tú | -as |
| él | -a |
| ella | -a |
| Ud. | -a |
| nosotros | -amos |
| nosotras | -amos |
| ellos | -an |
| ellas | -an |
| Uds. | -an |

**estudiar** [ehs-too-DYAHR]  to study

| I study | **yo estudio** | yoh ehs-TOO-dyoh |
|---------|----------------|-------------------|
| you study | **tú estudias** | too ehs-TOO-dyahs |
| he studies | **él estudia** | ehl ehs-TOO-dyah |
| she studies | **ella estudia** | EH-yah ehs-TOO-dyah |
| you study | **Ud. estudia** | oos-TEHD ehs-TOO-dyah |
| we study | **nosotros estudiamos** | noh-SOH-trohs ehs-too-DYAH-mohs |
| we study | **nosotras estudiamos** | noh-SOH-trahs ehs-too-DYAH-mohs |
| they study | **ellos estudian** | EH-yohs ehs-TOO-dyahn |
| they study | **ellas estudian** | EH-yahs ehs-TOO-dyahn |
| you (*plural*) study | **Uds. estudian** | oos-TEH-dehs ehs-TOO-dyahn |

- Verbs ending in **-er**

| PRONOUN | VERB ENDING |
|---------|-------------|
| yo | -o |
| tú | -es |
| él | -e |
| ella | -e |
| Ud. | -e |
| nosotros | -emos |
| nosotras | -emos |
| ellos | -en |
| ellas | -en |
| Uds. | -en |

**correr** [koh-RREHR]  to run

| I run | yo corro | yoh KOH-rroh |
|---|---|---|
| you run | tú corres | too KOH-rrehs |
| he runs | él corre | ehl KOH-rreh |
| she runs | ella corre | EH-yah KOH-rreh |
| you run | Ud. corre | OOS-TEHD KOH-rreh |
| we run | nosotros corremos | noh-SOH-trohs koh-RREH-mohs |
| we run | nosotras corremos | noh-SOH-trahs koh-RREH-mohs |
| they run | ellos corren | EH-yohs KOH-rrehn |
| they run | ellas corren | EH-yahs KOH-rrehn |
| you (*plural*) run | Uds. corren | OOS-TEH-dehs KOH-rrehn |

- Verbs ending in **-ir**

| PRONOUN | VERB ENDING |
|---|---|
| **yo** | -o |
| **tú** | -es |
| **él** | -e |
| **ella** | -e |
| **Ud.** | -e |
| **nosotros** | -imos |
| **nosotras** | -imos |
| **ellos** | -en |
| **ellas** | -en |
| **Uds.** | -en |

**escribir** [ehs-kree-BEER]  to write

| I run | yo escribo | yoh ehs-KREE-boh |
|---|---|---|
| you run | tú escribes | too ehs-KREE-behs |
| he runs | él escribe | ehl ehs-KREE-beh |
| she runs | ella escribe | EH-yah ehs-KREE-beh |
| you run | Ud. escribe | OOS-TEHD ehs-KREE-beh |
| we run | nosotros escribimos | noh-SOH-trohs ehs-kree-BEE-mohs |
| we run | nosotras escribimos | noh-SOH-trahs ehs-kree-BEE-mohs |
| they run | ellos escriben | EH-yohs ehs-KREE-behn |
| they run | ellas escriben | EH-yahs ehs-KREE-behn |
| you (*plural*) run | Uds. escriben | OOS-TEH-dehs ehs-KREE-behn |

## Practice I-2

**A** Determine all possible subjects of each verb below and write them in Spanish on the lines provided. There may be more than one answer for some items.

1. estudiamos    _____

2. corre    _____

3. escriben    _____

4. estudias    _____

5. escribo    _____

6. corren    _____

**B** Conjugate each of the following regular verbs according to the subject given. These verbs may be new to you, so you will need to pay attention to the verb endings.

1. comprender

    ellos _____

    yo _____

    nosotros _____

2. recibir

    tú _____

    Uds. _____

    ella _____

3. terminar

    yo _____

    Ud. _____

    nosotras _____

**C** Translate the conjugated verbs from Exercise B.

1. _____

    _____

    _____

2. _____

    _____

    _____

3. _____

_____

_____

**D** *Write all of the possible translations for the following sentences.*

1. Escribo una novela.

_____

2. ¿Estudias muy poco?

_____

3. Corremos en el parque mañana.

_____

**Verbs with Special Changes**  In this section you will learn about changes that need to be made to the stem of some verbs in order to conjugate them in the present tense. In the present tense, changes to the stem of these verbs occur in all persons except the **nosotros** [noh-SOH-trohs] and **nosotras** [noh-SOH-trahs] form. The three patterns of stem changes are shown below.

- e > ie
- o > ue
- e > i

In this book, the infinitive form in vocabulary lists will be followed by **(ie)**, **(ue)**, or **(i)** to indicate which stem change is needed, as shown here.

| | | |
|---|---|---|
| to close | **cerrar (ie)** | seh-RRAHR |
| to sleep | **dormir (ue)** | dohr-MEER |
| to serve | **servir (i)** | sehr-BEER |

**cerrar (ie)** [seh-RRAHR]  to close

| I close | **yo cierro** | yoh SYEH-rroh |
|---|---|---|
| you close | **tú cierras** | too SYEH-rrahs |
| he closes | **él cierra** | ehl SYEH-rrah |
| she closes | **ella cierra** | EH-yah SYEH-rrah |
| you close | **Ud. cierra** | oos-TEHD SYEH-rrah |
| we close | **nosotros cerramos** | noh-SOH-trohs seh-RRAH-mohs |
| we close | **nosotras cerramos** | noh-SOH-trahs seh-RRAH-mohs |
| they close | **ellos cierran** | EH-yohs SYEH-rrahn |
| they close | **ellas cierran** | EH-yahs SYEH-rrahn |
| you (*plural*) close | **Uds. cierran** | oos-TEH-dehs SYEH-rrahn |

## dormir (ue) [dohr-MEER] to sleep

| I sleep | yo duermo | yoh DWEHR-moh |
| you sleep | tú duermes | too DWEHR-mehs |
| he sleeps | él duerme | ehl DWEHR-meh |
| she sleeps | ella duerme | EH-yah DWEHR-meh |
| you sleep | Ud. duerme | OOS-TEHD DWEHR-meh |
| we sleep | nosotros dormimos | noh-SOH-trohs dohr-MEE-mohs |
| we sleep | nosotras dormimos | noh-SOH-trahs dohr-MEE-mohs |
| they sleep | ellos duermen | EH-yohs DWEHR-mehn |
| they sleep | ellas duermen | EH-yahs DWEHR-mehn |
| you (plural) sleep | Uds. duermen | OOS-TEH-dehs DWEHR-mehn |

## servir (i) [sehr-BEER] to serve

| I serve | yo sirvo | yoh SEER-boh |
| you serve | tú sirves | too SEER-behs |
| he serves | él sirve | ehl SEER-beh |
| she serves | ella sirve | EH-yah SEER-beh |
| you serve | Ud. sirve | OOS-TEHD SEER-beh |
| we serve | nosotros servimos | noh-SOH-trohs sehr-BEE-mohs |
| we serve | nosotras servimos | noh-SOH-trahs sehr-BEE-mohs |
| they serve | ellos sirven | EH-yohs SEER-behn |
| they serve | ellas sirven | EH-yahs SEER-behn |
| you (plural) serve | Uds. sirven | OOS-TEH-dehs SEER-behn |

Some of the most common verbs in each category are listed below.

### e > ie

| to begin | comenzar | koh-mehn-SAHR |
| to begin | empezar | ehm-peh-SAHR |
| to lose | perder | pehr-DEHR |
| to recommend | recomendar | rreh-koh-mehn-DAHR |
| to think | pensar | pehn-SAHR |
| to understand | entender | ehn-tehn-DEHR |

### o > ue

| to be able | poder | poh-DEHR |
| to cost | costar | kohs-TAHR |
| to count, tell | contar | kohn-TAHR |
| to die | morir | moh-REER |
| to eat lunch | almorzar | ahl-mohr-SAHR |
| to find | encontrar | ehn-kohn-TRAHR |
| to play | jugar (u>ue) | hoo-GAHR |
| to remember | recordar | rreh-kohr-DAHR |
| to return, give back | devolver | deh-bohl-BEHR |

| to return, go back | **volver** | bohl-BEHR |
| to show | **demostrar** | deh-mohs-TRAHR |

**e > i**

| to dress | **vestir** | behs-TEER |
| to repeat | **repetir** | rreh-peh-TEER |
| to request, ask for | **pedir** | peh-DEER |

## Practice I-3

**A** *Write the correct form of each of the following verbs according to the subject given.*

1. (cerrar)     ellos _____

2. (volver)     nosotros _____

3. (vestir)     tú _____

4. (servir)     yo _____

5. (dormir)     nosotras _____

6. (pensar)     ella _____

7. (encontrar)  Uds. _____

8. (jugar)      él _____

9. (pedir)      nosotros _____

10. (comenzar)  yo _____

**B** *Study the verbs with special changes, then complete the translation of each of the following sentences with the correct form of the appropriate verb.*

1. *You close the door.*

   Tú _____ la puerta.

2. *They do not sleep much.*

   Ellos no _____ mucho.

3. *We serve lunch early.*

   Nosotros _____ el almuerzo temprano.

4. *She repeats the words.*

   Ella _____ las palabras.

5. *I don't understand anything.*

   Yo no _____ nada.

6. *We return all the books.*

   Nosotros _____ todos los libros.

7. *The notebook costs a lot.*

   El cuaderno _____ mucho.

8. *We start at nine.*

   Nosotros _____ a las nueve.

9. *Do you play in the park?*

   ¿_____ Uds. en el parque?

10. *I return tomorrow.*

   Yo _____ mañana.

## Commands

**Telling Someone to Do Something (Ud./Uds.)** Spanish has only a few irregular formal command forms. Therefore, it will be easier for you to become familiar with giving commands in Spanish if you use only the **Ud./Uds.** [oos-TEHD/ oos-TEH-dehs] form for commands at first.

For all verbs that end in **-o** in the **yo** form of the present tense, the **Ud./Uds.** command is formed by removing the **-o** ending from the **yo** form of the present tense and adding endings as follows.

- For **-ar** verbs

  Add **-e** if the command is given to one person.
  Add **-en** if the command is given to more than one person.

| | |
|---|---|
| Walk slowly. *(to one person)* | **Camine Ud. despacio.**<br>kah-MEE-neh oos-TEHD dehs-PAH-syoh |
| Walk slowly. *(to more than one person)* | **Caminen Uds. despacio.**<br>kah-MEE-nehn oos-TEH-dehs dehs-PAH-syoh |

- For **-er** verbs

  Add **-a** if the command is given to one person.
  Add **-an** if the command is given to more than one person.

| | |
|---|---|
| Run fast. *(to one person)* | **Corra Ud. rápido.**<br>KOH-rrah oos-TEHD RRAH-pee-doh |
| Run fast. *(to more than one person)* | **Corran Uds. rápido.**<br>KOH-rrahn oos-TEH-dehs RRAH-pee-doh |

- For **-ir** verbs

  Add **-a** if the command is given to one person.
  Add **-an** if the command is given to more than one person.

| | |
|---|---|
| Write on the chalkboard. *(to one person)* | **Escriba Ud. en la pizarra.** ehs-KREE-bah oos-TEHD ehn lah pee-SAH-rrah |
| Write on the chalkboard. *(to more than one person)* | **Escriban Uds. en la pizarra.** ehs-KREE-bahn oos-TEH-dehs ehn lah pee-SAH-rrah |

In summary, the rules above can be used to form the formal **(Ud./Uds.** [oos-TEHD/oos-TEH-dehs]) command forms for any verb for which the **yo** [yoh] form of the present tense ends in **-o**.

| yo FORM | Ud. COMMAND | Uds. COMMAND |
|---|---|---|
| **caminar** (to walk) | | |
| **camino** kah-MEE-noh | camine kah-MEE-neh | caminen kah-MEE-nehn |
| **correr** (to run) | | |
| **corro** KOH-rroh | corra KOH-rrah | corran KOH-rrahn |
| **escribir** (to write) | | |
| **escribo** ehs-KREE-boh | escriba ehs-KREE-bah | escriban ehs-KREE-bahn |
| **hacer** (to do, make) | | |
| **hago** AH-goh | haga AH-gah | hagan AH-gahn |
| **poner** (to put) | | |
| **pongo** POHN-goh | ponga POHN-gah | pongan POHN-gahn |
| **salir** (to leave, go out) | | |
| **salgo** SAHL-goh | salga SAHL-gah | salgan SAHL-gahn |
| **traducir** (to translate) | | |
| **traduzco** trah-DOOS-koh | traduzca trah-DOOS-kah | traduzcan trah-DOOS-kahn |
| **traer** (to bring) | | |
| **traigo** TRAH-ee-goh | traiga TRAH-ee-gah | traigan TRAH-ee-gahn |
| **ver** (to see) | | |
| **veo** BEH-oh | vea BEH-ah | vean BEH-ahn |

If the **yo** form of the present tense does not end in **-o**, the command form will be irregular. The following verbs have irregular command forms.

| yo ꜰᴏʀᴍ | Ud. ᴄᴏᴍᴍᴀɴᴅ | Uds. ᴄᴏᴍᴍᴀɴᴅ |
|---|---|---|
| **dar** (to give) | | |
| **doy** | **dé** | **den** |
| DOH-ee | deh | dehn |
| **estar** (to be) | | |
| **estoy** | **esté** | **estén** |
| ehs-TOH-ee | ehs-TEH | ehs-TEHN |
| **ir** (to go) | | |
| **voy** | **vaya** | **vayan** |
| BOH-ee | BAH-yah | BAH-yahn |
| **saber** (to know) | | |
| **sé** | **sepa** | **sepan** |
| seh | SEH-pah | SEH-pahn |
| **ser** (to be) | | |
| **soy** | **sea** | **sean** |
| SOH-ee | SEH-ah | SEH-ahn |

**Telling Someone Not to Do Something (Ud./Uds.)**  When you want to tell someone *not* to do something, you use a negative formal (**Ud./Uds.** [ᴏᴏs-TEHD/ᴏᴏs-TEH-dehs]) command, which is formed by adding **no** before the affirmative formal (**Ud./Uds.**) command. The conjugated verb does not change.

| Don't sign the form. | **No firme Ud. el formulario.** |
|---|---|
| | noh FEER-meh ᴏᴏs-TEHD ehl fohr-moo-LAH-ryoh |
| Don't read the book now. | **No lea Ud. el libro ahora.** |
| | noh LEH-ah ᴏᴏs-TEHD ehl LEE-broh ah-OH-rah |
| Don't open the door. | **No abran Uds. la puerta.** |
| | noh AH-brahn ᴏᴏs-TEH-dehs lah PWEHR-tah |

## Practice I-4

**A** *Write the* **Ud.** *and* **Uds.** *command forms of the following verbs.*

|  | Usted | Ustedes |
|---|---|---|
| 1. caminar (*to walk*) | _____ | _____ |
| 2. leer (*to read*) | _____ | _____ |

|                          | **Usted** | **Ustedes** |
|--------------------------|-----------|-------------|
| 3. ir (*to go*)          | _____ | _____ |
| 4. asistir (*to attend*) | _____ | _____ |
| 5. dar (*to give*)       | _____ | _____ |
| 6. saber (*to know*)     | _____ | _____ |
| 7. estar (*to be*)       | _____ | _____ |
| 8. escuchar (*to listen*)| _____ | _____ |
| 9. ser (*to be*)         | _____ | _____ |
| 10. beber (*to drink*)   | _____ | _____ |
| 11. traducir (*to translate*) | _____ | _____ |
| 12. traer (*to bring*)   | _____ | _____ |

**B** Explain how you would make the commands in Exercise A negative. What changes would you need to make to the verb?

_____

_____

**C** Complete the following commands. Try to remember the new words that appear in the sentences.

1. *Walk quickly.*

   _____ Ud. rápido.

2. *Be good.*

   _____ (Ser) Uds. buenos.

3. *Give the homework to the teacher.*

   _____ Ud. la tarea al maestro.

4. *Go to the office.*

   _____ Uds. a la oficina.

5. *Attend the meeting.*

   _____ Ud. a la reunión.

6. *Listen to the announcements.*

   _____ Uds. los anuncios.

7. *Read the book.*

   _____ Uds. el libro.

8. *Erase the chalkboard.*

   _____ Ud. la pizarra.

9. *Run carefully.*

   _____ Ud. con cuidado.

10. *Be here on time.*

    _____ (Estar) Uds. aquí temprano.

**D** *Although you would not want to give some of the commands in Exercise C to your students, practice changing them to the negative form here.*

1. _____

2. _____

3. _____

4. _____

5. _____

6. _____

7. _____

8. _____

9. _____

10. _____

**Telling Someone to Do Something (tú)**  To tell someone to do something with the informal **tú** [too] command, you use the **él** [ehl] form of the present tense (but without including the word **él** [ehl]).

| Review the sentences. | **Repasa las oraciones.** |
|---|---|
|  | rreh-PAH-sah lahs oh-rah-SYOH-nehs |
| Understand my situation. | **Comprende mi situación.** |
|  | kohm-PREHN-deh mee see-twah-SYOHN |

Several important verbs have irregular **tú** commands.

**ser** (to be)                     **sé** [seh]
**venir** (to come)                 **ven** [behn]
**hacer** (to do)                   **haz** [ahs]
**ir** (to go)                      **ve** [beh]
**salir** (to leave, go out)        **sal** [sahl]
**poner** (to put)                  **pon** [pohn]
**decir** (to tell)                 **di** [dee]

## Practice I-5

*Complete the following sentences using the informal* **tú** *command.*

1. *Do the homework.*

   _____ la tarea.

2. *Leave now.*

   _____ ahora.

3. *Be good.*

   _____ bueno.

4. *Put the books on the shelf.*

   _____ los libros en el estante.

5. *Come early.*

   _____ temprano.

6. *Tell the truth.*

   _____ la verdad.

7. *Go with me.*

   _____ conmigo.

**Telling Someone Not to Do Something (tú)** If you want to use the informal (**tú** [too]) command to tell someone *not* to do something, use the negative **tú** [too] command, which is formed by adding **-s** to the negative **Ud.** [oos-TEHD] command.

| ENGLISH COMMAND | NEGATIVE Ud. COMMAND | NEGATIVE tú COMMAND |
|---|---|---|
| Don't eat in the hallway. | **No coma en el pasillo.** noh KOH-mah ehn ehl pah-SEE-yoh | **No comas en el pasillo.** noh KOH-mahs ehn ehl pah-SEE-yoh |
| Don't walk in the street. | **No camine en la calle.** noh kah-MEE-neh ehn lah KAH-yeh | **No camines en la calle.** noh kah-MEE-nehs ehn lah KAH-yeh |

## Practice I-6

**A** Review the affirmative and negative **tú** commands, then write the correct command form in each column. Focus on their meanings, since some of them may be new to you.

| | Affirmative **tú** | Negative **tú** |
|---|---|---|
| 1. escuchar (to listen) | _____ | _____ |
| 2. salir (to leave) | _____ | _____ |
| 3. hacer (to do) | _____ | _____ |
| 4. escribir (to write) | _____ | _____ |
| 5. ser (to be) | _____ | _____ |
| 6. comer (to eat) | _____ | _____ |
| 7. poner (to put) | _____ | _____ |
| 8. ir (to go) | _____ | _____ |

**B** Complete the following sentences with the correct **tú** command form of the verb.

1. Eat slowly.

   _____ despacio.

2. Speak louder.

   _____ más alto.

3. Don't run in the hallway.

   No _____ en el pasillo.

4. Come at three.

   _____ a las tres.

5. Don't listen to that program.

   No _____ ese programa.

6. Copy the instructions.

   _____ las instrucciones.

7. Learn all the words.

   _____ todas las palabras.

8. Bring the computer.

   _____ la computadora.

9. *Don't erase the chalkboard.*

   No _____ la pizarra.

10. *Don't open the books.*

    No _____ los libros.

11. *Repeat the answers.*

    _____ las respuestas.

12. *Don't be absent.*

    No _____ (estar) ausente.

## Asking Questions

**Questions Asking for a Yes or No Answer**  The simplest way to ask yes/no questions in Spanish is to raise the pitch of your voice at the end of the sentence.

Do you run in the park?    **¿Corres en el parque?**
                           KOH-rrehs ehn ehl PAHR-keh

You can also use the questions **¿verdad?** [behr-DAHD] or **¿no?** [noh] at the end of a statement, meaning "right?", when you want confirmation or rejection of what you have said. Again, raise the pitch of your voice when saying **¿verdad?** [behr-DAHD] or **¿no?** [noh].

You run in the park, right?    **Corres en el parque, ¿verdad?**
                               KOH-rrehs ehn ehl PAHR-keh, behr-DAHD

When answering yes/no questions, follow the patterns below.

Yes, I run in the park.         **Sí, corro en el parque.**
                                see, KOH-rroh ehn ehl PAHR-keh

No, I do not run in the park.    **No, no corro en el parque.**
                                 noh, noh KOH-rroh ehn ehl PAHR-keh

No, I walk in the park.          **No, camino en el parque.**
                                 noh, kah-MEE-noh ehn ehl PAHR-keh

Note that negative sentences in Spanish are formed by placing **no** in front of the conjugated verb.

I do not speak much in class.    **No hablo mucho en la clase.**
                                 noh AH-bloh MOO-choh ehn lah KLAH-seh

Other negative words that can be used to express negative sentences are found in Chapter 7, page 260.

## Practice I-7

**A** *Form a question from each of the following strings of words. Remember to change the infinitive to a conjugated form of the verb that agrees with the subject. The words are not given in any particular order.*

1. español / hablar / verdad / tú

   _____

2. asistir a / Uds. / la clase de física

   _____

3. en el parque / ellos / correr

   _____

4. nosotros / la tarea / terminar

   _____

5. en la clase / ella / mucho / aprender / no

   _____

**B** *Answer the questions you wrote in Exercise A as if you are the person to whom the question is addressed. Answer at least two of the questions with the negative form.*

1. _____
2. _____
3. _____
4. _____
5. _____

**Questions Asking for a Specific Piece of Information**   Use the following question words to obtain specific information.

| Where? | **¿Dónde?** |
| | DOHN-deh |
| From where? | **¿De dónde?** |
| | deh DOHN-deh |
| To where? | **¿Adónde?** |
| | ah-DOHN-deh |

| | |
|---|---|
| When? | **¿Cuándo?**<br>KWAHN-doh |
| For when? | **¿Para cuándo?**<br>PAH-rah KWAHN-doh |
| What? | **¿Qué?**<br>keh |
| With what? | **¿Con qué?**<br>kohn keh |
| For what? | **¿Para qué?**<br>PAH-rah keh |
| Who? | **¿Quién?** (*singular*)<br>kyehn |
| | **¿Quiénes?** (*plural*)<br>KYEH-nehs |
| Whose? | **¿De quién?** (*singular*)<br>deh kyehn |
| | **¿De quiénes?** (*plural*)<br>deh KYEH-nehs |
| With whom? | **¿Con quién?** (*singular*)<br>kohn kyehn |
| | **¿Con quiénes?** (*plural*)<br>kohn KYEH-nehs |
| For whom? | **¿Para quién?** (*singular*)<br>PAH-rah kyehn |
| | **¿Para quiénes?** (*plural*)<br>PAH-rah KYEH-nehs |
| Why? | **¿Por qué?**<br>pohr keh |
| How? | **¿Cómo?**<br>KOH-moh |
| How many? | **¿Cuántos? / ¿Cuántas?**<br>KWAHN-tohs / KWAHN-tahs |
| How much? | **¿Cuánto? / ¿Cuánta?**<br>KWAHN-toh / KWAHN-tah |
| Where is the principal's office? | **¿Dónde está la oficina del director / de la directora?**<br>DOHN-deh ehs-TAH lah oh-fee-SEE-nah dehl dee-rehk-TOHR / deh lah dee-rehk-TOH-rah |

| | |
|---|---|
| Where is the new student from? | **¿De dónde es el nuevo estudiante?**<br>deh DOHN-deh ehs ehl NWEH-boh<br>ehs-too-DYAHN-teh |
| (To) where are you going? | **¿Adónde va Ud.?**<br>ah-DOHN-deh bah oos-TEHD |
| When does the class begin? | **¿Cuándo empieza la clase?**<br>KWAHN-doh ehm-PYEH-sah lah KLAH-seh |
| Whose is the notebook? | **¿De quién es el cuaderno?**<br>deh kyehn ehs ehl kwah-DEHR-noh |
| Whose is the office? | **¿De quiénes es la oficina?**<br>deh KYEH-nehs ehs lah oh-fee-SEE-nah |

Note that to answer a question asking "Why?" (**¿Por qué?** [pohr keh]), you use **porque** [POHR-keh], meaning "because."

| | |
|---|---|
| Why don't you go to the meeting? | **¿Por qué no vas a la reunión?**<br>por keh noh bahs ah lah rreh-oo-NYOHN |
| Because I don't have time. | **Porque no tengo tiempo.**<br>POHR-keh noh TEHN-goh TYEHM-poh |
| With whom are you going to the party? | **¿Con quién vas a la fiesta?**<br>kohn kyehn bahs ah lah FYEHS-tah |
| I am going with you. | **Voy contigo.**<br>BOH-ee kohn-TEE-goh |

Note that in Spanish "with me" is **conmigo** [kohn-MEE-goh] and "with you" is **contigo** [kohn-TEE-goh]. Pronouns used with **con** [kohn] are listed below.

| | |
|---|---|
| **conmigo** | kohn-MEE-goh |
| **contigo** | kohn-TEE-goh |
| **con él** | kohn ehl |
| **con ella** | kohn EH-yah |
| **con Ud.** | kohn oos-TEHD |
| **con nosotros** | kohn noh-SOH-trohs |
| **con nosotras** | kohn noh-SOH-trahs |
| **con ellos** | kohn EH-yohs |
| **con ellas** | kohn EH-yahs |
| **con Uds.** | kohn oos-TEH-dehs |

## Practice I-8

**A** *Complete the following crossword puzzle.*

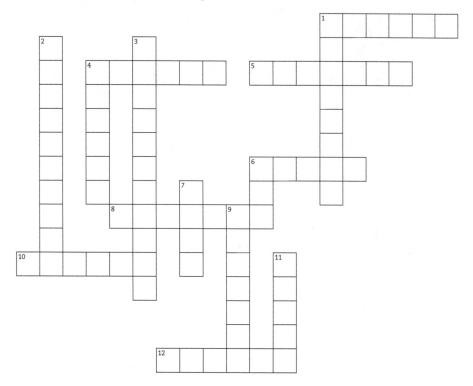

**Across**
1. when
4. how much
5. how many (*fem.*)
6. who
8. from where
10. why
12. to where

**Down**
1. with whom
2. for when
3. for whom
4. with what
6. what
7. how
9. whose
11. where

**B** Read each of the following pairs of questions and answers carefully, paying particular attention to the underlined part of the answer, which identifies the information being requested. Then write the question word needed to complete each question.

1. ¿_____ estudian?

   Elena y Juan estudian.

2. ¿_____ estudias?

   Yo estudio matemáticas.

3. ¿_____ no vas a la fiesta?

   Porque tengo un examen.

4. ¿_____ está la oficina?

   La oficina está en la calle Victoria.

5. ¿_____ es Juan?

   Juan es de Bolivia.

6. ¿_____ cuesta el libro?

   El libro cuesta cinco dólares.

7. ¿_____ es tu amigo?

   Mi amigo es Alfonso.

8. ¿_____ es la clase de inglés?

   La clase de inglés es ahora.

9. ¿_____ estás tú?

   Yo estoy bien, gracias.

10. ¿_____ vas al concierto?

    Yo voy con mis amigas.

## Summary Practice

*Each of the following sentences illustrates a situation that brings together much of what has been taught in this chapter. This summary should help you identify areas you may want to practice further. Write what you would say in Spanish in the following situations.*

1. You need to introduce your principal to a new parent.

   _____

2. You want to wish a parent a nice day.

   _____

3. Tell a student that you will see him/her next week.

   _____

4. You need to tell a parent to sign a form. [*Use the* **Ud.** *command.*]

   _____

5. Tell a student to write on the chalkboard.

   _____

6. Tell a student not to run in the hallways.

   _____

7. Ask a student where Mr. Smith is.

   _____

8. Ask a student whose book it is.

   _____

# 1

## Information Parents Need to Enroll Their Children in School

*La información que los padres necesitan para matricular a sus niños en la escuela*

31

## General Information Form

*El formulario de información*

---

**General Information**
*Información general*

Last name of the child _____ Name _____
*Apellido del niño/de la niña*            *Nombre*

Date of birth _____ Sex _____
*Fecha de nacimiento*      *Sexo*

Street address _____
*Dirección*

City _____ State _____ Zip Code _____
*Ciudad*              *Estado*      *Código postal*

Last name of the father/mother/guardian _____
*Apellido del padre/de la madre/del tutor*

Name _____
*Nombre*

Home telephone _____ Work telephone _____
*Teléfono de la casa*      *Teléfono del trabajo*

Person responsible in case of emergency _____
*Persona responsable en caso de emergencia*

Telephone number _____
*Número de teléfono*

---

## General Questions

*Las preguntas generales*

You can get almost all of the information above by asking general questions
(**las preguntas generales** [lahs preh-GOON-tahs heh-neh-RAH-lehs]) using the following pattern.

| | |
|---|---|
| What is _____? | **¿Cuál es _____?** <br> kwahl ehs |
| What is the child's date of birth? | **¿Cuál es la fecha de nacimiento del niño?** <br> kwahl ehs lah FEH-chah deh <br> nah-see-MYEHN-toh dehl NEE-nyoh |

| | |
|---|---|
| What is the phone number at work? | **¿Cuál es el número de teléfono del trabajo?**<br>kwahl ehs ehl NOO-meh-roh deh teh-LEH-foh-noh dehl trah-BAH-hoh |
| What is your address? | **¿Cuál es su dirección?**<br>kwahl ehs soo dee-rehk-SYOHN |
| In what city / state / zip code do you live? | **¿En qué ciudad / estado / código postal vive Ud.?**<br>ehn keh see-oo-DAHD / ehs-TAH-doh / KOH-dee-goh pohs-TAHL BEE-beh OOS-TEHD |

## GRAMMAR · Talking About Age

You can find out the age of a child by using the following idiomatic expression in Spanish.

| | |
|---|---|
| How old is he/she? | **¿Cuántos años tiene él/ella?**<br>KWAHN-tohs AH-nyohs TYEH-neh ehl/EH-yah |

The response, stating the age of someone, uses the following pattern.

| | |
|---|---|
| He/She is (six) years old. | **Él/Ella tiene (seis) años.**<br>ehl/EH-yah TYEH-neh (SEH-ees) AH-nyohs |

If a child is just one year old, you would express it as follows.

| | |
|---|---|
| He/She is one year old. | **Él/Ella tiene un año.**<br>ehl/EH-yah TYEH-neh oon AH-nyoh |

The idiomatic expression used to express age is one of several with the verb **tener** [teh-NEHR], meaning "to have." You will soon be introduced to more of these expressions, so it is a good idea for you to become familiar with the conjugation of the present tense of **tener**.

**tener** *(irreg.)* [teh-NEHR] to have

| | | |
|---|---|---|
| I have | **yo tengo** | yoh TEHN-goh |
| you have | **tú tienes** | too TYEH-nehs |
| he has | **él tiene** | ehl TYEH-neh |
| she has | **ella tiene** | EH-yah TYEH-neh |
| you have | **Ud. tiene** | OOS-TEHD TYEH-neh |
| we have | **nosotros tenemos** | noh-SOH-trohs teh-NEH-mohs |
| we have | **nosotras tenemos** | noh-SOH-trahs teh-NEH-mohs |
| they have | **ellos tienen** | EH-yohs TYEH-nehn |
| they have | **ellas tienen** | EH-yahs TYEH-nehn |
| you *(plural)* have | **Uds. tienen** | OOS-TEH-dehs TYEH-nehn |

Some of the other important expressions with the verb **tener** [teh-NEHR] follow. The English translation is sometimes "to feel" instead of "to be."

| | |
|---|---|
| to be (very) hungry | **tener (mucha) hambre** |
| | teh-NEHR (MOO-chah) AHM-breh |
| to be (very) thirsty | **tener (mucha) sed** |
| | teh-NEHR (MOO-chah) sehd |
| to be (very) cold | **tener (mucho) frío** |
| | teh-NEHR (MOO-choh) FREE-oh |
| to be (very) sleepy | **tener (mucho) sueño** |
| | teh-NEHR (MOO-choh) SWEH-nyoh |
| to be (very) afraid | **tener (mucho) miedo** |
| | teh-NEHR (MOO-choh) MYEH-doh |
| to be in a (big) hurry | **tener (mucha) prisa** |
| | teh-NEHR (MOO-chah) PREE-sah |
| to be (very) lucky | **tener (mucha) suerte** |
| | teh-NEHR (MOO-chah) SWEHR-teh |
| | |
| I am hungry. | **Yo tengo hambre.** |
| | yoh TEHN-goh AHM-breh |
| She feels very cold. | **Ella tiene mucho frío.** |
| | EH-yah TYEH-neh MOO-choh FREE-oh |

## Practice 1-1

*Using the English phrase in parentheses as a clue, fill in the blanks from the strings of scrambled letters below.*

1. tfnoems
   (*we are cold*)

   | e | | | o | | | r | í | |
   |---|---|---|---|---|---|---|---|---|

2. tsuieenñoe
   (*you [pl.] are sleepy*)

   | | | | | n | | | | |
   |---|---|---|---|---|---|---|---|---|

3. tuertngoe
   (*I am lucky*)

   | | e | | | | s | | | |
   |---|---|---|---|---|---|---|---|---|

4. tpiisenaes
   (*you are in a hurry*)

   | | | | | | | r | | |
   |---|---|---|---|---|---|---|---|---|

5. tamiebrne
   (*she is hungry*)

   | | | | | e | h | | | |
   |---|---|---|---|---|---|---|---|---|

6. tedees
(*we are thirsty*)

|  |  | n |  | m | o |  | s |  |  |
|---|---|---|---|---|---|---|---|---|---|

7. teidno
(*I am afraid*)

|  |  |  | g | o | m |  | e |  |  |
|---|---|---|---|---|---|---|---|---|---|

8. tinaeñdozs
(*he is ten years old*)

|  |  | e |  |  |  | i | e |  |  |  |  |
|---|---|---|---|---|---|---|---|---|---|---|---|

## Asking for More Information

*Para pedir más información*

You may also want to familiarize yourself with the following questions in order to ask for more information (**para pedir más información** [PAH-rah peh-DEER mahs een-fohr-mah-SYOHN]).

How many people live in your house?
**¿Cuántas personas viven en su casa?**
KWAHN-tahs pehr-SOH-nahs BEE-behn ehn soo KAH-sah

Do both parents live with the child?
**¿Viven ambos padres con el niño / la niña?**
BEE-behn AHM-bohs PAH-drehs kohn ehl NEE-nyoh / lah NEE-nyah

Who is the person responsible for your child?
**¿Quién está a cargo de su hijo/hija?**
kyehn ehs-TAH ah KAHR-goh deh soo EE-hoh/EE-hah

Does your child have brothers and sisters (siblings)?
**¿Tiene su hijo/hija hermanos?**
TYEH-neh soo EE-hoh/EE-hah ehr-MAH-nohs

How many brothers and sisters (siblings) does your child have?
**¿Cuántos hermanos tiene su hijo/hija?**
KWAHN-tohs ehr-MAH-nohs TYEH-neh soo EE-hoh/EE-hah

What language(s) do you speak at home?
**¿Qué lengua(s) hablan en casa?**
keh LEHN-gwah(s) AH-blahn ehn KAH-sah

Is your child attending / Has your child attended a preschool program?
**¿Asiste / Ha asistido su hijo/hija a un programa preescolar?**
ah-SEES-teh / ah ah-sees-TEE-doh soo EE-hoh/EE-hah ah oon proh-GRAH-mah preh-ehs-koh-LAHR

## Practice 1-2

*Study the questions in the General Questions section (pages 32–33) and the Asking for More Information section (page 35). Then write the appropriate question in Spanish to request the following information directly from a Spanish-speaking adult.*

1. the age of one of the students

   _____

2. a parent's address

   _____

3. if the child has any brothers and sisters

   _____

4. the child's date of birth

   _____

5. who the person responsible for the child is

   _____

6. the phone number at work

   _____

## GRAMMAR · Possessive Adjectives: my, your

You may have noticed the possessive adjective **su** [soo], meaning "your," in some of the example questions. Each subject pronoun has its equivalent possessive adjective. For now, you need only become familiar with **mi** [mee] ("my"), **tu** [too] ("your" familiar), and **su** [soo] ("your" formal). Later you will learn all the others. The plural of **mi** is **mis** [mees] ("my"), the plural of **tu** is **tus** [toos] ("your" familiar), and the plural of **su** is **sus** [soos] ("your" formal). The plural forms have nothing to do with the person or persons who possess something. Instead, you will need to use the plural form when what is possessed is plural.

| Who lives in your house? | **¿Quiénes viven en su casa?** |
| | KYEH-nehs BEE-behn ehn soo KAH-sah |
| My husband, my children, and I live in my house. | **Mi esposo, mis hijos y yo vivimos en mi casa.** |
| | mee ehs-POH-soh, mees EE-hohs ee yoh bee-BEE-mohs ehn mee KAH-sah |

For more information about possessive adjectives, see Chapter 3, page 113.

## Family Members and Relatives

*Los miembros de la familia y los parientes*

So far, you have learned how to request certain information about the child and his/her parents. Nowadays, however, a child's caretaker might be someone other than a parent—any of many family members and relatives (**los miembros de la familia y los parientes** [lohs MYEHM-brohs deh lah fah-MEE-lyah ee lohs pah-RYEHN-tehs]). Always remember the importance of family for Hispanics. In Spanish-speaking countries, there are many relatives who are considered close members of the family whom you might not consider to be part of your own immediate family.

Here is a list of family members and relatives that you will find very useful as you get to know the families with whom you work.

| aunt | **la tía** | lah TEE-ah |
|---|---|---|
| boyfriend | **el novio** | ehl NOH-byoh |
| brother | **el hermano** | ehl ehr-MAH-noh |
| brother-in-law | **el cuñado** | ehl koo-NYAH-doh |
| cousin | **el primo / la prima** | ehl PREE-moh / lah PREE-mah |
| daughter | **la hija** | lah EE-hah |
| daughter-in-law | **la nuera** | lah NWEH-rah |
| father | **el padre** | ehl PAH-dreh |
| father-in-law | **el suegro** | ehl SWEH-groh |
| girlfriend | **la novia** | lah NOH-byah |
| goddaughter | **la ahijada** | lah ah-ee-HAH-dah |
| godfather | **el padrino / el compadre** | ehl pah-DREE-noh / ehl kohm-PAH-dreh |
| godmother | **la madrina / la comadre** | lah mah-DREE-nah / lah koh-MAH-dreh |
| godson | **el ahijado** | ehl ah-ee-HAH-doh |
| granddaughter | **la nieta** | lah NYEH-tah |
| grandfather | **el abuelo** | ehl ah-BWEH-loh |
| grandmother | **la abuela** | lah ah-BWEH-lah |
| grandson | **el nieto** | ehl NYEH-toh |
| husband | **el esposo** | ehl ehs-POH-soh |
| mother | **la madre** | lah MAH-dreh |
| mother-in-law | **la suegra** | lah SWEH-grah |
| nephew | **el sobrino** | ehl soh-BREE-noh |
| niece | **la sobrina** | lah soh-BREE-nah |

| relative | **el pariente** | ehl pah-RYEHN-teh |
| sister | **la hermana** | lah ehr-MAH-nah |
| sister-in-law | **la cuñada** | lah koo-NYAH-dah |
| son | **el hijo** | ehl EE-hoh |
| son-in-law | **el yerno** | ehl YEHR-noh |
| stepbrother | **el hermanastro** | ehl ehr-mah-NAHS-troh |
| stepdaughter | **la hijastra** | lah ee-HAHS-trah |
| stepfather | **el padrastro** | ehl pah-DRAHS-troh |
| stepmother | **la madrastra** | lah mah-DRAHS-trah |
| stepsister | **la hermanastra** | lah ehr-mah-NAHS-trah |
| stepson | **el hijastro** | ehl ee-HAHS-troh |
| uncle | **el tío** | ehl TEE-oh |
| wife | **la esposa** | lah ehs-POH-sah |

Sometimes a masculine plural noun refers to both male and female persons.

| the parents | **los padres** | lohs PAH-drehs |
| the grandparents | **los abuelos** | lohs ah-BWEH-lohs |

## Practice 1-3

**A** *Find the words in the list below within the grid of letters. Words can appear horizontally, vertically, diagonally, and backwards.*

abuelo
hermanastra
madrina
padrino
suegra
ahijada
esposa
hijo
novio
pariente
compadre
hermana
madre
padrastro
prima
yerno

```
T B H E R M A N A S T R A X V
M A V G O R M G N O V I O W P
L Z E V O L E U B A E V F S A
W Y E R M O D O N I R D A P D
S E U V D D V T A U D S U O R
U R N F F A A O A O A B V M A
E N F M I U P M J H M J Z C S
G O T L A C K M I I D M E E T
R T A T H D A U O R H G S T R
A P T I D I R N H C P L P N O
R G X Y Y I Q I A L R W O E S
T W W L B J Y C N M L L S I Q
B V J E J E O B H A R Q A R R
A D A J I H A A L D U E M A K
D L X T C U Y K C W D K H P B
```

**B** *¿Quién es? Complete the following sentences with the missing word.*

1. El hermano de mi madre es mi _____.

2. La esposa de mi hermano es mi _____.

3. La madre de mi padre es mi _____.

4. El hijo de mi hermana es mi _____.

5. El _____ de mi madre es mi hermano.

6. Mi _____ es la hija de mi tío.

7. La hija de mi tío es la _____ de mi abuela.

8. Mi futura esposa es mi _____ ahora.

## GRAMMAR · Gender of Nouns and Articles

Unlike English nouns, all Spanish nouns are either masculine or feminine. In most cases, the gender of a noun has to be memorized, but here are some helpful guidelines.

- Nouns that refer to males are masculine. Example: **el hombre** [ehl OHM-breh] "the man."
- Nouns that refer to females are feminine. Example: **la mujer** [lah moo-HEHR] "the woman."
- Nouns ending in **-ista** can be either masculine or feminine. Examples: **el artista** (*male*) / **la artista** (*female*) [ehl ahr-TEES-tah / lah ahr-TEES-tah] "the artist."
- Nouns ending in **-dad, -tad, -tud, -ción,** and **-sión** are feminine. Examples: **la ciudad** [lah see-oo-DAHD] "the city," **la imaginación** [lah ee-mah-hee-nah-SYOHN] "the imagination."
- Nouns ending in **-o** are usually masculine. Example: **el cuaderno** [ehl kwah-DEHR-noh] "the notebook."
- Nouns ending in **-a** are usually feminine. Example: **la pluma** [lah PLOO-mah] "the pen."

In order to more easily remember the gender of a noun, it is helpful to learn it with its definite article. In Spanish, the article also has a masculine or feminine form, determined by the gender of the noun to which it is related. Vocabulary lists in this book always list each noun with its definite article.

## GRAMMAR · The Definite Article

The definite article has four forms in Spanish, all of which mean "the."

- Two singular forms: **el** (*masculine*) and **la** (*feminine*)
- Two plural forms: **los** (*masculine*) and **las** (*feminine*)

| | |
|---|---|
| MASCULINE SINGULAR | **el lápiz** ("the pencil") |
| | ehl LAH-pees |
| FEMININE SINGULAR | **la pizarra** ("the chalkboard") |
| | lah pee-SAH-rrah |
| MASCULINE PLURAL | **los lápices** ("the pencils") |
| | lohs LAH-pee-sehs |
| FEMININE PLURAL | **las pizarras** ("the chalkboards") |
| | lahs pee-SAH-rrahs |

In Spanish, there are two contractions formed with the definite article **el**.

- **a + el = al**

  I'm going to the gym.     **Voy al gimnasio.**
       BOH-ee ahl heem-NAH-syoh

- **de + el = del**

  It's the principal's wallet.     **Es la cartera del director.**
       ehs lah kahr-TEH-rah dehl dee-rehk-TOHR

## GRAMMAR · The Indefinite Article

The indefinite article has four forms in Spanish.

- Two singular forms: **un** (*masculine*) and **una** (*feminine*), meaning "a" or "an"
- Two plural forms: **unos** (*masculine*) and **unas** (*feminine*), meaning "some"

| | |
|---|---|
| MASCULINE SINGULAR | **un lápiz** ("a pencil") |
| | oon LAH-pees |
| FEMININE SINGULAR | **una pizarra** ("a chalkboard") |
| | oo-nah pee-SAH-rrah |
| MASCULINE PLURAL | **unos lápices** ("some pencils") |
| | oo-nohs LAH-pee-sehs |
| FEMININE PLURAL | **unas pizarras** ("some chalkboards") |
| | oo-nahs pee-SAH-rrahs |

## Nationalities

*Las nacionalidades*

Although parents are not usually asked to identify their native country, if you express an interest in knowing this information, it will show your interest in them and it can be a point of departure for a pleasant conversation.

A Hispanic family can come from any of the countries in the Spanish-speaking world. Remember that it is always a good idea to use the **usted (Ud.)** [oos-TEHD] form to address the parents; with students you may use the familiar **tú** [too] form. A conversation about nationality (**la nacionalidad** [lah nah-syoh-nah-lee-DAHD]) might include the following questions and responses.

| | |
|---|---|
| Where are you from? | **¿De dónde eres tú / es Ud.?** <br> deh DOHN-deh EH-rehs too / ehs oos-TEHD |
| I am from _____. | **Soy de _____.** <br> SOH-ee deh |
| What is your nationality? | **¿Cuál es tu/su nacionalidad?** <br> kwahl ehs too/soo <br> nah-syoh-nah-lee-DAHD |
| I am Panamanian. | **Soy panameño/panameña.** <br> SOH-ee pah-nah-MEH-nyoh/ <br> pah-nah-MEH-nyah |
| What nationality is he/she? | **¿De qué nacionalidad es él/ella?** <br> deh keh nah-syoh-nah-lee-DAHD <br> ehs ehl/EH-yah |
| He is Cuban. | **Él es cubano.** <br> ehl ehs koo-BAH-noh |
| She is Cuban. | **Ella es cubana.** <br> EH-yah ehs koo-BAH-nah |

### GRAMMAR · Using the Verb "To Be" to Express Origin

To ask about or to state the nationality of someone (or something), use the verb **ser** [sehr], meaning "to be."

The present tense of the verb **ser** [sehr] follows.

**ser** (*irreg.*) [sehr]  to be

| I am | **yo soy** | yoh SOH-ee |
|------|-----------|------------|
| you are | **tú eres** | too EH-rehs |
| he is | **él es** | ehl ehs |
| she is | **ella es** | EH-yah ehs |
| you are | **Ud. es** | oos-TEHD ehs |
| we are | **nosotros somos** | noh-SOH-trohs SOH-mohs |
| we are | **nosotras somos** | noh-SOH-trahs SOH-mohs |
| they are | **ellos son** | EH-yohs sohn |
| they are | **ellas son** | EH-yahs sohn |
| you (*plural*) are | **Uds. son** | oos-TEH-dehs sohn |

If you have an idea about where a person is from and would like to verify the information, you can also use the question that follows.

| Are you from (Chile)? | **¿Eres tú de (Chile)? / ¿Es Ud. de (Chile)?** |
|------|------|
| | EH-rehs too deh (CHEE-leh) / |
| | ehs oos-TEHD deh (CHEE-leh) |

Possible responses include the following.

| Yes, I am from (Chile). | **Sí, soy de (Chile).** |
|------|------|
| | see, SOH-ee deh (CHEE-leh) |
| No, I am not from (Chile). | **No, no soy de (Chile).** |
| | noh, noh SOH-ee deh (CHEE-leh) |
| I am from (Mexico). | **Soy de (México).** |
| | SOH-ee de (MEH-hee-koh) |
| I am (Mexican). (*male*) | **Soy (mexicano).** |
| | SOH-ee (meh-hee-KAH-noh) |
| I am (Mexican). (*female*) | **Soy (mexicana).** |
| | SOH-ee (meh-hee-KAH-nah) |

## Spanish-Speaking Countries and Nationalities

### *Los países de habla hispana y las nacionalidades*

A list of Spanish-speaking countries and nationalities (**los países de habla hispana y las nacionalidades** [lohs pah-EE-sehs deh AH-blah ees-PAH-nah ee lahs nah-syoh-nah-lee-DAH-dehs]) follows. In most cases, if you change the final -**o** of the masculine adjective denoting nationality to an -a, you will have the feminine form of the nationality. However, note that the adjective for someone from Costa Rica or from Nicaragua is the same in both the masculine and feminine forms. Also pay particular attention to the masculine and feminine forms of nationality for someone who comes from Spain.

**Argentina**
ahr-hehn-TEE-nah

**argentino / argentina**
ahr-hehn-TEE-noh / ahr-hehn-TEE-nah

**Bolivia**
boh-LEE-byah

**boliviano / boliviana**
boh-lee-BYAH-noh / boh-lee-BYAH-nah

**Chile**
CHEE-leh

**chileno / chilena**
chee-LEH-noh / chee-LEH-nah

**Colombia**
koh-LOHM-byah

**colombiano / colombiana**
koh-lohm-BYAH-noh / koh-lohm-BYAH-nah

**Costa Rica**
KOHS-tah RREE-kah

**costarricense**
kohs-tah-rree-SEHN-seh

**Cuba**
KOO-bah

**cubano / cubana**
koo-BAH-noh / koo-BAH-nah

**Ecuador**
eh-kwah-DOHR

**ecuatoriano / ecuatoriana**
eh-kwah-toh-RYAH-noh / eh-kwah-toh-RYAH-nah

**El Salvador**
ehl sahl-bah-DOHR

**salvadoreño / salvadoreña**
sahl-bah-doh-REH-nyoh / sahl-bah-doh-REH-nyah

**España**
ehs-PAH-nyah

**español / española**
ehs-pah-NYOHL / ehs-pah-NYOH-lah

**Guatemala**
gwah-teh-MAH-lah

**guatemalteco / guatemalteca**
gwah-teh-mahl-TEH-koh /
gwah-teh-mahl-TEH-kah

**Honduras**
ohn-DOO-rahs

**hondureño / hondureña**
ohn-doo-REH-nyoh / ohn-doo-REH-nyah

**México**
MEH-hee-koh

**mexicano / mexicana**
meh-hee-KAH-noh / meh-hee-KAH-nah

**Nicaragua**
nee-kah-RAH-gwah

**nicaragüense**
nee-kah-rah-GWEHN-seh

**Panamá**
pah-nah-MAH

**panameño / panameña**
pah-nah-MEH-nyoh / pah-nah-MEH-nyah

**Paraguay**
pah-rah-GWAH-ee

**paraguayo / paraguaya**
pah-rah-GWAH-yoh / pah-rah-GWAH-yah

**Perú**
peh-ROO

**peruano / peruana**
peh-RWAH-noh / peh-RWAH-nah

**Puerto Rico**
PWEHR-toh RREE-koh

**puertorriqueño / puertorriqueña**
pwehr-toh-rree-KEH-nyoh /
pwehr-toh-rree-KEH-nyah

**República Dominicana**
rreh-POO-blee-kah
doh-mee-nee-KAH-nah

**dominicano / dominicana**
doh-mee-nee-KAH-noh / doh-mee-nee-KAH-nah

| Uruguay | uruguayo / uruguaya |
|---|---|
| oo-roo-GWAH-ee | oo-roo-GWAH-yoh / oo-roo-GWAH-yah |
| **Venezuela** | **venezolano / venezolana** |
| beh-neh-SWEH-lah | beh-neh-soh-LAH-noh / beh-neh-soh-LAH-nah |

Unlike English, nationalities are not capitalized in Spanish.

## Practice 1-4

**A** Find the words in the list below within the grid of letters. Words can appear horizontally, vertically, and backwards, but not diagonally. Then fill in the blanks below with the first 20 unused letters from the grid, beginning at the top left. What sentence is spelled out?

argentina
chilena
colombiana
cubano
dominicana
ecuatoriano
guatemalteco
mexicano
panameño
peruano
puertorriqueña
venezolano

```
T O D O P A N A M E Ñ O S S O
M D O M I N I C A N A O S A M
O C E T L A M E T A U G E R I
O C A N O S E W D K A G Q N P
N F A N A I B M O L O C C A E
A R S C E E M W X D R X C Z R
L F O N A C I X E M X I H A U
O X F H B W N K N W D Y I N A
Z X F Q X Q R P V L H R L I N
E V O N A I R O T A U C E T O
N Z V V T Z G H E K L M N N S
E A O Y H C U B A N O X A E N
V X K Q B E P Y L W G D D G Y
H P B J R B E B D L T O K R B
P U E R T O R R I Q U E Ñ A P
```

\_\_ \_\_ \_\_ \_\_    \_\_ \_\_ \_\_ \_\_    \_\_ \_\_ \_\_ \_\_ \_\_ \_\_

**B** Decode the message below by determining the correct letter substitutions. Here's a hint: In the decoded message, every L becomes S and every R becomes D, as shown in the grid below.

| A | B | C | D | E | F | G | H | I | J | K | L | M | N | O | P | Q | R | S | T | U | V | W | X | Y | Z |
|---|---|---|---|---|---|---|---|---|---|---|---|---|---|---|---|---|---|---|---|---|---|---|---|---|---|
|   |   |   |   |   |   |   |   |   |   |   | S |   |   |   |   |   | D |   |   |   |   |   |   |   |   |

¿\_\_ \_\_   \_\_ \_\_ \_\_ \_\_ \_\_   \_\_ \_\_ \_\_ \_\_ ?   \_\_ \_\_ \_\_   \_\_ \_\_   \_\_ \_\_ \_\_
 R F    R J A R F    F E F L    L J I   R F   D J L

\_\_ \_\_ \_\_ \_\_ \_\_ \_\_ \_\_   \_\_ \_\_ \_\_ \_\_ \_\_ \_\_ .
F L K W R J L    X A V R J L

**C** *Form a sentence from each of the following strings of words. Remember to conjugate the verb and to change the ending of the nationality for gender agreement, if necessary.*

1. ¿? / Ud. / ser / dónde / de

   _____

2. ¿? / ser / de / tú / Colombia

   _____

3. ¿? / él / nacionalidad / de / ser / qué

   _____

4. ser / nosotras / español

   _____

5. Nicaragua / yo / ser / de

   _____

## GRAMMAR · Position and Gender of Adjectives

Unlike English adjectives, Spanish adjectives usually follow the noun, as is shown here.

the Peruvian president    **el presidente peruano**
                          ehl preh-see-DEHN-teh peh-RWAH-noh

Another important difference is that in Spanish, adjectives also have masculine and feminine forms, determined by the gender of the noun to which they are related. Here are some general guidelines for adjectives.

- Adjectives ending in **-o** in the masculine singular change the **-o** to **-a** in the feminine singular.

  the Mexican man      **el hombre mexicano**
                       ehl OHM-breh meh-hee-KAH-noh
  the Mexican woman    **la mujer mexicana**
                       lah moo-HEHR meh-hee-KAH-nah

- Most other adjectives have the same form for the masculine and the feminine.

  the intelligent man    **el hombre inteligente**
                         ehl OHM-breh een-teh-lee-HEHN-teh
  the intelligent woman  **la mujer inteligente**
                         lah moo-HEHR een-teh-lee-HEHN-teh

## Grammar · Plural of Nouns and Adjectives

For Spanish nouns, the concept of number (that is, whether the word is singular or plural) works just like it does in English. The singular form is used when referring to one person, place, or thing, and the plural form is used when referring to two or more. Unlike English, however, in Spanish the article and the adjective are also number sensitive (singular or plural).

The plurals of nouns and adjectives are formed in the following ways.

- Add **-s** to nouns and adjectives ending in a vowel.

  the black bag            **la bolsa negra**
                           lah BOHL-sah NEH-grah

  the black bags          **las bolsas negras**
                           lahs BOHL-sahs NEH-grahs

- Add **-es** to nouns and adjectives ending in a consonant.

  the easy exam          **la prueba fácil**
                           lah PRWEH-bah FAH-seel

  the easy exams        **las pruebas fáciles**
                           lahs PRWEH-bahs FAH-see-lehs

## Practice 1-5

**A** *Express the following phrases in Spanish.*

1. the Mexican girl          _____

2. the white papers        _____

3. the intelligent students    _____

4. the (*female*) Guatemalan   _____
   doctor

5. the big chalkboards       _____

6. the Cuban man             _____

**B** *Change the phrases in Exercise A to the plural if the phrase is singular and to the singular if it is plural.*

1. _____

2. _____

3. _____

4. _____

5. _____

6. _____

## Family Income

*Los ingresos de la familia*

Knowing the economic situation of a family is an important key to providing the right help to both the child and the parents. Among other things, information about family income (**los ingresos de la familia** [lohs een-GREH-sohs deh lah fah-MEE-lyah]) is necessary in order for many schools to decide if the child will receive discounted or free breakfast and/or lunch.

Here are some questions that will help you find out this information.

| | |
|---|---|
| How much money do you earn a week / a month / a year? | **¿Cuánto dinero gana Ud. a la semana / al mes / al año?**<br>KWAHN-toh dee-NEH-roh GAH-nah OOS-TEHD ah lah seh-MAH-nah / ahl mehs / ahl AH-nyoh |
| Do you have any other income? | **¿Tiene Ud. otros ingresos?**<br>TYEH-neh OOS-TEHD OH-trohs een-GREH-sohs |
| Do you receive food stamps? | **¿Recibe Ud. cupones para alimentos?**<br>rreh-SEE-beh OOS-TEHD koo-POH-nehs PAH-rah ah-lee-MEHN-tohs |

## Communication with Parents and Health Information

*La comunicación con los padres y la información sobre la salud*

The well-being of the students is crucial to their academic and social success while in school. School personnel must be familiar with any situation that may require special attention. Thus good communication with parents (**la comunicación con los padres** [lah koh-moo-nee-kah-SYOHN kohn lohs PAH-drehs]) is essential. Although the following list is not exhaustive, it includes questions about health information (**la información sobre la salud** [lah een-fohr-mah-SYOHN SOH-breh lah sah-LOOD]) that you may need to ask the students' parents.

| | |
|---|---|
| Does your child have any condition that requires special attention? | **¿Tiene su hijo/hija alguna condición que requiere atención especial?**<br>TYEH-neh soo EE-hoh/EE-hah ahl-GOO-nah kohn-dee-SYOHN keh rreh-KYEH-reh ah-tehn-SYOHN ehs-peh-SYAHL |

| | |
|---|---|
| Does he/she have problems with ...? | ¿Tiene problemas con...? TYEH-neh proh-BLEH-mahs kohn |
| eyesight | la vista lah BEES-tah |
| hearing | el oído ehl oh-EE-doh |
| speaking | el habla ehl AH-blah |
| Does he/she have ... problems? | ¿Tiene problemas...? TYEH-neh proh-BLEH-mahs |
| developmental | de desarrollo deh deh-sah-RROH-yoh |
| emotional | emocionales eh-moh-syoh-NAH-lehs |
| physical | físicos FEE-see-kohs |
| Does your child have any illness? | ¿Tiene su hijo/hija alguna enfermedad? TYEH-neh soo EE-hoh/EE-hah ahl-GOO-nah ehn-fehr-meh-DAHD |
| Is your child taking any medication? | ¿Está tomando su hijo/hija alguna medicina? ehs-TAH toh-MAHN-doh soo EE-hoh/ EE-hah ahl-GOO-nah meh-dee-SEE-nah |
| Does your child have any allergies? | ¿Tiene su hijo/hija alguna alergia? TYEH-neh soo EE-hoh/EE-hah ahl-GOO-nah ah-LEHR-hyah |
| Is he/she allergic ...? | ¿Es alérgico/alérgica...? ehs ah-LEHR-hee-koh/ah-LEHR-hee-kah |
| to antibiotics | a los antibióticos ah lohs ahn-tee-BYOH-tee-kohs |
| to aspirin | a la aspirina ah lah ahs-pee-REE-nah |
| to bee stings | a la mordedura de las abejas ah lah mohr-deh-DOO-rah deh lahs ah-BEH-hahs |
| to dust | al polvo ahl POHL-boh |
| to grass | a la hierba ah la YEHR-bah |
| to peanuts | al maní / a los cacahuetes ahl mah-NEE / ah lohs kah-kah-WEH-tehs |

| | |
|---|---|
| to pollen | **al polen** |
| | ahl POH-lehn |
| to shellfish | **a los mariscos** |
| | ah lohs mah-REES-kohs |
| Is your (*male*) child allergic to anything else? | **¿Es su hijo alérgico a otra cosa?** |
| | ehs soo EE-hoh ah-LEHR-hee-koh ah OH-trah KOH-sah |
| Is your (*female*) child allergic to anything else? | **¿Es su hija alérgica a otra cosa?** |
| | ehs soo EE-hah ah-LEHR-hee-kah ah OH-trah KOH-sah |

## The Physical Examination

### El *reconocimiento médico*

All children who attend school need to have a comprehensive physical examination (**el reconocimiento médico** [ehl rreh-koh-noh-see-MYEHN-toh MEH-dee-koh]). If complete information is not turned in to the school, the admission of the child to school may be delayed. Here are some items that must be included in the medical examination.

| | |
|---|---|
| height | **la estatura** |
| | lah ehs-tah-TOO-rah |
| weight | **el peso** |
| | ehl PEH-soh |
| blood pressure | **la tensión arterial** |
| | lah tehn-SYOHN ahr-teh-RYAHL |
| medical history | **la historia médica** |
| | lah ees-TOH-ryah MEH-dee-kah |
| nutritional evaluation | **la evaluación nutritiva** |
| | lah eh-bah-lwah-SYOHN noo-tree-TEE-bah |
| anemia screening | **el examen de anemia** |
| | ehl ehk-SAH-mehn deh ah-NEH-myah |
| dental screening | **el examen dental** |
| | ehl ehk-SAH-mehn dehn-TAHL |
| hearing screening | **el examen del oído** |
| | ehl ehk-SAH-mehn dehl oh-EE-doh |
| vision screening | **el examen de la vista** |
| | ehl ehk-SAH-mehn deh lah BEES-tah |
| developmental assessment | **la evaluación del desarrollo** |
| | lah eh-bah-lwah-SYOHN dehl deh-sah-RROH-yoh |

| lead poisoning assessment | **la evaluación de envenenamiento de plomo** |
| | lah eh-bah-lwah-SYOHN deh ehn-beh-neh-nah-MYEHN-toh deh PLOH-moh |
| tuberculosis test | **el examen de tuberculosis** |
| | ehl ehk-SAH-mehn deh too-behr-koo-LOH-sees |

## In Case of Emergency or Illness

### En caso de emergencia o enfermedad

The following questions will be helpful if you need to ask whom to contact in case of emergency or illness (**en caso de emergencia o enfermedad** [ehn KAH-soh deh eh-mehr-HEHN-syah oh ehn-fehr-meh-DAHD]).

| In case of an emergency, whom should we call? | **En caso de emergencia, ¿a quién debemos llamar?** |
| | ehn KAH-soh deh eh-mehr-HEHN-syah, ah kyehn deh-BEH-mohs yah-MAHR |
| What is his/her phone number at home / at work? | **¿Cuál es su número de teléfono en casa / en el trabajo?** |
| | kwahl ehs soo NOO-meh-roh deh teh-LEH-foh-noh ehn KAH-sah / ehn ehl trah-BAH-hoh |

## Health Insurance

### El seguro de enfermedad

In many instances it is important to know if the child has health insurance (**el seguro de enfermedad** [ehl seh-GOO-roh deh ehn-fehr-meh-DAHD]).

| Do you have health insurance? | **¿Tiene Ud. seguro de enfermedad?** |
| | TYEH-neh oos-TEHD seh-GOO-roh deh ehn-fehr-meh-DAHD |

| | |
|---|---|
| Is your (*male*) child included in the health insurance? | **¿Está incluido su hijo en su seguro de enfermedad?**<br>ehs-TAH een-kloo-EE-doh soo EE-hoh ehn soo seh-GOO-roh deh ehn-fehr-meh-DAHD |
| Is your (*female*) child included in the health insurance? | **¿Está incluida su hija en su seguro de enfermedad?**<br>ehs-TAH een-kloo-EE-dah soo EE-hah ehn soo seh-GOO-roh deh ehn-fehr-meh-DAHD |
| Do you have Medicaid? | **¿Tiene Ud. seguro de enfermedad del estado (Medicaid)?**<br>TYEH-neh oos-TEHD seh-GOO-roh deh ehn-fehr-meh-DAHD dehl ehs-TAH-doh (meh-dee-KEH-eed) |

There may be times when it is necessary to use an English word, for example, "Medicaid," since it may be the only way that parents will know what program you're asking about. For more information related to health issues, see Chapter 6.

## Proof of Residency

*Para comprobar el domicilio*

Most schools require parents to provide proof of residency (**para comprobar el domicilio** [PAH-rah kohm-proh-BAHR ehl doh-mee-SEE-lyoh]). This would include proof of the family's address, proof of the child's previous schooling, and/or proof of his/her age. You must tell the parents which documents are acceptable as proof. The following will help you express these ideas.

| | |
|---|---|
| To verify your address, you can bring … | **Para comprobar su dirección puede traer…**<br>PAH-rah kohm-proh-BAHR soo dee-rehk-SYOHN PWEH-deh trah-EHR |
| the electricity/gas/telephone bill | **la cuenta de la electricidad / del gas / del teléfono**<br>lah KWEHN-tah deh lah eh-lehk-tree-see-DAHD / dehl gahs / dehl teh-LEH-foh-noh |
| the health insurance card | **la tarjeta de su seguro de enfermedad**<br>lah tahr-HEH-tah deh soo seh-GOO-roh deh ehn-fehr-meh-DAHD |

| | |
|---|---|
| To verify your address, you can bring … | **Para comprobar su dirección puede traer…** PAH-rah kohm-proh-BAHR SOO dee-rehk-SYOHN PWEH-deh trah-EHR |
| the last income tax form | **el último formulario de declaración de impuestos** ehl OOL-tee-moh fohr-moo-LAH-ryoh deh deh-klah-rah-SYOHN deh eem-PWEHS-tohs |
| the driver's license | **la licencia de conducir** lah lee-SEHN-syah deh kohn-doo-SEER |
| To verify your child's previous schooling, you can bring a school transcript. | **Para comprobar la enseñanza previa de su hijo/hija puede traer la relación de notas de la escuela.** PAH-rah kohm-proh-BAHR lah ehn-seh-NYAHN-sah PREH-byah deh SOO EE-hoh/EE-hah PWEH-deh trah-EHR lah rreh-lah-SYOHN deh NOH-tahs deh lah ehs-KWEH-lah |
| To verify your child's age, you can bring … | **Para comprobar la edad de su hijo/hija puede traer…** PAH-rah kohm-proh-BAHR lah eh-DAHD deh SOO EE-hoh/EE-hah PWEH-deh trah-EHR |
| the child's birth certificate | **el certificado de nacimiento del niño / de la niña** ehl sehr-tee-fee-KAH-doh deh nah-see-MYEHN-toh dehl NEE-nyoh / deh lah NEE-nyah |
| the child's baptismal certificate | **el certificado de bautismo del niño / de la niña** ehl sehr-tee-fee-KAH-doh deh bah-oo-TEES-moh dehl NEE-nyoh / deh lah NEE-nyah |
| the child's passport | **el pasaporte del niño / de la niña** ehl pah-sah-POHR-teh dehl NEE-nyoh / deh lah NEE-nyah |

## Vaccinations

### Las vacunas

Students who are ready to enroll in any school must have a physical exam and proof of immunizations or vaccinations (**las vacunas** [lahs bah-KOO-nahs]) before they will be allowed to enroll in school.

| You need to bring ... | Necesita traer... |
|---|---|
| | neh-seh-SEE-tah trah-EHR |
| the last physical exam report | **el reporte del último examen físico** |
| | ehl rreh-POHR-teh dehl OOL-tee-moh ehk-SAH-mehn FEE-see-koh |
| the report showing all vaccinations | **el reporte de todas las vacunas** |
| | ehl rreh-POHR-teh deh TOH-dahs lahs bah-KOO-nahs |

## Practice 1-6

**A** *Complete each of the following sentences with the missing Spanish words, using the English cues in parentheses.*

1. ¿Tiene Ud. _____ (other income)?

2. ¿Tiene problemas con _____ (hearing)?

3. ¿Está tomando su hijo _____ (any medicine)?

4. En caso de emergencia, ¿_____ (whom should we call)?

5. ¿Tiene Ud. _____ (health insurance)?

6. Para comprobar su dirección, _____ (you can bring) la licencia de conducir.

7. Necesita traer _____ (the report showing all vaccinations).

**B** Using the English cues in parentheses, unscramble each string of letters to form a Spanish word or expression, including its definite article. Then use the numbered letters to fill in the blanks below. What does the question ask?

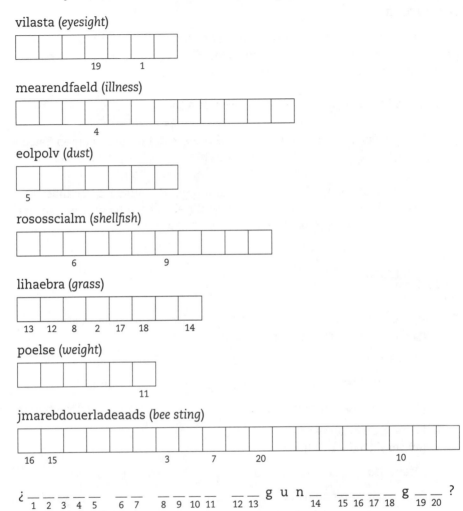

vilasta (eyesight)

| | | | | | | |
|---|---|---|---|---|---|---|
| | | | 19 | | 1 | |

mearendfaeld (illness)

| | | | | | | | | | | |
|---|---|---|---|---|---|---|---|---|---|---|
| | | | 4 | | | | | | | |

eolpolv (dust)

| | | | | | | |
|---|---|---|---|---|---|---|
| 5 | | | | | | |

rososscialm (shellfish)

| | | | | | | | | | | |
|---|---|---|---|---|---|---|---|---|---|---|
| | | 6 | | | 9 | | | | | |

lihaebra (grass)

| | | | | | | | |
|---|---|---|---|---|---|---|---|
| 13 | 12 | 8 | 2 | 17 | 18 | | 14 |

poelse (weight)

| | | | | | |
|---|---|---|---|---|---|
| | | | 11 | | |

jmarebdouerladeaads (bee sting)

| | | | | | | | | | | | | | | | | | | | |
|---|---|---|---|---|---|---|---|---|---|---|---|---|---|---|---|---|---|---|---|
| 16 | 15 | | | 3 | | 7 | | 20 | | | | | | 10 | | | | | |

¿ __ __ __ __ __   __ __   __ __ __ __   __ __ g u n __   __ __ __ __ g __ __ ?
1 2 3 4 5  6 7  8 9 10 11  12 13      14  15 16 17 18  19 20

## Traveling to School by Bus or by Car

*Para viajar a la escuela en autobús o en coche/carro*

Children often travel to school by school bus (**viajar a la escuela en autobús** [byah-HAHR ah lah ehs-KWEH-lah ehn ah-oo-toh-BOOS]) or are driven to school by car (**en coche/carro** [ehn KOH-cheh/KAH-rroh]) by their parents. The following will be helpful when communicating with parents about travel to and from school.

| | |
|---|---|
| How does your child get to school? | **¿Cómo llega su hijo/hija a la escuela?** KOH-moh YEH-gah soo EE-hoh/EE-hah ah lah ehs-KWEH-lah |
| Who brings / picks up your child? | **¿Quién trae/recoge a su hijo/hija?** kyehn TRAH-eh/rreh-KOH-heh ah soo EE-hoh/EE-hah |

A parent may have questions about travel to and from school, and may ask you questions similar to those that follow.

| | |
|---|---|
| At what time should I bring / pick up my child? | **¿A qué hora debo traer/recoger a mi hijo/hija?** ah keh OH-rah DEH-boh trah-EHR/ rreh-koh-HEHR ah mee EE-hoh/EE-hah |
| Where do I drop off / pick up my child at school? | **¿Dónde dejo/recojo a mi hijo/hija en la escuela?** DOHN-deh DEH-hoh/rreh-KOH-hoh ah mee EE-hoh/EE-hah ehn lah ehs-KWEH-lah |
| At what time does the bus leave for school / for home? | **¿A qué hora sale el autobús para la escuela / para casa?** ah keh OH-rah SAH-leh ehl ah-oo-toh-BOOS PAH-rah lah ehs-KWEH-lah / PAH-rah KAH-sah |
| How long does it take to get to school? | **¿Cuánto tiempo dura el viaje a la escuela?** KWAHN-toh TYEHM-poh DOO-rah ehl BYAH-heh ah lah ehs-KWEH-lah |
| Where does the bus pick up the children? | **¿Dónde recoge el autobús a los niños?** DOHN-deh rreh-KOH-heh ehl ah-oo-toh-BOOS ah lohs NEE-nyohs |
| Where does he/she get off the bus? | **¿Dónde se baja del autobús?** DOHN-deh seh BAH-hah dehl ah-oo-toh-BOOS |

## Verbs

| to arrive | **llegar** | yeh-GAHR |
| to get off | **bajar de** | bah-HAHR deh |
| to get on | **subir a** | soo-BEER ah |
| to leave | **salir** (*irreg.*) | sah-LEER |
| to pick up | **recoger** (*irreg.*) | rreh-koh-HEHR |
| to return | **regresar** | rreh-greh-SAHR |
| to return | **volver (ue)** | bohl-BEHR |

Older children may either take public transportation or walk to school. Here is some important advice for students when they are traveling to school.

| Get to the bus stop on time. | **Llega a tiempo a la parada.** YEH-gah ah TYEHM-poh ah lah pah-RAH-dah |
| Wait for the bus at the designated stop. | **Espera la llegada del autobús en la parada indicada.** ehs-PEH-rah lah yeh-GAH-dah dehl ah-oo-toh-BOOS ehn lah pah-RAH-dah een-dee-KAH-dah |
| Walk—don't run—when getting to or getting off the bus. | **Camina, no corras, para llegar al autobús ni tampoco al salir.** kah-MEE-nah, noh KOH-rrahs, PAH-rah yeh-GAHR ahl ah-oo-toh-BOOS nee tahm-POH-koh ahl sah-LEER |
| Don't stand near the curb. | **No te pares cerca del contén.** noh teh PAH-rehs SEHR-kah dehl kohn-TEHN |
| Don't push. | **No empujes.** noh ehm-POO-hehs |
| Stay seated. | **Manténte sentado.** mahn-TEHN-teh sehn-TAH-doh |
| Always obey the driver. | **Obedece siempre al chofer.** oh-beh-DEH-seh SYEHM-preh ahl choh-FEHR |
| Cross at the corner. | **Cruza en la esquina.** KROO-sah ehn lah ehs-KEE-nah |
| Wait for the green light. | **Espera la luz verde.** ehs-PEH-rah lah loos BEHR-deh |

| | |
|---|---|
| Wait for a signal from the driver before crossing. | **Espera la señal del chofer antes de cruzar.**<br>ehs-PEH-rah lah seh-NYAHL dehl choh-FEHR AHN-tehs deh kroo-SAHR |
| Cross at least ten feet in front of the bus. | **Cruza siempre al menos diez pies delante del autobús.**<br>KROO-sah SYEHM-preh ahl MEH-nohs dyehs pyehs deh-LAHN-teh dehl ah-oo-toh-BOOS |

Some useful words for places and things around the neighborhood (**el barrio** [ehl BAH-rryoh]) follow.

| | |
|---|---|
| alley | **el callejón**<br>ehl kah-yeh-HOHN |
| apartment building | **el edificio de apartamentos**<br>ehl eh-dee-FEE-syoh deh ah-pahr-tah-MEHN-tohs |
| avenue | **la avenida**<br>lah ah-beh-NEE-dah |
| block | **la cuadra**<br>lah KWAH-drah |
| bridge | **el puente**<br>ehl PWEHN-teh |
| building | **el edificio**<br>ehl eh-dee-FEE-syoh |
| bus stop | **la parada de autobuses**<br>lah pah-RAH-dah deh ah-oo-toh-BOO-sehs |
| corner (outside) | **la esquina**<br>lah ehs-KEE-nah |
| fence | **la cerca**<br>lah SEHR-kah |
| intersection | **la bocacalle**<br>lah boh-kah-KAH-yeh |
| sidewalk | **la acera**<br>lah ah-SEH-rah |
| sign | **el letrero**<br>ehl leh-TREH-roh |

| | |
|---|---|
| street | **la calle**<br>lah KAH-yeh |
| street light | **el farol**<br>ehl fah-ROHL |
| subway station | **la estación de metro**<br>lah ehs-tah-SYOHN deh MEH-troh |
| traffic | **el tránsito**<br>ehl TRAHN-see-toh |
| traffic sign | **la señal de tráfico**<br>lah seh-NYAHL deh TRAH-fee-koh |

## Traffic Signs

*Las señales de tráfico*

| | |
|---|---|
| one-way street | **la calle de dirección única**<br>lah KAH-yeh deh dee-rehk-SYOHN<br>oo-nee-kah |
| two-way street | **la calle de doble sentido**<br>lah KAH-yeh deh DOH-bleh sehn-TEE-doh |
| pedestrian crossing | **el paso de peatones**<br>ehl PAH-soh deh peh-ah-TOH-nehs |
| railroad crossing | **el cruce de ferrocarril**<br>ehl KROO-seh deh feh-rroh-kah-RREEL |
| school crossing sign | **la señal de cruce escolar**<br>lah seh-NYAHL deh KROO-seh<br>ehs-koh-LAHR |
| stop sign | **la señal de parar**<br>lah seh-NYAHL deh pah-RAHR |
| traffic light | **el semáforo**<br>ehl seh-MAH-foh-roh |
| Do not cross! | **¡Prohibido cruzar!**<br>proh-ee-BEE-doh kroo-SAHR |
| Do not enter! | **¡Paso prohibido!**<br>PAH-soh proh-ee-BEE-doh |
| School crossing! | **¡Cruce escolar!**<br>KROO-seh ehs-koh-LAHR |
| Stop! | **¡Pare!**<br>PAH-reh |
| Yield! | **¡Ceda!**<br>SEH-dah |

At times, a parent may ask for directions or for help getting to school or to some other place. Following are some of the things that a parent may ask or say.

| | |
|---|---|
| I am lost. | **Estoy perdido/perdida.** |
| | ehs-TOH-ee pehr-DEE-doh/pehr-DEE-dah |
| Would you tell me where _____ is? | **¿Podría decirme dónde está _____?** |
| | poh-DREE-ah deh-SEER-meh DOHN-deh |
| | ehs-TAH |
| Would you explain to me how to get to _____? | **Podría explicarme cómo llegar/ir a _____?** |
| | poh-DREE-ah ehs-plee-KAHR-meh |
| | KOH-moh yeh-GAHR/eer ah |

## GRAMMAR · Using the Verb "To Be" to Express Location

**estar** (*irreg.*) [ehs-TAHR] to be

| | | |
|---|---|---|
| I am | **yo estoy** | yoh ehs-TOH-ee |
| you are | **tú estás** | too ehs-TAHS |
| he is | **él está** | ehl ehs-TAH |
| she is | **ella está** | EH-yah ehs-TAH |
| you are | **Ud. está** | oos-TEHD ehs-TAH |
| we are | **nosotros estamos** | noh-SOH-trohs ehs-TAH-mohs |
| we are | **nosotras estamos** | noh-SOH-trahs ehs-TAH-mohs |
| they are | **ellos están** | EH-yohs ehs-TAHN |
| they are | **ellas están** | EH-yahs ehs-TAHN |
| you (*plural*) are | **Uds. están** | oos-TEH-dehs ehs-TAHN |

To tell where something (or someone) is located, use the verb **estar** [ehs-TAHR], meaning "to be," + the location.

| | |
|---|---|
| It is ... | **Está...** |
| | ehs-TAH |
| at the intersection of | **en el cruce de** |
| | ehn ehl KROO-seh deh |
| down the street | **calle abajo** |
| | KAH-yeh ah-BAH-hoh |
| facing | **frente a** |
| | FREHN-teh ah |
| far away | **lejos (de aquí)** |
| | LEH-hohs (deh ah-KEE) |
| nearby | **cerca (de aquí)** |
| | SEHR-kah (deh ah-KEE) |

| It is ... | Está...<br>ehs-TAH |
|---|---|
| (four) minutes away | **a (cuatro) minutos**<br>ah (KWAH-troh) mee-NOO-tohs |
| (five) blocks away | **a (cinco) cuadras**<br>ah (SEEN-koh) KWAH-drahs |
| in the next block | **en la próxima cuadra**<br>ehn lah PROHK-see-mah KWAH-drah |
| on the corner | **en la esquina**<br>ehn lah ehs-KEE-nah |
| to the east | **al este**<br>ahl EHS-teh |
| to the north | **al norte**<br>ahl NOHR-teh |
| to the south | **al sur**<br>ahl soor |
| to the west | **al oeste**<br>ahl oh-EHS-teh |
| up the street | **calle arriba**<br>KAH-yeh ah-RREE-bah |

For more expressions indicating location, see Chapter 2, pages 77–78.

## Practice 1-7

**A** *Find the words in the list below within the grid of letters. Words can appear horizontally, vertically, or diagonally.*

acera
avenida
calle
callejón
cuadra
edificio
esquina
fuente
manzana
puente
rascacielos
vitrina

```
L Y X Z B P J C U I G X F Q X
F S C S W J O I C I F I D E V
U A C E R A A E B N K Y P R N
E A W E I E C V E A N S A E K
N R R I M T T M E J U B W W T
T D N A D L K N I N A V D M J
E A V O S Y S J E E I I G G J
D U I A J C Y V A U H D G G E
E C T X K E A S D N P S A V L
F D R U C H L C N W I B W U L
D S I J D U N L I G P U D N A
C U N O C Z H B A E S H Q G C
K J A B K C M N J C L I Y S X
A N A Z N A M J C C Y O U N E
H O Q C I M G O W M K Y S D T
```

**B**  *Complete the following crossword puzzle.*

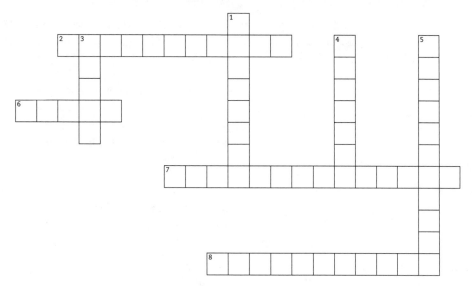

**Across**
2. at the intersection of
6. west
7. pedestrian crossing
8. nearby

**Down**
1. traffic light
3. north
4. facing
5. far from here

**C**  *While on a bus trip, you need to give some instructions to your students. What would you say to them? Review the **Ud./Uds.** command forms, and write the correct command for each instruction given.*

1. to wait for the green light

   _____

2. to get on the bus

   _____

3. not to push

   _____

4. to walk, not run

   _____

5. not to shout

   _____

## Grammar · Expressing What Someone Has to Do

To tell someone what he or she has to do, use the pattern "you have to" + infinitive (**Ud. tiene que** [oos-TEHD TYEH-neh keh] or **tú tienes que** [too TYEH-nehs keh] + infinitive).

| | |
|---|---|
| You have to cross at the corner. | **Ud. tiene que cruzar en la esquina.** |
| | oos-TEHD TYEH-neh keh kroo-SAHR ehn lah ehs-KEE-nah |
| | **Tú tienes que cruzar en la esquina.** |
| | too TYEH-nehs keh kroo-SAHR ehn lah ehs-KEE-nah |

For the present tense of the verb **tener**, see page 33 in this chapter.

When giving instructions to someone traveling on foot, you can use the following expressions.

| | |
|---|---|
| You have to … | **Usted tiene que…** |
| | oos-TEHD TYEH-neh keh |
| | **Tú tienes que…** |
| | too TYEH-nehs keh |
| continue straight ahead | **seguir derecho** |
| | seh-GEER deh-REH-choh |
| cross | **cruzar** |
| | kroo-SAHR |
| go up to | **ir hasta** |
| | eer AHS-tah |
| go down to | **bajar hasta** |
| | bah-HAHR AHS-tah |
| turn right | **doblar a la derecha** |
| | doh-BLAHR ah lah deh-REH-chah |
| turn left | **doblar a la izquierda** |
| | doh-BLAHR ah lah ees-KYEHR-dah |

If someone is taking public transportation, use the following expressions.

| You should take ... | **Ud. debe tomar...** |
|---|---|
| | OOS-TEHD DEH-beh toh-MAHR |
| | **Tú debes tomar...** |
| | too DEH-behs toh-MAHR |
| the bus | **el autobús** |
| | ehl ah-oo-toh-BOOS |
| the (a) cab | **el (un) taxi** |
| | ehl (oon) TAHK-see |
| the train/subway | **el tren/metro** |
| | ehl trehn/MEH-troh |
| You should get off at _____. | **Ud. debe bajarse en _____.** |
| | OOS-TEHD DEH-beh bah-HAHR-seh ehn |

## Practice 1-8

*To complete the following exercise, write the correct form of the verb **tener** in the first blank. Then, using the English cues in parentheses, choose the correct expression from the list below and write it in the second blank.*

| | |
|---|---|
| ir hasta la esquina | llegar a tiempo a la parada |
| doblar a la izquierda | cruzar la calle |
| esperar la luz verde | tomar el metro |
| doblar a la derecha | |

1. Juan, _____ (tú) que _____.
   (cross the street)

2. Nosotros _____ que _____.
   (wait for the green light)

3. Ellos _____ que _____.
   (get to the bus stop on time)

4. Ella _____ que _____.
   (go up to the corner)

5. Yo _____ que _____.
   (turn right)

## Summary Practice

*Using the correct form of the verb(s) in parentheses, write a sentence in Spanish that is equivalent to each of the following.*

1. Does your child have any condition that requires special attention? **(tener/requerir)**

   _____

2. How many people live in your house? **(vivir)**

   _____

3. I am in a hurry. **(tener)**

   _____

4. How old is she? **(tener)**

   _____

5. The office is two blocks away. **(estar)**

   _____

6. Where are you **(Ud.)** from? **(ser)**

   _____

7. You **(Ud.)** have to continue straight ahead. **(tener)**

   _____

8. How does your daughter get to school? **(llegar)**

   _____

9. You **(Ud.)** have to wait for the bus at the designated stop. **(tener)**

   _____

10. I am lost. **(estar)**

   _____

11. Wait **(Ud.)** for a signal from the driver before crossing. **(esperar)**

   _____

# 2

# The School Building

*La escuela*

## School Personnel/Staff

*El personal de la escuela*

Many people work in a school or in occupations that bring them into daily contact with school-age children. Here are some typical positions of school personnel (**el personal de la escuela** [ehl pehr-soh-NAHL deh lah ehs-KWEH-lah]).

| | |
|---|---|
| administrator | **el administrador / la administradora**<br>ehl ahd-mee-nees-trah-DOHR /<br>lah ahd-mee-nees-trah-DOH-rah |
| advisor | **el consejero / la consejera**<br>ehl kohn-seh-HEH-roh /<br>lah kohn-seh-HEH-rah |
| aide | **el/la asistente**<br>ehl/lah ah-sees-TEHN-teh |
| assistant principal | **el/la asistente al director / a la directora**<br>ehl/lah ah-sees-TEHN-teh<br>ahl dee-rehk-TOHR / ah lah dee-rek-TOH-rah |
| board member | **el miembro de la junta directiva**<br>ehl MYEHM-broh deh lah HOON-tah<br>dee-rehk-TEE-bah |
| bus driver | **el conductor / la conductora de autobús**<br>ehl kohn-dook-TOHR / lah kohn-dook-TOH-<br>rah deh ah-oo-toh-BOOS |
| cashier | **el cajero / la cajera**<br>ehl kah-HEH-roh / lah kah-HEH-rah |
| chairperson (of the _____ department) | **el jefe / la jefa (de la cátedra de _____)**<br>ehl HEH-feh / lah HEH-fah<br>(deh lah KAH-teh-drah deh) |
| coach (sports) | **el entrenador / la entrenadora**<br>ehl ehn-treh-nah-DOHR /<br>lah ehn-treh-nah-DOH-rah |
| cook | **el cocinero / la cocinera**<br>ehl koh-see-NEH-roh / lah koh-see-NEH-rah |
| counselor | **el consejero / la consejera**<br>ehl kohn-seh-HEH-roh /<br>lah kohn-seh-HEH-rah |
| crossing guard | **la persona encargada de ayudar a los niños a cruzar la calle**<br>lah pehr-SOH-nah ehn-kahr-GAH-dah<br>deh ah-yoo-DAHR ah lohs NEE-nyohs<br>ah kroo-SAHR lah KAH-yeh |

| | |
|---|---|
| custodian | **el guardián / la guardiana**<br>ehl gwahr-DYAHN /<br>lah gwahr-DYAH-nah |
| headmaster/headmistress | **el director / la directora**<br>ehl dee-rehk-TOHR /<br>lah dee-rehk-TOH-rah |
| instructor | **el instructor / la instructora**<br>ehl eens-trook-TOHR /<br>lah eens-trook-TOH-rah |
| interpreter | **el/la intérprete**<br>ehl/lah een-TEHR-preh-teh |
| janitor | **el/la conserje**<br>ehl/lah kohn-SEHR-heh |
| librarian | **el bibliotecario / la bibliotecaria**<br>ehl bee-blyoh-teh-KAH-ryoh /<br>lah bee-blyoh-teh-KAH-ryah |
| nurse | **el enfermero / la enfermera**<br>ehl ehn-fehr-MEH-roh /<br>lah ehn-fehr-MEH-rah |
| principal | **el director / la directora**<br>ehl dee-rehk-TOHR /<br>lah dee-rehk-TOH-rah |
| psychologist | **el psicólogo / la psicóloga**<br>ehl see-KOH-loh-goh /<br>lah see-KOH-loh-gah |
| receptionist | **el/la recepcionista**<br>ehl/lah rreh-sehp-syoh-NEES-tah |
| secretary | **el secretario / la secretaria**<br>ehl seh-kreh-TAH-ryoh /<br>lah seh-kreh-TAH-ryah |
| security guard | **el/la guardia de seguridad**<br>ehl/lah GWAHR-dyah deh<br>seh-goo-ree-DAHD |
| superintendent | **el/la superintendente**<br>ehl/lah soo-peh-reen-tehn-DEHN-teh |
| supervisor | **el supervisor / la supervisora**<br>ehl soo-pehr-bee-SOHR /<br>lah soo-pehr-bee-SOH-rah |
| teacher | **el maestro / la maestra**<br>ehl mah-EHS-troh / lah mah-EHS-trah |

| | |
|---|---|
| teacher's aide | **el/la asistente del maestro /**<br>**de la maestra**<br>ehl/lah ah-sees-TEHN-teh dehl<br>mah-EHS-troh / deh lah mah-EHS-trah |
| therapist | **el/la terapista**<br>ehl/lah teh-rah-PEES-tah |
| trainer | **el entrenador / la entrenadora**<br>ehl ehn-treh-nah-DOHR /<br>lah ehn-treh-nah-DOH-rah |
| translator | **el traductor / la traductora**<br>ehl trah-dook-TOHR /<br>lah trah-dook-TOH-rah |
| volunteer | **el voluntario / la voluntaria**<br>ehl boh-loon-TAH-ryoh /<br>lah boh-loon-TAH-ryah |

## GRAMMAR · To Find Out "Who?"

When you need to find out who is in charge or who does a particular job in the school building, you will need to ask the following questions.

| | |
|---|---|
| Who is _____? | **¿Quién es _____?**<br>kyehn ehs |
| Who are _____? | **¿Quiénes son _____?**<br>KYEH-nehs sohn |

Note that **quiénes** [KYEH-nehs] is used when you expect the answer to be more than one person.

| | |
|---|---|
| Who is the teacher? | **¿Quién es el maestro / la maestra?**<br>kyehn ehs ehl mah-EHS-troh /<br>lah mah-EHS-trah |
| It is Mr. _____ /<br>Mrs. _____ / Miss _____. | **Es el señor _____ /**<br>**la señora _____ / la señorita _____.**<br>ehs ehl seh-NYOHR / lah seh-NYOH-rah /<br>lah seh-nyoh-REE-tah |
| Who are the members of the school board? | **¿Quiénes son los miembros de la junta directiva?**<br>KYEH-nehs sohn lohs MYEHM-brohs deh<br>lah HOON-tah dee-rehk-TEE-bah |
| Several parents are the members of the school board. | **Varios padres son los miembros de la junta directiva.**<br>BAH-ryohs PAH-drehs sohn lohs<br>MYEHM-brohs deh lah HOON-tah<br>dee-rehk-TEE-bah |

## Practice 2-1

*Write the Spanish words that identify the people being described. Remember to use the appropriate definite articles.*

1. Who works in the library? _____

2. Who fixes problems with the boiler? _____

3. Who cleans the school building? _____

4. Who translates? _____

5. Who helps the children cross the street? _____

6. Who answers the phones? _____

7. Who maintains the security? _____

8. Who works in the cafeteria? _____

9. Who instructs the students in a sport? _____

10. Who drives the bus? _____

# School Supplies

### Los materiales necesarios para la escuela

Here is a list of many of the supplies needed for school (**los materiales necesarios para la escuela** [lohs mah-teh-RYAH-lehs neh-seh-SAH-ryohs PAH-rah lah ehs-KWEH-lah]).

| | |
|---|---|
| backpack | **la mochila** <br> lah moh-CHEE-lah |
| bag | **la bolsa** <br> lah BOHL-sah |
| ballpoint pen | **el bolígrafo** <br> ehl boh-LEE-grah-foh |
| book | **el libro** <br> ehl LEE-broh |
| brush (artist's) | **el pincel** <br> ehl peen-SEHL |
| calculator | **la calculadora** <br> lah kahl-koo-lah-DOH-rah |
| compass | **el compás** <br> ehl kohm-PAHS |

| | |
|---|---|
| computer | **la computadora**<br>lah kohm-poo-tah-DOH-rah |
| dictionary | **el diccionario**<br>ehl deek-syoh-NAH-ryoh |
| electronic organizer | **el organizador electrónico**<br>ehl ohr-gah-nee-sah-DOHR<br>eh-lehk-TROH-nee-koh |
| eraser (rubber) | **la goma de borrar**<br>lah GOH-mah deh boh-RRAHR |
| file folder | **la carpeta**<br>lah kahr-PEH-tah |
| highlighter | **el marcador**<br>ehl mahr-kah-DOHR |
| lock | **el candado**<br>ehl kahn-DAH-doh |
| notebook | **el cuaderno**<br>ehl kwah-DEHR-noh |
| paper | **el papel**<br>ehl pah-PEHL |
| pen | **la pluma**<br>lah PLOO-mah |
| pencil | **el lápiz**<br>ehl LAH-pees |
| pencil sharpener | **el sacapuntas**<br>ehl sah-kah-POON-tahs |
| ruler | **la regla**<br>lah RREH-glah |
| scissors | **las tijeras**<br>lahs tee-HEH-rahs |

## GRAMMAR · Using the Verb "To Be" to Express Identification

At this point you may want to learn how to identify objects around you. There are two basic questions you can use, depending on whether you are asking about one object or about more than one object: "What is _____?" and "What are _____?" You always use the Spanish verb **ser** [sehr], meaning "to be."

| | |
|---|---|
| What is it? (*singular*) | **¿Qué es?**<br>keh ehs |
| What are they? (*plural*) | **¿Qué son?**<br>keh sohn |
| It is _____. | **Es** _____.<br>ehs |

| They are _____. | **Son** _____. |
| | sohn |
| What is this/that? | **¿Qué es esto/eso?** |
| | keh ehs EHS-toh/EH-soh |
| It is a highlighter. | **Es un marcador.** |
| | ehs oon mahr-kah-DOHR |

For the conjugation of the present tense of the verb **ser** [sehr], see Chapter 1, page 42.

## Practice 2-2

*Identify each of the following objects usually found in a classroom. Write a complete sentence using the verb **ser** to identify each one.*

1.  _____

2.  _____

3.  _____

4. _____

5.  _____

6.  _____

## More School-Related Vocabulary

*Más vocabulario relacionado con la escuela*

Here is a list of additional school-related vocabulary (**el vocabulario relacionado con la escuela** [ehl boh-kah-boo-LAH-ryoh rreh-lah-syoh-NAH-doh kohn lah ehs-KWEH-lah]) that will prove very useful to you.

| elementary school | **la escuela primaria**<br>lah ehs-KWEH-lah pree-MAH-ryah |
| --- | --- |
| grade (level) | **el grado**<br>ehl GRAH-doh |
| grade (mark) | **la nota**<br>lah NOH-tah |
| graduation | **la graduación**<br>lah grah-dwah-SYOHN |
| high school | **la escuela secundaria**<br>lah ehs-KWEH-lah seh-koon-DAH-ryah |
| homework | **la tarea**<br>lah tah-REH-ah |
| lesson | **la lección**<br>lah lehk-SYOHN |
| recess | **el recreo**<br>ehl rreh-KREH-oh |
| report | **el informe**<br>ehl een-FOHR-meh |
| report card | **el boletín**<br>ehl boh-leh-TEEN |

| | |
|---|---|
| schedule | **el horario** <br> ehl oh-RAH-ryoh |
| school year | **el año escolar** <br> ehl AH-nyoh ehs-koh-LAHR |
| semester | **el semestre** <br> ehl seh-MEHS-treh |
| student | **el/la estudiante** <br> ehl/lah ehs-too-DYAHN-teh |
| subject | **la asignatura** <br> lah ah-seeg-nah-TOO-rah |
| test | **el examen / la prueba** <br> ehl ehk-SAH-mehn / lah PRWEH-bah |

# The School Building

## La escuela

If you are familiar with the vocabulary related to the school building itself, you will be able to talk about where many things are located. It will also help you when you need to give directions. The following lists deal with both the building itself and its surroundings, and they will help you to communicate about situations in and around the school (**dentro y alrededor de la escuela** [DEHN-troh ee ahl-rreh-deh-DOHR deh lah ehs-KWEH-lah]).

## Rooms in the School
### Los cuartos de la escuela

| | |
|---|---|
| auditorium | **el auditorio** <br> ehl ah-oo-dee-TOH-ryoh <br> **el salón / la sala de actos** <br> ehl sah-LOHN / <br> lah SAH-lah deh AHK-tohs |
| basement | **el sótano** <br> ehl SOH-tah-noh |
| bathroom | **el cuarto de baño** <br> ehl KWAHR-toh deh BAH-nyoh |
| boiler room | **la sala de calderas** <br> lah SAH-lah deh kahl-DEH-rahs |
| cafeteria | **la cafetería** <br> lah kah-feh-teh-REE-ah |
| classroom | **el salón de clases / el aula** <br> ehl sah-LOHN deh KLAH-sehs / <br> ehl AH-oo-lah |

| | |
|---|---|
| computer lab | **el laboratorio de computadoras** |
| | ehl lah-boh-rah-TOH-ryoh deh |
| | kohm-poo-tah-DOH-rahs |
| copy machine room | **el cuarto de la copiadora** |
| | ehl KWAHR-toh deh lah |
| | koh-pyah-DOH-rah |
| counseling office | **la oficina del consejero / de la consejera** |
| | lah oh-fee-SEE-nah |
| | dehl kohn-seh-HEH-roh / |
| | deh lah kohn-seh-HEH-rah |
| gymnasium | **el gimnasio** |
| | ehl heem-NAH-syoh |
| laboratory | **el laboratorio** |
| | ehl lah-boh-rah-TOH-ryoh |
| library | **la biblioteca** |
| | lah bee-blyoh-TEH-kah |
| locker room | **el vestuario** |
| | ehl behs-TWAH-ryoh |
| mail room | **el cuarto de correo** |
| | ehl KWAHR-toh deh koh-RREH-oh |
| nurse's office | **la oficina del enfermero / de la enfermera** |
| | lah oh-fee-SEE-nah |
| | dehl ehn-fehr-MEH-roh / |
| | deh lah ehn-fehr-MEH-rah |
| staff room | **la sala de maestros** |
| | lah SAH-lah deh mah-EHS-trohs |

## In and Around the School Building
*Dentro y alrededor de la escuela*

| | |
|---|---|
| air conditioning | **el aire acondicionado** |
| | ehl AH-ee-reh |
| | ah-kohn-dee-syoh-NAH-doh |
| carpet | **la alfombra** |
| | lah ahl-FOHM-brah |
| ceiling | **el techo** |
| | ehl TEH-choh |
| corridor | **el pasillo** |
| | ehl pah-SEE-yoh |
| door | **la puerta** |
| | lah PWEHR-tah |

| | |
|---|---|
| driveway | **la entrada (para carros)** |
| | lah ehn-TRAH-dah (PAH-rah KAH-rrohs) |
| elevator | **el ascensor** |
| | ehl ah-sehn-SOHR |
| entrance | **la entrada** |
| | lah ehn-TRAH-dah |
| escalator | **la escalera mecánica** |
| | lah ehs-kah-LEH-rah meh-KAH-nee-kah |
| exit | **la salida** |
| | lah sah-LEE-dah |
| fence | **la cerca** |
| | lah SEHR-kah |
| fire extinguisher | **el extintor** |
| | ehl ehs-teen-TOHR |
| flag | **la bandera** |
| | lah bahn-DEH-rah |
| floor (ground surface, flooring) | **el suelo** |
| | ehl SWEH-loh |
| floor (story) | **el piso** |
| | ehl PEE-soh |
| gate | **la verja** |
| | lah BEHR-hah |
| hallway | **el pasillo** |
| | ehl pah-SEE-yoh |
| heat | **la calefacción** |
| | lah kah-leh-fahk-SYOHN |
| light | **la luz** |
| | lah loos |
| lobby | **el vestíbulo** |
| | ehl behs-TEE-boo-loh |
| locker | **el cajón con llave** |
| | ehl kah-HOHN kohn YAH-beh |
| parking lot | **el estacionamiento** |
| | ehl ehs-tah-syoh-nah-MYEHN-toh |
| playground | **el patio de recreo** |
| | ehl PAH-tyoh deh rreh-KREH-oh |
| roof | **el techo** |
| | ehl TEH-choh |
| staircase | **la escalera** |
| | lah ehs-kah-LEH-rah |

| | |
|---|---|
| wall | **la pared**<br>lah pah-REHD |
| water fountain | **la fuente de agua potable**<br>lah FWEHN-teh deh AH-gwah<br>poh-TAH-bleh |
| window | **la ventana**<br>lah behn-TAH-nah |
| window shade/blind | **la persiana**<br>lah pehr-SYAH-nah |

## In the Bathroom
### En el cuarto de baño

In a school, the bathrooms (**los cuartos de baño** [lohs KWAHR-tohs deh BAH-nyoh]) that are used by the students are usually separate from those used by the adults.

| | |
|---|---|
| boys' bathroom | **el baño para niños**<br>ehl BAH-nyoh PAH-rah NEE-nyohs |
| girls' bathroom | **el baño para niñas**<br>ehl BAH-nyoh PAH-rah NEE-nyahs |
| men's bathroom | **el baño para caballeros**<br>ehl BAH-nyoh PAH-rah kah-bah-YEH-rohs |
| women's bathroom | **el baño para damas**<br>ehl BAH-nyoh PAH-rah DAH-mahs |

Here are some of the items you will typically find in the bathroom.

| | |
|---|---|
| mirror | **el espejo**<br>ehl ehs-PEH-hoh |
| paper towel | **la toalla de papel**<br>lah toh-AH-yah deh pah-PEHL |
| sink | **el lavamanos**<br>ehl lah-bah-MAH-nohs |
| soap | **el jabón**<br>ehl hah-BOHN |
| toilet | **el servicio**<br>ehl sehr-BEE-syoh |
| toilet paper | **el papel higiénico**<br>ehl pah-PEHL ee-HYEH-nee-koh |
| urinal | **el orinal**<br>ehl oh-ree-NAHL |

## Verbs

| to ask for permission | **pedir (i) permiso** | peh-DEER pehr-MEE-soh |
| to dry your hands | **secarse las manos** | seh-KAHR-seh lahs MAH-nohs |
| to flush the toilet | **descargar** | dehs-kahr-GAHR |
| to wash your hands | **lavarse las manos** | lah-BAHR-seh lahs MAH-nohs |

## GRAMMAR · To Find Out "Where?"

If the parents or students you encounter are not familiar with the school building, you will probably be asked questions such as the following, depending on whether someone is asking about the location of one thing or about the location of more than one thing: "Where is _____?" or "Where are _____?"

Remember that to tell the location of a person, place, or thing, you use the verb **estar** [ehs-TAHR], meaning "to be."

| Where is _____? (*singular*) | **¿Dónde está _____?**<br>DOHN-deh ehs-TAH |
| Where are _____? (*plural*) | **¿Dónde están _____?**<br>DOHN-deh ehs-TAHN |
| Where is the bathroom? | **¿Dónde está el cuarto de baño?**<br>DOHN-deh ehs-TAH ehl KWAHR-toh<br>deh BAH-nyoh |
| It is there. | **Está allí.**<br>ehs-TAH ah-YEE |
| Where are the elevators? | **¿Dónde están los ascensores?**<br>DOHN-deh ehs-TAHN lohs<br>ah-sehn-SOH-rehs |
| They are over there. | **Están allá.**<br>ehs-TAHN ah-YAH |

You will also need to become familiar with several expressions that indicate location or give directions. Here is a list of several of them.

| It is … / They are … | **Está…/Están…**<br>ehs-TAH/ehs-TAHN |
| behind | **detrás de**<br>deh-TRAHS deh |
| downstairs | **abajo**<br>ah-BAH-hoh |
| in front of | **enfrente de**<br>ehn-FREHN-teh deh |
| in the corner | **en el rincón**<br>ehn ehl rreen-KOHN |

| It is … / They are … | Está…/Están…<br>ehs-TAH/ehs-TAHN |
|---|---|
| inside | **adentro**<br>ah-DEHN-troh |
| next to | **al lado de**<br>ahl LAH-doh deh |
| on the corner | **en la esquina**<br>ehn lah ehs-KEE-nah |
| on the first/second/third floor | **en el primer/segundo/tercer piso**<br>ehn ehl pree-MEHR/seh-GOON-doh/<br>tehr-SEHR PEE-soh |
| outside | **afuera**<br>ah-FWEH-rah |
| over there | **allá**<br>ah-YAH |
| there | **allí**<br>ah-YEE |
| to the right | **a la derecha**<br>ah lah deh-REH-chah |
| to the left | **a la izquierda**<br>ah lah ees-KYEHR-dah |
| at the end of | **al final de**<br>ahl fee-NAHL deh |
| upstairs | **arriba**<br>ah-RREE-bah |

For more expressions indicating location, see Chapter 1, pages 59–60.

## In the Classroom / In the Office
*En la sala de clase / En la oficina*

Many of the objects you find in a classroom (**la sala de clase** [lah SAH-lah deh KLAH-seh]) can also be found in any office (**la oficina** [lah oh-fee-SEE-nah]). The following list will come in handy when you are talking about either place.

| bell (electric) | **el timbre**<br>ehl TEEM-breh |
|---|---|
| bell (hand) | **la campana**<br>lah kahm-PAH-nah |
| bookcase | **la estantería**<br>lah ehs-tahn-teh-REE-ah |
| box | **la caja**<br>lah KAH-hah |

| | |
|---|---|
| chair | **la silla** |
| | lah SEE-yah |
| chalk | **la tiza** |
| | lah TEE-sah |
| chalkboard | **la pizarra** |
| | lah pee-SAH-rrah |
| clock | **el reloj** |
| | ehl rreh-LOH |
| closet | **el armario** |
| | ehl ahr-MAH-ryoh |
| computer | **la computadora** |
| | lah kohm-poo-tah-DOH-rah |
| copy machine | **la copiadora** |
| | lah koh-pyah-DOH-rah |
| copy machine toner | **la tinta de copiar** |
| | lah TEEN-tah deh koh-PYAHR |
| counter | **el mostrador** |
| | ehl mohs-trah-DOHR |
| desk | **el escritorio** |
| | ehl ehs-kree-TOH-ryoh |
| desk (student) | **el pupitre** |
| | ehl poo-PEE-treh |
| drawer | **el cajón** |
| | ehl kah-HOHN |
| envelope | **el sobre** |
| | ehl SOH-breh |
| eraser (chalkboard) | **el borrador (de la pizarra)** |
| | ehl boh-rrah-DOHR |
| | (deh lah pee-SAH-rrah) |
| fax machine | **el telefax** |
| | ehl teh-leh-FAHKS |
| file cabinet | **el fichero** |
| | ehl fee-CHEH-roh |
| file folder | **la carpeta** |
| | lah kahr-PEH-tah |
| files | **el archivo** |
| | ehl ahr-CHEE-boh |
| ink | **la tinta** |
| | lah TEEN-tah |
| letter | **la carta** |
| | lah KAHR-tah |
| loudspeaker | **el altavoz** |
| | ehl ahl-tah-BOHS |

| | |
|---|---|
| overhead projector | **el retroproyector**<br>ehl rreh-troh-proh-yehk-TOHR |
| paper | **el papel**<br>ehl pah-PEHL |
| paper clip | **el sujetapapeles**<br>ehl soo-heh-tah-pah-PEH-lehs |
| pass (permission) | **el pase / el permiso**<br>ehl PAH-seh / ehl pehr-MEE-soh |
| picture | **el cuadro**<br>ehl KWAH-droh |
| poster | **el cartel**<br>ehl kahr-TEHL |
| printer | **la impresora**<br>lah eem-preh-SOH-rah |
| rug | **la alfombra**<br>lah ahl-FOHM-brah |
| sheet of paper | **la hoja de papel**<br>lah OH-hah deh pah-PEHL |
| stamp | **el sello**<br>ehl SEH-yoh |
| staple | **la grapa**<br>lah GRAH-pah |
| stapler | **la grapadora**<br>lah grah-pah-DOH-rah |
| table | **la mesa**<br>lah MEH-sah |
| telephone | **el teléfono**<br>ehl teh-LEH-foh-noh |
| trash can | **el cubo de la basura**<br>ehl KOO-boh deh lah bah-SOO-rah |
| wastepaper basket | **la papelera**<br>lah pah-peh-LEH-rah |

## Verbs

| | | |
|---|---|---|
| to announce | **anunciar** | ah-noon-SYAHR |
| to call | **llamar** | yah-MAHR |
| to copy | **copiar** | koh-PYAHR |
| to fax | **mandar por fax** | mahn-DAHR pohr fahks |
| to file | **archivar** | ahr-chee-BAHR |
| to fill out | **llenar** | yeh-NAHR |
| to photocopy | **fotocopiar** | foh-toh-koh-PYAHR |
| to staple | **sujetar con grapas** | soo-heh-TAHR kohn GRAH-pahs |

## Practice 2-3

**A** *Using the English cues in parentheses, unscramble each string of letters to form a Spanish word or expression, including its definite article. Then use the numbered letters to fill in the blanks below. What is the phrase?*

aaucrñeoetlbod (*bathroom*)

| | | | | | | | | | | | | | | |
|---|---|---|---|---|---|---|---|---|---|---|---|---|---|---|
| | | | 4 | | | | | | | | | | | |

dallaearsotamses (*staff room*)

| | | | | | | | | | | | | | | | |
|---|---|---|---|---|---|---|---|---|---|---|---|---|---|---|---|
| | | | | | | | | | | | 7 | | | | |

ontasoel (*basement*)

| | | | | | | | |
|---|---|---|---|---|---|---|---|
| | | 10 | | | | | |

soellasnceadsle (*classroom*)

| | | | | | | | | | | | | | | | |
|---|---|---|---|---|---|---|---|---|---|---|---|---|---|---|---|
| | | | | 9 | | | | | | | | | | | |

aciltboalbei (*library*)

| | | | | | | | | | | | |
|---|---|---|---|---|---|---|---|---|---|---|---|
| | | | | | 8 | | | | | | |

tadilioouer (*auditorium*)

| | | | | | | | | | | |
|---|---|---|---|---|---|---|---|---|---|---|
| | | 5 | | | | | | | | |

dreuecltreocoora (*mail room*)

| | | | | | | | | | | | | | | | |
|---|---|---|---|---|---|---|---|---|---|---|---|---|---|---|---|
| 12 | 1 | 17 | 18 | 14 | | | | 11 | 15 | | | | 19 | | |

onsigemlia (*gymnasium*)

| | | | | | | | | | |
|---|---|---|---|---|---|---|---|---|---|
| | | | | | 6 | | | | |

lvisuraoete (*locker room*)

| | | | | | | | | | | |
|---|---|---|---|---|---|---|---|---|---|---|
| | | 3 | | | | | | | | |

feioienrnsdcjoacaleol (*counselor's office*)

| | | | | | | | | | | | | | | | | | | | | |
|---|---|---|---|---|---|---|---|---|---|---|---|---|---|---|---|---|---|---|---|---|
| 13 | 21 | 2 | | | | | | | 20 | | | 16 | | | | | | | | |

___ ___ ___    ___ ___ ___ ___ ___ ___ ___    ___ ___    ___ ___    ___ ___ ___ ___ ___ ___ ___
1  2  3      4  5  6  7  8  9  10      11 12    13 14    15 16 17 18 19 20 21

**B** *Complete the following crossword puzzle.*

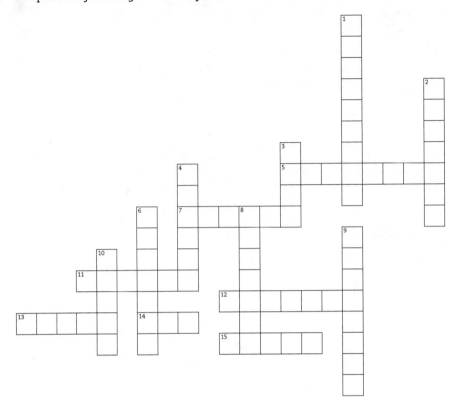

**Across**
5. carpet
7. mirror
11. exit
12. flag
13. ceiling
14. light
15. wall

**Down**
1. sink
2. window
3. bathroom
4. door
6. hallway
8. entrance
9. staircase
10. soap

**C** *Using the English cues in parentheses, write complete sentences in Spanish to tell where the following people, places, or things are located. Use the verb* **estar**.

1. ¿Dónde está el gimnasio? *(in the basement)*

_____

2. ¿Dónde están las fuentes de agua potable? *(there)*

_____

3. ¿Dónde están las toallas de papel? (*in the drawer*)

_____

4. ¿Dónde está la oficina del director? (*in front of the auditorium*)

_____

5. ¿Dónde está el sujetapapeles? (*next to the printer*)

_____

6. ¿Dónde está el cubo de la basura? (*in the corner*)

_____

7. ¿Dónde están los carteles? (*on the wall*)

_____

8. ¿Dónde está la consejera? (*next to the nurse*)

_____

9. ¿Dónde está el escritorio? (*in front of the students' desks*)

_____

10. ¿Dónde están las estanterías? (*behind the copy machine*)

_____

**D** *Write the correct English word for the people, places, or things that are being asked about in each item in Exercise C.*

1. _____

2. _____

3. _____

4. _____

5. _____

6. _____

7. _____

8. _____

9. _____

10. _____

## In the Library
*En la biblioteca*

| | |
|---|---|
| book | **el libro**<br>ehl LEE-broh |
| fine | **la multa**<br>lah MOOL-tah |
| library card | **la tarjeta de biblioteca**<br>lah tahr-HEH-tah deh bee-blyoh-TEH-kah |
| magazine | **la revista**<br>lah rreh-BEES-tah |
| newspaper | **el periódico**<br>ehl peh-RYOH-dee-koh |
| page | **la página**<br>lah PAH-hee-nah |
| return date | **la fecha de devolución**<br>lah FEH-chah deh deh-boh-loo-SYOHN |
| shelf | **el estante**<br>ehl ehs-TAHN-teh |
| subscription | **la suscripción**<br>lah soos-kreep-SYOHN |
| volume (book) | **el tomo**<br>ehl TOH-moh |

## Verbs

| | | |
|---|---|---|
| to borrow | **pedir (i) prestado/prestada** | peh-DEER prehs-TAH-doh/<br>prehs-TAH-dah |
| to find | **encontrar (ue)** | ehn-kohn-TRAHR |
| to keep silent | **guardar silencio** | gwahr-DAHR see-LEHN-syoh |
| to look for | **buscar** | boos-KAHR |
| to lose | **perder (ie)** | pehr-DEHR |
| to pay the fine | **pagar la multa** | pah-GAHR lah MOOL-tah |
| to research | **investigar** | een-behs-tee-GAHR |
| to return, give back | **devolver (ue)** | deh-bohl-BEHR |

## In the Auditorium
*En el auditorio / el salón de actos / la sala de actos*

| | |
|---|---|
| aisle | **el pasillo**<br>ehl pah-SEE-yoh |
| box office | **la taquilla**<br>lah tah-KEE-yah |

| curtain | **el telón** |
| | ehl teh-LOHN |
| lighting | **las luces** |
| | lahs LOO-sehs |
| microphone | **el micrófono** |
| | ehl mee-KROH-foh-noh |
| row | **la fila** |
| | lah FEE-lah |
| seat | **la butaca** |
| | lah boo-TAH-kah |
| stage | **el escenario** |
| | ehl eh-seh-NAH-ryoh |

## Verbs

| to applaud | **aplaudir** | ah-plah-oo-DEER |
| to listen | **escuchar** | ehs-koo-CHAHR |
| to watch | **mirar** | mee-RAHR |

## Practice 2-4

*Write the Spanish word for what is being described. Remember to use the correct definite article.*

1. where the student's grades appear

   _____

2. where we buy tickets for a play

   _____

3. where we sit in a theatre

   _____

4. what we have to pay when we have an overdue book

   _____

5. the break students get during the school day

   _____

6. what teachers give students to do at home

   _____

7. what we read to get the news every day

   _____

8. what students take to see what they have learned

   _____

9. the list of classes and times they meet

   _____

10. the number or letter students get on an exam

    _____

## In the Cafeteria
*En la cafetería*

### Meals · *Las comidas*

Meals (**las comidas** [lahs koh-MEE-dahs]) served to students in the school cafeteria are typically lunch (**el almuerzo** [ehl ahl-MWEHR-soh]), snacks (**la merienda** [lah meh-RYEHN-dah]), and sometimes breakfast (**el desayuno** [ehl deh-sah-YOO-noh]). Students rarely eat dinner (**la cena** [lah SEH-nah]) at school.

Foodstuffs (**los comestibles** [lohs koh-mehs-TEE-blehs]) that you may find in the cafeteria include the following.

| | |
|---|---|
| bread | **el pan**<br>ehl pahn |
| chicken | **el pollo**<br>ehl POH-yoh |
| fish | **el pescado**<br>ehl pehs-KAH-doh |
| hamburger | **la hamburguesa**<br>lah ahm-boor-GEH-sah |
| hot dog | **el perro caliente**<br>ehl PEH-rroh kah-LYEHN-teh |
| meat | **la carne**<br>lah KAHR-neh |
| pepper | **la pimienta**<br>lah pee-MYEHN-tah |
| rice | **el arroz**<br>ehl ah-RROHS |
| salad | **la ensalada**<br>lah ehn-sah-LAH-dah |
| salt | **la sal**<br>lah sahl |

| sandwich | **el emparedado / el sándwich**<br>ehl ehm-pah-reh-DAH-doh /<br>ehl SAHND-weech |
| soup | **la sopa**<br>lah SOH-pah |
| spaghetti | **los espaguetis**<br>lohs ehs-pah-GEH-tees |
| vegetables | **los vegetales**<br>los beh-heh-TAH-lehs |

The following list includes some popular (and some not so popular) vegetables (**los vegetales** [lohs beh-heh-TAH-lehs]) that you may find in school cafeterias.

| bean | **el frijol**<br>ehl free-HOHL |
| broccoli | **el brécol**<br>ehl BREH-kohl |
| carrot | **la zanahoria**<br>lah sah-nah-OH-ryah |
| corn | **el maíz**<br>ehl mah-EES |
| cucumber | **el pepino**<br>ehl peh-PEE-noh |
| green pea | **el guisante**<br>ehl gee-SAHN-teh |
| lettuce | **la lechuga**<br>lah leh-CHOO-gah |
| potato | **la papa / la patata**<br>lah PAH-pah / lah pah-TAH-tah |
| spinach | **la espinaca**<br>lah ehs-pee-NAH-kah |
| tomato | **el tomate**<br>ehl toh-MAH-teh |

## Dessert · El postre

You may find the following desserts (**los postres** [lohs POHS-trehs]) in a school cafeteria.

| | |
|---|---|
| cake | **el bizcocho** |
| | ehl bees-KOH-choh |
| cookie | **la galletita** |
| | lah gah-yeh-TEE-tah |
| fruit | **la fruta** |
| | lah FROO-tah |

Some fruits (**las frutas** [lahs FROO-tahs]) that might be found in the school cafeteria are the following.

| | |
|---|---|
| apple | **la manzana** |
| | lah mahn-SAH-nah |
| banana | **el plátano** |
| | ehl PLAH-tah-noh |
| grape | **la uva** |
| | lah OO-bah |
| melon | **el melón** |
| | ehl meh-LOHN |
| orange | **la naranja** |
| | lah nah-RAHN-hah |
| peach | **el melocotón** |
| | ehl meh-loh-koh-TOHN |
| pear | **la pera** |
| | lah PEH-rah |
| strawberry | **la fresa** |
| | lah FREH-sah |

## Drinks · Las bebidas

Here are some drinks (**las bebidas** [lahs beh-BEE-dahs]) that you may find in the cafeteria.

| | |
|---|---|
| juice | **el jugo** |
| | ehl HOO-goh |
| lemonade | **la limonada** |
| | lah lee-moh-NAH-dah |

| | |
|---|---|
| milk | **la leche**<br>lah LEH-cheh |
| punch | **el ponche**<br>ehl POHN-cheh |
| soft drink | **el refresco**<br>ehl rreh-FREHS-koh |
| water | **el agua**<br>ehl AH-gwah |

## GRAMMAR · "There Is" and "There Are"

**Hay...** [AH-ee] means "There is ..." and "There are ...".
**¿Hay...?** [AH-ee] means "Is there ...?" and "Are there ...?"

| | |
|---|---|
| Is there soup today? | **¿Hay sopa hoy?**<br>AH-ee SOH-pah OH-ee |
| Yes, there is chicken soup. | **Sí, hay sopa de pollo.**<br>see, AH-ee SOH-pah deh POH-yoh |
| How many bottles of water are there on the table? | **¿Cuántas botellas de agua hay en la mesa?**<br>KWAHN-tahs boh-TEH-yahs deh AH-gwah AH-ee ehn lah MEH-sah |
| There are two. | **Hay dos.**<br>AH-ee dohs |

## *More Information* · *Más información*

In many school cafeterias you will find Spanish-speaking personnel. It is a good idea to talk to them in Spanish. You will make them feel good, and at the same time you will be practicing your Spanish. And, who knows? You may get an extra apple.

| | |
|---|---|
| How much does it cost? | **¿Cuánto cuesta?**<br>KWAHN-toh KWEHS-tah |
| What is for dessert today? | **¿Cuál es el postre hoy?**<br>kwahl ehs ehl POHS-treh OH-ee |
| What is today's special? | **¿Cuál es el plato del día?**<br>kwahl ehs ehl PLAH-toh dehl DEE-ah |

### Breakfast · El desayuno

Breakfast (**el desayuno** [ehl deh-sah-YOO-noh]) is considered to be the most important meal of the day, and yet many students do not eat a good breakfast. Included below is a separate section dedicated to breakfast.

| | |
|---|---|
| What do you eat for breakfast? | **¿Qué comes de desayuno?**<br>keh KOH-mehs deh deh-sah-YOO-noh |
| For breakfast I eat _____. | **De desayuno yo como _____.**<br>deh deh-sah-YOO-noh yoh KOH-moh |
| What do you want for breakfast? | **¿Qué quieres de desayuno?**<br>keh KYEH-rehs deh deh-sah-YOO-noh |
| For breakfast I want _____. | **De desayuno yo quiero _____.**<br>deh deh-sah-YOO-noh yoh KYEH-roh |
| Do you bring your breakfast/ lunch from home? | **¿Traes el desayuno / el almuerzo de tu casa?**<br>TRAH-ehs ehl deh-sah-YOO-noh /<br>ehl ahl-MWEHR-soh deh too KAH-sah |
| Do you eat breakfast at home? | **¿Desayunas en casa?**<br>deh-sah-YOO-nahs ehn KAH-sah |

### Typical Breakfast Foods · La comida típica del desayuno

Although a big breakfast is usually left for the weekend, even a weekday "American" breakfast is much heavier than what is usually eaten in Spanish-speaking countries. A typical breakfast in a Spanish-speaking country is likely to be coffee (**el café** [ehl kah-FEH]) and some type of bread (**el pan** [ehl pahn]).

Some typical breakfast foods (**la comida típica del desayuno** [lah koh-MEE-dah TEE-pee-kah dehl deh-sah-YOO-noh]) in the United States are the following.

| | |
|---|---|
| bacon | **el tocino**<br>ehl toh-SEE-noh |
| bread | **el pan**<br>ehl pahn |
| butter | **la mantequilla**<br>lah mahn-teh-KEE-yah |
| cereal | **el cereal**<br>ehl seh-reh-AHL |
| cheese | **el queso**<br>ehl KEH-soh |
| coffee | **el café**<br>ehl kah-FEH |

| cream cheese | **el queso crema** |
| | ehl KEH-soh KREH-mah |
| egg | **el huevo** |
| | ehl WEH-boh |
| ham | **el jamón** |
| | ehl hah-MOHN |
| margarine | **la margarina** |
| | lah mahr-gah-REE-nah |
| milk | **la leche** |
| | lah LEH-cheh |
| oatmeal | **la avena** |
| | lah ah-BEH-nah |
| omelet | **la tortilla** |
| | lah tohr-TEE-yah |
| roll | **el panecillo** |
| | ehl pah-neh-SEE-yoh |
| sausage | **la salchicha** |
| | lah sahl-CHEE-chah |
| skim milk | **la leche desnatada** |
| | lah LEH-cheh dehs-nah-TAH-dah |
| tea | **el té** |
| | ehl teh |
| toast | **el pan tostado** |
| | ehl pahn tohs-TAH-doh |
| yogurt | **el yogurt** |
| | ehl yoh-GOOR |

## Verbs

| to bring | **traer** (*irreg.*) | trah-EHR |
| to chew | **masticar** | mahs-tee-KAHR |
| to clean | **limpiar** | leem-PYAHR |
| to cost | **costar** (ue) | kohs-TAHR |
| to drink | **beber** | beh-BEHR |
| to eat | **comer** | koh-MEHR |
| to eat breakfast | **desayunar** | deh-sah-yoo-NAHR |
| to eat lunch | **almorzar** (ue) | ahl-mohr-SAHR |
| to eat dinner | **cenar** | seh-NAHR |
| to pay | **pagar** | pah-GAHR |
| to pick up | **recoger** (*irreg.*) | rreh-koh-HEHR |
| to share | **compartir** | kohm-pahr-TEER |
| to swallow | **tragar** | trah-GAHR |

## Grammar · Expressing "To Like"

In Spanish, the verb **gustar** [goos-TAHR] is used to convey "to like," but its usage is slightly different from the other verbs you have encountered. You will use only two forms of the verb **gustar**: **gusta** [goos-tah] and **gustan** [goos-tahn].

When you want to express what you like *to do,* use **gusta** [goos-tah]. If you want to say that you like a certain *thing* use **gusta** [goos-tah]. However, if you want to say that you like *more than one thing,* use **gustan** [goos-tahn].

The pronouns **me, te, le, nos, les** [meh, teh, leh, nohs, lehs] are placed before the verb in order to indicate the person who is expressing his or her opinion.

| I like | **me gusta/gustan** | meh goos-tah/goos-tahn |
| you (*familiar*) like | **te gusta/gustan** | teh goos-tah/goos-tahn |
| he likes | **le gusta/gustan** | leh goos-tah/goos-tahn |
| she likes | **le gusta/gustan** | leh goos-tah/goos-tahn |
| you (*formal*) like | **le gusta/gustan** | leh goos-tah/goos-tahn |
| we like | **nos gusta/gustan** | nohs goos-tah/goos-tahn |
| they like | **les gusta/gustan** | lehs goos-tah/goos-tahn |
| you (*plural*) like | **les gusta/gustan** | lehs goos-tah/goos-tahn |

| | |
|---|---|
| I like the music class. | **Me gusta la clase de música.** meh goos-tah lah KLAH-seh deh MOO-see-kah |
| She likes to study in the evening. | **Le gusta estudiar por la noche.** leh goos-tah ehs-too-DYAHR pohr lah NOH-cheh |

Remember that when you like more than one thing, **gustan** [goos-tahn] is used instead of **gusta** [goos-tah].

| | |
|---|---|
| I like hardworking students. | **Me gustan los estudiantes trabajadores.** meh goos-tahn lohs ehs-too-DYAHN-tehs trah-bah-hah-DOH-rehs |

Read the examples above again. Did you notice that when a noun follows **gusta** [goos-tah] or **gustan** [goos-tahn], its definite article (**el, la, los, las** [ehl, lah, lohs, lahs]) is always included?

When talking about what you *don't* like, put **no** [noh] before **me, te, le, nos, les** [meh, teh, leh, nohs, lehs].

| | |
|---|---|
| I don't like to study in the library. | **No me gusta estudiar en la biblioteca.** noh meh goos-tah ehs-too-DYAHR ehn lah bee-blyoh-TEH-kah |

| | |
|---|---|
| She does not like homework. | **No le gusta la tarea.**<br>noh leh GOOS-tah lah tah-REH-ah |
| We don't like tests. | **No nos gustan las pruebas.**<br>noh nohs GOOS-tahn lahs PRWEH-bahs |

## Practice 2-5

**A** *Read the following lists, then circle the word that does not belong in each group.*

1. la zanahoria | la lechuga | la carne | el pepino

2. el huevo | la salchicha | el tocino | la sopa

3. el pollo | la carne | el maíz | el perro caliente

4. la manzana | el arroz | la piña | la uva

5. comer | traer | masticar | tragar

6. la leche | el pescado | el jugo | el agua

7. la naranja | la sal | el ajo | la cebolla

8. el pollo | la avena | el cereal | la leche

9. almorzar | limpiar | cenar | desayunar

10. queso | yogurt | mantequilla | jamón

**B** *Write complete sentences in Spanish to answer the following questions truthfully.*

1. ¿Te gusta beber té?

   _____

2. ¿Le gustan las fresas?

   _____

3. ¿Les gusta comer en la cafetería?

   _____

4. ¿Le gustan a Ud. los postres?

   _____

5. ¿Le gusta el melocotón?

   _____

**C** *You want to find out what all of your students, as a group, like. What would you ask them?*

   _____

## Summary Practice

*Write the Spanish question you will need to ask in order to find out the following information.*

1. who the students in the hallway are

   _____

2. if a particular student likes to share his/her lunch

   _____

3. if there is salad for (**para**) lunch

   _____

4. where the women's bathroom is

   _____

5. what the dessert is

   _____

6. if the students, as a group, don't like to bring their lunch from home

   _____

7. where the pencil sharpener is

   _____

8. what those (**esos**) papers are

   _____

9. if the principal's office is to the right of the entrance

   _____

10. if there is a light in the parking lot

   _____

# 3

# The Primary Grades

*Los grados primarios*

In preschool or nursery school (**la guardería** [lah gwahr-deh-REE-ah]), kindergarten (**el kinder / el jardín de infancia** [ehl KEEN-dehr / ehl hahr-DEEN deh een-FAHN-syah]), and the early years of elementary school (**la escuela primaria** [lah ehs-KWEH-lah pree-MAH-ryah]), children are busy learning about the world around them and they increase their vocabulary daily. Among many other things, they learn about the city or town in which they live and the people who are found there. Some important areas of learning for young children are the following.

| | |
|---|---|
| animals | **los animales** <br> lohs ah-nee-MAH-lehs |
| body | **el cuerpo** <br> ehl KWEHR-poh |
| buildings | **los edificios** <br> lohs eh-dee-FEE-syohs |
| city | **la ciudad** <br> lah see-oo-DAHD |
| clothing | **la ropa** <br> lah RROH-pah |
| colors | **los colores** <br> lohs koh-LOH-rehs |
| date (on calendar) | **la fecha** <br> lah FEH-chah |
| days of the week | **los días de la semana** <br> lohs DEE-ahs deh lah seh-MAH-nah |
| family | **la familia** <br> lah fah-MEE-lyah |
| food | **la comida** <br> lah koh-MEE-dah |
| holidays | **los días feriados** <br> lohs DEE-ahs feh-RYAH-dohs |
| home | **el hogar** <br> ehl oh-GAHR |
| house | **la casa** <br> lah KAH-sah |
| months of the year | **los meses del año** <br> lohs MEH-sehs dehl AH-nyoh |
| musical instruments | **los instrumentos musicales** <br> lohs eens-troo-MEHN-tohs moo-see-KAH-lehs |
| occupations | **las profesiones** <br> lahs proh-feh-SYOH-nehs |

| people | **la gente / las personas** |
| | lah HEHN-teh / lahs pehr-SOH-nahs |
| seasons of the year | **las estaciones del año** |
| | lahs ehs-tah-SYOH-nehs dehl ah-nyoh |
| sports | **los deportes** |
| | lohs deh-POHR-tehs |
| time (clock) | **la hora** |
| | lah OH-rah |
| town | **el pueblo** |
| | ehl PWEH-bloh |
| transportation | **el transporte** |
| | ehl trahns-POHR-teh |
| weather | **el tiempo** |
| | ehl TYEHM-poh |

Health and safety are also important topics in all grades. For these topics, see Chapter 6.

# The School Calendar

*El calendario escolar*

The school calendar (**el calendario escolar** [ehl kah-lehn-DAH-ryoh ehs-koh-LAHR]), together with the schedule of classes, is an important document with which parents and students must become very familiar. Families plan their vacations around the school calendar. It is also important to be familiar with the different holidays so that when students have a day off from school, someone will be taking care of them. Important vocabulary and expressions relating to the school calendar follow.

## Months

*Los meses*

To express dates in Spanish, you first need to know the months (**los meses** [lohs MEH-sehs]) of the year. Note that in Spanish, the months of the year are not capitalized.

| January | **enero** | eh-NEH-roh |
| February | **febrero** | feh-BREH-roh |
| March | **marzo** | MAHR-soh |
| April | **abril** | ah-BREEL |
| May | **mayo** | MAH-yoh |
| June | **junio** | HOO-nyoh |

| July | **julio** | HOO-lyoh |
| August | **agosto** | ah-GOHS-toh |
| September | **septiembre** | sehp-TYEHM-breh |
| October | **octubre** | ohk-TOO-breh |
| November | **noviembre** | noh-BYEHM-breh |
| December | **diciembre** | dee-SYEHM-breh |

## Expressing Dates
*Para expresar la fecha*

There are a different ways you can phrase a question when you want to find out the date (**la fecha** [lah FEH-chah]).

| What is today's date? | **¿Cuál es la fecha de hoy?** |
| | kwahl ehs lah FEH-chah deh OH-ee |
| | **¿A cómo estamos hoy?** |
| | ah KOH-moh ehs-TAH-mohs OH-ee |

To respond with what date it is, use the following patterns.

| Today is the fourth of March. | **Hoy es el cuatro de marzo.** |
| | OH-ee ehs ehl KWAH-troh deh MAHR-soh |
| | **Estamos a cuatro de marzo.** |
| | ehs-TAH-mohs ah KWAH-troh deh MAHR-soh |

To find out on what date an event takes place, you may ask a question as follows.

| What is the date of _____? | **¿Cuál es la fecha de _____?** |
| | kwahl ehs lah FEH-chah deh |
| What is the date of the exam? | **¿Cuál es la fecha del examen?** |
| | kwahl ehs lah FEH-chah dehl ehk-SAH-mehn |
| The exam is on June 3. | **El examen es el tres de junio.** |
| | ehl ehk-SAH-mehn ehs ehl trehs deh HOO-nyoh |

Note that "on" + (*day of the month*) is translated as **el** [ehl] + (*day of the month*).

A complete date is expressed in the following manner.

| June 1, 2006 | **el primero de junio del dos mil seis** |
| | ehl pree-MEH-roh deh HOO-nyoh dehl dohs meel SEH-ehs |

In Spanish you will only use an ordinal number for the first of the month (**el primero del mes** [ehl pree-MEH-roh dehl mehs]). For all other dates you must use cardinal numbers.

For a complete list of numbers, see Chapter 4, pages 157–158.

## Holidays
*Los días feriados*

Here is a list of holidays (**los días feriados** [lohs DEE-ahs feh-RYAH-dohs]), many of which are recognized by schools in the United States; several are public holidays.

| | |
|---|---|
| Christmas | **la Navidad**<br>lah nah-bee-DAHD |
| Columbus Day | **el día de la Raza**<br>ehl DEE-ah deh lah RRAH-sah |
| Easter | **la Pascua de Resurrección**<br>lah PAHS-kwah deh<br>rreh-soo-rrehk-SYOHN |
| Father's Day | **el día de los Padres**<br>ehl DEE-ah deh lohs PAH-drehs |
| Halloween | **la Víspera de Todos los Santos**<br>lah BEES-peh-rah deh TOH-dohs lohs<br>SAHN-tohs |
| Hanukkah | **la Fiesta de las Luces**<br>lah FYEHS-tah deh lahs LOO-sehs |
| Labor Day | **el día del Trabajador**<br>ehl DEE-ah dehl trah-bah-hah-DOHR |
| Mother's Day | **el día de las Madres**<br>ehl DEE-ah deh lahs MAH-drehs |
| New Year's Day | **el día de Año Nuevo**<br>ehl DEE-ah deh AH-nyoh NWEH-boh |
| Passover | **la Pascua (de los judíos)**<br>lah PAHS-kwah (deh lohs hoo-DEE-ohs) |
| President's Day | **el día de los Presidentes**<br>ehl DEE-ah deh lohs preh-see-DEHN-tehs |
| Ramadan | **Ramadán**<br>rrah-mah-DAHN |
| Rosh Hashanah | **el día de Año Nuevo Judío**<br>ehl DEE-ah deh AH-nyoh NWEH-boh<br>hoo-DEE-oh |
| Thanksgiving | **el día de Acción de Gracias**<br>ehl DEE-ah deh ahk-SYOHN deh<br>GRAH-syahs |

| Valentine's Day | el día de los Enamorados |
|---|---|
| | ehl DEE-ah deh lohs |
| | eh-nah-moh-RAH-dohs |

To express good wishes, say **feliz** [feh-LEES], meaning "happy," followed by the name of the holiday. In these cases you don't use the definite article.

| Happy New Year! | **¡Feliz Año Nuevo!** |
|---|---|
| | feh-LEES AH-nyoh NWEH-boh |

## Days of the Week
*Los días de la semana*

In Spanish, the days of the week (**los días de la semana** [lohs DEE-ahs deh lah seh-MAH-nah]) are always masculine and, like the months of the year, they are not capitalized. You will also find it helpful to know that in the Spanish-speaking world, the week begins on Monday.

| Monday | **lunes** | LOO-nehs |
|---|---|---|
| Tuesday | **martes** | MAHR-tehs |
| Wednesday | **miércoles** | MYEHR-koh-lehs |
| Thursday | **jueves** | HWEH-behs |
| Friday | **viernes** | BYEHR-nehs |
| Saturday | **sábado** | SAH-bah-doh |
| Sunday | **domingo** | doh-MEEN-goh |

If you want to find out the day of an event, you may ask a question using the following pattern.

| What day is _____? | **¿Qué día es _____?** |
|---|---|
| | keh DEE-ah ehs |
| What day is the meeting? | **¿Qué día es la reunión?** |
| | keh DEE-ah ehs lah rreh-oo-NYOHN |
| The art class is on Monday. | **La clase de arte es el lunes.** |
| | lah KLAH-seh deh AHR-teh ehs ehl LOO-nehs |
| The art class is on Mondays. | **La clase de arte es los lunes.** |
| | lah KLAH-seh deh AHR-teh ehs lohs LOO-nehs |

Note that "on" is translated as **el** [ehl] when used with the day of the week in its singular form, but it is translated as **los** [lohs] when the day of the week is in the plural form, as indicated by the definite article.

# Telling Time
## *Para expresar la hora*

Learning how to tell time (**expresar la hora** [ehs-preh-SAHR lah OH-rah]) in Spanish is quite simple. Remember that you will always use the verb **ser** [sehr], and that you will use only two forms of the verb. You will use **es** [ehs] between one o'clock and one thirty, and **son** [sohn] for stating all other times.

To ask or state what time it is, use the following patterns.

| | |
|---|---|
| What time is it? | **¿Qué hora es?** <br> keh OH-rah ehs |
| It's one o'clock. | **Es la una.** <br> ehs lah oo-nah |
| It's two o'clock. | **Son las dos.** <br> sohn lahs dohs |

The Spanish word **y** [ee], meaning "and," is used to tell time between the hour and half past the hour, when you want to say how many minutes after the hour it is.

| | |
|---|---|
| It is one ten. | **Es la una y diez.** <br> ehs lah oo-nah ee dyehs |
| It's nine twenty. | **Son las nueve y veinte.** <br> sohn lahs NWEH-beh ee BEH-een-teh |

The Spanish word **menos** [MEH-nohs], meaning "minus," is used after the half hour to tell how many minutes it is before the next hour.

| | |
|---|---|
| It's one thirty-five (twenty-five minutes until two). | **Son las dos menos veinte y cinco.** <br> sohn lahs dohs MEH-nohs BEH-een-teh ee SEEN-koh |

The quarter-hour and half-hour in Spanish can be expressed by using specific words instead of the number of minutes they represent.

| | |
|---|---|
| quarter | **cuarto** <br> KWAHR-toh |
| half | **media** <br> MEH-dyah |
| It's a quarter to one. | **Es la una menos cuarto.** <br> ehs lah oo-nah MEH-nohs KWAHR-toh |
| It's half past twelve. | **Son las doce y media.** <br> sohn lahs DOH-seh ee MEH-dyah |

If you want to differentiate between morning, afternoon, and evening, use the following expressions.

| in the morning | **de la mañana** |
| | deh lah mah-NYAH-nah |
| in the afternoon | **de la tarde** |
| | deh lah TAHR-deh |
| in the evening | **de la noche** |
| | deh lah NOH-cheh |
| It is seven o'clock in the morning. | **Son las siete de la mañana.** |
| | sohn lahs SYEH-teh deh lah mah-NYAH-nah |

To ask at what time an event takes place, you can pattern your question as follows.

| (At) what time is _____? | **¿A qué hora es _____?** |
| | ah keh OH-rah ehs |
| (At) what time is the English class? | **¿A qué hora es la clase de inglés?** |
| | ah keh OH-rah ehs lah KLAH-seh deh een-GLEHS |
| (It is) at two o'clock. | **(Es) a las dos.** |
| | (ehs) ah lahs dohs |
| (It is) at one o'clock. | **(Es) a la una.** |
| | (ehs) ah lah OO-nah |

To express noon (**el mediodía** [ehl meh-dyoh-DEE-ah]) and midnight (**la medianoche** [lah meh-dyah-NOH-cheh]), you use the following specific expressions.

| at noon | **al mediodía** |
| | ahl meh-dyoh-DEE-ah |
| at midnight | **a la medianoche** |
| | ah lah meh-dyah-NOH-cheh |

The following expressions related to telling time will prove very useful.

| at about | **a eso de** |
| | ah EH-soh deh |
| sharp / on the dot | **en punto** |
| | ehn POON-toh |

## GRAMMAR · To Find Out "When?"

If you do not need to know a specific time or date when something is taking place, use **¿Cuándo?** [KWAHN-doh] to ask "When?"

| | |
|---|---|
| When is the fair? | **¿Cuándo es el festival?**<br>KWAHN-doh ehs ehl fehs-tee-BAHL |
| It is at the beginning of December. | **Es a principios de diciembre.**<br>ehs ah preen-SEE-pyohs deh dee-SYEHM-breh |

The following expressions can be used to answer the question "When?" (**¿Cuándo?** [KWAHN-doh]). When you answer, you will be giving a specific time period.

| | |
|---|---|
| at the beginning of | **a principios de**<br>ah preen-SEE-pyohs deh |
| at the end of | **a fines de**<br>ah FEE-nehs deh |
| daily | **a diario / diariamente**<br>ah DYAH-ryoh / dyah-ryah-MEHN-teh |
| each day | **cada día**<br>KAH-dah DEE-ah |
| every day | **todos los días**<br>TOH-dohs lohs DEE-ahs |
| in a minute / an hour | **en un minuto / una hora**<br>ehn oon mee-NOO-toh / oo-nah OH-rah |
| in/about the middle of | **a mediados de**<br>ah meh-DYAH-dohs deh |
| now | **ahora**<br>ah-OH-rah |
| right now | **ahora mismo**<br>ah-OH-rah MEES-moh |
| starting from (one o'clock) on | **a partir de (la una)**<br>ah pahr-TEER deh (lah oo-nah) |

The following words and phrases also answer questions asked with **¿Cuándo?**
[KWAHN-doh], but they are not as specific as the expressions included in the list
above.

| | |
|---|---|
| afterward | **después**<br>dehs-PWEHS |
| already | **ya**<br>yah |
| at once | **en seguida**<br>ehn seh-GEE-dah |
| before | **antes**<br>AHN-tehs |
| from time to time | **de vez en cuando**<br>deh behs ehn KWAHN-doh |
| immediately | **inmediatamente**<br>een-meh-dyah-tah-MEHN-teh |
| not yet | **todavía no**<br>toh-dah-BEE-ah noh |
| often | **a menudo**<br>ah meh-NOO-doh |
| soon | **pronto**<br>PROHN-toh |
| whenever you can | **cuando pueda**<br>KWAHN-do PWEH-dah |
| whenever you have time | **cuando tenga tiempo**<br>KWAHN-doh TEHN-gah TYEHM-poh |
| whenever you like | **cuando quiera**<br>KWAHN-doh KYEH-rah |

## Practice 3-1

**A** *Express the following dates in Spanish. (If you need help with numbers, see Chapter 4, pages 157–158.)*

1. September 15, 1990  _____

2. October 25, 2001  _____

3. July 1, 2006  _____

4. January 31, 1984  _____

**B** Fill in the missing days of the week. Remember that in Spanish-speaking countries, the week begins on Monday.

_____ martes _____ jueves

_____ sábado _____

**C** Write complete sentences to express the following times in Spanish. Remember to use the verb **ser**.

1. 9:10 A.M. _____

2. noon _____

3. 2:35 P.M. _____

4. 5:00 P.M. _____

5. midnight _____

6. 7:30 P.M. _____

7. 11:15 A.M. _____

**D** Complete the following sentences with the Spanish word(s) for the expressions in parentheses.

1. Nosotros desayunamos _____ (every day).

2. Ella visita a sus parientes _____ (at the beginning of) marzo.

3. Uds. tienen que leer _____ (right now).

4. Las vacaciones son _____ (starting from) hoy.

5. Tenemos un examen _____ (about the middle of) abril.

**E** Write a question in Spanish to ask for the following information.

1. the time

_____

2. today's date

_____

3. when an event is taking place

_____

4. the time of the Spanish class

_____

## Talking About the Weather

*Para hablar del tiempo*

It is a good idea to become familiar with the different ways to talk about the weather (**el tiempo** [ehl TYEHM-poh]). Let's begin by becoming familiar with the seasons (**las estaciones** [lahs ehs-tah-SYOH-nehs]).

| | | |
|---|---|---|
| spring | **la primavera** | lah pree-mah-BEH-rah |
| summer | **el verano** | ehl beh-RAH-noh |
| autumn | **el otoño** | ehl oh-TOH-nyoh |
| winter | **el invierno** | ehl een-BYEHR-noh |

If you want to ask about the weather in a specific season, you might ask the question as follows.

| | |
|---|---|
| What is the weather like in the spring? | **¿Qué tiempo hace en la primavera?** <br> keh TYEHM-poh AH-seh ehn lah pree-mah-BEH-rah |

The verb **hacer** [ah-SEHR] is used in many idiomatic expressions dealing with the weather. To talk about what the weather is like, use **hacer** as follows.

| | |
|---|---|
| How is the weather? | **¿Qué tiempo hace?** <br> keh TYEHM-poh AH-seh |
| The weather is good. | **Hace buen tiempo.** <br> AH-seh bwehn TYEHM-poh |
| The weather is bad. | **Hace mal tiempo.** <br> AH-seh mahl TYEHM-poh |
| It is (very) cold. | **Hace (mucho) frío.** <br> AH-seh (MOO-choh) FREE-oh |
| It is (very) hot. | **Hace (mucho) calor.** <br> AH-seh (MOO-choh) kah-LOHR |
| It is cool. | **Hace fresco.** <br> AH-seh FREHS-koh |
| It is sunny. | **Hace sol.** <br> AH-seh sohl |
| It is windy. | **Hace viento.** <br> AH-seh BYEHN-toh |

To talk about what the weather was like in the past, use **hizo** [EE-soh] instead of **hace** [AH-seh].

| | |
|---|---|
| What was the weather like yesterday? | **¿Qué tiempo hizo ayer?**<br>keh TYEHM-poh EE-soh ah-YEHR |
| It was hot yesterday. | **Hizo calor ayer.**<br>EE-soh kah-LOHR ah-YEHR |

To find some words and expressions that are useful when talking about the past, see Chapter 6, pages 231–232.

To talk about what the weather will be like in the future, use **va a hacer** [bah ah ah-SEHR] instead of **hace** [AH-seh].

| | |
|---|---|
| What is the weather going to be like tomorrow? | **¿Qué tiempo va a hacer mañana?**<br>keh TYEHM-poh bah ah ah-SEHR<br>mah-NYAH-nah |
| Tomorrow it is going to be windy. | **Mañana va a hacer viento.**<br>mah-NYAH-nah bah ah ah-SEHR<br>BYEHN-toh |

To find some words and expressions that are useful when talking about the future, see Chapter 5, pages 197–198.

With the following weather expressions, you need to use the verb **estar** [ehs-TAHR], meaning "to be."

| | |
|---|---|
| It is cloudy. | **Está nublado.**<br>ehs-TAH noo-BLAH-doh |
| It is clear. | **Está despejado.**<br>ehs-TAH dehs-peh-HAH-doh |
| It is sunny. | **Está soleado.**<br>ehs-TAH soh-leh-AH-doh |
| It is rainy. | **Está lluvioso.**<br>ehs-TAH yoo-BYOH-soh |
| It is snowing. | **Está nevando.**<br>ehs-TAH neh-BAHN-doh |
| It is drizzling. | **Está lloviznando.**<br>ehs-TAH yoh-bees-NAHN-doh |
| It is raining. | **Está lloviendo.**<br>ehs-TAH yoh-BYEHN-doh |

Remember to use **va a estar** [bah ah ehs-TAHR] instead of **está** [ehs-TAH] when you want to use these **estar** expressions to talk about what the weather will be like in the future.

| Tomorrow it is going to be cloudy. | **Mañana va a estar nublado.** mah-NYAH-nah bah ah ehs-TAHR noo-BLAH-doh |
|---|---|

Other weather-related events that you will want to know how to express are the following.

| downpour | **el aguacero** ehl ah-gwah-SEH-roh |
|---|---|
| hail | **el granizo** ehl grah-NEE-soh |
| lightning | **el relámpago** ehl rreh-LAHM-pah-goh |
| rain | **la lluvia** lah YOO-byah |
| snow | **la nieve** lah NYEH-beh |
| thunder | **el trueno** ehl TRWEH-noh |
| weather forecast | **el pronóstico del tiempo** ehl proh-NOHS-tee-koh dehl TYEHM-poh |

## Practice 3-2

*What would you say in the following situations? Express the following ideas in Spanish, either by translating a sentence or by phrasing a question to find out information.*

1. You want to know what the weather was like yesterday.

   _____

2. It is cold and cloudy.

   _____

3. It is a rainy, windy day. How would you describe the weather in general?

   _____

4. You want to tell your students that tomorrow the weather is going to be good.

_____

5. It is snowing.

_____

# Clothing

### La ropa

The weather affects the clothing (**la ropa** [lah RROH-pah]) that people wear. Nowadays a lot of the clothing that children wear is the same for boys and girls.

## Articles of Clothing for Boys and Girls
### Las prendas de vestir para niños y niñas

The following list includes some articles of clothing (**las prendas de vestir** [lahs PREHN-dahs deh behs-TEER] that both boys (**los niños** [lohs NEE-nyohs]) and girls (**las niñas** [lahs NEE-nyahs]) may wear in many different situations.

| | |
|---|---|
| coat | **el abrigo / el sobretodo**<br>ehl ah-BREE-goh / ehl soh-breh-TOH-doh |
| jacket | **el saco / la chaqueta**<br>ehl SAH-koh / lah chah-KEH-tah |
| jeans | **los blue jeans / los vaqueros**<br>lohs bloo yeens / lohs bah-KEH-rohs |
| pajamas | **el piyama**<br>ehl pee-YAH-mah |
| pants | **los pantalones**<br>lohs pahn-tah-LOH-nehs |
| raincoat | **la gabardina / el impermeable**<br>lah gah-bar-DEE-nah /<br>ehl eem-pehr-mch-AH-bleh |
| shirt | **la camisa**<br>lah kah-MEE-sah |
| shorts | **los pantalones cortos**<br>lohs pahn-tah-LOH-nehs KOHR-tohs |

| socks | **los calcetines** |
| | lohs kahl-seh-TEE-nehs |
| suit | **el traje** |
| | ehl TRAH-heh |
| sweater | **el suéter** |
| | ehl SWEH-tehr |
| sweatshirt | **la sudadera** |
| | lah soo-dah-DEH-rah |
| tee shirt | **la camiseta** |
| | lah kah-mee-SEH-tah |
| uniform | **el uniforme** |
| | ehl oo-nee-FOHR-meh |

## For Girls · *Para las niñas*

| blouse | **la blusa** |
| | lah BLOO-sah |
| bra | **el sostén** |
| | ehl sohs-TEHN |
| dress | **el vestido** |
| | ehl behs-TEE-doh |
| panties | **las bragas** |
| | lahs BRAH-gahs |
| pantyhose | **los pantis / las pantimedias** |
| | lohs PAHN-tees / |
| | lahs pahn-tee-MEH-dyahs |
| skirt | **la falda** |
| | lah FAHL-dah |
| tights | **los leotardos** |
| | lohs leh-oh-TAHR-dohs |

## For Boys · *Para los niños*

| briefs | **los calzoncillos** |
| | lohs kahl-sohn-SEE-yohs |
| undershirt | **la camiseta** |
| | lah kah-mee-SEH-tah |

## Clothing Accessories
*Los complementos para la ropa*

| | |
|---|---|
| accessories | **los complementos** <br> lohs kohm-pleh-MEHN-tohs |
| backpack | **la mochila** <br> lah moh-CHEE-lah |
| belt | **el cinturón** <br> ehl seen-too-ROHN |
| cap | **la gorra** <br> lah GOH-rrah |
| glove | **el guante** <br> ehl GWAHN-teh |
| handkerchief | **el pañuelo** <br> ehl pah-NYWEH-loh |
| hat | **el sombrero** <br> ehl sohm-BREH-roh |
| pocket | **el bolsillo** <br> ehl bohl-SEE-yoh |
| purse | **el monedero / el portamonedas** <br> ehl moh-neh-DEH-roh / <br> ehl pohr-tah-moh-NEH-dahs |
| scarf | **la bufanda** <br> lah boo-FAHN-dah |
| tie | **la corbata** <br> lah kohr-BAH-tah |
| wallet | **la billetera / la cartera** <br> lah bee-yeh-TEH-rah / lah kahr-TEH-rah |

## Verbs

| | | |
|---|---|---|
| to button up | **abrocharse** | ah-broh-CHAHR-seh |
| to fix | **arreglar** | ah-rreh-GLAHR |
| to get dressed | **vestirse (i)** | behs-TEER-seh |
| to put on | **ponerse** (*irreg.*) | poh-NEHR-seh |
| to show | **mostrar (ue)** | mohs-TRAHR |
| to take off | **quitarse** | kee-TAHR-seh |
| to tie one's shoes | **abrocharse los zapatos** | ah-broh-CHAHR-seh lohs <br> sah-PAH-tohs |
| to try on | **probarse (ue)** | proh-BAHR-seh |
| to undress | **desvestirse (i)** | dehs-behs-TEER-seh |
| to wear | **llevar** | yeh-BAHR |

## Grammar · Expressing Ownership

In Spanish, when you want to find out who owns something, you use the following patterns.

| Whose _____ is it? | **¿De quién es _____?** |
| | deh kyehn ehs |
| Whose _____ are they? | **¿De quién son _____?** |
| | deh kyehn sohn |
| Whose book is it? | **¿De quién es el libro?** |
| | deh kyehn ehs ehl LEE-broh |
| Whose books are they? | **¿De quién son los libros?** |
| | deh kyehn sohn lohs LEE-brohs |

In English, when you want to find out who owns something, you use the word "whose" regardless of whether you think the item is possessed by one person or by more than one person.

In Spanish, when you think there is more than one owner, you ask the question as follows.

| Whose _____ is it? | **¿De quiénes es _____?** |
| | deh KYEH-nehs ehs |
| Whose _____ are they? | **¿De quiénes son _____?** |
| | deh KYEH-nehs sohn |
| Whose ball is it? | **¿De quiénes es la pelota?** |
| | deh KYEH-nehs ehs lah peh-LOH-tah |
| Whose balls are they? | **¿De quiénes son las pelotas?** |
| | deh KYEH-nehs sohn lahs peh-LOH-tahs |

Note that Spanish always includes the definite article for the item possessed, though English typically does not.

To state who owns something, use the following pattern.

| It is / They are _____. | **Es de / Son de _____.** |
| | ehs deh / sohn deh |
| It is / They are Ana's. | **Es de / Son de Ana.** |
| | ehs deh / sohn deh AH-nah |
| It is / They are Ana's and Paco's. | **Es de / Son de Ana y Paco.** |
| | ehs deh / sohn deh AH-nah ee PAH-koh |
| Whose is the coat? | **¿De quién es el abrigo?** |
| | deh kyehn ehs ehl ah-BREE-goh |
| It is Felipe's. | **Es de Felipe.** |
| | ehs deh feh-LEE-peh |

## GRAMMAR · Possessive Adjectives

Possessive adjectives are used to express ownership. In Spanish, the adjective must agree with the noun (object) that is possessed. As in English, the possessive adjectives are placed before the noun. In Chapter 1, you learned three possessive adjectives, **mi** [mee], **tu** [too], and **su** [soo].

Here is a list showing all the possessive adjectives you will need.

| ONE ITEM POSSESSED | MORE THAN ONE ITEM POSSESSED |
|---|---|
| **mi mochila**  (my backpack)<br>mee moh-CHEE-lah | **mis mochilas**  (my backpacks)<br>mees moh-CHEE-lahs |
| **tu mochila**  (your [*familiar*] backpack)<br>too moh-CHEE-lah | **tus mochilas**  (your backpacks)<br>toos moh-CHEE-lahs |
| **su mochila**  (your [*formal*] backpack)<br>soo moh-CHEE-lah | **sus mochilas**  (your backpacks)<br>soos moh-CHEE-lahs |
| **su mochila**  (his backpack)<br>soo moh-CHEE-lah | **sus mochilas**  (his backpacks)<br>soos moh-CHEE-lahs |
| **su mochila**  (her backpack)<br>soo moh-CHEE-lah | **sus mochilas**  (her backpacks)<br>soos moh-CHEE-lahs |
| **nuestra mochila**  (our backpack)<br>NWEHS-trah moh-CHEE-lah | **nuestras mochilas**  (our backpacks)<br>NWEHS-trahs moh-CHEE-lahs |
| **su mochila**  (their backpack)<br>soo moh-CHEE-lah | **sus mochilas**  (their backpacks)<br>soos moh-CHEE-lahs |

You will notice that **nuestro** [NWEHS-troh] is the only possessive adjective that has a feminine form: **nuestra** [NWEHS-trah].

| our t-shirt | **nuestra camiseta**<br>NWEHS-trah kah-mee-SEH-tah |
|---|---|
| our pants | **nuestros pantalones**<br>NWEHS-trohs pahn-tah-LOH-nehs |

## GRAMMAR · Using the Verb "To Be" to Express a Characteristic

To find out about the characteristics of someone or something, ask a question using the following patterns.

| What is _____ like? | **¿Cómo es _____?**<br>KOH-moh ehs |
|---|---|
| What are _____ like? | **¿Cómo son _____?**<br>KOH-moh sohn |

| | |
|---|---|
| What is the sweater like? | **¿Cómo es el suéter?** |
| | ᴋᴏʜ-moh ehs ehl sᴡᴇʜ-tehr |
| What are the pants like? | **¿Cómo son los pantalones?** |
| | ᴋᴏʜ-moh sohn lohs pahn-tah-ʟᴏʜ-nehs |

When describing a person, a place, or a thing (for example, an article of clothing), use the verb **ser** [sehr] + an adjective.

| | |
|---|---|
| The sweater is pretty. | **El suéter es bonito.** |
| | ehl sᴡᴇʜ-tehr ehs boh-ɴᴇᴇ-toh |
| The pants are expensive. | **Los pantalones son caros.** |
| | lohs pahn-tah-ʟᴏʜ-nehs sohn ᴋᴀʜ-rohs |

Some adjectives that you can use to describe clothing are listed here.

| | |
|---|---|
| dressy | **vistoso** |
| | bees-ᴛᴏʜ-soh |
| expensive | **caro** |
| | ᴋᴀʜ-roh |
| inexpensive | **barato** |
| | bah-ʀᴀʜ-toh |
| long | **largo** |
| | ʟᴀʜʀ-goh |
| pretty | **lindo / bonito** |
| | ʟᴇᴇɴ-doh / boh-ɴᴇᴇ-toh |
| short | **corto** |
| | ᴋᴏʜʀ-toh |
| ugly | **feo** |
| | ғᴇʜ-oh |

## Gʀᴀᴍᴍᴀʀ · Agreement of Noun and Adjective

A Spanish adjective agrees with the noun it describes in both gender and number.

| | |
|---|---|
| The dress is long. | **El vestido es largo.** |
| | ehl behs-ᴛᴇᴇ-doh ehs ʟᴀʜʀ-goh |
| The skirts are long. | **Las faldas son largas.** |
| | lahs ғᴀʜʟ-dahs sohn ʟᴀʜʀ-gahs |

For more information about gender and number of nouns and adjectives, see Chapter 1, page 45.

## Verbs

| | | |
|---|---|---|
| to be in style | **estar** (*irreg.*) **de moda** | ehs-TAHR deh MOH-dah |
| to be out of style | **estar** (*irreg.*) **pasado de moda** | ehs-TAHR pah-SAH-doh deh MOH-dah |
| to fit (well) | **quedarle bien** | keh-DAHR-leh byehn |
| to fit (poorly) | **quedarle mal** | keh-DAHR-leh mahl |
| to fit loosely | **quedarle ancho** | keh-DAHR-leh AHN-choh |
| to fit tightly | **quedarle estrecho** | keh-DAHR-leh ehs-TREH-choh |
| to look good | **lucir** (*irreg.*) **bien** | loo-SEER byehn |
| to look bad | **lucir** (*irreg.*) **mal** | loo-SEER mahl |
| to match | **hacer** (*irreg.*) **juego con** | ah-SEHR HWEH-goh kohn |

The indirect object pronoun **le** [leh], meaning "you," "him," or "her," can be either attached to an infinitive or placed before a conjugated verb.

| | |
|---|---|
| The pants seem to fit you/him/her well. | **Los pantalones parecen quedarle bien.** lohs pahn-tah-LOH-nehs pah-REH-sehn keh-DAHR-leh byehn |
| The pants fit you/him/her well. | **Los pantalones le quedan bien.** lohs pahn-tah-LOH-nehs leh KEH-dahn byehn |

## Materials
*Las telas*

Some favorite materials (**las telas** [lahs TEH-lahs]) for clothing are the following.

| | |
|---|---|
| cotton | **algodón** ahl-goh-DOHN |
| denim | **mezclilla** mehs-KLEE-yah |
| flannel | **franela** frah-NEH-lah |
| leather | **cuero** KWEH-roh |
| polyester | **poliéster** poh-LYEHS-tehr |
| wool | **lana** LAH-nah |

To find out what material something (whether it is clothes or something else) is made of, ask a question as follows.

| | |
|---|---|
| What is _____ made of? | **¿De qué es _____?**<br>deh keh ehs |
| What is the blouse made of? | **¿De qué es la blusa?**<br>deh keh ehs lah BLOO-sah |

To tell about the material of which something is made, you can use the following pattern.

| | |
|---|---|
| It is (made) of _____. | **Es de _____.**<br>ehs deh |
| They are (made) of _____. | **Son de _____.**<br>sohn deh |
| The blouse is made of cotton. | **La blusa es de algodón.**<br>lah BLOO-sah ehs deh ahl-goh-DOHN |
| The pants are made of wool. | **Los pantalones son de lana.**<br>lohs pahn-tah-LOH-nehs sohn deh LAH-nah |

## Colors
*Los colores*

Here is a list of colors (**los colores** [lohs koh-LOH-rehs]).

| | | |
|---|---|---|
| black | **negro** | NEH-groh |
| blue | **azul** | ah-SOOL |
| brown | **marrón** | mah-RROHN |
| gray | **gris** | grees |
| green | **verde** | BEHR-deh |
| navy blue | **azul marino** | ah-SOOL mah-REE-noh |
| orange | **anaranjado** | ah-nah-rahn-HAH-doh |
| pink | **rosado** | rroh-SAH-doh |
| purple | **morado** | moh-RAH-doh |
| red | **rojo** | RROH-hoh |
| violet | **morado** | moh-RAH-doh |
| white | **blanco** | BLAHN-koh |
| yellow | **amarillo** | ah-mah-REE-yoh |

To talk about the color of an object in Spanish, use the following patterns.

| | |
|---|---|
| What color is _____? | **¿De qué color es _____?** |
| | deh keh koh-LOHR ehs |
| What color are _____? | **¿De qué color son _____?** |
| | deh keh koh-LOHR sohn |
| What color is the blouse? | **¿De qué color es la blusa?** |
| | deh keh koh-LOHR ehs lah BLOO-sah |
| The blouse is white. | **La blusa es blanca.** |
| | lah BLOO-sah ehs BLAHN-kah |
| What color are the sweaters? | **¿De qué color son los suéteres?** |
| | deh keh koh-LOHR sohn lohs |
| | SWEH-teh-rehs |
| The sweaters are black. | **Los suéteres son negros.** |
| | lohs SWEH-teh-rehs sohn NEH-grohs |

## GRAMMAR · Position of Adjectives

In Spanish, adjectives are generally placed after the noun they modify. Remember that colors, as adjectives, agree with the noun they modify in gender and number.

| | |
|---|---|
| He is wearing a white shirt and black pants. | **Lleva una camisa blanca y unos pantalones negros.** |
| | YEH-bah oo-nah kah-MEE-sah |
| | BLAHN-kah ee oo-nohs |
| | pahn-tah-LOH-nehs NEH-grohs |

## Practice 3-3

**A** *What article of clothing would these people wear in each specified situation?*

1. Hace mucho calor. Llevo _____.

2. Hace fresco. Lleva _____.

3. Está lloviendo. Llevamos _____.

4. Está nevando. Llevan _____.

5. Hace viento. Llevas _____.

**B** *Write complete sentences to answer the following questions, using the cues in parentheses.*

1. ¿De quién es la camiseta? (Juan)

   _____

2. ¿De quiénes son los calcetines? (Alberto *and* Pedro)

   _____

3. ¿De quién es la falda? (Graciela)

   _____

4. ¿De quién son los calzoncillos? (David)

   _____

5. ¿De quiénes son las chaquetas? (Diego *and* Tina)

   _____

**C** *Complete the following sentences with the Spanish words for the English cues in parentheses.*

1. _____ (*my*) abrigo es _____ (*blue*).

2. _____ (*our*) guantes son _____ (*black*).

3. _____ (*his*) mochila es _____ (*yellow*).

4. _____ (*your* [familiar]) pañuelos son _____ (*white*).

5. _____ (*their*) pantalones son _____ (*red*).

## Curriculum

### El plan de estudio

It is useful to learn to express the subject areas in which students in the primary grades generally receive academic instruction. A list of the typical subject areas of the primary school curriculum (**el plan de estudio** [ehl plahn deh ehs-TOO-dyoh]) follows.

| | |
|---|---|
| art | **el arte**<br>ehl AHR-teh |
| language arts | **el lenguaje**<br>ehl lehn-GWAH-heh |
| mathematics | **las matemáticas**<br>lahs mah-teh-MAH-tee-kahs |

| | |
|---|---|
| music | **la música**<br>lah MOO-see-kah |
| physical education | **la educación física**<br>lah eh-doo-kah-SYOHN FEE-see-kah |
| science | **la ciencia**<br>lah SYEHN-syah |
| social studies | **los estudios sociales**<br>lohs ehs-TOO-dyohs soh-SYAH-lehs |

The following vocabulary will be useful as you are helping your students to become fluent in English.

| | |
|---|---|
| How do you spell _____? | **¿Cómo se escribe / se deletrea _____?**<br>KOH-moh seh ehs-KREE-beh /<br>seh deh-leh-TREH-ah |
| alphabet | **el abecedario**<br>ehl ah-beh-seh-DAH-ryoh |
| handwriting | **la caligrafía / la escritura**<br>lah kah-lee-grah-FEE-ah /<br>lah ehs-kree-TOO-rah |
| pronunciation | **la pronunciación**<br>lah proh-noon-syah-SYOHN |
| reading | **la lectura**<br>lah lehk-TOO-rah |
| spelling | **la ortografía**<br>lah ohr-toh-grah-FEE-ah |
| spelling book | **el abecedario**<br>ehl ah-beh-seh-DAH-ryoh |

Reading time is an important learning time, as well as a relaxing activity. Children love to hear (**oír** [oh-EER]) and to tell (**contar** [kohn-TAHR]) stories (**cuentos** [KWEHN-tohs]). By the early grades they begin to read (**leer** [leh-EHR]) for themselves. Here are useful words that are related to reading.

| | |
|---|---|
| answer | **la respuesta**<br>lah rrehs-PWEHS-tah |
| beginning | **el principio**<br>ehl preen-SEE-pyoh |
| chapter | **el capítulo**<br>ehl kah-PEE-too-loh |
| character | **el personaje**<br>ehl pehr-soh-NAH-heh |

| end | **el fin**<br>ehl feen |
|---|---|
| page | **la página**<br>lah PAH-hee-nah |
| problem | **el problema**<br>ehl proh-BLEH-mah |
| question | **la pregunta**<br>lah preh-GOON-tah |
| summary | **el resumen**<br>ehl rreh-SOO-mehn |
| theme | **el tema**<br>ehl TEH-mah |
| title | **el título**<br>ehl TEE-too-loh |
| word | **la palabra**<br>lah pah-LAH-brah |

## Verbs

| to hear / listen to stories | **oír** (*irreg.*) / **escuchar cuentos**<br>oh-EER / ehs-koo-CHAHR KWEHN-tohs |
|---|---|
| to learn | **aprender**<br>ah-prehn-DEHR |
| to print (write in block letters) | **escribir en letra de molde**<br>ehs-kree-BEER ehn LEH-trah deh MOHL-deh |
| to read | **leer** (*irreg.*)<br>leh-EHR |
| to spell (letter by letter) | **deletrear/escribir**<br>deh-leh-treh-AHR/ehs-kree-BEER |
| to tell stories | **contar (ue) cuentos**<br>kohn-TAHR KWEHN-tohs |
| to write (in longhand) | **escribir (a mano / en cursiva)**<br>ehs-kree-BEER (ah MAH-noh /<br>ehn koor-SEE-bah) |

For a more complete list of school subjects and vocabulary related to each subject, see Chapter 4.

## GRAMMAR · Verbs That Are Irregular in the yo Form

Some important verbs that are irregular only in the **yo** [yoh] form are listed here.

| to be acquainted with | **conocer**<br>koh-noh-SEHR | **yo conozco**<br>yoh koh-NOHS-koh |
|---|---|---|

| to bring | **traer** | **yo traigo** |
| | trah-EHR | yoh TRAH-ee-goh |
| to do, make | **hacer** | **yo hago** |
| | ah-SEHR | yoh AH-goh |
| to fall | **caerse** | **yo me caigo** |
| | kah-EHR-seh | yoh meh KAH-ee-goh |
| to give | **dar** | **yo doy** |
| | dahr | yoh DOH-ee |
| to go out, leave | **salir** | **yo salgo** |
| | sah-LEER | yoh SAHL-goh |
| to know facts | **saber** | **yo sé** |
| | sah-BEHR | yoh seh |
| to put, place | **poner** | **yo pongo** |
| | poh-NEHR | yoh POHN-goh |
| to see | **ver** | **yo veo** |
| | behr | yoh VEH-oh |
| to translate | **traducir** | **yo traduzco** |
| | trah-doo-SEER | yoh trah-DOOS-koh |

The verbs above are regular in all other forms of the present tense. Look carefully at the complete conjugation of the verb **traer**.

**traer** ( *irreg.*) [trah-EHR]  to bring

| I bring | **yo traigo** | yoh TRAH-ee-goh |
| you bring | **tú traes** | too TRAH-ehs |
| he brings | **él trae** | ehl TRAH-eh |
| she brings | **ella trae** | EH-yah TRAH-eh |
| you bring | **Ud. trae** | OOS-TEHD TRAH-eh |
| we bring | **nosotros traemos** | noh-SOH-trohs trah-EH-mohs |
| we bring | **nosotras traemos** | noh-SOH-trahs trah-EH-mohs |
| they bring | **ellos traen** | EH-yohs TRAH-ehn |
| they bring | **ellas traen** | EH-yahs TRAH-ehn |
| you (*plural*) bring | **Uds. traen** | OOS-TEH-dehs TRAH-ehn |

| What do you bring to school? | **¿Qué traes a la escuela?** |
| | keh TRAH-ehs ah lah ehs-KWEH-lah |
| I bring a notebook and a pencil. | **Traigo un cuaderno y un lápiz.** |
| | TRAH-ee-goh oon kwah-DEHR-noh ee |
| | oon LAH-pees |

For a list of additional objects that you might find in the classroom, see Chapter 2, pages 69–70 and 78–80.

## Art Projects

### Los proyectos de arte

Art projects (**los proyectos de arte** [lohs proh-YEHK-tohs deh AHR-teh]) are an everyday activity in early childhood education. When doing art projects, a student may wear an apron (**un delantal** [oon deh-lahn-TAHL]).

Some materials that are typically used in art projects are the following.

| | |
|---|---|
| brush (artist's) | **el pincel**<br>ehl peen-SEHL |
| coloring book | **el libro de colorear**<br>ehl LEE-broh deh koh-loh-reh-AHR |
| crayons | **los lápices para pintar**<br>lohs LAH-pee-sehs PAH-rah peen-TAHR |
| glue | **la cola**<br>lah KOH-lah |
| modeling clay | **la plasticina**<br>lah plahs-tee-SEE-nah |
| paper (colored) | **el papel (de colores)**<br>ehl pah-PEHL (deh koh-LOH-rehs) |
| scissors (plastic) | **las tijeras (de plástico)**<br>lahs tee-HEH-rahs (deh PLAHS-tee-koh) |

### Verbs

| | | |
|---|---|---|
| to color | **colorear** | koh-loh-reh-AHR |
| to cut | **cortar** | kohr-TAHR |
| to draw | **dibujar** | dee-boo-HAHR |
| to fold | **doblar** | doh-BLAHR |
| to paint | **pintar** | peen-TAHR |
| to paste | **pegar** | peh-GAHR |
| to tie | **amarrar** | ah-mah-RRAHR |

## Cleaning Up the Classroom

### Para limpiar el aula

At the end of each day, and usually at the end of any art project, the children will have to gather what they have used and clean up. Some items that will be needed for cleaning up the classroom (**limpiar el aula** [leem-PYAHR ehl AH-oo-lah]) are listed here.

| | | |
|---|---|---|
| broom | **la escoba** | lah ehs-KOH-bah |
| bucket | **el balde / el cubo** | ehl BAHL-deh / ehl KOO-boh |
| dust rag | **el trapo** | ehl TRAH-poh |
| dustpan | **el recogedor de basura** | ehl rreh-koh-heh-DOHR deh bah-soo-rah |
| mop | **el trapeador** | ehl trah-peh-ah-DOHR |
| paper towel | **la toalla de papel** | lah toh-AH-yah deh pah-PEHL |
| sponge | **la esponja** | lah ehs-POHN-hah |
| towel | **la toalla** | lah toh-AH-yah |
| trash can | **el basurero** | ehl bah-soo-REH-roh |
| water | **el agua** | ehl AH-gwah |

Here are some familiar commands you will find useful when asking a child to clean up.

| | | |
|---|---|---|
| Dust. | **Sacude.** | sah-KOO-deh |
| Pick up. | **Recoge.** | rreh-KOH-heh |
| Sweep. | **Barre.** | BAH-rreh |

To review the formation of commands, see the Introduction, pages 16–18, 20, and 21.

## Verbs

| | | |
|---|---|---|
| to clean | **limpiar** | leem-PYAHR |
| to dust | **sacudir** | sah-koo-DEER |
| to mop | **trapear** | trah-peh-AHR |
| to pick up | **recoger** (*irreg.*) | rreh-koh-HEHR |
| to put | **poner** (*irreg.*) | poh-NEHR |
| to put away | **guardar** | gwahr-DAHR |
| to sweep | **barrer** | bah-RREHR |
| to throw away | **tirar** | tee-RAHR |
| to throw away | **botar** | boh-TAHR |
| to wash | **lavar** | lah-BAHR |

## Practice 3-4

*Answer the following questions truthfully, using complete sentences.*

1. ¿Sabes deletrear en español?

   _____

2. ¿Traes un sacapuntas a la escuela?

   _____

3. ¿A qué hora sales de la escuela?

   _____

4. ¿Conoces a todos los estudiantes de la escuela?

   _____

5. ¿Das mucha tarea a los estudiantes?

   _____

6. ¿Haces mucho trabajo en la escuela?

   _____

## Toys and Playthings

### Los juguetes y otras cosas para jugar

In early childhood programs, a good part of the day is spent in playtime and rest. There are often many toys and playthings (**los juguetes y otras cosas para jugar** [lohs hoo-GEH-tehs ee OH-trahs KOH-sahs PAH-rah hoo-GAHR]) in the classroom. The children may also have many of these playthings at home.

| | |
|---|---|
| ball | **la pelota**<br>lah peh-LOH-tah |
| balloon | **el globo**<br>ehl GLOH-boh |
| blocks (wooden) | **los bloques (de madera)**<br>lohs BLOH-kehs (deh mah-DEH-rah) |
| cart (small) | **el carretón**<br>ehl kah-rreh-TOHN |
| costume | **el disfraz**<br>ehl dees-FRAHS |

| | |
|---|---|
| doll | **la muñeca** |
| | lah moo-NYEH-kah |
| jump rope | **la cuerda de saltar** |
| | lah KWEHR-dah deh sahl-TAHR |
| puppet | **el títere** |
| | ehl TEE-teh-reh |
| puzzle (jigsaw) | **el rompecabezas** |
| | ehl rrohm-peh-kah-BEH-sahs |
| stuffed animal | **el animal de peluche** |
| | ehl ah-nee-MAHL deh peh-LOO-cheh |
| toy train | **el tren de juguete** |
| | ehl trehn deh hoo-GEH-teh |
| toy truck | **el camión de juguete** |
| | ehl kah-MYOHN deh hoo-GEH-teh |

Spanish speakers often use the ending **-ito**, which indicates that something is little or small in size, when referring to toys.

| | |
|---|---|
| boat | **el barquito** |
| | ehl bahr-KEE-toh |
| car | **el carrito** |
| | ehl kah-RREE-toh |
| train | **el trencito** |
| | ehl trehn-SEE-toh |
| truck | **el camioncito** |
| | ehl kah-myohn-SEE-toh |

It is also common to use the ending **-ito** when referring to stuffed animals, but in this case it is used to indicate endearment. For example, a toy bear is **el osito** [ehl oh-SEE-toh], a toy cat is **el gatito** [ehl gah-TEE-toh], and a toy dog is **el perrito** [ehl peh-RREE-toh]. The ending **-ito** can also be used with people's names (especially children) to indicate endearment, for example, **Pedrito** instead of **Pedro** or **Juanita** instead of **Juana**.

Here is a list of other toys or playthings that children may have at home.

| | |
|---|---|
| bicycle | **la bicicleta** |
| | lah bee-see-KLEH-tah |
| kite | **la cometa** |
| | lah koh-MEH-tah |
| skates | **los patines** |
| | lohs pah-TEE-nehs |

| sled | **el trineo** |
| | ehl tree-NEH-oh |
| toy soldier | **el soldado de juguete** |
| | ehl sohl-DAH-doh deh hoo-GEH-teh |
| tricycle | **el triciclo** |
| | ehl tree-SEE-kloh |

Spanish-speaking children, like their English-speaking counterparts, often use English brand names to identify their favorite playthings (las Barbies, el Nintendo, los Legos, etc.).

## Verbs

| to bounce (the ball) | **hacer** (*irreg.*) **rebotar (la pelota)** | ah-SEHR rreh-boh-TAHR (lah peh-LOH-tah) |
| to play | **jugar (ue)** | hoo-GAHR |
| to ride | **montar** | mohn-TAHR |
| to throw | **tirar** | tee-RAHR |
| to throw | **lanzar** | lahn-SAHR |

## Pets in the Classroom

### Los animales domésticos en el aula

There are often pets (**los animales domésticos** [lohs ah-nee-MAH-lehs doh-MEHS-tee-kohs]) in an early childhood classroom. Some common ones are listed here.

| fish | **el pez / los peces** |
| | ehl PEHS / lohs PEH-sehs |
| frog | **la rana** |
| | lah RRAH-nah |
| hamster | **el hámster** |
| | ehl HAHMS-tehr |
| snake | **la culebra** |
| | lah koo-LEH-brah |
| turtle | **la tortuga** |
| | lah tohr-TOO-gah |

## On the Playground

*En el patio de recreo*

Naps (**la siesta** [lah SYEHS-tah]), snacks (**la merienda** [lah meh-RYEHN-dah]), and recess (**el recreo** [ehl rreh-KREH-oh]) are very important in early childhood education.

Here are some things you may find on an early childhood playground (**el patio de recreo** [ehl PAH-tyoh deh rreh-KREH-oh]).

| | |
|---|---|
| bench | **el banco**<br>ehl BAHN-koh |
| merry-go-round | **el tiovivo**<br>ehl tee-oh-BEE-boh |
| sandbox | **el cajón de arena**<br>ehl kah-HOHN deh ah-REH-nah |
| seesaw | **el subibaja**<br>ehl soo-bee-BAH-hah |
| slide | **el tobogán**<br>ehl toh-boh-GAHN |
| swing | **el columpio**<br>ehl koh-LOOM-pyoh |
| water fountain | **la fuente de agua potable**<br>lah FWEHN-teh deh AH-gwah<br>poh-TAH-bleh |

During playtime, young children also like to do these activities.

| | |
|---|---|
| to play "dress up" | **jugar a disfrazarse**<br>hoo-GAHR ah dees-frah-SAHR-seh |
| to play hide and seek | **jugar al escondite**<br>hoo-GAHR ahl ehs-kohn-DEE-teh |
| to play "house" | **jugar a la casita**<br>hoo-GAHR ah lah kah-SEE-tah |
| to put puzzles together | **armar rompecabezas**<br>ahr-MAHR rrohm-peh-kah-BEH-sahs |

As children get older, they often enjoy table games (**los juegos de mesa** [lohs HWEH-gohs deh MEH-sah]), some of which are listed here.

| | |
|---|---|
| cards | **las cartas**<br>lahs KAHR-tahs |

| | |
|---|---|
| checkers | **las damas** |
| | lahs DAH-mahs |
| chess | **el ajedrez** |
| | ehl ah-heh-DREHS |

Here is a list of some of the things that you may say to the children.

| | |
|---|---|
| It's time (to) … | **Es hora de…** |
| | ehs OH-rah deh |
| to get up | **levantarse** |
| | leh-bahn-TAHR-seh |
| to go to the park | **ir al parque** |
| | eer ahl PAHR-keh |
| to nap | **dormir la siesta** |
| | dohr-MEER lah SYEHS-tah |
| to play (a game) | **jugar a (un juego)** |
| | hoo-GAHR ah (oon HWEH-goh) |
| to relax | **relajarse** |
| | rreh-lah-HAHR-seh |
| to rest | **descansar** |
| | dehs-kahn-SAHR |

Some commands that you may want to give a child are the following.

| | |
|---|---|
| Behave. | **Pórtate bien.** |
| | POHR-tah-teh byehn |
| Get up. | **Levántate.** |
| | leh-BAHN-tah-teh |
| Go to sleep. | **Duérmete.** |
| | DWEHR-meh-teh |
| Lie down. | **Acuéstate.** |
| | ah-KWEHS-tah-teh |
| Don't be afraid. | **No tengas miedo.** |
| | noh TEHN-gahs MYEH-doh |
| Don't cry. | **No llores.** |
| | noh YOH-rehs |

When children are at play, things do not always go as they should. You will sometimes need to tell a child not to behave in a certain way.

| | |
|---|---|
| Don't behave badly. | **No te portes mal.** |
| | noh teh POHR-tehs mahl |
| Don't bite. | **No muerdas.** |
| | noh MWEHR-dahs |

| | | |
|---|---|---|
| Don't fight. | **No pelees.** | |
| | | noh peh-LEH-ehs |
| Don't hit. | **No pegues.** | |
| | | noh PEH-gehs |
| Don't jump. | **No saltes.** | |
| | | noh SAHL-tehs |
| Don't push. | **No empujes.** | |
| | | noh ehm-POO-hehs |
| Don't run. | **No corras.** | |
| | | noh KOH-rrahs |

## Verbs

| | | |
|---|---|---|
| to argue | **discutir** | dees-koo-TEER |
| to break | **romper** | rrohm-PEHR |
| to curse | **decir** (*irreg.*) **malas palabras** | deh-SEER MAH-lahs pah-LAH-brahs |
| to grab | **agarrar** | ah-gah-RRAHR |
| to hit | **pegar** | peh-GAHR |
| to hit | **golpear** | gohl-peh-AHR |
| to hit (against) | **dar** (*irreg.*) **(contra)** | dahr (KOHN-trah) |
| to hit (against) | **chocar (contra)** | choh-KAHR (KOHN-trah) |
| to jump | **saltar** | sahl-TAHR |
| to kick | **patear** | pah-teh-AHR |
| to pull | **tirar de** | tee-RAHR deh |
| to pull | **jalar** | hah-LAHR |
| to push | **empujar** | ehm-poo-HAHR |
| to run | **correr** | koh-RREHR |
| to shake | **sacudir** | sah-koo-DEER |
| to spit | **escupir** | ehs-koo-PEER |
| to yell | **gritar** | gree-TAHR |

For an explanation of how to form commands, see the Introduction, pages 16–18, 20, and 21.

## GRAMMAR · Reflexive Verbs I

When Spanish speakers talk about many of their daily activities, you will find that they often need to use reflexive verbs. These verbs are called "reflexive" because they indicate that the subject is acting upon himself/herself. You will recognize reflexive verbs by the **se** [seh] that is attached to the infinitive form.

| | | |
|---|---|---|
| to behave oneself | **portarse bien** | pohr-TAHR-seh byehn |
| to brush one's hair | **cepillarse el pelo** | seh-pee-YAHR-seh ehl PEH-loh |
| to brush one's teeth | **cepillarse los dientes** | seh-pee-YAHR-seh lohs DYEHN-tehs |

| to get up | **levantarse** | leh-bahn-TAHR-seh |
| to go to sleep | **dormirse (ue)** | dohr-MEER-seh |
| to lie down, go to bed | **acostarse (ue)** | ah-kohs-TAHR-seh |
| to misbehave | **portarse mal** | pohr-TAHR-seh mahl |
| to sit down | **sentarse (ie)** | sehn-TAHR-seh |
| to wake up | **despertarse (ie)** | dehs-pehr-TAHR-seh |
| to wash up | **lavarse** | lah-BAHR-seh |

When used without the **se**, many reflexive verbs change meaning. For example, **dormir** [dohr-MEER] means "to sleep," **levantar** [leh-bahn-TAHR] means "to raise," and **portar** [pohr-TAHR] means "to carry."

Many sections of this book have lists of verbs that are related to the theme of a particular section. Remember that the reflexive verbs will have **se** [seh] attached to the infinitive ending. When you use these verbs, don't forget to use the reflexive pronouns, shown here.

| myself | **me** | meh | ourselves | **nos** | nohs |
| yourself (*familiar*) | **te** | teh | | | |
| himself | **se** | seh | themselves (*masc.*) | **se** | seh |
| herself | **se** | seh | themselves (*fem.*) | **se** | seh |
| yourself (*formal*) | **se** | seh | yourselves | **se** | seh |

**levantarse** [leh-bahn-TAHR-seh]  to get up (raise oneself)

| I get up | **(yo) me levanto** | meh leh-BAHN-toh |
| you get up | **(tú) te levantas** | teh leh-BAHN-tahs |
| he gets up | **(él) se levanta** | seh leh-BAHN-tah |
| she gets up | **(ella) se levanta** | seh leh-BAHN-tah |
| you get up | **(Ud.) se levanta** | seh leh-BAHN-tah |
| we get up | **(nosotros) nos levantamos** | nohs leh-bahn-TAH-mohs |
| we get up | **(nosotras) nos levantamos** | nohs leh-bahn-TAH-mohs |
| they get up | **(ellos) se levantan** | seh leh-BAHN-tahn |
| they get up | **(ellas) se levantan** | seh leh-BAHN-tahn |
| you (*plural*) get up | **(Uds.) se levantan** | seh leh-BAHN-tahn |

Yesterday you (*plural*) behaved. **Ayer se portaron bien.**
ah-YEHR seh pohr-TAH-rohn byehn

Are you going to wake up early? **¿Te vas a despertar temprano?**
teh bahs ah dehs-pehr-TAHR tehm-PRAH-noh

Don't get up. **No te levantes.**
noh teh leh-BAHN-tehs

Note that reflexive pronouns are usually placed immediately before a conjugated verb. The only exception to this placement is with an affirmative command. The reflexive pronoun is attached to the end of an affirmative command.

| Do not lie down. | **No te acuestes.** |
|---|---|
| | noh teh ah-KWEHS-tehs |
| Lie down. | **Acuéstate.** |
| | ah-KWEHS-tah-teh |

## GRAMMAR · Direct Object Pronouns

In Spanish, as in English, direct object pronouns can replace nouns representing the person or thing that is the direct object of the verb. Here is a list of the direct object pronouns.

| | | | | | |
|---|---|---|---|---|---|
| me | **me** | meh | us | **nos** | nohs |
| you (*familiar*) | **te** | teh | | | |
| him | **lo** | loh | them (*masc.*) | **los** | lohs |
| her | **la** | lah | them (*fem.*) | **las** | lahs |
| you (*formal, masc.*) | **lo** | loh | you (*formal, masc.*) | **los** | lohs |
| you (*formal, fem.*) | **la** | lah | you (*formal, fem.*) | **las** | lahs |
| it (*masc.*) | **lo** | loh | them (*masc.*) | **los** | lohs |
| it (*fem.*) | **la** | lah | them (*fem.*) | **las** | lahs |

With the exception of affirmative commands, direct object pronouns are placed directly before a conjugated verb.

| Did you buy the book? | **¿Compraste el libro?** |
|---|---|
| | kohm-PRAHS-teh ehl LEE-broh |
| Yes, I bought it. | **Sí, lo compré.** |
| | see, loh kohm-PREH |

With an affirmative command, the direct object pronoun follows and is attached to the command.

| Return it! | **¡Devuélvelo!** |
|---|---|
| | deh-BWEHL-beh-loh |

Note that when a direct object pronoun is attached to an affirmative command, a written accent is used in order to keep the stress on the same syllable of the verb that carries the stress in the non-command form. Verbs that only have one syllable do not need this accent.

In a negative sentence, the direct object pronoun is preceded by **no**.

| I did not buy it. | **No lo compré.** |
|---|---|
| | noh loh kohm-PREH |
| Do not buy it! | **¡No lo compres!** |
| | noh loh KOHM-prehs |

## GRAMMAR · Personal *a*

When the direct object of the verb is a person, the word **a** [ah] is placed before the word that represents the person. This **a** is called *the personal a* and it is not translated into English.

I know Pedro.                    **Conozco a Pedro.**
                                 koh-NOHS-koh ah PEH-droh

When the direct object pronoun is used for a person, it replaces both the personal **a** and the direct object noun.

Do you know Elena?               **¿Conoces a Elena?**
                                 koh-NOH-sehs ah eh-LEH-nah

No, I do not know her.           **No, no la conozco.**
                                 noh, noh lah koh-NOHS-koh

## Practice 3-5

**A** *Using the English phrase in parentheses as a clue, fill in the blanks from the strings of letters below.*

1. eemurdet
   (*go to sleep*)

2. rolsel
   (*don't cry*)        n o

3. attenaelv
   (*get up*)

4. sleepe
   (*don't fight*)      n o

5. srarco
   (*don't run*)        n o

6. ratelopmets
   (*don't behave badly*)   n o

7. eatcestau
   (*lie down*)

8. obeitranept
   (*behave*)

**B** *Write the reflexive pronoun that completes each phrase.*

1. Yo _____ porto bien.

2. Ellos _____ levantan a las diez.

3. Nosotros _____ acostamos a las once.

4. Tú _____ cepillas el pelo.

5. Ella _____ despierta a las siete.

**C** *Answer each of the following questions by replacing the underlined words with the correct pronoun.*

1. ¿Conoces a Juan? Sí, _____ conozco.

2. ¿Lees las novelas? No, no _____ leo.

3. ¿Me vas a despertar a las diez? Sí, _____ voy a despertar a las ocho.

4. ¿Visitas a tu tía? Sí, _____ visito.

5. ¿Empujas a tus amigos? No, no _____ empujo.

**D** *Write the personal* **a** *on the line provided if it is needed to complete the sentence. If it is not needed, just write an X.*

1. Conocen _____ los estudiantes.

2. Traigo _____ los lápices.

3. Nosotros dormimos _____ la siesta.

4. El director visita _____ los profesores.

5. Juan se cepilla _____ los dientes.

6. Tú ves _____ tus compañeros de clase.

## Summary Practice

*What would you say in the following situations? Write your responses in Spanish, using complete sentences.*

1. You want to know if a student knows the principal.

   _____

2. You need to find out when the meeting is.

   _____

3. You ask someone what the weather is going to be like tomorrow.

   _____

4. You tell a friend that it is raining.

   _____

5. You tell your students that your scarf is black and red.

   _____

6. You want to find out to whom the coat belongs.

   _____

7. You tell a student that the dress is in style.

   _____

8. You ask a student what the color of a shirt is.

   _____

9. You tell a student to write it [*masculine*] on the chalkboard.

   _____

10. Tell a student not to put them [*feminine*] in his/her backpack.

    _____

11. Tell your students to put away the toys.

    _____

12. Tell your students to behave.

    _____

# 4

## The Curriculum

*El plan de estudio*

## School Subjects

### Las asignaturas

The following is an extensive, though not exhaustive, list of school subjects (**las asignaturas** [lahs ah-seeg-nah-TOO-rahs] that a typical student encounters in the school curriculum (**el plan de estudio** [ehl plahn deh ehs-TOO-dyoh]), together with some useful related vocabulary.

| | |
|---|---|
| algebra | **el álgebra**<br>ehl AHL-heh-brah |
| arithmetic | **la aritmética**<br>lah ah-reet-MEH-tee-kah |
| art | **el arte**<br>ehl AHR-teh |
| astronomy | **la astronomía**<br>lah ahs-troh-noh-MEE-ah |
| biology | **la biología**<br>lah byoh-loh-HEE-ah |
| calculus | **el cálculo**<br>ehl KAHL-koo-loh |
| chemistry | **la química**<br>lah KEE-mee-kah |
| Chinese | **el chino**<br>ehl CHEE-noh |
| computer science | **la informática**<br>lah een-fohr-MAH-tee-kah |
| dance | **el baile**<br>ehl BAH-ee-leh |
| drama | **el drama**<br>ehl DRAH-mah |
| economics | **la economía**<br>lah eh-koh-noh-MEE-ah |
| English | **el inglés**<br>ehl een-GLEHS |
| French | **el francés**<br>ehl frahn-SEHS |

| geography | **la geografía** |
| | lah heh-oh-grah-FEE-ah |
| geometry | **la geometría** |
| | lah heh-oh-meh-TREE-ah |
| German | **el alemán** |
| | ehl ah-leh-MAHN |
| history | **la historia** |
| | lah ees-TOH-ryah |
| Italian | **el italiano** |
| | ehl ee-tah-LYAH-noh |
| Korean | **el coreano** |
| | ehl koh-reh-AH-noh |
| Latin | **el latín** |
| | ehl lah-TEEN |
| literature | **la literatura** |
| | lah lee-teh-rah-TOO-rah |
| mathematics | **las matemáticas** |
| | lahs mah-teh-MAH-tee-kahs |
| music | **la música** |
| | lah MOO-see-kah |
| physical education | **la educación física** |
| | lah eh-doo-kah-SYOHN FEE-see-kah |
| physics | **la física** |
| | lah FEE-see-kah |
| science | **la ciencia** |
| | lah SYEHN-syah |
| social studies | **los estudios sociales** |
| | lohs ehs-TOO-dyohs soh-SYAH-lehs |
| Spanish | **el español** |
| | ehl ehs-pah-NYOHL |
| theater | **el teatro** |
| | ehl teh-AH-troh |
| trigonometry | **la trigonometría** |
| | lah tree-goh-noh-meh-TREE-ah |

## GRAMMAR · The Verb "To Know"

In Spanish, there are two verbs that mean "to know," but these two verbs are not interchangeable.

**Saber** [sah-BEHR] is used to express the idea of knowing a *fact*, such as where a place is, a lesson, a rule, etc.

| | |
|---|---|
| I know there are no classes today. | **Yo sé que no hay clases hoy.** <br> yoh seh keh noh AH-ee KLAH-sehs OH-ee |

To express the idea of knowing *how* to do something, use **saber** [sah-BEHR] followed by an infinitive.

| | |
|---|---|
| We know how to play the guitar. | **Nosotros sabemos tocar la guitarra.** <br> noh-SOH-trohs sah-BEH-mohs toh-KAHR lah gee-TAH-rrah |

To express knowing a place or a person in the sense of being *acquainted with* or *familiar with*, you will always use **conocer** [koh-noh-SEHR].

| | |
|---|---|
| She knows the school very well. | **Ella conoce la escuela muy bien.** <br> EH-yah koh-NOH-seh lah ehs-KWEH-lah MOO-ee byehn |
| I know the biology teacher. | **Yo conozco al maestro de biología / a la maestra de biología.** <br> yoh koh-NOHS-koh ahl mah-EHS-troh deh byoh-loh-HEE-ah / ah lah mah-EHS-trah deh byoh-loh-HEE-ah |

Remember that when **conocer** [koh-noh-SEHR] is followed by a person, as in the example above, you must add the personal **a** [ah] after the verb. If **a** [ah] is followed by **el** [ehl], remember to use the contraction **al** [ahl].

Following is the present tense of the two Spanish verbs that mean "to know."

**saber** (*irreg.*) [sah-BEHR] to know (information, facts, how to do something)

| I know | **yo sé** | yoh seh |
|---|---|---|
| you know | **tú sabes** | too SAH-behs |
| he knows | **él sabe** | ehl SAH-beh |
| she knows | **ella sabe** | EH-yah SAH-beh |
| you know | **Ud. sabe** | oos-TEHD SAH-beh |
| we know | **nosotros sabemos** | noh-SOH-trohs sah-BEH-mohs |
| we know | **nosotras sabemos** | noh-SOH-trahs sah-BEH-mohs |
| they know | **ellos saben** | EH-yohs SAH-behn |
| they know | **ellas saben** | EH-yahs SAH-behn |
| you (*plural*) know | **Uds. saben** | oos-TEH-dehs SAH-behn |

**conocer** (*irreg.*) [koh-noh-SEHR] to know, be acquainted/familiar with

| I know | **yo conozco** | yoh koh-NOHS-koh |
|---|---|---|
| you know | **tú conoces** | too koh-NOH-sehs |
| he knows | **él conoce** | ehl koh-NOH-seh |
| she knows | **ella conoce** | EH-yah koh-NOH-seh |
| you know | **Ud. conoce** | OOS-TEHD koh-NOH-seh |
| we know | **nosotros conocemos** | noh-SOH-trohs koh-noh-SEH-mohs |
| we know | **nosotras conocemos** | noh-SOH-trahs koh-noh-SEH-mohs |
| they know | **ellos conocen** | EH-yohs koh-NOH-sehn |
| they know | **ellas conocen** | EH-yahs koh-NOH-sehn |
| you (*plural*) know | **Uds. conocen** | OOS-TEH-dehs koh-NOH-sehn |

## Practice 4-1

*Complete the following sentences with the correct form of* **saber** *or* **conocer**.

1. Yo no _____ a tus padres.

2. Nosotros _____ la respuesta a la pregunta.

3. Ellos _____ jugar al tenis.

4. ¿_____ tú a mi familia?

5. El director no _____ quién es el presidente del club.

6. Yo _____ hablar español muy bien.

7. Uds. _____ los restaurantes buenos en Lima.

8. Ella _____ a todos los profesores de la escuela.

## In Language Class

### En la clase de lenguas

Following is vocabulary that is particularly relevant to language class (**la clase de lenguas** [lah KLAH-seh deh LEHN-gwahs]).

| accent | **el acento** |
|---|---|
| | ehl ah-SEHN-toh |
| adjective | **el adjetivo** |
| | ehl ahd-heh-TEE-boh |
| adverb | **el adverbio** |
| | ehl ahd-BEHR-byoh |
| colon | **los dos puntos** |
| | lohs dohs POON-tohs |

| | |
|---|---|
| comma | **la coma**<br>lah KOH-mah |
| command | **el mandato**<br>ehl mahn-DAH-toh |
| composition | **la composición**<br>lah kohm-poh-see-SYOHN |
| conjugation | **la conjugación**<br>lah kohn-hoo-gah-SYOHN |
| conjunction | **la conjunción**<br>lah kohn-hoon-SYOHN |
| consonant | **la consonante**<br>lah kohn-soh-NAHN-teh |
| essay | **el ensayo**<br>ehl ehn-SAH-yoh |
| gerund | **el gerundio**<br>ehl heh-ROON-dyoh |
| grammar | **la gramática**<br>lah grah-MAH-tee-kah |
| infinitive | **el infinitivo**<br>ehl een-fee-nee-TEE-boh |
| interjection | **la interjección**<br>lah een-tehr-hehk-SYOHN |
| language | **el lenguaje**<br>ehl lehn-GWAH-heh |
| letter (alphabet) | **la letra**<br>lah LEH-trah |
| letter (capital) | **la letra mayúscula**<br>lah LEH-trah mah-YOOS-koo-lah |
| letter (lowercase) | **la letra minúscula**<br>lah LEH-trah mee-NOOS-koo-lah |
| meaning | **el significado**<br>ehl seeg-nee-fee-KAH-doh |
| noun | **el sustantivo**<br>ehl soos-tahn-TEE-boh |
| paragraph | **el párrafo**<br>ehl PAH-rrah-foh |
| participle | **el participio**<br>ehl pahr-tee-SEE-pyoh |
| passive voice | **la voz pasiva**<br>lah bohs pah-SEE-bah |
| period | **el punto**<br>ehl POON-toh |

| preposition | **la preposición** |
| | lah preh-poh-see-SYOHN |
| pronoun | **el pronombre** |
| | ehl proh-NOHM-breh |
| semicolon | **el punto y coma** |
| | ehl POON-toh ee KOH-mah |
| sentence | **la oración / la frase completa** |
| | lah oh-rah-SYOHN / |
| | lah FRAH-seh kohm-PLEH-tah |
| subject | **el sujeto** |
| | ehl soo-HEH-toh |
| syllable | **la sílaba** |
| | lah SEE-lah-bah |
| tense | **el tiempo** |
| | ehl TYEHM-poh |
| verb | **el verbo** |
| | ehl BEHR-boh |
| vocabulary | **el vocabulario** |
| | ehl boh-kah-boo-LAH-ryoh |
| vowel | **la vocal** |
| | lah boh-KAHL |
| word | **la palabra** |
| | lah pah-LAH-brah |
| writing | **la escritura** |
| | lah ehs-kree-TOO-rah |

## In Literature Class

### En la clase de literatura

Following is vocabulary that is particularly relevant to literature class (**la clase de literatura** [lah KLAH-seh deh lee-teh-rah-TOO-rah]).

| anonymous | **anónimo** |
| | ah-NOH-nee-moh |
| anthology | **la antología** |
| | lah ahn-toh-loh-HEE-ah |
| author | **el autor / la autora** |
| | ehl ah-oo-TOHR / lah ah-oo-TOH-rah |
| best seller | **el libro de gran éxito / el bestseller** |
| | ehl LEE-broh deh grahn EHK-see-toh / |
| | ehl behst-SEH-lehr |

| | |
|---|---|
| biography | **la biografía** <br> lah byoh-grah-FEE-ah |
| chapter | **el capítulo** <br> ehl kah-PEE-too-loh |
| character | **el personaje** <br> ehl pehr-soh-NAH-heh |
| comedy | **la comedia** <br> lah koh-MEH-dyah |
| edition | **la edición** <br> lah eh-dee-SYOHN |
| hero | **el héroe** <br> ehl EH-roh-eh |
| heroine | **la heroína** <br> lah eh-roh-EE-nah |
| in print | **en venta** <br> ehn BEHN-tah |
| index | **el índice** <br> ehl EEN-dee-seh |
| literary prize | **el premio literario** <br> ehl PREH-myoh lee-teh-RAH-ryoh |
| literature | **la literatura** <br> lah lee-teh-rah-TOO-rah |
| masterpiece | **la obra maestra** <br> lah OH-brah mah-EHS-trah |
| narrator | **el narrador / la narradora** <br> ehl nah-rrah-DOHR / <br> lah nah-rrah-DOH-rah |
| novel | **la novela** <br> lah noh-BEH-lah |
| out of print | **agotado** <br> ah-goh-TAH-doh |
| paperback | **el libro de bolsillo** <br> ehl LEE-broh deh bohl-SEE-yoh |
| period (literary) | **el período** <br> ehl peh-REE-oh-doh |
| play | **la obra de teatro** <br> lah OH-brah deh teh-AH-troh |
| plot | **el argumento** <br> ehl ahr-goo-MEHN-toh |
| poetry | **la poesía** <br> lah poh-eh-SEE-ah |

| | |
|---|---|
| prose | **la prosa** |
| | lah PROH-sah |
| reader | **el lector / la lectora** |
| | ehl lehk-TOHR / lah lehk-TOH-rah |
| reading | **la lectura** |
| | lah lehk-TOO-rah |
| script | **el guión** |
| | ehl gee-OHN |
| short story | **el cuento** |
| | ehl KWEHN-toh |
| style | **el estilo** |
| | ehl ehs-TEE-loh |
| theme | **el tema** |
| | ehl TEH-mah |
| title | **el título** |
| | ehl TEE-too-loh |
| tragedy | **la tragedia** |
| | lah trah-HEH-dyah |
| volume | **el volumen** |
| | ehl boh-LOO-mehn |
| work (of art) | **la obra (de arte)** |
| | lah OH-brah (deh AHR-teh) |

## Poetry
*La poesía*

| | |
|---|---|
| metaphor | **la metáfora** |
| | lah meh-TAH-foh-rah |
| ode | **la oda** |
| | lah OH-dah |
| poem | **el poema** |
| | ehl poh-EH-mah |
| poet | **el poeta / la poetiza** |
| | ehl poh-EH-tah / lah poh-eh-TEE-sah |
| rhyme | **la rima** |
| | lah RREE-mah |
| sonnet | **el soneto** |
| | ehl soh-NEH-toh |
| stanza | **la estrofa** |
| | lah ehs-TROH-fah |
| verse | **el verso** |
| | ehl BEHR-soh |

## In Social Studies Class

### En la clase de estudios sociales

Following are general topics that are particularly relevant to social studies class (**la clase de estudios sociales** [lah KLAH-seh deh ehs-TOO-dyohs soh-SYAH-lehs]).

| | |
|---|---|
| ages | **las edades**<br>lahs eh-DAH-dehs |
| compass points | **los puntos cardinales**<br>lohs POON-tohs kahr-dee-NAH-lehs |
| eras | **las eras**<br>lahs EH-rahs |
| geography | **la geografía**<br>lah heh-oh-grah-FEE-ah |
| government | **el gobierno**<br>ehl goh-BYEHR-noh |
| history | **la historia**<br>lah ees-TOH-ryah |
| monarchy | **la monarquía**<br>lah moh-nahr-KEE-ah |
| religion | **la religión**<br>lah rreh-lee-HYOHN |
| war and conflict | **la guerra y el conflicto**<br>lah GEH-rrah ee ehl kohn-FLEEK-toh |

## Eras/Ages

### Las eras / Las edades

| | |
|---|---|
| Age of Enlightenment | **el Siglo de las Luces**<br>ehl SEE-gloh deh lahs LOO-sehs |
| Bronze Age | **la Edad de Bronce**<br>lah eh-DAHD deh BROHN-seh |
| Feudalism | **el feudalismo**<br>ehl feh-oo-dah-LEES-moh |
| Golden Age | **el Siglo de Oro**<br>ehl SEE-gloh deh OH-roh |
| Middle Ages | **la Edad Media**<br>lah eh-DAHD MEH-dyah |
| Renaissance | **el Renacimiento**<br>ehl rreh-nah-see-MYEHN-toh |
| Stone Age | **la Edad de Piedra**<br>lah eh-DAHD deh PYEH-drah |

## Government
*El gobierno*

| | |
|---|---|
| congress | **el congreso**<br>ehl kohn-GREH-soh |
| council | **el concilio**<br>ehl kohn-SEE-lyoh |
| coup d'etat | **el golpe de estado**<br>ehl GOHL-peh deh ehs-TAH-doh |
| court | **la corte**<br>lah KOHR-teh |
| house of representatives | **la cámara de representantes**<br>lah KAH-mah-rah deh<br>rreh-preh-sehn-TAHN-tehs |
| leader | **el jefe / la jefa**<br>ehl HEH-feh / lah HEH-fah |
| | **el/la líder**<br>ehl/lah LEE-dehr |
| nation | **la nación**<br>lah nah-SYOHN |
| parliament | **el parlamento**<br>ehl pahr-lah-MEHN-toh |
| policy | **la política**<br>lah poh-LEE-tee-kah |
| possession | **la posesión**<br>lah poh-seh-SYOHN |
| power | **la potencia**<br>lah poh-TEHN-syah |
| president | **el presidente**<br>ehl preh-see-DEHN-teh |
| prime minister | **el primer ministro / la primera ministra**<br>ehl pree-MEHR mee-NEES-troh /<br>lah pree-MEH-rah mee-NEES-trah |
| republic | **la república**<br>lah rreh-POO-blee-kah |
| ruler | **el/la gobernante**<br>ehl/lah goh-behr-NAHN-teh |
| senate | **el senado**<br>ehl seh-NAH-doh |
| state | **el estado**<br>ehl ehs-TAH-doh |

| | |
|---|---|
| statesman | **el hombre de estado / la mujer de estado**<br>ehl OHM-breh deh ehs-TAH-doh /<br>lah moo-HEHR deh ehs-TAH-doh |

## Monarchy
*La monarquía*

| | |
|---|---|
| castle | **el castillo**<br>ehl kahs-TEE-yoh |
| coronation | **la coronación**<br>lah koh-roh-nah-SYOHN |
| court | **la corte**<br>lah KOHR-teh |
| crown | **la corona**<br>lah koh-ROH-nah |
| heir | **el heredero**<br>ehl eh-reh-DEH-roh |
| king | **el rey**<br>ehl RREH-ee |
| queen | **la reina**<br>lah RREH-ee-nah |
| reign | **el reinado**<br>ehl rreh-ee-NAH-doh |
| throne | **el trono**<br>ehl TROH-noh |

## Religion
*La religión*

| | |
|---|---|
| atheism | **el ateísmo**<br>ehl ah-teh-EES-moh |
| Bible | **la Biblia**<br>lah BEE-blyah |
| Catholicism | **el catolicismo**<br>ehl kah-toh-lee-SEES-moh |
| Christianity | **el cristianismo**<br>ehl krees-tyah-NEES-moh |
| church | **la iglesia**<br>lah ee-GLEH-syah |
| faith | **la fe**<br>lah feh |
| God | **Dios**<br>dyohs |

| | |
|---|---|
| Hinduism | **el hinduismo**<br>ehl een-doo-EES-moh |
| Imam | **el imán**<br>ehl ee-MAHN |
| Islam | **el Islam**<br>ehl ees-LAHM |
| Judaism | **el judaísmo**<br>ehl hoo-dah-EES-moh |
| minister | **el/la ministro**<br>ehl/lah mee-NEES-troh |
| New/Old Testament | **el Nuevo / el Antiguo Testamento**<br>ehl NWEH-boh / ehl ahn-TEE-gwoh<br>tehs-tah-MEHN-toh |
| paganism | **el paganismo**<br>ehl pah-gah-NEES-moh |
| pope | **el papa**<br>ehl PAH-pah |
| priest | **el sacerdote / el cura**<br>ehl sah-sehr-DOH-teh / ehl KOO-rah |
| Protestantism | **el protestantismo**<br>ehl proh-tehs-tahn-TEES-moh |
| rabbi | **el rabino**<br>ehl rrah-BEE-noh |

# War and Conflict
*La guerra y el conflicto*

| | |
|---|---|
| ally | **el aliado**<br>ehl ah-LYAH-doh |
| army | **el ejército**<br>ehl eh-HEHR-see-toh |
| battle | **la batalla**<br>lah bah-TAH-yah |
| century | **el siglo**<br>ehl SEE-gloh |
| civil war | **la guerra civil**<br>lah GEH-rrah see-BEEL |
| conqueror | **el conquistador / la conquistadora**<br>ehl kohn-kees-tah-DOHR /<br>lah kohn-kees-tah-DOH-rah |
| defeat | **la derrota**<br>lah deh-RROH-tah |

| dynasty | **la dinastía**<br>lah dee-nahs-TEE-ah |
| empire | **el imperio**<br>ehl eem-PEH-ryoh |
| enemy | **el enemigo / la enemiga**<br>ehl eh-neh-MEE-goh / lah eh-neh-MEE-gah |
| execution | **la ejecución**<br>lah eh-heh-koo-SYOHN |
| invasion | **la invasión**<br>lah een-bah-SYOHN |
| navy | **la armada**<br>lah ahr-MAH-dah |
| patriot | **el/la patriota**<br>ehl/lah pah-TRYOH-tah |
| peace | **la paz**<br>lah pahs |
| rebel | **el/la rebelde**<br>ehl/lah rreh-BEHL-deh |
| revolution | **la revolución**<br>lah rreh-boh-loo-SYOHN |
| settler | **el colonizador / la colonizadora**<br>ehl koh-loh-nee-sah-DOHR /<br>lah koh-loh-nee-sah-DOH-rah |
| siege | **el sitio**<br>ehl SEE-tyoh |
| slave | **el esclavo / la esclava**<br>ehl ehs-KLAH-boh / lah ehs-KLAH-bah |
| slavery | **la esclavitud**<br>lah ehs-klah-bee-TOOD |
| succession | **la sucesión**<br>lah soo-seh-SYOHN |
| surrender | **la rendición**<br>lah rrehn-dee-SYOHN |
| traitor | **el traidor / la traidora**<br>ehl trah-ee-DOHR / lah trah-ee-DOH-rah |
| treason | **la traición**<br>lah trah-ee-SYOHN |
| treaty | **el tratado**<br>ehl trah-TAH-doh |
| unity | **la unidad**<br>lah oo-nee-DAHD |
| victory | **la victoria**<br>lah beek-TOH-ryah |

## Verbs

| | | |
|---|---|---|
| to conquer | **conquistar** | kohn-kees-TAHR |
| to defeat | **derrotar** | deh-rroh-TAHR |
| to execute | **ejecutar** | eh-heh-koo-TAHR |
| to found | **fundar** | foon-DAHR |
| to invade | **invadir** | een-bah-DEER |
| to rebel | **rebelarse** | rreh-beh-LAHR-seh |
| to restore | **restaurar** | rrehs-tah-oo-RAHR |
| to rule | **gobernar (ie)** | goh-behr-NAHR |
| to surrender | **rendirse (i)** | rrehn-DEER-seh |

# Geography

*La geografía*

atmosphere **la atmósfera**
lah aht-MOHS-feh-rah

bay **la bahía**
lah bah-EE-ah

beach **la playa**
lah PLAH-yah

cave **la caverna / la cueva**
lah kah-BEHR-nah / lah KWEH-bah

coastline **el litoral**
ehl lee-toh-RAHL

continent **el continente**
ehl kohn-tee-NEHN-teh

desert **el desierto**
ehl deh-SYEHR-toh

earth **la tierra**
lah TYEH-rrah

earthquake **el terremoto**
ehl teh-rreh-MOH-toh

forest **la selva**
lah SEHL-bah

gulf **el golfo**
ehl GOHL-foh

hill **la colina**
lah koh-LEE-nah

island **la isla**
lah EES-lah

jungle **la jungla**
lah HOON-glah

| | | |
|---|---|---|
| lake | **el lago** | |
| | ehl LAH-goh | |
| land | **la tierra** | |
| | lah TYEH-rrah | |
| map | **el mapa** | |
| | ehl MAH-pah | |
| mountain | **la montaña** | |
| | lah mohn-TAH-nyah | |
| mountain range | **la cordillera** | |
| | lah kohr-dee-YEH-rah | |
| ocean | **el océano** | |
| | ehl oh-SEH-ah-noh | |
| peninsula | **la península** | |
| | lah peh-NEEN-soo-lah | |
| plain | **la llanura** | |
| | lah yah-NOO-rah | |
| region | **la región** | |
| | lah rreh-HYOHN | |
| river | **el río** | |
| | ehl RREE-oh | |
| sea | **el mar** | |
| | ehl mahr | |
| stream | **el arroyo** | |
| | ehl ah-RROH-yoh | |
| valley | **el valle** | |
| | ehl BAH-yeh | |
| vegetation | **la vegetación** | |
| | lah beh-heh-tah-SYOHN | |
| volcano | **el volcán** | |
| | ehl bohl-KAHN | |
| woods | **el bosque** | |
| | ehl BOHS-keh | |

## Compass Points
*Los puntos cardinales*

| | | |
|---|---|---|
| north | **el norte** | ehl NOHR-teh |
| south | **el sur** | ehl soor |
| east | **el este** | ehl EHS-teh |
| west | **el oeste** | ehl oh-EHS-teh |

# In Mathematics Class

## En la clase de matemáticas

Among other areas of study, mathematics class (**la clase de matemáticas** [lah KLAH-seh deh mah-teh-MAH-tee-kahs]) may include the following.

| | |
|---|---|
| algebra | **el álgebra** |
| | ehl AHL-heh-brah |
| arithmetic | **la aritmética** |
| | lah ah-reet-MEH-tee-kah |
| calculus | **el cálculo** |
| | ehl KAHL-koo-loh |
| geometry | **la geometría** |
| | lah heh-oh-meh-TREE-ah |
| trigonometry | **la trigonometría** |
| | lah tree-goh-noh-meh-TREE-ah |

Here is some additional vocabulary that is particularly useful when talking about mathematics.

| | |
|---|---|
| arithmetical operations | **las operaciones aritméticas** |
| | lahs oh-peh-rah-SYOH-nehs |
| | ah-reet-MEH-tee-kahs |
| arithmetical signs | **los signos aritméticos** |
| | lohs SEEG-nohs ah-reet-MEH-tee-kohs |
| decimal | **el número decimal** |
| | ehl NOO-meh-roh deh-see-MAHL |
| denominator | **el denominador** |
| | ehl deh-noh-mee-nah-DOHR |
| difference | **la diferencia** |
| | lah dee-feh-REHN-syah |
| dividend | **el dividendo** |
| | ehl dee-bee-DEHN-doh |
| divisor | **el divisor** |
| | ehl dee-bee-SOHR |
| equation | **la ecuación** |
| | lah eh-kwah-SYOHN |
| factor | **el factor** |
| | ehl fahk-TOHR |

| fraction | **el quebrado / la fracción**<br>ehl keh-BRAH-doh / lah frahk-SYOHN |
|---|---|
| geometric figures | **las figuras geométricas**<br>lahs fee-GOO-rahs heh-oh-MEH-tree-kahs |
| integer | **el número entero**<br>ehl NOO-meh-roh ehn-TEH-roh |
| logarithm | **el logaritmo**<br>ehl loh-gah-REET-moh |
| multiple | **el múltiplo**<br>ehl MOOL-tee-ploh |
| number | **el número**<br>ehl NOO-meh-roh |
| numerator | **el numerador**<br>ehl noo-mee-rah-DOHR |
| operation | **la operación**<br>lah oh-peh-rah-SYOHN |
| parenthesis | **el paréntesis**<br>ehl pah-REHN-teh-sees |
| problem | **el problema**<br>ehl proh-BLEH-mah |
| product | **el producto**<br>ehl proh-DOOK-toh |
| proportion | **la proporción**<br>lah proh-pohr-SYOHN |
| quantity | **la cantidad**<br>lah kahn-tee-DAHD |
| quotient | **el cociente**<br>ehl koh-SYEHN-teh |
| remainder | **el resto**<br>ehl RREHS-toh |
| result | **el resultado**<br>ehl rreh-sool-TAH-doh |
| ruler | **la regla**<br>lah RREH-glah |
| solution | **la solución**<br>lah soh-loo-SYOHN |
| sum | **la suma**<br>lah SOO-mah |
| table | **la tabla**<br>lah TAH-blah |
| total | **el total**<br>ehl toh-TAHL |

## Arithmetical Signs
*Los signos aritméticos*

addition sign
**el signo de la suma**
ehl SEEG-noh deh lah SOO-mah

division sign
**el signo de la división**
ehl SEEG-noh deh lah dee-bee-SYOHN

equal sign
**el signo de igualdad**
ehl SEEG-noh deh ee-gwahl-DAHD

multiplication sign
**el signo de la multiplicación**
ehl SEEG-noh deh lah
mool-tee-plee-kah-SYOHN

subtraction sign
**el signo de la resta**
ehl SEEG-noh deh lah RREHS-tah

## Arithmetical Operations
*Las operaciones aritméticas*

addition
**la suma**
lah SOO-mah

divided by
**dividido por**
dee-bee-DEE-doh pohr

division
**la división**
lah dee-bee-SYOHN

minus
**menos**
MEH-nohs

multiplication
**la multiplicación**
lah mool-tee-plee-kah-SYOHN

multiplied by
**multiplicado por**
mool-tee-plee-KAH-doh pohr

plus
**más**
mahs

subtraction
**la resta**
lah RREHS-tah

## Geometry
*La geometría*

Some terms used in geometry class are the following.

acute angle
**el ángulo agudo**
ehl AHN-goo-loh ah-GOO-doh

altitude
**la altura**
lah ahl-TOO-rah

angle
**el ángulo**
ehl AHN-goo-loh

arc
**el arco**
ehl AHR-koh

area
**el área**
ehl AH-reh-ah

axiom
**el axioma**
ehl ahk-SYOH-mah

base
**la base**
lah BAH-seh

center
**el centro**
ehl SEHN-troh

chord
**la cuerda**
lah KWEHR-dah

circumference
**la circunferencia**
lah seer-koon-feh-REHN-syah

curve
**la curva**
lah KOOR-bah

diagonal
**diagonal**
dyah-goh-NAHL

diameter
**el diámetro**
ehl DYAH-meh-troh

dimension
**la dimensión**
lah dee-mehn-SYOHN

ellipse
**el elipse**
ehl eh-LEEP-seh

equilateral
**equilátero**
eh-kee-LAH-teh-roh

geometric figures
**las figuras geométricas**
lahs fee-GOO-rahs heh-oh-MEH-tree-kahs

height
**la altura**
lah ahl-TOO-rah

horizontal
**horizontal**
oh-ree-sohn-TAHL

hyperbola
**la hipérbola**
lah ee-PEHR-boh-lah

hypotenuse
**la hipotenusa**
lah ee-poh-teh-NOO-sah

intersection
**la intersección**
lah een-tehr-sehk-SYOHN

| | |
|---|---|
| length | **la longitud**<br>lah lohn-hee-TOOD |
| line | **la línea**<br>lah LEE-neh-ah |
| line segment | **el segmento de la línea**<br>ehl sehg-MEHN-toh deh lah LEE-neh-ah |
| obtuse angle | **el ángulo obtuso**<br>ehl AHN-goo-loh ohb-TOO-soh |
| parabola | **la parábola**<br>lah pah-RAH-boh-lah |
| parallel | **paralelo**<br>pah-rah-LEH-loh |
| perpendicular | **perpendicular**<br>pehr-pehn-dee-koo-LAHR |
| plane | **el plano**<br>ehl PLAH-noh |
| point | **el punto**<br>ehl POON-toh |
| radius | **el radio**<br>ehl RRAH-dyoh |
| right angle | **el ángulo recto**<br>ehl AHN-goo-loh RREHK-toh |
| secant | **la secante**<br>lah seh-KAHN-teh |
| side | **el lado**<br>ehl LAH-doh |
| symmetry | **la simetría**<br>lah see-meh-TREE-ah |
| tangent | **la tangente**<br>lah tahn-HEHN-teh |
| vertical | **vertical**<br>behr-tee-KAHL |

## Geometric Figures · *Las figuras geométricas*

| | |
|---|---|
| circle | **el círculo**<br>ehl SEER-koo-loh |
| parallelogram | **el paralelogramo**<br>ehl pah-rah-leh-loh-GRAH-moh |
| pentagon | **el pentágono**<br>ehl pehn-TAH-goh-noh |
| polygon | **el polígono**<br>ehl poh-LEE-goh-noh |

| quadrilateral | **el cuadrilátero** |
|---|---|
| | ehl kwah-dree-LAH-teh-roh |
| rectangle | **el rectángulo** |
| | ehl rrehk-TAHN-goo-loh |
| rhombus | **el rombo** |
| | ehl RROHM-boh |
| semicircle | **el semicírculo** |
| | ehl seh-mee-SEER-koo-loh |
| square | **el cuadrado** |
| | ehl kwah-DRAH-doh |
| trapezoid | **el trapezoide** |
| | ehl trah-peh-SOH-ee-deh |
| triangle | **el triángulo** |
| | ehl TRYAHN-goo-loh |

## Verbs

| to add | **sumar** | SOO-MAHR |
|---|---|---|
| to be correct | **estar** (*irreg.*) **correcto** | ehs-TAHR koh-RREHK-toh |
| to be incorrect | **estar** (*irreg.*) **incorrecto** | ehs-TAHR een-koh-RREHK-toh |
| to be incorrect | **equivocarse** | eh-kee-boh-KAHR-seh |
| to bring down (a number) | **bajar (un número)** | bah-HAHR (oon NOO-meh-roh) |
| to calculate | **calcular** | kahl-koo-LAHR |
| to carry (a number) | **llevarse (un número)** | yeh-BAHR-seh (oon NOO-meh-roh) |
| to check | **comprobar (ue)** | kohm-proh-BAHR |
| to count | **contar (ue)** | kohn-TAHR |
| to divide | **dividir** | dee-bee-DEER |
| to multiply | **multiplicar** | mool-tee-plee-KAHR |
| to prove | **probar (ue)** | proh-BAHR |
| to solve | **resolver (ue)** | rreh-sohl-BEHR |
| to subtract | **restar** | rrehs-TAHR |

## Numbers

*Los números*

To describe numbers (**los números** [lohs NOO-meh-rohs], use these terms.

| cardinal | **cardinal** |
|---|---|
| | kahr-dee-NAHL |
| composite | **compuesto** |
| | kohm-PWEHS-toh |

| even | **par** |
| | pahr |
| integral | **entero** |
| | ehn-TEH-roh |
| irrational | **irracional** |
| | ee-rrah-syoh-NAHL |
| odd | **impar** |
| | eem-PAHR |
| ordinal | **ordinal** |
| | ohr-dee-NAHL |
| prime | **primo** |
| | PREE-moh |
| rational | **racional** |
| | rrah-syoh-NAHL |

## Cardinal Numbers · *Los números cardinales*

| 0 | **cero** | SEH-roh | 16 | **dieciséis** | dyeh-see-SEH-ees |
| 1 | **uno** | OO-noh | 17 | **diecisiete** | dyeh-see-SYEH-teh |
| 2 | **dos** | dohs | 18 | **dieciocho** | dyeh-see-OH-choh |
| 3 | **tres** | trehs | 19 | **diecinueve** | dyeh-see-NWEH-beh |
| 4 | **cuatro** | KWAH-troh | 20 | **veinte** | BEH-een-teh |
| 5 | **cinco** | SEEN-koh | 21 | **veinte y uno** | BEH-een-teh ee OO-noh |
| 6 | **seis** | SEH-ees | 22 | **veinte y dos** | BEH-een-teh ee dohs |
| 7 | **siete** | SYEH-teh | 23 | **veinte y tres** | BEH-een-teh ee trehs |
| 8 | **ocho** | OH-choh | 24 | **veinte y cuatro** | BEH-een-teh ee KWAH-troh |
| 9 | **nueve** | NWEH-beh | 25 | **veinte y cinco** | BEH-een-teh ee SEEN-koh |
| 10 | **diez** | dyehs | 26 | **veinte y seis** | BEH-een-teh ee SEH-ees |
| 11 | **once** | OHN-seh | 27 | **veinte y siete** | BEH-een-teh ee SYEH-teh |
| 12 | **doce** | DOH-seh | 28 | **veinte y ocho** | BEH-een-teh ee OH-choh |
| 13 | **trece** | TREH-seh | 29 | **veinte y nueve** | BEH-een-teh ee NWEH-beh |
| 14 | **catorce** | kah-TOHR-seh | 30 | **treinta** | TREH-een-tah |
| 15 | **quince** | KEEN-seh | | | |

| 40 | **cuarenta** | kwah-REHN-tah |
| 50 | **cincuenta** | seen-KWEHN-tah |
| 60 | **sesenta** | seh-SEHN-tah |
| 70 | **setenta** | seh-TEHN-tah |
| 80 | **ochenta** | oh-CHEHN-tah |
| 90 | **noventa** | noh-BEHN-tah |
| 100 | **ciento/cien** | SYEHN-toh/syehn |

| 101 | **ciento uno** | SYEHN-toh OO-noh |
| 102 | **ciento dos** | SYEHN-toh dohs |
| 200 | **doscientos/doscientas** | doh-SYEHN-tohs/doh-SYEHN-tahs |
| 300 | **trescientos/trescientas** | treh-SYEHN-tohs/treh-SYEHN-tahs |
| 400 | **cuatrocientos/cuatrocientas** | kwah-troh-SYEHN-tohs/<br>kwah-troh-SYEHN-tahs |
| 500 | **quinientos/quinientas** | kee-NYEHN-tohs/kee-NYEHN-tahs |
| 600 | **seiscientos/seiscientas** | seh-ee-SYEHN-tohs/seh-ee-SYEHN-tahs |
| 700 | **setecientos/setecientas** | seh-teh-SYEHN-tohs/seh-teh-SYEHN-tahs |
| 800 | **ochocientos/ochocientas** | oh-choh-SYEHN-tohs/oh-choh-SYEHN-tahs |
| 900 | **novecientos/novecientas** | noh-beh-SYEHN-tohs/noh-beh-SYEHN-tahs |

| 1,000 | **mil** | meel |
| 2,000 | **dos mil** | dohs meel |
| 100,000 | **cien mil** | syehn meel |
| 200,000 | **doscientos mil /**<br>**doscientas mil** | doh-SYEHN-tohs meel /<br>doh-SYEHN-tahs meel |
| 1,000,000 | **un millón** | oon mee-YOHN |
| 2,000,000 | **dos millones** | dohs mee-YOH-nehs |
| 1,000,000,000 | **mil millones** | meel mee-YOH-nehs |

To express a quantity in terms of millions or billions, you use a **de** [deh] + noun construction as follows: a million books is **un millón de libros** [oon mee-YOHN deh LEE-brohs]; two million balls is **dos millones de pelotas** [dohs mee-YOH-nehs deh peh-LOH-tahs]; a billion dollars is **mil millones de dólares** [meel mee-YOH-nehs deh DOH-lah-rehs].

## Fractions · *Las fracciones*

| ½ | **un medio** | oon MEH-dyoh |
| 1½ | **uno y medio** | oo-noh ee MEH-dyoh |
| ⅓ | **un tercio** | oon TEHR-syoh |
| ⅔ | **dos tercios** | dohs TEHR-syohs |
| ¼ | **un cuarto** | oon KWAHR-toh |
| ¾ | **tres cuartos** | trehs KWAHR-tohs |
| ⅕ | **un quinto** | oon KEEN-toh |
| ⅘ | **cuatro quintos** | KWAH-troh KEEN-tohs |
| ⅙ | **un sexto** | oon SEHS-toh |
| ⅚ | **cinco sextos** | SEEN-koh SEHS-tohs |
| ⅐ | **un séptimo** | oon SEHP-tee-moh |

| | | |
|---|---|---|
| ⁶⁄₇ | **seis séptimos** | SEH-ees SEHP-tee-mohs |
| ⅛ | **un octavo** | oon ohk-TAH-boh |
| ⅞ | **siete octavos** | SYEH-teh ohk-TAH-bohs |
| ⅑ | **un noveno** | oon noh-BEH-noh |
| ⁸⁄₉ | **ocho novenos** | OH-choh noh-BEH-nohs |
| ⅒ | **un décimo** | oon DEH-see-moh |
| ⁹⁄₁₀ | **nueve décimos** | NWEH-beh DEH-see-mohs |

## Ordinal Numbers · *Los números ordinales*

| | | |
|---|---|---|
| first | **primero/primera** | pree-MEH-roh/pree-MEH-rah |
| second | **segundo/segunda** | seh-GOON-doh/seh-GOON-dah |
| third | **tercero/tercera** | tehr-SEH-roh/tehr-SEH-rah |
| fourth | **cuarto/cuarta** | KWAHR-toh/KWAHR-tah |
| fifth | **quinto/quinta** | KEEN-toh/KEEN-tah |
| sixth | **sexto/sexta** | SEHS-toh/SEHS-tah |
| seventh | **séptimo/séptima** | SEHP-tee-moh/SEHP-tee-mah |
| eighth | **octavo/octava** | ohk-TAH-boh/ohk-TAH-bah |
| ninth | **noveno/novena** | noh-BEH-noh/noh-BEH-nah |
| tenth | **décimo/décima** | DEH-see-moh/DEH-see-mah |

However, to express "first" or "third" before a masculine singular noun, you use **primer** [pree-MEHR] and **tercer** [tehr-SEHR].

# In Computer Science Class

## *En la clase de informática*

Many terms associated with computers are English words. In computer science class (**la clase de informática** [lah KLAH-seh deh een-fohr-MAH-tee-kah], students learn that although "download" is translated as **bajar** [bah-HAHR], many people use the English word "download" [DAH-oon-loh-ood].

| | |
|---|---|
| @ | **la arroba** |
| | lah ah-RROH-bah |
| address book | **la libreta de direcciones** |
| | lah lee-BREH-tah deh dee-rehk-SYOH-nehs |
| antivirus | **el antivirus** |
| | ehl ahn-tee-BEE-roos |

| | |
|---|---|
| attached file | **el archivo adjunto**<br>ehl ahr-CHEE-boh ahd-HOON-toh |
| backup disk | **el disco de respaldo**<br>ehl DEES-koh deh rrehs-PAHL-doh |
| backup file | **el archivo de reserva**<br>ehl ahr-CHEE-boh deh rreh-SEHR-bah |
| button | **el botón**<br>ehl boh-TOHN |
| computer | **la computadora**<br>lah kohm-poo-tah-DOH-rah |
| database | **la base de datos**<br>lah BAH-seh deh DAH-tohs |
| disk | **el disco**<br>ehl DEES-koh |
| disk drive | **la unidad de discos**<br>lah oo-nee-DAHD deh DEES-kohs |
| e-mail | **el correo electrónico**<br>ehl koh-RREH-oh eh-lehk-TROH-nee-koh |
| e-mail address | **la dirección de correo electrónico**<br>lah dee-rehk-SYOHN deh koh-RREH-oh<br>eh-lehk-TROH-nee-koh |
| exit | **la salida**<br>lah sah-LEE-dah |
| file | **el archivo / el fichero**<br>ehl ahr-CHEE-boh / ehl fee-CHEH-roh |
| file transfer | **la transferencia de ficheros**<br>lah trahns-feh-REHN-syah deh<br>fee-CHEH-rohs |
| floppy disk | **el disco flexible**<br>ehl DEES-koh flehk-SEE-bleh |
| folder | **la carpeta**<br>lah kahr-PEH-tah |
| handle (nickname) | **el apodo**<br>ehl ah-POH-doh |
| hard disk | **el disco duro**<br>ehl DEES-koh DOO-roh |
| home page | **la página principal / la página inicial**<br>lah PAH-hee-nah preen-see-PAHL /<br>lah PAH-hee-nah ee-nee-SYAHL |
| inkjet printer | **la impresora de chorro de tinta**<br>lah eem-preh-SOH-rah deh CHOH-rroh<br>deh TEEN-tah |

| | |
|---|---|
| Internet | **la red / el internet** |
| | lah rrehd / ehl een-tehr-NEHT |
| key | **la tecla** |
| | lah TEH-klah |
| keyboard | **el teclado** |
| | ehl teh-KLAH-doh |
| keyword | **la palabra clave** |
| | lah pah-LAH-brah KLAH-beh |
| laser printer | **la impresora por láser** |
| | lah eem-preh-SOH-rah pohr LAH-sehr |
| link | **el enlace / el vínculo** |
| | ehl ehn-LAH-seh / ehl BEEN-koo-loh |
| memory | **la memoria** |
| | lah meh-MOH-ryah |
| menu | **el menú** |
| | ehl meh-NOO |
| modem | **el módem** |
| | ehl MOH-dehm |
| monitor | **la consola** |
| | lah kohn-SOH-lah |
| mouse | **el ratón** |
| | ehl rrah-TOHN |
| mouse button | **el botón del ratón** |
| | ehl boh-TOHN dehl rrah-TOHN |
| mouse pad | **la alfombrilla de ratón** |
| | lah ahl-fohm-BREE-yah deh rrah-TOHN |
| password | **la contraseña** |
| | lah kohn-trah-SEH-nyah |
| printer | **la impresora** |
| | lah eem-preh-SOH-rah |
| screen | **la pantalla** |
| | lah pahn-TAH-yah |
| search engine | **el motor de búsqueda** |
| | ehl moh-TOHR deh BOOS-keh-dah |
| shift lock | **el sujetador de mayúsculas** |
| | ehl soo-heh-tah-DOHR deh mah-YOOS-koo-lahs |
| space bar | **el espaciador** |
| | ehl ehs-pah-syah-DOHR |
| spam | **el mensaje no deseado** |
| | ehl mehn-SAH-heh noh deh-seh-AH-doh |

| toolbar | **la barra de herramientas** |
| | lah BAH-rrah deh eh-rrah-MYEHN-tahs |
| user name | **el nombre de usuario** |
| | ehl NOHM-breh deh oo-SWAH-ryoh |
| virus | **el virus** |
| | ehl BEE-roos |
| Web page | **la página web** |
| | lah PAH-hee-nah wehb |
| Web site | **el sitio web** |
| | ehl SEE-tyoh wehb |
| window | **la ventana** |
| | lah behn-TAH-nah |

## Verbs

| to attach | **adjuntar** | ahd-hoon-TAHR |
| to attach | **unir** | OO-NEER |
| to back up | **hacer** (*irreg.*) **un backup** | ah-SEHR oon BAHK-ahp |
| to backspace | **retroceder** | rreh-troh-seh-DEHR |
| to chat | **conversar** | kohn-behr-SAHR |
| to chat | **charlar** | chahr-LAHR |
| to check | **verificar** | beh-ree-fee-KAHR |
| to check | **examinar** | ehk-sah-mee-NAHR |
| to clear | **borrar** | boh-RRAHR |
| to clear | **despejar** | dehs-peh-HAHR |
| to click | **pulsar** | pool-SAHR |
| to compute | **computar** | kohm-poo-TAHR |
| to delete | **borrar** | boh-RRAHR |
| to download | **hacer** (*irreg.*) **un download** | ah-SEHR oon DAH-oon-loh-ood |
| to download | **bajar archivos** | bah-HAHR ahr-CHEE-bohs |
| to drag | **arrastrar** | ah-rrahs-TRAHR |
| to file | **archivar** | ahr-chee-BAHR |
| to file | **guardar** | gwahr-DAHR |
| to go back | **regresar** | rreh-greh-SAHR |
| to load | **cargar** | kahr-GAHR |
| to log on | **comenzar** (**ie**) **una sesión** | koh-mehn-SAHR oo-nah seh-SYOHN |
| to log out | **terminar la sesión** | tehr-mee-NAHR lah seh-SYOHN |
| to paste | **pegar** | peh-GAHR |
| to print | **imprimir** | eem-pree-MEER |
| to quit | **salir** (*irreg.*) | sah-LEER |
| to save a file | **hacer** (*irreg.*) **un archivo de reserva** | ah-SEHR oon ahr-CHEE-boh deh rreh-SEHR-bah |
| to surf | **navegar** | nah-beh-GAHR |

| | | |
|---|---|---|
| to upload | **subir** | SOO-BEER |
| to upload | **cargar** | kahr-GAHR |
| to upload | **copiar** | koh-PYAHR |

## In Chemistry Class

*En la clase de química*

| | | |
|---|---|---|
| acid | **el ácido** | ehl AH-see-doh |
| atom | **el átomo** | ehl AH-toh-moh |
| atomic | **atómico** | ah-TOH-mee-koh |
| chemical | **químico** | KEE-mee-koh |
| chemical reaction | **la reacción química** | lah rreh-ahk-SYOHN KEE-mee-kah |
| dioxide | **el dióxido** | ehl dee-OHK-see-doh |
| element | **el elemento** | ehl eh-leh-MEHN-toh |
| flask | **el frasco de laboratorio** | ehl FRAHS-koh deh lah-boh-rah-TOH-ryoh |
| gas | **el gas** | ehl gahs |
| gaseous | **gaseoso** | gah-seh-OH-soh |
| inorganic | **inorgánico** | ee-nohr-GAH-nee-koh |
| matter | **la materia** | lah mah-TEH-ryah |
| molecule | **la molécula** | la moh-LEH-koo-lah |
| nitrate | **el nitrato** | ehl nee-TRAH-toh |
| organic | **orgánico** | ohr-GAH-nee-koh |
| oxide | **el óxido** | ehl OHK-see-doh |
| particle | **la partícula** | lah pahr-TEE-koo-lah |

| | |
|---|---|
| salt | **la sal**<br>lah sahl |
| solid | **sólido**<br>SOH-lee-doh |
| substance | **la sustancia**<br>lah SOOS-TAHN-syah |
| test tube | **la probeta**<br>lah proh-BEH-tah |

## Chemical Elements
*Los elementos químicos*

| | |
|---|---|
| aluminum | **el aluminio**<br>ehl ah-loo-MEE-nyoh |
| barium | **el bario**<br>ehl BAH-ryoh |
| calcium | **el calcio**<br>ehl KAHL-syoh |
| carbon | **el carbono**<br>ehl kahr-BOH-noh |
| chlorine | **el cloro**<br>ehl KLOH-roh |
| chromium | **el cromo**<br>ehl KROH-moh |
| copper | **el cobre**<br>ehl KOH-breh |
| gold | **el oro**<br>ehl OH-roh |
| helium | **el helio**<br>ehl EH-lyoh |
| hydrogen | **el hidrógeno**<br>ehl ee-DROH-heh-noh |
| iodine | **el yodo**<br>ehl YOH-doh |
| iron | **el hierro**<br>ehl YEH-rroh |
| lead | **el plomo**<br>ehl PLOH-moh |
| magnesium | **el magnesio**<br>ehl mahg-NEH-syoh |
| mercury | **el mercurio**<br>ehl mehr-KOO-ryoh |

| oxygen | **el oxígeno** |
| | ehl ohk-SEE-heh-noh |
| potassium | **el potasio** |
| | ehl poh-TAH-syoh |
| radium | **el radio** |
| | ehl RRAH-dyoh |
| silicon | **el silicio** |
| | ehl see-LEE-syoh |
| silver | **la plata** |
| | lah PLAH-tah |
| sodium | **el sodio** |
| | ehl SOH-dyoh |
| sulfur | **el azufre** |
| | ehl ah-SOO-freh |
| tin | **el estaño** |
| | ehl ehs-TAH-nyoh |
| zinc | **el zinc** |
| | ehl seenk |

## Verbs

| to balance (an equation) | **balancear (una ecuación)** |
| | bah-lahn-seh-AHR (OO-nah eh-kwah-SYOHN) |
| to do an experiment | **hacer (*irreg.*) un experimento** |
| | ah-SEHR oon ehs-peh-ree-MEHN-toh |
| to mix | **mezclar** |
| | mehs-KLAHR |

# In Art Class

## *En la clase de arte*

| abstract | **abstracto** |
| | ahbs-TRAHK-toh |
| art | **el arte** |
| | ehl AHR-teh |
| artist | **el/la artista** |
| | ehl/lah ahr-TEES-tah |
| artwork | **la obra de arte** |
| | lah OH-brah deh AHR-teh |
| background | **el fondo** |
| | ehl FOHN-doh |

| | |
|---|---|
| brush | **el pincel** |
| | ehl peen-SEHL |
| bust | **el busto** |
| | ehl BOOS-toh |
| canvas | **el lienzo** |
| | ehl LYEHN-soh |
| chisel | **el cincel** |
| | ehl seen-SEHL |
| clay | **la arcilla** |
| | lah ahr-SEE-yah |
| color | **el color** |
| | ehl koh-LOHR |
| design | **el diseño** |
| | ehl dee-SEH-nyoh |
| drawing | **el dibujo** |
| | ehl dee-BOO-hoh |
| easel | **el caballete** |
| | ehl kah-bah-YEH-teh |
| exhibit | **la exposición** |
| | lah ehs-poh-see-SYOHN |
| gallery | **la galería** |
| | lah gah-leh-REE-ah |
| illustration | **la ilustración** |
| | lah ee-loos-trah-SYOHN |
| landscape | **el paisaje** |
| | ehl pah-ee-SAH-heh |
| light | **la luz** |
| | lah loos |
| marble | **el mármol** |
| | ehl MAHR-mohl |
| model | **el/la modelo** |
| | ehl/lah moh-DEH-loh |
| oil paint | **el óleo** |
| | ehl OH-leh-oh |
| oil painting | **el cuadro al óleo** |
| | ehl KWAH-droh ahl OH-leh-oh |
| paint | **la pintura** |
| | lah peen-TOO-rah |
| painter | **el pintor / la pintora** |
| | ehl peen-TOHR / lah peen-TOH-rah |

| | |
|---|---|
| painting (activity) | **la pintura**<br>lah peen-TOO-rah |
| painting (picture) | **la pintura / el cuadro**<br>lah peen-TOO-rah / ehl KWAH-droh |
| palette | **la paleta**<br>lah pah-LEH-tah |
| portrait | **el retrato**<br>ehl rreh-TRAH-toh |
| pottery | **la cerámica**<br>lah seh-RAH-mee-kah |
| sculptor | **el escultor / la escultora**<br>ehl ehs-kool-TOHR / lah ehs-kool-TOH-rah |
| sculpture | **la escultura**<br>lah ehs-kool-TOO-rah |
| shadow | **la sombra**<br>lah SOHM-brah |
| statue | **la estatua**<br>lah ehs-TAH-twah |
| still life | **el bodegón / la naturaleza muerta**<br>ehl boh-deh-GOHN /<br>lah nah-too-rah-LEH-sah MWEHR-tah |
| stone | **la piedra**<br>lah PYEH-drah |
| style | **el estilo**<br>ehl ehs-TEE-loh |
| watercolor paint | **la acuarela**<br>lah ah-kwah-REH-lah |

## Verbs

| | | |
|---|---|---|
| to admire | **admirar** | ahd-mee-RAHR |
| to carve | **tallar** | tah-YAHR |
| to cast | **fundir** | foon-DEER |
| to comment on | **comentar sobre** | koh-mehn-TAHR SOH-breh |
| to criticize | **criticar** | kree-tee-KAHR |
| to model | **modelar** | moh-deh-LAHR |
| to paint | **pintar** | peen-TAHR |
| to see | **ver** (*irreg.*) | behr |
| to watch | **mirar** | mee-RAHR |

## In Music Class

*En la clase de música*

Following is vocabulary that is particularly relevant to music class (**la clase de música** [lah KLAH-seh deh MOO-see-kah]).

| | |
|---|---|
| auditorium | **el auditorio**<br>ehl ah-oo-dee-TOH-ryoh<br>**el salón / la sala de actos**<br>ehl sah-LOHN / lah SAH-lah deh AHK-tohs |
| band | **el conjunto**<br>ehl kohn-HOON-toh |
| baton | **la batuta**<br>lah bah-TOO-tah |
| choir | **el coro**<br>ehl KOH-roh |
| composer | **el compositor / la compositora**<br>ehl kohm-poh-see-TOHR /<br>lah kohm-poh-see-TOH-rah |
| concert | **el concierto**<br>ehl kohn-SYEHR-toh |
| conductor | **el director / la directora de orquesta**<br>ehl dee-rehk-TOHR /<br>lah dee-rehk-TOH-rah deh ohr-KEHS-tah |
| harmony | **la armonía**<br>lah ahr-moh-NEE-ah |
| key | **la tecla**<br>lah TEH-klah |
| keyboard | **el teclado**<br>ehl teh-KLAH-doh |
| melody | **la melodía**<br>lah meh-loh-DEE-ah |
| music | **la música**<br>lah MOO-see-kah |
| musical instruments | **los instrumentos musicales**<br>lohs eens-troo-MEHN-tohs<br>moo-see-KAH-lehs |
| musical staff | **el pentagrama**<br>ehl pehn-tah-GRAH-mah |
| musical styles | **los estilos de música**<br>lohs ehs-TEE-lohs deh MOO-see-kah |

| | |
|---|---|
| musician | **el músico / la música** |
| | ehl MOO-see-koh / lah MOO-see-kah |
| note | **la nota** |
| | lah NOH-tah |
| orchestra | **la orquesta** |
| | lah ohr-KEHS-tah |
| refrain | **el estribillo** |
| | ehl ehs-tree-BEE-yoh |
| rhythm | **el ritmo** |
| | ehl RREET-moh |
| scale | **la escala** |
| | lah ehs-KAH-lah |
| score | **la partitura** |
| | lah pahr-tee-TOO-rah |
| singer | **el/la cantante** |
| | ehl/lah kahn-TAHN-teh |
| song | **la canción** |
| | lah kahn-SYOHN |
| sound | **el sonido** |
| | ehl soh-NEE-doh |
| theory | **la teoría** |
| | lah teh-oh-REE-ah |
| tune | **la melodía** |
| | lah meh-loh-DEE-ah |
| voice | **la voz** |
| | lah bohs |

## Musical Styles
*Los estilos de música*

| | |
|---|---|
| blues | **los blues** |
| | lohs bloos |
| chamber music | **la música de cámara** |
| | lah MOO-see-kah deh KAH-mah-rah |
| classical music | **la música clásica** |
| | lah MOO-see-kah KLAH-see-kah |
| country music | **la música country** |
| | lah MOO-see-kah KOHN-tree |
| folk music | **la música folk** |
| | lah MOO-see-kah FOH-ook |
| jazz | **la música de jazz** |
| | lah MOO-see-kah deh yahs |

| opera | **la ópera**<br>la OH-peh-rah |
| popular music | **la música popular**<br>lah MOO-see-kah poh-POO-LAHR |
| rock | **la música rock**<br>lah MOO-see-kah rrohk |

## Musical Instruments
*Los instrumentos musicales*

| accordion | **el acordeón**<br>ehl ah-kohr-deh-OHN |
| bassoon | **el bajón**<br>ehl bah-HOHN |
| castanets | **las castañuelas**<br>lahs kahs-tah-NYWEH-lahs |
| cello | **el violoncelo**<br>ehl byoh-lohn-SEH-loh |
| clarinet | **el clarinete**<br>ehl klah-ree-NEH-teh |
| drum | **el tambor**<br>ehl tahm-BOHR |
| drums (set) | **la batería**<br>lah bah-teh-REE-ah |
| electric guitar | **la guitarra eléctrica**<br>lah gee-TAH-rrah eh-LEHK-tree-kah |
| flute | **la flauta**<br>lah FLAH-oo-tah |
| guitar | **la guitarra**<br>lah gee-TAH-rrah |
| horn | **la trompa**<br>lah TROHM-pah |
| oboe | **el oboe**<br>ehl oh-BOH-eh |
| organ | **el órgano**<br>ehl OHR-gah-noh |
| piano | **el piano**<br>ehl PYAH-noh |
| saxophone | **el saxofón**<br>ehl sahk-soh-FOHN |
| trombone | **el trombón**<br>ehl trohm-BOHN |

| trumpet | **la trompeta** |
| | lah trohm-PEH-tah |
| tuba | **la tuba** |
| | lah TOO-bah |
| viola | **la viola** |
| | lah BYOH-lah |
| violin | **el violín** |
| | ehl byoh-LEEN |

## Verbs

| to applaud | **aplaudir** | ah-plah-oo-DEER |
| to hear | **oír** (*irreg.*) | oh-EER |
| to listen | **escuchar** | ehs-koo-CHAHR |
| to play (a musical instrument) | **tocar** | toh-KAHR |
| to sing | **cantar** | kahn-TAHR |
| to sound | **sonar (ue)** | soh-NAHR |
| to tune (a musical instrument) | **afinar** | ah-fee-NAHR |

## In Dance Class

### En la clase de baile

Following is vocabulary that is particularly relevant to dance class (**la clase de baile** [lah KLAH-seh deh BAH-ee-leh]).

| ballet | **el ballet** |
| | ehl bah-LEH |
| choreographer | **el coreógrafo / la coreógrafa** |
| | ehl koh-reh-OH-grah-foh / |
| | lah koh-reh-OH-grah-fah |
| choreography | **la coreografía** |
| | lah koh-reh-oh-grah-FEE-ah |
| dancer | **el bailarín / la bailarina** |
| | ehl bah-ee-lah-REEN / |
| | lah bah-ee-lah-REE-nah |
| ethnic | **étnico** |
| | EHT-nee-koh |
| jump | **el salto** |
| | ehl SAHL-toh |
| modern | **moderno** |
| | moh-DEHR-noh |
| movement | **el movimiento** |
| | ehl moh-bee-MYEHN-toh |

| partner | **el compañero / la compañera** |
| | ehl kohm-pah-NYEH-roh / |
| | lah kohm-pah-NYEH-rah |
| slippers | **las zapatillas** |
| | lahs sah-pah-TEE-yahs |
| step | **el paso** |
| | ehl PAH-soh |
| tap | **el tap** |
| | ehl tahp |

### Verbs

| to choreograph | **coreografiar** | koh-reh-oh-grah-fee-AHR |
| to dance | **bailar** | bah-ee-LAHR |
| to move | **moverse (ue)** | moh-BEHR-seh |

## In Drama Class

### En la clase de drama

Following is vocabulary that is particularly relevant to drama class (**la clase de drama** [lah KLAH-seh deh DRAH-mah]).

| act | **el acto** |
| | ehl AHK-toh |
| actor | **el actor** |
| | ehl ahk-TOHR |
| actress | **la actriz** |
| | lah ahk-TREES |
| applause | **el aplauso** |
| | ehl ah-PLAH-oo-soh |
| audience | **el público** |
| | ehl POO-blee-koh |
| character | **el personaje** |
| | ehl pehr-soh-NAH-heh |
| comedy | **la comedia** |
| | lah koh-MEH-dyah |
| costumes | **el vestuario** |
| | ehl behs-TWAH-ryoh |
| dialogue | **el diálogo** |
| | ehl DYAH-loh-goh |
| director | **el director / la directora** |
| | ehl dee-rehk-TOHR / |
| | lah dee-rehk-TOH-rah |

| | |
|---|---|
| end | **el fin** |
| | ehl FEEN |
| ending | **el final** |
| | ehl fee-NAHL |
| performance | **la función** |
| | lah foon-SYOHN |
| play | **la obra de teatro** |
| | lah OH-brah deh teh-AH-troh |
| playwright | **el dramaturgo / la dramaturga** |
| | ehl drah-mah-TOOR-goh / |
| | lah drah-mah-TOOR-gah |
| plot | **la trama** |
| | lah TRAH-mah |
| row | **la fila** |
| | lah FEE-lah |
| scene | **la escena** |
| | lah eh-SEH-nah |
| screen | **la pantalla** |
| | lah pahn-TAH-yah |
| script | **el guión** |
| | ehl gee-OHN |
| seat | **el asiento** |
| | ehl ah-SYEHN-toh |
| show | **la función** |
| | lah foon-SYOHN |
| stage | **el escenario** |
| | ehl eh-seh-NAH-ryoh |
| theme | **el tema** |
| | ehl TEH-mah |
| title | **el título** |
| | ehl TEE-too-loh |
| tragedy | **la tragedia** |
| | lah trah-HEH-dyah |

## Verbs

| | |
|---|---|
| to build scenery | **construir** (*irreg.*) **un escenario** |
| | kohns-troo-EER oon eh-seh-NAH-ryoh |
| to play (perform) a role | **hacer** (*irreg.*) / **representar un papel** |
| | ah-SEHR / rreh-preh-sehn-TAHR oon pah-PEHL |
| to put on a play | **representar una obra** |
| | rreh-preh-sehn-TAHR oo-nah OH-brah |

## In Physical Education Class

*En la clase de educación física*

Following is vocabulary that is particularly relevant to physical education class (**la clase de educación física** [lah KLAH-seh deh eh-doo-kah-SYOHN FEE-see-kah]).

| | |
|---|---|
| gym | **el gimnasio**<br>ehl heem-NAH-syoh |
| sports | **los deportes**<br>lohs deh-POHR-tehs |
| stadium | **el estadio**<br>ehn ehl ehs-TAH-dyoh |

### Sports
*Los deportes*

| | |
|---|---|
| athletics | **el atletismo**<br>ehl ah-tleh-TEES-moh |
| baseball | **el béisbol**<br>ehl BEH-ees-bohl |
| basketball | **el básquetbol**<br>ehl BAHS-keht-bohl |
| fencing | **la esgrima**<br>lah ehs-GREE-mah |
| football | **el fútbol americano**<br>ehl FOOT-bohl ah-meh-ree-KAH-noh |
| ice hockey | **el hockey sobre (el) hielo**<br>ehl HOH-kee SOH-breh (ehl) YEH-loh |
| race (contest) | **la carrera**<br>lah kah-RREH-rah |
| soccer | **el fútbol**<br>ehl FOOT-bohl |
| sport | **el deporte**<br>ehl deh-POHR-teh |
| swimming | **la natación**<br>lah nah-tah-SYOHN |
| tennis | **el tenis**<br>ehl TEH-nees |
| volleyball | **el volibol**<br>ehl boh-lee-BOHL |

| weightlifting | **el levantamiento de pesas** |
| | ehl leh-bahn-tah-MYEHN-toh deh |
| | PEH-sahs |
| wrestling | **la lucha libre** |
| | lah LOO-chah LEE-breh |

## At the Stadium / At the Gym
*En el estadio / En el gimnasio*

| athlete | **el/la atleta** |
| | ehl/lah ah-TLEH-tah |
| ball | **la pelota / el balón** |
| | lah peh-LOH-tah / ehl bah-LOHN |
| baseball | **la pelota de béisbol** |
| | lah peh-LOH-tah deh BEH-ees-bohl |
| basketball | **el balón de básquetbol** |
| | ehl bah-LOHN deh BAHS-keht-bohl |
| soccer ball | **el balón de fútbol** |
| | ehl bah-LOHN deh FOOT-bohl |
| tennis ball | **la pelota de tenis** |
| | lah peh-LOH-tah deh TEH-nees |
| basket | **la canasta** |
| | lah kah-NAHS-tah |
| bat | **el bate** |
| | ehl BAH-teh |
| champion | **el campeón / la campeona** |
| | ehl kahm-peh-OHN / |
| | lah kahm-peh-OH-nah |
| coach | **el entrenador / la entrenadora** |
| | ehl ehn-treh-nah-DOHR / |
| | lah ehn-treh-nah-DOH-rah |
| court | **la cancha** |
| | lah KAHN-chah |
| exercise | **el ejercicio** |
| | ehl eh-hehr-SEE-syoh |
| field | **el campo deportivo** |
| | ehl KAHM-poh deh-pohr-TEE-boh |
| game | **el partido / el encuentro** |
| | ehl pahr-TEE-doh / ehl ehn-KWEHN-troh |
| helmet | **el casco** |
| | ehl KAHS-koh |

| match | **el partido / el encuentro** |
| | ehl pahr-TEE-doh / ehl ehn-KWEHN-troh |
| net | **la red** |
| | lah rrehd |
| player | **el jugador / la jugadora** |
| | ehl hoo-gah-DOHR / lah hoo-gah-DOH-rah |
| racket | **la raqueta** |
| | lah rrah-KEH-tah |
| referee | **el árbitro** |
| | ehl AHR-bee-troh |
| runner | **el corredor / la corredora** |
| | ehl koh-rreh-DOHR / |
| | lah koh-rreh-DOH-rah |
| team | **el equipo** |
| | ehl eh-KEE-poh |
| tournament | **el torneo** |
| | ehl tohr-NEH-oh |
| track | **la pista** |
| | lah PEES-tah |
| trainer | **el entrenador / la entrenadora** |
| | ehl ehn-treh-nah-DOHR / |
| | lah ehn-treh-nah-DOH-rah |

## Verbs

| to bat | **batear** | bah-teh-AHR |
| to bowl | **bolear** | boh-leh-AHR |
| to catch | **coger** (*irreg.*) | koh-HEHR |
| to catch | **agarrar** | ah-gah-RRAHR |
| to dive | **clavar** | klah-BAHR |
| to do aerobics | **hacer** (*irreg.*) **ejercicios aeróbicos** | ah-SEHR eh-hehr-SEE-syohs ah-eh-ROH-bee-kohs |
| to exercise | **hacer** (*irreg.*) **ejercicios** | ah-SEHR eh-hehr-SEE-syohs |
| to get in shape | **ponerse** (*irreg.*) **en forma** | poh-NEHR-seh ehn FOHR-mah |
| to jog | **trotar** | troh-TAHR |
| to jump | **saltar** | sahl-TAHR |
| to keep score | **apuntar los tantos** | ah-poon-TAHR lohs TAHN-tohs |
| to lift weights | **levantar pesas** | leh-bahn-TAHR PEH-sahs |
| to lose | **perder** (ie) | pehr-DEHR |
| to play a game/ match | **jugar** (ue) **un partido** | hoo-GAHR oon pahr-TEE-doh |
| to practice | **practicar** | prahk-tee-KAHR |
| to run | **correr** | koh-RREHR |
| to score a goal | **marcar un tanto** | mahr-KAHR oon TAHN-toh |

| to skate | **patinar** | pah-tee-NAHR |
| to sweat | **sudar** | SOO-DAHR |
| to swim | **nadar** | nah-DAHR |
| to throw | **lanzar** | lahn-SAHR |
| to train | **entrenarse** | ehn-treh-NAHR-seh |
| to win | **ganar** | gah-NAHR |

## Extracurricular Activities

### Las actividades extracurriculares

The number of extracurricular activities (**las actividades extracurriculares** [lahs ahk-tee-bee-DAH-dehs ehs-trah-koo-rree-koo-LAH-rehs]) varies from school to school, but this is a list of the most common activities that take place during or after school.

| the ... club | **el club de...** |
| | ehl kloob deh |
| chess | **ajedrez** |
| | ah-heh-DREHS |
| computer | **informática** |
| | een-fohr-MAH-tee-kah |
| dance | **baile** |
| | BAH-ee-leh |
| debate | **debate** |
| | deh-BAH-teh |
| drama | **drama** |
| | DRAH-mah |
| ecology | **ecología** |
| | eh-koh-loh-HEE-ah |
| film | **cine** |
| | SEE-neh |
| foreign languages | **lenguas extranjeras** |
| | LEHN-gwahs ehs-trahn-HEH-rahs |
| history | **historia** |
| | ees-TOH-ryah |
| mathematics | **matemáticas** |
| | mah-teh-MAH-tee-kahs |
| poetry | **poesía** |
| | poh-eh-SEE-ah |
| science | **ciencias** |
| | SYEHN-syahs |

Encouraging students to take part in extracurricular activities allows them to make new friends and learn new information.

| | |
|---|---|
| Do you want to participate in the _____ club? | **¿Quieres participar en el club de _____?**<br>KYEH-rehs pahr-tee-see-PAHR ehn ehl kloob deh |
| The club's meetings take place at (time). | **Las reuniones del club tienen lugar a la(s) (time).**<br>lahs rreh-oo-NYOH-nehs dehl kloob TYEH-nehn loo-GAHR ah lah(s) |
| When does the club meet? | **¿Cuándo se reúne el club?**<br>KWAHN-doh seh rreh-oo-neh ehl kloob |
| The meeting is at three thirty. | **La reunión es a las tres y media.**<br>lah rreh-oo-NYOHN ehs ah lahs trehs ee MEH-dyah |
| Who is the advisor to the club? | **¿Quién es el consejero / la consejera del club?**<br>kyehn ehs ehl kohn-seh-HEH-roh / lah kohn-seh-HEH-rah dehl kloob |
| The requirements for the club are _____. | **Los requisitos para el club son _____.**<br>lohs rreh-kee-SEE-tohs PAH-rah ehl kloob sohn |
| There are no requirements to belong to the club. | **No hay requisitos para pertenecer al club.**<br>noh AH-ee rreh-kee-SEE-tohs PAH-rah pehr-teh-neh-SEHR ahl kloob |

Many students like to get involved in their community and can join organizations through the school.

| | |
|---|---|
| In our school we have an organization to help ... | **En nuestra escuela tenemos una organización para ayudar a...**<br>ehn NWEHS-trah ehs-KWEH-lah teh-NEH-mohs oo-nah ohr-gah-nee-sah-SYOHN PAH-rah ah-yoo-DAHR ah |
| avoid drinking and driving | **evitar beber y conducir**<br>eh-bee-TAHR beh-BEHR ee kohn-doo-SEER |
| build houses | **construir casas**<br>kohns-TRWEER KAH-sahs |

| the elderly | **los ancianos** |
| | lohs ahn-SYAH-nohs |
| the homeless | **los destituidos** |
| | lohs dehs-tee-TWEE-dohs |
| people with AIDS | **las personas con SIDA** |
| | lahs pehr-SOH-nahs kohn SEE-dah |
| to raise money | **recaudar fondos** |
| | rreh-kah-oo-DAHR FOHN-dohs |
| students with academic problems | **los estudiantes con problemas académicos** |
| | lohs ehs-too-DYAHN-tehs kohn proh-BLEH-mahs ah-kah-DEH-mee-kohs |

Clubs and other organizations often have fundraisers, which may include events such as the following.

| auction | **la subasta** |
| | lah soo-BAHS-tah |
| banquet | **el banquete** |
| | ehl bahn-KEH-teh |
| carnival | **el carnaval** |
| | ehl kahr-nah-BAHL |
| contest | **el concurso** |
| | ehl kohn-KOOR-soh |
| dance | **el baile** |
| | ehl BAH-ee-leh |
| fair | **la feria** |
| | lah FEH-ryah |
| party | **la fiesta** |
| | lah FYEHS-tah |
| performance | **la función** |
| | lah foon-SYOHN |
| raffle | **la rifa / el sorteo** |
| | lah RREE-fah / ehl sohr-TEH-oh |
| show | **la función / el espectáculo** |
| | lah foon-SYOHN / ehl ehs-pehk-TAH-koo-loh |
| trip | **el viaje** |
| | ehl BYAH-heh |

## On a Trip

### De excursión

Regardless of the grade you teach, there is often an opportunity to take trips outside of school. There is a lot of planning that takes place before any trip (**la excursión** [lah ehs-koor-SYOHN]). Here are some phrases that will prove useful.

| | |
|---|---|
| You have to take the permission letter home. | **Tienes que llevar la carta de permiso a casa.**<br>TYEH-nehs keh yeh-BAHR lah KAHR-tah deh pehr-MEE-soh ah KAH-sah |
| One of your parents has to sign the letter. | **Uno de tus padres tiene que firmar la carta.**<br>OO-noh deh toos PAH-drehs TYEH-neh keh feer-MAHR lah KAHR-tah |
| Your guardian has to sign the letter. | **Tu tutor tiene que firmar la carta.**<br>too too-TOHR TYEH-neh keh feer-MAHR lah KAHR-tah |
| You have to bring your lunch. | **Tienes que traer el almuerzo.**<br>TYEH-nehs keh trah-EHR ehl ahl-MWEHR-soh |
| You have to be here on time. | **Tienes que estar aquí a tiempo.**<br>TYEH-nehs keh ehs-TAHR ah-KEE ah TYEHM-poh |
| We are going to leave at (time). | **Vamos a salir a la(s)** (time).<br>BAH-mohs ah sah-LEER a lah(s) |
| We are going to return at (time). | **Vamos a regresar a la(s)** (time).<br>BAH-mohs ah rreh-greh-SAHR ah lah(s) |

## Permission Form

### El formulario de permiso

Most schools require a permission form (**el formulario de permiso** [ehl fohr-moo-LAH-ryoh deh pehr-MEE-soh]) before a student is allowed to go on a school trip. The form letter and permission form on page 181 can be sent home with students. Other phrases you may need to include, depending on the situation, are included on the following pages.

Note that in many Spanish-speaking countries you will find the date written as DD/MM/YY, rather than as MM/DD/YY, which you are more used to. When in doubt, write the date with the name of the month spelled out, as shown here.

June 7, 2005                    **Junio 7, 2005**

(*Date*)

Dear Mr./Mrs. _____ ,
*Estimado Sr. / Estimada Sra.,*

On _____ (*date*) our class is going to participate in a visit to
_____ (*place*).
*El* _____ (date) *nuestra clase va a participar en una visita a*
_____ (place).

We are going to leave school at _____ (*time*) and we are going to
return at _____ (*time*).
*Vamos a salir de la escuela a la(s)* _____ (time) *y vamos a regresar
a la(s)* _____ (time).

All of the students have to bring their lunch, since we are not going to be able
to eat lunch in the school cafeteria.
*Todos los estudiantes tienen que traer el almuerzo ya que no vamos a poder
almorzar en la cafetería de la escuela.*

Please sign the form below and return it with your child before
_____ (*date*) .
*Por favor, firme el formulario abajo y devuélvalo con su hijo/hija antes del*
_____ (date).

Sincerely,
*Sinceramente,*

_____

-------------------------------------------------------------------------------------------------

_____ (*student's name*) has my permission to attend the field
trip to _____ (*place*) on _____ (*date*).
_____ (student's name) *tiene mi permiso para asistir a la
excursión a* _____ (place) *el* _____ (date).

_____
Parent/Guardian signature
*Firma del padre / de la madre / del tutor*

Other sentences you may need to include or say are the following.

| | |
|---|---|
| Each student must pay for the entrance fee. | **Cada estudiante tiene que pagar la entrada.**<br>KAH-dah ehs-too-DYAHN-teh TYEH-neh keh pah-GAHR lah ehn-TRAH-dah |
| The cost is _____. | **El costo es de _____.**<br>ehl KOHS-toh ehs deh |
| Please enclose a check or cash. | **Por favor, incluya un cheque o dinero en efectivo.**<br>pohr fah-BOHR, een-KLOO-yah oon CHEH-keh oh dee-NEH-roh ehn eh-fehk-TEE-boh |
| If you send a check, make it payable to _____. | **Si envía un cheque, hágalo a nombre de _____.**<br>see ehn-BEE-ah oon CHEH-keh, AH-gah-loh ah NOHM-breh deh |
| If you can't afford it, please send me a note. | **Si Ud. no puede hacer este gasto, por favor envíeme una nota.**<br>see oos-TEHD noh PWEH-deh ah-SEHR EHS-teh GAHS-toh, pohr fah-BOHR ehn-BEE-eh-meh oo-nah NOH-tah |
| We can use the school's funds to cover the cost. | **Podemos usar los fondos de la escuela para cubrir el costo.**<br>poh-DEH-mohs oo-SAHR lohs FOHN-dohs deh lah ehs-KWEH-lah PAH-rah koo-BREER ehl KOHS-toh |
| We need volunteers. | **Necesitamos voluntarios.**<br>neh-seh-see-TAH-mohs boh-loon-TAH-ryohs |
| Please let me know if you are willing to accompany us on the trip. | **Por favor, avíseme si Ud. está dispuesto a acompañarnos en el viaje.**<br>por fah-BOHR, ah-BEE-seh-meh see oos-TEHD ehs-TAH dees-PWEHS-toh ah ah-kohm-pah-NYAHR-nohs ehn ehl BYAH-heh |
| All students have to bring _____. | **Todos los estudiantes tienen que traer _____.**<br>TOH-dohs lohs ehs-too-DYAHN-tehs TYEH-nehn keh trah-EHR |

Please remind your child that he/she must respect all the school's rules of behavior during the trip.

**Por favor, recuérdele a su hijo/hija que tiene que respetar todas las reglas de comportamiento de la escuela durante el viaje.**

pohr fah-BOHR, rreh-KWEHR-deh-leh ah soo EE-hoh/EE-hah keh TYEH-neh keh rrehs-peh-TAHR TOH-dahs lahs RREH-glahs deh kohm-pohr-tah-MYEHN-toh deh lah ehs-KWEH-lah doo-RAHN-teh ehl BYAH-heh

If you have any questions, you can call me at (*phone number*) between (*time*) and (*time*).

**Si Ud. tiene alguna pregunta, me puede llamar a (*phone number*) entre la(s) (*time*) y la(s) (*time*).**

see OOS-TEHD TYEH-neh ahl-GOO-nah preh-GOON-tah, meh PWEH-deh yah-MAHR ahl NOO-meh-roh (*number*) EHN-treh lah(s) (*time*) ee lah(s) (*time*)

These are some places you may visit on a school trip.

amusement park

**el parque de atracciones**
ehl PAHR-keh deh ah-trahk-SYOH-nehs

aquarium

**el acuario**
ehl ah-KWAH-ryoh

beach

**la playa**
lah PLAH-yah

botanical garden

**el jardín botánico**
ehl hahr-DEEN boh-TAH-nee-koh

city hall

**el ayuntamiento**
ehl ah-yoon-tah-MYEHN-toh

courthouse

**la corte**
lah KOHR-teh

factory

**la fábrica**
lah FAH-bree-kah

farm

**la granja**
lah GRAHN-hah

firehouse

**la casa de bomberos**
lah KAH-sah deh bohm-BEH-rohs

library

**la biblioteca**
lah bee-blyoh-TEH-kah

| movie theater | **el cine** |
| | ehl SEE-neh |
| museum | **el museo** |
| | ehl moo-SEH-oh |
| park | **el parque** |
| | ehl PAHR-keh |
| police station | **el cuartel de policía** |
| | ehl kwahr-TEHL deh poh-lee-SEE-ah |
| restaurant | **el restaurante** |
| | ehl rrehs-tah-oo-RAHN-teh |
| theater | **el teatro** |
| | ehl teh-AH-troh |
| zoo | **el parque zoológico** |
| | ehl PAHR-keh soh-LOH-hee-koh |

Here are some things you may want to say to some of the students who may not be familiar with English. The commands included here address a group (more than one person). You may want to refer to the Introduction, pages 16–18, 20, and 21, to review the singular commands.

| We have arrived. | **Hemos llegado.** |
| | EH-mohs yeh-GAH-doh |
| Does anyone have to go to the bathroom? | **¿Alguien tiene que ir al baño?** |
| | AHL-gyehn TYEH-neh keh eer ahl BAH-nyoh |
| Get off the bus. | **Bájense del autobús.** |
| | BAH-hehn-seh dehl ah-oo-toh-BOOS |
| Line up. | **Pónganse en fila.** |
| | POHN-gahn-seh ehn FEE-lah |
| Take your partner by the hand. | **Tomen a su compañero de la mano.** |
| | TOH-mehn ah soo kohm-pah-NYEH-roh deh lah MAH-noh |
| Do not separate from the group. | **No se separen del grupo.** |
| | noh seh seh-PAH-rehn dehl GROO-poh |
| Hurry up. | **Apúrense. / Dense prisa.** |
| | ah-POO-rehn-seh / DEHN-seh PREE-sah |
| Get on the bus. | **Súbanse al autobús.** |
| | soo-bahn-seh ahl ah-oo-toh-BOOS |

## Practice 4-2

**A** List *four activities that you could suggest to your students as a way to raise funds for a club.*

1. _____

2. _____

3. _____

4. _____

**B** Write in Spanish where you would take your students if they wanted to do the following things.

1. visit an art exhibit

   _____

2. see animals in their habitat

   _____

3. have fun and go on different rides

   _____

4. visit the office of the mayor

   _____

5. learn about fire prevention

   _____

6. learn about books and do research

   _____

**C** You and your students are taking a trip. Write three sentences in Spanish in which you tell the students or their parents what they must do before the trip.

1. _____

2. _____

3. _____

**D** *While on a trip, students need to know the rules. Write what you would tell them if you wanted them to do the following things. Use the Spanish command form.*

1. walk in pairs

   _____

2. get on the bus

   _____

3. walk in a line

   _____

# Success in School: Enlisting Parental Support

*El éxito en la escuela:*
*para ganarse el apoyo de los padres*

Most teachers communicate regularly with parents in order to enlist their support (**ganarse el apoyo de los padres** [gah-NAHR-seh ehl ah-POH-yoh deh lohs PAH-drehs]). Most parents will gladly help if they know what they can do to help their child reach his/her full potential and enjoy success in school (**el éxito en la escuela** [ehl EHK-see-toh ehn lah ehs-KWEH-lah]). One important area in which parents can help is school attendance (**la asistencia a la escuela** [lah ah-sees-TEHN-syah ah lah ehs-KWEH-lah]).

# School/Class Attendance

## *La asistencia a la escuela / a las clases*

Children can't learn if they are not in class. It is of primary importance to communicate the need to attend school and arrive on time. Let's begin with some things you can tell the parents.

| | |
|---|---|
| School attendance is mandatory. | **La asistencia a la escuela es obligatoria.** <br> lah ah-sees-TEHN-syah ah lah ehs-KWEH-lah ehs oh-blee-gah-TOH-ryah |
| Your child must arrive on time. | **Su hijo/hija tiene que llegar a tiempo.** <br> soo EE-hoh/EE-hah TYEH-neh keh yeh-GAHR ah TYEHM-poh |
| If your child is absent, call the school at (*phone number*). | **Si su hijo/hija está ausente, llame a la escuela al número** (*phone number*). <br> see soo EE-hoh/EE-hah ehs-TAH ah-oo-SEHN-teh, YAH-meh ah lah ehs-KWEH-lah ahl NOO-meh-roh |
| Upon returning, your child must bring a note signed by you. | **Al regresar, su hijo/hija tiene que traer una nota firmada por Ud.** <br> ahl rreh-greh-SAHR, soo EE-hoh/EE-hah TYEH-neh keh trah-EHR oo-nah NOH-tah feer-MAH-dah pohr oos-TEHD |
| If possible, your child should call a classmate in order to find out the assignment. | **Si es posible, su hijo/hija debe llamar a un compañero de clase para saber la tarea.** <br> see ehs poh-SEE-bleh, soo EE-hoh/EE-hah DEH-beh yah-MAHR ah oon kohm-pah-NYEH-roh deh KLAH-seh PAH-rah sah-BEHR lah tah-REH-ah |
| If the absence is prolonged, you should call the teacher. | **Si la ausencia es larga, Ud. debe llamar al maestro / a la maestra.** <br> see lah ah-oo-SEHN-syah ehs LAHR-gah, oos-TEHD DEH-beh yah-MAHR ahl mah-EHS-troh / ah lah mah-EHS-trah |

| | |
|---|---|
| If the absence is more than (number) days, your child needs a note from the doctor. | **Si la ausencia es de más de** (number) **días, su hijo/hija necesita una nota del médico / de la médica.** |

see lah ah-oo-SEHN-syah ehs deh mahs deh… DEE-ahs, soo EE-hoh/EE-hah neh-seh-SEE-tah oo-nah NOH-tah dehl MEH-dee-koh / deh lah MEH-dee-kah

# Classroom Rules

## Las reglas de la clase

Another area in which parents can help is in adherence to classroom rules (**las reglas de la clase** [lahs RREH-glahs deh lah KLAH-seh]). You can begin the process by making them aware of the rules set by the administration and the teachers in your school so that they can understand what they can do to help. Here are some things that you might say to the parents.

| | |
|---|---|
| I need your help in making sure that your child follows the rules of our school. | **Necesito su ayuda para asegurar que su hijo/hija siga las reglas de nuestra escuela.** |

neh-seh-SEE-toh soo ah-YOO-dah PAH-rah ah-seh-goo-RAHR keh soo EE-hoh/EE-hah SEE-gah lahs RREH-glahs deh NWEHS-trah ehs-KWEH-lah

There are general behavior rules that can apply to most situations.

| | |
|---|---|
| It is important … | **Es importante…** |
| | ehs eem-pohr-TAHN-teh |
| to ask permission | **pedir permiso** |
| | peh-DEER pehr-MEE-soh |
| to be respectful | **ser respetuoso/respetuosa** |
| | sehr rrehs-peh-TWOH-soh/ rrehs-peh-TWOH-sah |
| to behave | **portarse bien** |
| | pohr-TAHR-seh byehn |
| to pay attention | **prestar atención** |
| | prehs-TAHR ah-tehn-SYOHN |

## GRAMMAR · Impersonal Expressions + Infinitive

Using an impersonal expression such as "it is important" (**es importante** [ehs eem-pohr-TAHN-teh]) followed by an infinitive, as shown in the examples above, is one way to express how students are expected to behave. Using an impersonal expression allows you to make a general statement about expected behavior without addressing anyone in particular.

Here are some other impersonal expressions you can use this way.

| It is necessary … | **Es necesario…** |
| | ehs neh-seh-SAH-ryoh |
| It is better … | **Es mejor…** |
| | ehs meh-HOHR |
| It is advisable … | **Es aconsejable…** |
| | ehs ah-kohn-seh-HAH-bleh |
| It is good … | **Es bueno…** |
| | ehs BWEH-noh |
| It is bad … | **Es malo…** |
| | ehs MAH-loh |

# What Must Be Done

*Lo que hay que hacer*

Using the expression **hay que** [AH-ee keh], meaning "one must," + an infinitive is another way to express the rules of classroom behavior without addressing a particular person. It allows you to say what must be done (**lo que hay que hacer** [loh keh AH-ee keh ah-SEHR]).

| To speak, one must raise one's hand. | **Para hablar hay que levantar la mano.** |
| | PAH-rah ah-BLAHR AH-ee keh leh-bahn-TAHR lah MAH-noh |
| To leave the class, one must ask permission. | **Para salir de la clase hay que pedir permiso.** |
| | PAH-rah sah-LEER deh lah KLAH-seh AH-ee keh peh-DEER pehr-MEE-soh |
| To get good grades, one must … | **Para sacar buenas notas hay que…** |
| | PAH-rah sah-KAHR BWEH-nahs NOH-tahs AH-ee keh |
| study regularly | **estudiar regularmente** |
| | ehs-too-DYAHR rreh-goo-lahr-MEHN-teh |

| | |
|---|---|
| do the homework every day | **hacer la tarea todos los días**<br>ah-SEHR lah tah-REH-ah TOH-dohs lohs DEE-ahs |
| take notes in class | **hacer apuntes en la clase**<br>ah-SEHR ah-POON-tehs ehn KLAH-seh |
| bring the necessary supplies to class every day | **traer los materiales necesarios a clase todos los días**<br>trah-EHR lohs mah-teh-RYAH-lehs neh-seh-SAH-ryohs ah KLAH-seh TOH-dohs lohs DEE-ahs |
| pay attention in class | **prestar atención en clase**<br>prehs-TAHR ah-tehn-SYOHN ehn KLAH-seh |
| ask questions when one does not understand | **hacer preguntas cuando uno no entiende**<br>ah-SEHR preh-GOON-tahs KWAHN-doh oo-noh noh ehn-TYEHN-deh |

## Practice 5-1

*Use one of the impersonal expressions below to state what must be done or what students need to do in each case. Write complete sentences in Spanish.*

es mejor      es bueno
es aconsejable      es necesario
hay que

1. bring a note from your father

   _____

2. call a classmate

   _____

3. pay attention

   _____

4. do the homework every day

   _____

5. study regularly

   _____

## Rules of Behavior

*Las reglas de comportamiento*

In addition to classroom rules, all schools have general rules of behavior (**las reglas de comportamiento** [lahs RREH-glahs deh kohm-pohr-tah-MYEHN-toh]) that must be followed to ensure the safety and well-being of everyone in the school. Many of these rules apply to any school or any classroom, and they often specify what students cannot do (**lo que los estudiantes no pueden hacer** [loh que lohs ehs-too-DYAHN-tehs noh PWEH-dehn ah-SEHR]).

## What Students Cannot Do

*Lo que los estudiantes no pueden hacer*

| In our school, students cannot … | **En nuestra escuela los estudiantes no pueden…** |
|---|---|
| | ehn NWEHS-trah ehs-KWEH-lah lohs ehs-too-DYAHN-tehs noh PWEH-dehn |
| arrive late | **llegar tarde** |
| | yeh-GAHR TAHR-deh |
| be disrespectful to others | **faltarle el respeto a otros** |
| | fahl-TAHR-leh ehl rrehs-PEH-toh ah OH-trohs |
| bring cell phones | **traer teléfonos celulares** |
| | trah-EHR teh-LEH-foh-nohs seh-loo-LAH-rehs |
| cut class | **ausentarse de clase** |
| | ah-oo-sehn-TAHR-seh deh KLAH-seh |
| destroy school property | **destruir la propiedad de la escuela** |
| | dehs-troo-EER lah proh-pyeh-DAHD deh lah ehs-KWEH-lah |
| disobey school rules | **desobedecer las reglas de la escuela** |
| | dehs-oh-beh-deh-SEHR lahs RREH-glahs deh lah ehs-KWEH-lah |
| eat outside the cafeteria | **comer fuera de la cafetería** |
| | koh-MEHR FWEH-rah deh lah kah-feh-teh-REE-ah |

| | |
|---|---|
| fight with others | **pelear con otros** |
| | peh-leh-AHR kohn OH-trohs |
| leave without permission | **salir sin permiso** |
| | sah-LEER seen pehr-MEE-soh |
| play in the hallways | **jugar en los pasillos** |
| | hoo-GAHR ehn lohs pah-SEE-yohs |
| smoke | **fumar** |
| | foo-MAHR |
| speak in a loud voice | **hablar en voz alta** |
| | ah-BLAHR ehn bohs AHL-tah |
| use bad language | **usar malas palabras** |
| | oo-SAHR MAH-lahs pah-LAH-brahs |

If you want to express what behavior is forbidden in a way that is not intended for any particular student, use the expression **se prohíbe** [seh proh-EE-beh] + an infinitive.

| | |
|---|---|
| It is forbidden ... | **Se prohíbe...** |
| | seh proh-EE-beh |
| to fight | **pelear** |
| | peh-leh-AHR |
| to kick | **dar patadas** |
| | dahr pah-TAH-dahs |
| to laugh at another person | **reírse de otra persona** |
| | rreh-EER-seh deh OH-trah |
| | pehr-SOH-nah |
| to make fun of another person | **burlarse de otra persona** |
| | boor-LAHR-seh deh OH-trah |
| | pehr-SOH-nah |
| to push | **empujar** |
| | ehm-poo-HAHR |
| to spit | **escupir** |
| | ehs-koo-PEER |
| to yell | **gritar** |
| | gree-TAHR |

## GRAMMAR · Expressing What Someone Can(not) Do

You may have noticed that by using **(no)** + the present tense of the verb **poder** [poh-DEHR] + an infinitive, you can express many of the activities that students are and are not allowed to do in school.

**poder (ue)** [poh-DEHR]  to be able, can (present tense)

| I can | **yo puedo** | yoh PWEH-doh |
|-------|--------------|--------------|
| you can | **tú puedes** | too PWEH-dehs |
| he can | **él puede** | ehl PWEH-deh |
| she can | **ella puede** | EH-yah PWEH-deh |
| you can | **Ud. puede** | oos-TEHD PWEH-deh |
| we can | **nosotros podemos** | noh-SOH-trohs poh-DEH-mohs |
| we can | **nosotras podemos** | noh-SOH-trahs poh-DEH-mohs |
| they can | **ellos pueden** | EH-yohs PWEH-dehn |
| they can | **ellas pueden** | EH-yahs PWEH-dehn |
| you (*plural*) can | **Uds. pueden** | oos-TEH-dehs PWEH-dehn |

For example, if you are addressing only one student, you use **(no) puedes** [(noh) PWEH-dehs].

| You may (not) bring ... to school. | **(No) puedes traer... a la escuela.** noh PWEH-dehs trah-EHR... ah lah ehs-KWEH-lah |
|---|---|
| a beeper | **un bíper** oon BEE-pehr |
| a game | **un juego** oon HWEH-goh |
| a gun | **un revólver** oon rreh-BOHL-behr |
| a knife | **un cuchillo** oon koo-CHEE-yoh |

## Practice 5-2

*Write the correct form of the verb* **poder** *to complete the following sentences.*

1. ¿_____ nosotros fumar en el patio?

2. Tú no _____ salir del aula ahora.

3. Ellos _____ estudiar en la biblioteca.

4. Él no _____ traer la mochila al gimnasio.

5. Yo no _____ traer mis CDs a la escuela.

6. Uds. _____ salir después de las clases.

## GRAMMAR · To Find Out "Why?"

It is important to know the reasons that a student takes certain actions. Here are some questions you will need to use when trying to find out why (**por qué** [pohr keh]) students do or don't do certain things in school.

| | |
|---|---|
| Why did you arrive late? | **¿Por qué llegaste tarde?**<br>pohr keh yeh-GAHS-teh TAHR-deh |
| Why were you absent? | **¿Por qué estuviste ausente?**<br>pohr keh ehs-too-BEES-teh ah-oo-SEHN-teh |
| Why didn't you go to (English) class? | **¿Por qué no fuiste a la clase de (inglés)?**<br>pohr keh noh FWEES-teh ah lah KLAH-seh deh (een-GLEHS) |
| Why didn't you do your homework? | **¿Por qué no hiciste la tarea?**<br>pohr keh noh ee-SEES-teh lah tah-REH-ah |
| Why didn't you study for the test? | **¿Por qué no estudiaste para el examen?**<br>pohr keh noh ehs-too-DYAHS-teh PAH-rah ehl ehk-SAH-mehn |
| Why didn't you come to _____? | **¿Por qué no viniste a _____?**<br>pohr keh noh bee-NEES-teh ah |

All of the verbs used in the questions above are in the preterite tense. For information about the formation of the preterite and a list of words and expressions that are useful when talking about the past, see Chapter 6, pages 230–232.

Remember that in order to find out the cause or reason for certain behavior, you can ask a question using **¿Por qué?** [pohr keh], meaning "Why?" The answer to the question may include the word **porque** [POHR-keh], meaning "because."

| | |
|---|---|
| I arrived late because the bus was late. | **Llegué tarde porque el autobús llegó tarde.**<br>yeh-GEH TAHR-deh POHR-keh ehl ah-oo-toh-BOOS yeh-GOH TAHR-deh |

## Practice 5-3

*Answer the following questions according to the model.*

MODELO    ¿Puedo fumar en la escuela?

*No, no puedes fumar. Se prohíbe fumar en la escuela.*

1. ¿Pueden ellos pelear en el patio?

_____

2. ¿Puedes tú llegar tarde?

_____

3. ¿Puedo yo comer fuera de la cafetería?

_____

4. ¿Puede ella salir sin permiso?

_____

5. ¿Podemos nosotros jugar en los pasillos?

_____

## Consequences

*Las consecuencias*

There are different types of consequences, depending on the severity of the infraction. There may be academic consequences (**las consecuencias académicas** [lahs kohn-seh-KWEHN-syahs ah-kah-DEH-mee-kahs]) or consequences resulting from behavior problems (**los problemas de comportamiento** [lohs proh-BLEH-mahs deh kohm-pohr-tah-MYEHN-toh]). Note that some of the same consequences may apply in both situations.

### Academic Consequences
*Las consecuencias académicas*

| You have to … | Tienes que...<br>TYEH-nehs keh |
|---|---|
| stay in school after classes | **quedarte en la escuela después de las clases**<br>keh-DAHR-teh ehn lah ehs-KWEH-lah dehs-PWEHS deh lahs KLAH-sehs |

| | |
|---|---|
| go to the detention room | **ir al aula de castigo** |
| | eer ahl AH-oo-lah deh kahs-TEE-goh |
| work with a private teacher | **trabajar con un maestro / una maestra particular** |
| | trah-bah-HAHR kohn oon mah-EHS-troh / oo-nah mah-EHS-trah pahr-tee-koo-LAHR |
| take the exam again | **hacer el examen otra vez** |
| | ah-SEHR ehl ehk-SAH-mehn OH-trah behs |
| attend review classes | **asistir a las clases de repaso** |
| | ah-sees-TEER ah lahs KLAH-sehs deh RREH-pah-soh |

As you can see, by using the expression **tener** [teh-NEHR] + **que** [keh] + an infinitive, you can express what a student *has to do*.

## GRAMMAR · The Simple Future

Spanish speakers use the present tense of the verb **ir** [eer] followed by the word **a** [ah] + an infinitive to express or ask about future actions.

| | |
|---|---|
| Are you going to study a lot tonight? | **¿Vas a estudiar mucho esta noche?** |
| | bahs ah ehs-too-DYAHR MOO-choh EHS-tah NOH-cheh |
| Yes, I am going to study a lot. | **Sí, voy a estudiar mucho.** |
| | see, BOH-ee ah ehs-too-DYAHR MOO-choh |

You may find the following words and expressions useful when talking about the future.

| | |
|---|---|
| later | **más tarde** |
| | mahs TAHR-deh |
| today | **hoy** |
| | OH-ee |
| tonight | **esta noche** |
| | EHS-tah NOH-cheh |
| tomorrow | **mañana** |
| | mah-NYAH-nah |
| tomorrow morning | **mañana por la mañana** |
| | mah-NYAH-nah pohr lah mah-NYAH-nah |
| tomorrow afternoon | **mañana por la tarde** |
| | mah-NYAH-nah pohr lah TAHR-deh |

| tomorrow night | **mañana por la noche** |
| | mah-NYAH-nah pohr lah NOH-cheh |
| the day after tomorrow | **pasado mañana** |
| | pah-SAH-doh mah-NYAH-nah |
| next week | **la semana próxima** |
| | lah seh-MAH-nah PROHK-see-mah |
| next month | **el mes próximo** |
| | ehl mehs PROHK-see-moh |
| next year | **el año próximo** |
| | ehl AH-nyoh PROHK-see-moh |

## GRAMMAR · "If" Clauses

Spanish speakers use the following pattern when they state under what conditions certain actions, events, or situations will take place: "if" + verb in present tense, verb in (simple) future tense (**si** [see] + verb in present tense, verb in (simple) future tense).

| | | ENGLISH | SPANISH |
|---|---|---|---|
| CONDITION | | If you do not study, | **Si no estudias,** |
| RESULT | | you are not going to succeed. | **no vas a tener éxito.** |
| | | | see noh ehs-TOO-dyahs, |
| | | | noh bahs ah teh-NEHR |
| | | | EHK-see-toh |
| CONDITION | | If you are late, | **Si llegas tarde,** |
| RESULT | | you will not learn. | **no vas a aprender.** |
| | | | see YEH-gahs TAHR-deh, |
| | | | noh bahs ah ah-prehn-DEHR |
| CONDITION | | If you use bad language, | **Si usas malas palabras,** |
| RESULT | | I am going to call your parents. | **voy a llamar a tus padres.** |
| | | | see OO-sahs MAH-lahs |
| | | | pah-LAH-brahs, BOH-ee ah |
| | | | yah-MAHR ah toos PAH-drehs |

## Practice 5-4

**A** *Answer the following questions in order to tell what the person has to do. Use the correct form of* **tener que** + *an infinitive in your answers.*

1. ¿Por qué no puedo ir a la cafetería? (*have to study now*)

   _____

2. ¿Por qué no podemos hacer el examen hoy? (*have to attend review classes*)

   _____

3. ¿Por qué no puedes llegar a tiempo? *(have to work with a private teacher)*

_____

4. ¿Por qué no pueden ellos ir a la clase de baile? *(have to stay in school after classes)*

_____

**B** *Using the strings of words below, write sentences expressing what the different people are going to do. The words are given in no particular order.*

1. nosotros / más tarde / estudiar / en la biblioteca / ir a

_____

2. ellos / mañana por la tarde / asistir a las clases de repaso / ir a

_____

3. tú / ir a / la semana próxima / hacer el examen

_____

4. yo / mañana por la mañana / ir a / hacer la tarea

_____

5. Ud. / ir a / pasado mañana / llamar al director

_____

**C** *Complete the following sentences with the correct form of the verb in parentheses.*

1. Si tú _____ (pelear) con tus amigos, tú _____ (ir) a quedarte en la escuela después de las clases.

2. Si nosotros no _____ (asistir) a clases, nosotros

_____ (ir) a salir mal.

3. Si él _____ (usar) malas palabras, él _____ (ir) a tener muchos problemas.

4. Si Uds. _____ (salir) sin permiso, el consejero

_____ (ir) a llamar a sus padres.

5. Si yo _____ (hablar) en voz alta, mis compañeros no

_____ (ir) a oír a la profesora.

## Other Consequences of Improper Conduct
*Otras consecuencias de conducta impropia*

Here are other consequences of improper conduct (**otras consecuencias de conducta impropia** [OH-trahs kohn-seh-KWEHN-syahs deh kohn-DOOK-tah eem-PROH-pyah]) that you might need to inform students about.

You can also express the consequence of certain behavior by stating what the person has to do.

| | |
|---|---|
| If you fight with others, you have to … | **Si peleas con otros, tienes que…** see peh-LEH-ahs kohn OH-trohs, TYEH-nehs keh |
| apologize | **disculparte / pedir perdón** dees-kool-PAHR-teh / peh-DEER pehr-DOHN |
| go to the principal's office | **ir a la oficina del director / de la directora** eer ah lah oh-fee-SEE-nah dehl dee-rehk-TOHR / deh lah dee-rehk-TOH-rah |

To describe some of the penalties for breaking the school rules, you should also become familiar with the following phrases.

| | |
|---|---|
| You have to return to school with one of your parents. | **Tienes que regresar a la escuela con uno de tus padres.** TYEH-nehs keh rreh-greh-SAHR ah lah ehs-KWEH-lah kohn oo-noh deh toos PAH-drehs |
| You cannot participate in extracurricular activities. | **No puedes participar en las actividades extracurriculares.** noh PWEH-dehs pahr-tee-see-PAHR ehn lahs ahk-tee-bee-DAH-dehs ehs-trah-koo-rree-koo-LAH-rehs |
| You are suspended for (number) days. | **Quedas suspendido por** (number) **días.** KEH-dahs soos-pehn-DEE-doh pohr… DEE-ahs |

# Praising a Student's Behavior and His/Her Work

*Para alabar el buen comportamiento y el trabajo*
*de un alumno / una alumna*

Letting the student's parents know when their child has done well is key to reinforcing the good behavior we expect from all students. Here are some phrases you may want to use to praise a student's behavior and work (**para alabar el buen comportamiento y el trabajo de un alumno / una alumna** [PAH-rah ah-lah-BAHR ehl bwehn kohm-pohr-tah-MYEHN-toh ee ehl trah-BAH-hoh deh oon ah-LOOM-noh / oo-nah ah-LOOM-nah]).

| | |
|---|---|
| You should be proud of (name). | **Ud. debe estar orgulloso/orgullosa de (name).**<br>OOS-TEHD DEH-beh ehs-TAHR ohr-goo-YOH-soh/ohr-goo-YOH-sah deh |
| He/She … | **Él/Ella...**<br>ehl/EH-yah |
| has improved his/her behavior | **ha mejorado su comportamiento**<br>ah meh-hoh-RAH-doh soo kohm-pohr-tah-MYEHN-toh |
| has improved his/her relationship with the other students | **ha mejorado su relación con otros estudiantes**<br>ah meh-hoh-RAH-doh soo rreh-lah-SYOHN kohn OH-trohs ehs-too-DYAHN-tehs |
| behaves well in class | **se comporta bien en clase**<br>seh kohm-POHR-tah byehn ehn KLAH-seh |
| has a positive attitude | **tiene una actitud positiva**<br>TYEH-neh oo-nah ahk-tee-TOOD poh-see-TEE-bah |
| completes his/her work on time | **completa su trabajo a tiempo**<br>kohm-PLEH-tah soo trah-BAH-hoh ah TYEHM-poh |
| helps others | **ayuda a otros**<br>ah-YOO-dah ah OH-trohs |
| works independently | **trabaja independientemente**<br>trah-BAH-hah een-deh-pehn-dyehn-teh-MEHN-teh |
| cooperates in class | **coopera en la clase**<br>koh-oh-PEH-rah ehn lah KLAH-seh |

| He/She ... | Él/Ella...<br>ehl/EH-yah |
|---|---|
| got a good grade on the last homework / the last test | **sacó una buena nota en la última tarea / el último examen**<br>sah-KOH OO-nah BWEH-nah NOH-tah ehn lah OOL-tee-mah tah-REH-ah / ehl OOL-tee-moh ehk-SAH-mehn |
| passed all his/her classes | **aprobó en todas sus clases**<br>ah-proh-BOH ehn TOH-dahs soos KLAH-sehs |

An easy way to praise the student and his/her work directly is by using ¡qué [keh] + an adjective!

| How marvelous! | **¡Qué maravilloso!**<br>keh mah-rah-bee-YOH-soh |
|---|---|
| How organized! | **¡Qué organizado/organizada!**<br>keh ohr-gah-nee-SAH-doh/ ohr-gah-nee-SAH-dah |
| How wonderful! | **¡Qué estupendo!**<br>keh ehs-too-PEHN-doh |

You may also include the noun that you are praising. In this case, the word **tan** [tahn] or **más** [mahs] usually precedes the adjective.

| What good homework! | **¡Qué tarea tan/más buena!**<br>keh tah-REH-ah tahn/mahs BWEH-nah |
|---|---|
| What a marvelous composition! | **¡Qué composición tan/más maravillosa!**<br>keh kohm-poh-see-SYOHN tahn/mahs mah-rah-bee-YOH-sah |

## Describing States and Conditions

*Para describir el estado de ánimo y condiciones*

When talking to parents, you will often need to describe how a student seems to be feeling at school. One way to express this idea is by using the verb **parecer** [pah-reh-SEHR] + an adjective, with the meaning of "to seem" + an adjective.

| In class your child seems ... | **En clase su hijo/hija parece...**<br>ehn KLAH-seh soo EE-hoh/EE-hah pah-REH-seh |
|---|---|
| anxious | **ansioso**<br>ahn-SYOH-soh |

| | |
|---|---|
| bored | **aburrido** |
| | ah-boo-RREE-doh |
| calm | **tranquilo** |
| | trahn-KEE-loh |
| exhausted | **agotado** |
| | ah-goh-TAH-doh |
| happy | **contento** |
| | kohn-TEHN-toh |
| nervous | **nervioso** |
| | nehr-BYOH-soh |
| relaxed | **relajado** |
| | rreh-lah-HAH-doh |
| tired | **cansado** |
| | kahn-SAH-doh |
| worried | **preocupado** |
| | preh-oh-koo-PAH-doh |

If the child to whom you are referring is a girl, all the Spanish adjectives listed above will end in **-a** instead of **-o**.

## GRAMMAR · Using the Verb "To Be" + Adjective to Express Conditions or States

The most common way to describe a condition or state in Spanish is to use the verb **estar** [ehs-TAHR] + an adjective. In addition to the adjectives listed above, other adjectives that are commonly used with **estar** are listed here.

| | |
|---|---|
| I am ... | **Estoy...** |
| | ehs-TOH-ee |
| angry | **enojado** |
| | eh-noh-HAH-doh |
| ashamed | **avergonzado** |
| | ah-behr-gohn-SAH-doh |
| busy | **ocupado** |
| | oh-koo-PAH-doh |
| grateful | **agradecido** |
| | ah-grah-deh-SEE-doh |
| healthy | **saludable** |
| | sah-loo-DAH-bleh |
| sad | **triste** |
| | TREES-teh |
| sick | **enfermo** |
| | ehn-FEHR-moh |

| I am ... | **Estoy...** |
| | ehs-TOH-ee |
| surprised | **sorprendido** |
| | sohr-prehn-DEE-doh |

Remember that the adjective ending may need to be changed to agree with the gender and number of the noun it describes.

| We are furious. | **Estamos furiosos.** |
| | ehs-TAH-mohs foo-RYOH-sohs |

For additional vocabulary about feelings and personal problems, see Chapter 7, pages 252–253 and 257–259.

To review the present tense of the verb **estar**, see Chapter 1, page 59.

## Practice 5-5

*Complete the following sentences with the Spanish translation for one of the adjectives below. Remember to change the ending if necessary. One of the adjectives will not be used.*

| surprised | furious |
| ashamed | tired |
| busy | healthy |
| anxious | bored |

1. Juan trabaja mucho. Él está _____.

2. Ellos tienen muchos exámenes hoy. Ellos están _____.

3. Nosotros salimos muy bien en el examen. Estamos _____.

4. Yo no estudié para el examen. Estoy _____.

5. La clase no es muy interesante. Uds. están _____.

6. Ella no puede ir al teatro porque tiene mucho trabajo. Está

   _____.

7. Estudio mucho pero no salgo bien. Estoy _____.

# Giving Advice to Students

*Para aconsejar a los estudiantes*

As a teacher, you will sometimes give advice to students (**aconsejar a los estudiantes** [ah-kohn-seh-HAHR ah lohs ehs-too-DYAHN-tehs]). Remember that you can use **(no) debes** [(noh) DEH-behs] + an infinitive, meaning "you should (not)" + the infinitive. Here are some expressions you may need.

| You should / ought to … | **Debes…** |
| --- | --- |
| | DEH-behs |
| do the homework carefully | **hacer la tarea con cuidado** |
| | ah-SEHR lah tah-REH-ah kohn kwee-DAH-doh |
| ask questions | **hacer preguntas** |
| | ah-SEHR preh-GOON-tahs |
| arrive at class early / on time | **llegar a la clase temprano / a tiempo** |
| | yeh-GAHR ah lah KLAH-seh tehm-PRAH-noh / ah TYEM-poh |
| pay attention in class | **prestar atención en clase** |
| | prehs-TAHR ah-tehn-SYOHN ehn KLAH-seh |
| participate in class | **participar en la clase** |
| | pahr-tee-see-PAHR ehn lah KLAH-seh |
| You should not / ought not … | **No debes…** |
| | noh DEH-behs |
| copy another student's homework | **copiar la tarea de otro estudiante** |
| | koh-PYAHR lah tah-REH-ah deh OH-troh ehs-too-DYAHN-teh |
| talk with your friends during class | **hablar con tus amigos durante la clase** |
| | ah-BLAHR kohn toos ah-MEE-gohs doo-RAHN-teh lah KLAH-seh |
| leave the class without permission | **salir de la clase sin permiso** |
| | sah-LEER deh lah KLAH-seh seen pehr-MEE-soh |
| get to class late | **llegar tarde a la clase** |
| | yeh-GAHR TAHR-deh ah lah KLAH-seh |
| look at another student's work during an exam | **mirar el trabajo de otro estudiante durante un examen** |
| | mee-RAHR ehl trah-BAH-hoh deh OH-troh ehs-too-DYAHN-teh doo-RAHN-teh oon ehk-SAH-mehn |

## Homework

### La tarea

Homework (**la tarea** [lah tah-REH-ah]) provides a link between school and home. Parents who come from Spanish-speaking countries are not always familiar with the type and length of homework assignments given in classrooms across the United States. It will prove helpful to share with them the reasons that homework is given and guidelines for what it should involve at home.

| | |
|---|---|
| Homework is given in order … | **La tarea se da para…**<br>lah tah-REH-ah seh dah PAH-rah |
| to know whether the students understood the lesson | **saber si los alumnos entendieron la lección**<br>sah-BEHR see lohs ah-LOOM-nohs ehn-tehn-DYEH-rohn lah lehk-SYOHN |
| to help the students understand and review what I presented in class | **ayudar a los alumnos a entender y repasar lo que yo expliqué en clase**<br>ah-yoo-DAHR ah lohs ah-LOOM-nohs ah ehn-tehn-DEHR ee rreh-pah-SAHR loh keh yoh ehs-plee-KEH ehn KLAH-seh |
| to help the students find more information on a topic | **ayudar a los alumnos a encontrar más información sobre un tema**<br>ah-yoo-DAHR ah lohs ah-LOOM-nohs ah ehn-kohn-TRAHR mahs een-fohr-mah-SYOHN SOH-breh oon TEH-mah |
| Your child should spend about (number) minutes a night on homework. | **Su hijo/hija debe pasar unos** (number) **minutos en la tarea cada noche.**<br>soo EE-hoh/EE-hah DEH-beh pah-SAHR oo-nohs… mee-NOO-tohs ehn lah tah-REH-ah KAH-dah NOH-cheh |
| Your child should spend about (number) hours a night on homework. | **Su hijo/hija debe pasar unas** (number) **horas en la tarea cada noche.**<br>soo EE-hoh/EE-hah DEH-beh pah-SAHR oo-nahs… OH-rahs ehn lah tah-REH-ah KAH-dah NOH-cheh |

Many of the suggestions in this chapter, such as the information about homework, could be sent home to the parents.

In order to succeed in school, children need to develop good study habits (**buenos hábitos de estudio** [BWEH-nohs AH-bee-tohs deh ehs-TOO-dyoh]) and attitudes that will help them to become lifelong learners. Teachers and parents are partners (**compañeros** [kohm-pah-NYEH-rohs]) in helping students to achieve this goal. Although you can use the direct command to tell the parents what to do, it is often better to tell them indirectly by using the subjunctive, which is explained below.

## GRAMMAR · The Present Subjunctive in Indirect Commands

Spanish speakers use the subjunctive to express a desire to influence the actions of others, that is, to give an indirect command.

| | |
|---|---|
| It is necessary for your child to study / do homework daily. | **Es necesario que su hijo/hija estudie / haga la tarea diariamente.** <br> ehs neh-seh-SAH-ryoh keh soo <br> EE-hoh/EE-hah ehs-TOO-dyeh / AH-gah <br> lah tah-REH-ah dyah-ryah-MEHN-teh |

### The Present Subjunctive: Regular Verbs

All verbs that end in **-o** in the **yo** [yoh] form of the present tense are formed regularly in the present subjunctive. The present subjunctive is formed by removing the **-o** from the **yo** form of the present tense and adding a set of endings as follows.

- For **-ar** verbs

  Add **-e, -es, -e, -emos, -en.**

- For **-er** and **-ir** verbs

  Add **-a, -as, -a, -amos, -an.**

Conjugations of some sample verbs that are regular in the present subjunctive follow.

**estudiar** [ehs-too-DYAHR] to study

| | | |
|---|---|---|
| yo | estudie | yoh ehs-TOO-dyeh |
| tú | estudies | too ehs-TOO-dyehs |
| él | estudie | ehl ehs-TOO-dyeh |
| ella | estudie | EH-yah ehs-TOO-dyeh |
| Ud. | estudie | oos-TEHD ehs-TOO-dyeh |
| nosotros | estudiemos | noh-SOH-trohs ehs-too-DYEH-mohs |
| nosotras | estudiemos | noh-SOH-trahs ehs-too-DYEH-mohs |
| ellos | estudien | EH-yohs ehs-TOO-dyehn |
| ellas | estudien | EH-yahs ehs-TOO-dyehn |
| Uds. | estudien | oos-TEH-dehs ehs-TOO-dyehn |

**leer** [leh-EHR] to read

| yo | lea | yoh LEH-ah |
| tú | leas | too LEH-ahs |
| él | lea | ehl LEH-ah |
| ella | lea | EH-yah LEH-ah |
| Ud. | lea | OOS-TEHD LEH-ah |
| nosotros | leamos | noh-SOH-trohs leh-AH-mohs |
| nosotras | leamos | noh-SOH-trahs leh-AH-mohs |
| ellos | lean | EH-yohs LEH-ahn |
| ellas | lean | EH-yahs LEH-ahn |
| Uds. | lean | OOS-TEH-dehs LEH-ahn |

**escribir** [ehs-kree-BEER] to read

| yo | escriba | yoh ehs-KREE-bah |
| tú | escribas | too ehs-KREE-bahs |
| él | escriba | ehl ehs-KREE-bah |
| ella | escriba | EH-yah ehs-KREE-bah |
| Ud. | escriba | OOS-TEHD ehs-KREE-bah |
| nosotros | escribamos | noh-SOH-trohs ehs-kree-BAH-mohs |
| nosotras | escribamos | noh-SOH-trahs ehs-kree-BAH-mohs |
| ellos | escriban | EH-yohs ehs-KREE-bahn |
| ellas | escriban | EH-yahs ehs-KREE-bahn |
| Uds. | escriban | OOS-TEH-dehs ehs-KREE-bahn |

**venir** [beh-NEER] to come

| yo | venga | yoh BEHN-gah |
| tú | vengas | too BEHN-gahs |
| él | venga | ehl BEHN-gah |
| ella | venga | EH-yah BEHN-gah |
| Ud. | venga | OOS-TEHD BEHN-gah |
| nosotros | vengamos | noh-SOH-trohs behn-GAH-mohs |
| nosotras | vengamos | noh-SOH-trahs behn-GAH-mohs |
| ellos | vengan | EH-yohs BEHN-gahn |
| ellas | vengan | EH-yahs BEHN-gahn |
| Uds. | vengan | OOS-TEH-dehs BEHN-gahn |

The teacher hopes that ...     **El maestro / La maestra espera que...**
ehl mah-EHS-troh / lah mah-EHS-trah
ehs-PEH-rah keh

we will study     **estudiemos**
ehs-too-DYEH-mohs

| I am reading the book | **yo lea el libro** |
| | yoh LEH-ah ehl LEE-broh |
| they will write the composition | **ellos escriban la composición** |
| | EH-yohs ehs-KREE-bahn lah kohm-poh-see-SYOHN |
| you are coming early | **tú vengas temprano** |
| | too BEHN-gahs tehm-PRAH-noh |

Note that the present subjunctive can express an action that is happening either at the same time as or after the action of the main verb.

## The Present Subjunctive: Irregular Verbs

If the **yo** [yoh] form of the present tense does not end in **-o**, the present subjunctive form is irregular. The following verbs are irregular in the present subjunctive.

**dar** [dahr]  to give

| yo | dé | yoh deh |
| tú | des | too dehs |
| él | dé | ehl deh |
| ella | dé | EH-yah deh |
| Ud. | dé | OOS-TEHD deh |
| nosotros | demos | noh-SOH-trohs DEH-mohs |
| nosotras | demos | noh-SOH-trahs DEH-mohs |
| ellos | den | EH-yohs dehn |
| ellas | den | EH-yahs dehn |
| Uds. | den | OOS-TEH-dehs dehn |

**estar** [ehs-TAHR]  to be

| yo | esté | yoh ehs-TEH |
| tú | estés | too ehs-TEHS |
| él | esté | ehl ehs-TEH |
| ella | esté | EH-yah ehs-TEH |
| Ud. | esté | OOS-TEHD ehs-TEH |
| nosotros | estemos | noh-SOH-trohs ehs-TEH-mohs |
| nosotras | estemos | noh-SOH-trahs ehs-TEH-mohs |
| ellos | estén | EH-yohs ehs-TEHN |
| ellas | estén | EH-yahs ehs-TEHN |
| Uds. | estén | OOS-TEH-dehs ehs-TEHN |

**ir** [eer]  to go

| yo | vaya | yoh BAH-yah |
| tú | vayas | too BAH-yahs |
| él | vaya | ehl BAH-yah |
| ella | vaya | EH-yah BAH-yah |
| Ud. | vaya | oos-TEHD BAH-yah |
| nosotros | vayamos | noh-SOH-trohs bah-YAH-mohs |
| nosotras | vayamos | noh-SOH-trahs bah-YAH-mohs |
| ellos | vayan | EH-yohs BAH-yahn |
| ellas | vayan | EH-yahs BAH-yahn |
| Uds. | vayan | oos-TEH-dehs BAH-yahn |

**ser** [sehr]  to be

| yo | sea | yoh SEH-ah |
| tú | seas | too SEH-ahs |
| él | sea | ehl SEH-ah |
| ella | sea | EH-yah SEH-ah |
| Ud. | sea | oos-TEHD SEH-ah |
| nosotros | seamos | noh-SOH-trohs seh-AH-mohs |
| nosotras | seamos | noh-SOH-trahs seh-AH-mohs |
| ellos | sean | EH-yohs SEH-ahn |
| ellas | sean | EH-yahs SEH-ahn |
| Uds. | sean | oos-TEH-dehs SEH-ahn |

**saber** [sah-BEHR]  to know

| yo | sepa | yoh SEH-pah |
| tú | sepas | too SEH-pahs |
| él | sepa | ehl SEH-pah |
| ella | sepa | EH-yah SEH-pah |
| Ud. | sepa | oos-TEHD SEH-pah |
| nosotros | sepamos | noh-SOH-trohs seh-PAH-mohs |
| nosotras | sepamos | noh-SOH-trahs seh-PAH-mohs |
| ellos | sepan | EH-yohs SEH-pahn |
| ellas | sepan | EH-yahs SEH-pahn |
| Uds. | sepan | oos-TEH-dehs SEH-pahn |

## Impersonal Expressions

Here are some impersonal expressions that can be used to give indirect commands when followed by a subject + a verb in the present subjunctive.

| It is advisable that ... | **Es aconsejable que...** |
| | ehs ah-kohn-seh-HAH-bleh keh |
| It is better that ... | **Es mejor que...** |
| | ehs meh-HOHR keh |

| | |
|---|---|
| It is important that … | **Es importante que…**<br>ehs eem-pohr-TAHN-teh keh |
| It is necessary that … | **Es necesario que…**<br>ehs neh-seh-SAH-ryoh keh |
| It is preferable that … | **Es preferible que…**<br>ehs preh-feh-REE-bleh keh |
| It is important that you come to school every day. | **Es importante que vengas a la escuela todos los días.**<br>ehs eem-pohr-TAHN-teh keh BEHN-gahs ah lah ehs-KWEH-lah TOH-dohs lohs DEE-ahs |

When you're making a general statement about expected behavior without referring to anyone in particular, impersonal expressions are followed by the infinitive because they are statements rather than indirect commands.

| | |
|---|---|
| It is important to come to school every day. | **Es importante venir a la escuela todos los días.**<br>ehs eem-pohr-TAHN-teh beh-NEER ah lah ehs-KWEH-lah TOH-dohs lohs DEE-ahs |

In addition to using impersonal expressions, you can give indirect commands by using the expression **Ojalá que** [oh-hah-LAH keh], meaning "I hope that," or by using conjugated forms of verbs that express a desire to influence the actions of another person. Some of those verbs are listed here.

| | | |
|---|---|---|
| to advise | **aconsejar** | ah-kohn-seh-HAHR |
| to forbid | **prohibir** | proh-ee-BEER |
| to hope | **esperar** | ehs-peh-RAHR |
| to recommend | **recomendar (ie)** | rreh-koh-mehn-DAHR |
| to want | **querer (ie)** | keh-REHR |
| to want | **desear** | deh-seh-AHR |

| | |
|---|---|
| I hope that you can help me. | **Espero que / Ojalá que Ud. me pueda ayudar.**<br>ehs-PEH-roh keh / oh-hah-LAH keh oos-TEHD meh PWEH-dah ah-yoo-DAHR |
| I recommend that your child do practice exercises. | **Recomiendo que su hijo/hija haga ejercicios de práctica.**<br>rreh-koh-MYEHN-doh keh soo EE-hoh/ EE-hah AH-gah eh-hehr-SEE-syohs deh PRAHK-tee-kah |

Other suggestions that you may want to make to parents follow.

| It is important that your child … | **Es importante que su hijo/hija…**<br>ehs eem-pohr-TAHN-teh keh soo<br>EE-hoh/EE-hah |
| turn in the homework | **entregue la tarea**<br>ehn-TREH-geh lah tah-REH-ah |
| review the lessons | **repase las lecciones**<br>rreh-PAH-seh lahs lehk-SYOH-nehs |
| read a book | **lea un libro**<br>LEH-ah oon LEE-broh |
| get at least (*number*) hours<br>of sleep each night | **duerma por lo menos** (*number*) **horas**<br>**cada noche**<br>DWEHR-mah pohr loh MEH-nohs…<br>OH-rahs KAH-dah NOH-cheh |

Long-term assignments, such as research papers and oral reports, often have deadlines that are weeks away, so it is important for parents to be aware of what their children need to do in order to handle such an assignment.

| It is important that you help<br>your child organize his/her<br>assignments by recording them<br>on calendars or planners, along<br>with due dates, etc. | **Es importante que ayude a su hijo/hija**<br>**a organizar sus tareas poniéndolas en**<br>**un calendario o planificador junto con**<br>**las fechas en que se deben entregar, etc.**<br>ehs eem-pohr-TAHN-teh keh<br>ah-YOO-deh ah soo EE-hoh/EE-hah ah<br>ohr-gah-nee-SAHR soos tah-REH-ahs<br>poh-NYEHN-doh-lahs ehn oon<br>kah-lehn-DAH-ryoh oh<br>plah-nee-fee-kah-DOHR HOON-toh kohn<br>lahs FEH-chahs ehn keh seh DEH-behn<br>ehn-treh-GAHR |
| This assignment is for (*day of<br>the week*). | **Esta tarea es para** (*day of the week*).<br>EHS-tah tah-REH-ah ehs PAH-rah |
| If he/she does not hand in the<br>assignment by that date … | **Si él/ella no entrega la tarea para esa**<br>**fecha…**<br>see ehl/EH-yah noh ehn-TREH-gah lah<br>tah-REH-ah PAH-rah EH-sah FEH-chah |
| I am not going to accept it | **no la voy a aceptar**<br>noh lah BOH-ee ah ah-sehp-TAHR |
| he/she will get a lower grade | **él/ella va a recibir una nota más baja**<br>ehl/EH-yah bah a rreh-see-BEER OO-nah<br>NOH-tah mahs BAH-hah |

## Practice 5-6

**A** *Circle the correct form of the verb from the two that are given to complete the following sentences. Once you are finished, you should say the sentence aloud so that you can practice the use of the subjunctive.*

1. Es necesario que ellos (vienen | vengan) antes de las clases.

2. Yo quiero que tú (leas | lees) esa novela.

3. El señor Thomas prohíbe que los estudiantes (comen | coman) en clase.

4. Es mejor que tú (entregues | entregas) la tarea hoy.

5. Ellos esperan que el examen no (es | sea) esta semana.

6. Yo recomiendo que Uds. (saben | sepan) el vocabulario.

7. La bibliotecaria desea que él no (habla | hable) en voz alta.

8. Es preferible que nosotros (repasemos | repasamos) la gramática.

**B** *Complete the following sentences with the Spanish translation for the phrase in parentheses.*

1. Es necesario que tú _____ (study early).

2. Yo espero que Uds. _____ (come on time).

3. Es mejor que tú _____ (study in the library).

4. Es aconsejable que los estudiantes

   _____ (don't go to the park today).

5. Es importante que yo _____
   (know when you are absent).

6. El director prohíbe que Uds. _____
   (eat in the hallways).

7. Yo recomiendo que ella _____
   (participate more in class).

8. El consejero desea que yo _____
   (speak with you).

9. Yo no quiero que ellos _____
   (copy another student's homework).

10. Tus padres esperan que tú _____
    (do well on the exam).

## The Home Environment

*El ambiente en casa*

Parents can also help to establish good study habits by providing a suitable home environment (**el ambiente en casa** [ehl ahm-BYEHN-teh ehn KAH-sah]) for doing homework and for studying. Here are some guidelines you may want to give them.

| | |
|---|---|
| Establish a regular time for studying and doing homework. | **Establezca una hora regular para estudiar y hacer la tarea.**<br>ehs-tah-BLEHS-kah OO-nah OH-rah RREH-goo-lahr PAH-rah ehs-too-DYAHR ee ah-SEHR lah tah-REH-ah |
| While your child is studying, the television should be turned off and any other distractions (e.g., e-mail, the Internet, calls from friends) should not be allowed. | **Mientras su hijo/hija estudia, el televisor debe estar apagado y no se debe permitir ninguna otra distracción (e.g., el correo electrónico, el internet, las llamadas de amigos).**<br>MYEHN-trahs soo EE-hoh/EE-hah ehs-TOO-dyah, ehl teh-leh-bee-SOHR DEH-beh ehs-TAHR ah-pah-GAH-doh ee noh seh DEH-beh pehr-mee-TEER neen-GOO-nah OH-trah dees-trahk-SYOHN (e.g., ehl koh-RREH-oh eh-lehk-TROH-nee-koh, ehl een-tehr-NEHT, lahs yah-MAH-dahs deh ah-MEE-gohs) |
| If possible, make sure that your child has a quiet, comfortable, well-lit study area to study and do homework. | **Si es posible, asegúrese de que su hijo/hija tenga un área de estudio tranquila y cómoda, con buena luz para estudiar y hacer la tarea.**<br>see ehs poh-SEE-bleh, ah-seh-GOO-reh-seh deh keh soo EE-hoh/EE-hah TEHN-gah oon AH-reh-ah deh ehs-TOO-dyoh trahn-KEE-lah ee KOH-moh-dah, kohn BWEH-nah loos PAH-rah ehs-too-DYAHR ee ah-SEHR lah tah-REH-ah |

| | |
|---|---|
| Make sure that your child has the school supplies he/she needs to do assignments. | **Asegúrese de que su hijo/hija tenga los materiales que necesita para hacer las tareas.**<br>ah-seh-GOO-reh-seh deh keh soo EE-hoh/EE-hah TEHN-gah lohs mah-teh-RYAH-lehs keh neh-seh-SEE-tah PAH-rah ah-SEHR lahs tah-REH-ahs |

## Preparing for Exams
*Para prepararse para los exámenes*

Increased accountability has moved many school districts and schools to increase the number of classroom tests, as well as standardized tests. Success on these tests depends not only on good instruction but also on parental support and hard work by students. In Chapter 7, pages 275–277, you will find information about the most common tests that you may need to explain to parents.

Children need help finding methods for study and review that work best for them as they prepare for exams (**prepararse para los exámenes** [preh-pah-RAHR-seh PAH-rah lohs ehk-SAH-meh-nehs]). For younger students, some recommendations for parents could be the following.

| | |
|---|---|
| Give your child practice tests. | **Haga exámenes de práctica con su hijo/hija.**<br>AH-gah ehk-SAH-meh-nehs deh PRAHK-tee-kah kohn soo EE-hoh/EE-hah |
| Help your child correct his/her work using the word list. | **Ayude a su hijo/hija a corregir su trabajo usando la lista de palabras.**<br>ah-YOO-deh ah soo EE-hoh/EE-hah ah koh-rreh-HEER soo trah-BAH-hoh oo-SAHN-doh lah LEES-tah deh pah-LAH-brahs |

The following recommendations are appropriate for children of all ages.

| | |
|---|---|
| Encourage your child … | **Anime a su hijo/hija a...**<br>ah-NEE-meh ah soo EE-hoh/EE-hah ah |
| to not leave studying for the last minute | **no dejar el estudio para el último momento**<br>noh deh-HAHR ehl ehs-TOO-dyoh PAH-rah ehl OOL-tee-moh moh-MEHN-toh |
| to prepare an exam study schedule | **preparar un horario de repaso para los exámenes**<br>preh-pah-RAHR oon oh-RAH-ryoh deh rreh-PAH-soh PAH-rah lohs ehk-SAH-meh-nehs |

| Encourage your child ... | **Anime a su hijo/hija a...** |
| | ah-NEE-meh ah soo EE-hoh/EE-hah ah |
| to read the instructions carefully | **leer las instrucciones con cuidado** |
| | leh-EHR lahs eens-trook-SYOH-nehs kohn kwee-DAH-doh |
| to answer the easiest questions first | **contestar a las preguntas más fáciles primero** |
| | kohn-tehs-TAHR ah lahs preh-GOON-tahs mahs FAH-see-lehs pree-MEH-roh |
| to avoid spending too much time on one question | **evitar el pasar mucho tiempo en una pregunta** |
| | eh-bee-TAHR ehl pah-SAHR MOO-choh TYEHM-poh ehn oo-nah preh-GOON-tah |

Being prepared for a test also includes many physical aspects. Here are some suggestions for parents.

| Make sure that your child ... | **Asegúrese de que su hijo/hija...** |
| | ah-seh-GOO-reh-seh deh keh soo EE-hoh/EE-hah |
| gets a good night's rest the night before a test | **duerma bastante la noche antes** |
| | DWEHR-mah bahs-TAHN-teh lah NOH-cheh AHN-tehs |
| eats a good breakfast | **se desayune bien** |
| | seh deh-sah-YOO-neh byehn |
| relaxes mentally | **se relaje mentalmente** |
| | seh rreh-LAH-heh mehn-tahl-MEHN-teh |

## Evaluating Students' Work

*Para evaluar el trabajo de los estudiantes*

As you work with students and parents, you will constantly be in the position of evaluating students' work (**evaluar el trabajo de los estudiantes** [eh-bah-LWAHR ehl trah-BAH-hoh deh lohs ehs-too-DYAHN-tehs]). To communicate about this with students and parents, you will need to be able to describe the student and his/her work.

By now you are familiar with many adjectives in Spanish. Some adjectives can be used with the verb **ser** [sehr], and others must be used with **estar** [ehs-TAHR]. If you remember that **estar** is used with an adjective to describe a condition or state, and **ser** is used with an adjective to describe a characteristic or inherent quality, you should have no problem making yourself understood.

# The Successful Student
*El estudiante que tiene éxito*

There are many qualities that can be used to describe a successful student (**el estudiante que tiene éxito** [ehl ehs-too-DYAHN-teh keh TYEH-neh EHK-see-toh]). A parent may ask you about the student as follows.

What is my child like in class?   **¿Cómo es mi hijo/hija en clase?**
KOH-moh ehs mee EE-hoh/EE-hah
ehn KLAH-seh

You may answer using one or more of the following descriptions.

Your child is ...    **Su hijo/hija es...**
SOO EE-hoh/EE-hah ehs

artistic    **artístico**
ahr-TEES-tee-koh

athletic    **atlético**
ah-TLEH-tee-koh

careful    **cuidadoso**
kwee-dah-DOH-soh

creative    **creativo**
kreh-ah-TEE-boh

hardworking    **trabajador / trabajadora**
trah-bah-hah-DOHR /
trah-bah-hah-DOH-rah

honest    **honesto**
oh-NEHS-toh

independent    **independiente**
een-deh-pehn-DYEHN-teh

inquisitive    **curioso**
koo-RYOH-soh

intelligent    **inteligente**
een-teh-lee-HEHN-teh

obedient    **obediente**
oh-beh-DYEHN-teh

organized    **organizado**
ohr-gah-nee-SAH-doh

punctual    **puntual**
poon-TWAHL

respectful    **respetuoso**
rrehs-peh-TWOH-soh

| | |
|---|---|
| Your child is … | **Su hijo/hija es…** |
| | soo EE-hoh/EE-hah ehs |
| studious | **estudioso / aplicado** |
| | ehs-too-DYOH-soh / ah-plee-KAH-doh |
| Your child is always … | **Su hijo/hija siempre está…** |
| | soo EE-hoh/EE-hah SYEHM-preh ehs-TAH |
| ready for class | **listo para la clase** |
| | LEES-toh PAH-rah lah KLAH-seh |
| well prepared | **bien preparado** |
| | byehn preh-pah-RAH-doh |
| His/Her homework is always … | **Su tarea siempre está…** |
| | soo tah-REH-ah SYEHM-preh ehs-TAH |
| complete | **completa** |
| | kohm-PLEH-tah |
| well done | **bien hecha** |
| | byehn EH-chah |

Remember that the ending of any adjective you use must agree in gender and number with the noun it is describing.

## The Student at Risk of Failing a Subject / the School Year
*El estudiante en riesgo de suspender una asignatura / el año escolar*

Many signals can indicate that a student is at risk academically, that he/she might be at risk of failing a subject or the school year (**en riesgo de suspender una asignatura o el año escolar** [ehn RRYEHS-goh deh soos-pehn-DEHR oo-nah ah-seeg-nah-TOO-rah oh ehl AH-nyoh ehs-koh-LAHR]). Here are some of the signals to discuss with parents.

| | |
|---|---|
| Your child … | **Su hijo/hija…** |
| | soo EE-hoh/EE-hah |
| arrives late to school / to class | **llega tarde a la escuela / a la clase** |
| | YEH-gah TAHR-deh ah lah |
| | ehs-KWEH-lah / ah lah KLAH-seh |
| misses school often | **falta a la escuela a menudo** |
| | FAHL-tah ah lah ehs-KWEH-lah ah |
| | meh-NOO-doh |
| is not attentive in class | **no presta atención en la clase** |
| | noh PREHS-tah ah-tehn-SYOHN ehn |
| | lah KLAH-seh |

| | |
|---|---|
| does not participate in class | **no participa en la clase**<br>noh pahr-tee-SEE-pah ehn lah KLAH-seh |
| misbehaves in school | **se porta mal en la escuela**<br>seh POHR-tah mahl ehn lah ehs-KWEH-lah |
| talks to his/her classmates during class | **habla con sus compañeros durante la clase**<br>AH-blah kohn soos kohm-pah-NYEH-rohs doo-RAHN-teh lah KLAH-seh |
| does not concentrate | **no se concentra**<br>noh seh kohn-SEHN-trah |

If you want to address the student directly, just add an **-s** at the end of the verb. For those sentences where **se** appears, you add the **-s** and also change **se** [seh] to **te** [teh].

| You ... | **Tú...**<br>too |
|---|---|
| arrive late to school | **llegas tarde a la escuela**<br>YEH-gahs TAHR-deh ah lah ehs-KWEH-lah |
| misbehave in school | **te portas mal en la escuela**<br>teh POHR-tahs mahl ehn lah ehs-KWEH-lah |

Other concerns you may want to share with parents are the following.

| Your child's homework is ... | **La tarea de su hijo/hija está...**<br>lah tah-REH-ah deh soo EE-hoh/EE-hah ehs-TAH |
|---|---|
| incomplete | **incompleta**<br>een-kohm-PLEH-tah |
| late | **atrasada**<br>ah-trah-SAH-dah |
| done carelessly | **hecha sin cuidado**<br>EH-chah seen kwee-DAH-doh |
| His/Her test grades are low. | **Su nota en los exámenes es baja.**<br>soo NOH-tah ehn lohs ehk-SAH-meh-nehs ehs BAH-hah |

To do well or not on a test or in a class is expressed in Spanish with **salir bien** [sah-LEER byehn] or **salir mal** [sah-LEER mahl].

| | |
|---|---|
| You did not do well on the test. | **No saliste bien en el examen.** |
| | noh sah-LEES-teh byehn ehn ehl ehk-SAH-mehn |

To receive good or bad grades in Spanish is expressed as follows.

| | |
|---|---|
| to get good grades | **sacar buenas notas** |
| | sah-KAHR BWEH-nahs NOH-tahs |
| to get bad grades | **sacar malas notas** |
| | sah-KAHR MAH-lahs NOH-tahs |
| He/She does not get good grades in (geography). | **Él/Ella no saca buenas notas en (geografía).** |
| | ehl/EH-yah noh SAH-kah BWEH-nahs NOH-tahs ehn (heh-oh-grah-FEE-ah) |
| All the students in the class got bad grades. | **Todos los estudiantes de la clase sacaron malas notas.** |
| | TOH-dohs lohs ehs-too-DYAHN-tehs deh lah KLAH-seh sah-KAH-rohn MAH-lahs NOH-tahs |

Note that the first example above uses the present tense, and the second example uses the preterite. It is important for you to become familiar with both tenses. In the Introduction, pages 9–15, and in Chapter 6, pages 230–232, you will find information about the formation and use of these two tenses. You may also refer to the Appendix, where you will find many common verbs fully conjugated.

Students who are at risk often exhibit frustration at home. The parents can be on the alert for signs of frustration.

| | |
|---|---|
| Does your child say that …? | **¿Dice su hijo/hija que…?** |
| | DEE-seh soo EE-hoh/EE-hah keh |
| the homework is too hard | **la tarea es demasiado difícil** |
| | lah tah-REH-ah ehs deh-mah-SYAH-doh dee-FEE-seel |
| he/she does not understand the instructions | **no comprende las instrucciones** |
| | noh kohm-PREHN-deh lahs eens-trook-SYOH-nehs |
| the homework takes too much time | **la tarea toma demasiado tiempo** |
| | lah tah-REH-ah TOH-mah deh-mah-SYAH-doh TYEHM-poh |

## Getting Academic Help

*Para recibir ayuda académica*

It's not easy to speak to parents of children who are at risk, whether it is regarding academics or behavior. They are often very upset and at a loss as to what they can do. You may find that you need to help them calm down before you can begin to share your concerns and recommendations. Some expressions that may be helpful are the following.

| | |
|---|---|
| Calm down. | **Tranquilícese.**<br>trahn-kee-LEE-seh-seh |
| Don't worry. | **No se preocupe.**<br>noh seh preh-oh-KOO-peh |
| There are several ways in which you can help your child. | **Hay varias maneras en que Ud. puede ayudar a su hijo/hija.**<br>AH-ee BAH-ryahs mah-NEH-rahs ehn keh OOS-TEHD PWEH-deh ah-yoo-DAHR ah soo EE-hoh/EE-hah |

Once the parents have calmed down, you will be able to suggest strategies for solving or lessening the problem, and for informing them of help that is available. The suggestions will depend on what the problem is, how severe it is, and what the needs of a particular child are. Some possibilities are the following.

| | |
|---|---|
| The school can provide help with the subject matter or the assignments. | **La escuela puede proporcionar ayuda con la materia o las tareas.**<br>lah ehs-KWEH-lah PWEH-deh proh-pohr-syoh-NAHR ah-YOO-dah kohn lah mah-TEH-ryah oh lahs tah-REH-ahs |
| If your child cannot do the homework, he/she can receive help by telephone. | **Si su hijo/hija no comprende la tarea, puede recibir ayuda por teléfono.**<br>see soo EE-hoh/EE-hah noh kohm-PREHN-deh lah tah-REH-ah, PWEH-deh rreh-see-BEER ah-YOO-dah pohr tch-LEH-foh-noh |
| The telephone number is *(phone number)*. | **El número de teléfono es** *(phone number)*.<br>ehl NOO-meh-roh deh teh-LEH-foh-noh ehs |

| | |
|---|---|
| Your child can go to the library and ask the librarian for suggestions. | **Su hijo/hija puede ir a la biblioteca y pedirle sugerencias al bibliotecario / a la bibliotecaria.** |

soo EE-hoh/EE-hah PWEH-deh eer
ah lah bee-blyoh-TEH-kah ee
peh-DEER-leh soo-heh-REHN-syahs
ahl bee-blyoh-teh-KAH-ryoh /
ah lah bee-blyoh-teh-KAH-ryah

You may also want to add a few suggestions such as the following.

| | |
|---|---|
| Keep in touch with me. | **Manténgase en contacto conmigo.** |

mahn-TEHN-gah-seh ehn kohn-TAHK-toh
kohn-MEE-goh

| | |
|---|---|
| If you have any concerns, call me at (phone number) between (time) and (time). | **Si tiene alguna preocupación, llámeme al (phone number) entre (time) y (time).** |

see TYEH-neh ahl-GOO-nah
preh-oh-koo-pah-SYOHN, YAH-meh-meh
ahl... EHN-treh... ee...

| | |
|---|---|
| Make an appointment to see me. | **Haga una cita para hablar conmigo.** |

AH-gah OO-nah SEE-tah PAH-rah ah-BLAHR
kohn-MEE-goh

| | |
|---|---|
| Come to see me during Parents' Night. | **Venga a verme durante la noche de la Reunión de Padres.** |

BEHN-gah ah BEHR-meh doo-RAHN-teh
lah NOH-cheh deh lah rreh-oo-NYOHN
deh PAH-drehs

When sensitive issues are involved, it is important to have an interpreter attend any meetings you have with a parent or member of the family who doesn't understand English. Students with serious personal or social problems are usually referred to a counselor. For more on this, see Chapter 7, "In the Counselor's Office."

## Summary Practice

*Express the following sentences in Spanish. You may want to review the chapter before doing the exercise. You may also need to consult the English-Spanish Glossary at the end of the book.*

1. Upon returning to school, your child must bring a note signed by you.

   _____

2. It is important to pay attention.

   _____

3. In order to do well, you (**tú**) must ask questions when you do not understand.

   _____

4. It is forbidden to yell in the hallways.

   _____

5. You (**tú**) have to take the exam again.

   _____

6. You (**Uds.**) are going to have a test next week.

   _____

7. If she behaves badly, she cannot participate in sports.

   _____

8. What wonderful homework!

   _____

9. I hope that you study a lot.

   _____

10. It is important that he sleep at least eight hours a night.

    _____

# Health, Medical Problems, and Emergencies

*La salud, los problemas médicos
y las emergencias*

Before entering school, children must have all their vaccinations (**las vacunas** [lahs bah- koo-nahs]) at a doctor's office (**la consulta del médico / de la médica** [lah kohn-sool-tah dehl meh-dee-koh / deh lah meh-dee-kah]) or at a clinic (**la clínica** [lah klee-nee-kah]).

The parent or guardian must also provide information about the child's general health (**la salud** [lah sah-lood]), as well as contact information in case of illness. For more about the information that may be required, see Chapter 1.

## In the Nurse's Office

### En la oficina del enfermero / de la enfermera

Most medical emergencies (**las emergencias** [lahs eh-mehr-hehn-syahs]) that take place in school, whether major or minor, will probably be dealt with first in the nurse's office (**en la oficina del enfermero / de la enfermera** [ehn lah oh-fee-see-nah dehl ehn-fehr-meh-roh / deh lah ehn-fehr-meh-rah]). There a student may rest in bed (**la cama** [lah kah-mah]), have his/her temperature taken with a thermometer (**el termómetro** [ehl tehr-moh-meh-troh]), and be evaluated by the nurse.

If a student needs to go to the nurse's office, you may say the following to him/her.

| | |
|---|---|
| Go to the nurse's office. | **Ve a la oficina del enfermero / de la enfermera.**<br>beh ah lah oh-fee-see-nah<br>dehl ehn-fehr-meh-roh /<br>deh lah ehn-fehr-meh-rah |

## Describing Symptoms

### Para describir los síntomas

One way to find out what a sick child is feeling is to ask him/her to describe symptoms (**describir los síntomas** [dehs-kree-beer lohs seen-toh-mahs]).

| | |
|---|---|
| What's wrong? | **¿Qué tienes? / ¿Qué te pasa?**<br>keh tyeh-nehs / keh teh pah-sah |

The child will likely describe his/her symptoms using an expression with **tener** [teh-nehr], as shown in the following pattern: "I have" + (*ailment*) (**Tengo** [tehn-goh] + (*ailment*)).

| | |
|---|---|
| I have a headache. | **Tengo dolor de cabeza.**<br>tehn-goh doh-lohr deh kah-beh-sah |

| | |
|---|---|
| I have a cough. | **Tengo tos.**<br>TEHN-goh tohs |

Here are some of the illnesses or conditions that may bring a student to the nurse's office.

| | |
|---|---|
| acne | **el acné**<br>ehl ahk-NEH |
| backache | **el dolor de espalda**<br>ehl doh-LOHR deh ehs-PAHL-dah |
| chills | **los escalofríos**<br>lohs ehs-kah-loh-FREE-ohs |
| constipation | **el estreñimiento**<br>ehl ehs-treh-nyee-MYEHN-toh |
| cough | **la tos**<br>lah tohs |
| cramps | **los calambres**<br>lohs kah-LAHM-brehs |
| diarrhea | **la diarrea**<br>lah dyah-RREH-ah |
| dizziness | **los mareos**<br>lohs mah-REH-ohs |
| earache | **el dolor de oído**<br>ehl doh-LOHR deh oh-EE-doh |
| fever | **la fiebre**<br>lah FYEH-breh |
| gas | **los gases**<br>los GAH-sehs |
| headache | **el dolor de cabeza**<br>ehl doh-LOHR deh kah-BEH-sah |
| hiccup(s) | **el hipo**<br>ehl EE-poh |
| indigestion | **la indigestión**<br>lah een-dee-hehs-TYOHN |
| infection | **la infección**<br>lah een-fehk-SYOHN |
| insect bite | **la picadura**<br>lah pee-kah-DOO-rah |
| itch | **la picazón**<br>lah pee-kah-SOHN |
| lice | **los piojos**<br>lohs PYOH-hohs |

| | |
|---|---|
| menstrual period | **el período / la regla**<br>ehl peh-REE-oh-doh / la RREH-glah |
| mucus | **la flema**<br>lah FLEH-mah |
| nausea | **la náusea**<br>lah NAH-oo-seh-ah |
| rash | **la erupción**<br>lah eh-roop-SYOHN |
| seizure | **la convulsión**<br>lah kohn-bool-SYOHN |
| sore throat | **el dolor de garganta**<br>ehl doh-LOHR deh gahr-GAHN-tah |
| stomachache | **el dolor de estómago**<br>doh-LOHR deh ehs-TOH-mah-goh |
| toothache | **el dolor de muelas**<br>ehl doh-LOHR deh MWEH-lahs |

Another way to find out how a child is feeling is to ask the following question.

| | |
|---|---|
| How are you? | **¿Cómo estás? / ¿Cómo te sientes?**<br>KOH-moh ehs-TAHS /<br>KOH-moh teh SYEHN-tehs |

In addition to answering your question with **tengo** [TEHN-goh] + *(ailment)*, a child may describe his/her symptoms using **estoy** [ehs-TOH-ee], meaning "I am," + an adjective or **me siento** [meh SYEHN-toh], meaning "I feel," + an adjective.

| | |
|---|---|
| I am sick. | **Estoy enfermo.**<br>ehs-TOH-ee ehn-FEHR-moh |
| I feel sick. | **Me siento enfermo.**<br>meh SYEHN-toh ehn-FEHR-moh |

For more information about describing a state of being, see Chapter 5, pages 203–204.

Remember that the verb **estar** [ehs-TAHR] is used with an adjective to indicate the physical or emotional condition of someone, and that for adjectives in the feminine form, the **-o** ending changes to **-a**.

| | |
|---|---|
| Elena is sick. | **Elena está enferma.**<br>eh-LEH-nah ehs-TAH ehn-FEHR-mah |

When making a determination about the nature and seriousness of an illness or injury, a nurse may ask the child to do the following.

| | |
|---|---|
| Breathe deeply. | **Respire profundamente.**<br>rrehs-PEE-reh proh-foon-dah-MEHN-teh |
| Exhale. | **Exhale.**<br>ehk-SAH-leh |
| Inhale. | **Inhale.**<br>ee-NAH-leh |
| Open your mouth. | **Abra la boca.**<br>AH-brah lah BOH-kah |
| Stick out your tongue. | **Saque la lengua.**<br>SAH-keh lah LEHN-gwah |
| Swallow. | **Trague.**<br>TRAH-geh |

For an explanation of how to form commands, see the Introduction, pages 16–18, 20, and 21.

Some situations will require a visit to the doctor (**el médico / la médica** [ehl MEH-dee-koh / lah MEH-dee-kah]), the dentist (**el/la dentista** [ehl/lah dehn-TEES-tah]), or even to the hospital emergency room (**la sala de emergencia del hospital** [lah SAH-lah deh eh-mehr-HEHN-syah dehl ohs-pee-TAHL]).

## Accidents

### Los accidentes

No matter how hard parents and teachers try to prevent them, accidents (**los accidentes** [lohs ahk-see-DEHN-tehs]) happen both at home and at school. You will need to use the preterite tense to talk about what happened in the past.

| | |
|---|---|
| What happened to him/her? | **¿Qué le pasó?**<br>keh leh pah-SOH |
| He/She fell. | **Él/Ella se cayó.**<br>ehl/EH-yah seh kah-YOH |

## Practice 6-1

*Find the words in the list below within the grid of letters. Words can appear horizontally, vertically, and backward, but not diagonally.*

agotado
débil
el dolor
el hipo
el oído
la erupción
la espalda
la fiebre
la flema
la garganta
la regla
la tos
los mareos
los piojos

```
U N M N L O S M A R E O S S E
Z Q R K S Z X X L O P C G H B
N G K D E A L G E R A L A L K
L H A D L A P S E A L C J A U
E L J O R S I I Y R C T D F T
R A D D E L D O L O R Z Y L W
B F N A L A T O S P P B D E G
E K U T L C E L H I P O L M U
I B M O Y A T N A G R A G A L
F O U G D Y E Z F K S D L Q P
A N L A N G L I B E D S N Q Y
L N Q C D E O D I O L E A K R
A D X R B V S O J O I P S O L
W D K K L A E R U P C I O N J
I L X O X P O X L R Z F K S W
```

## GRAMMAR · The Preterite Tense

The preterite tense can be used to talk about something that happened in the past. Regular Spanish verbs form the preterite tense by dropping the infinitive endings (-ar, -er, -ir) and adding a set of endings to the stem as follows.

- For verbs ending in **-ar**

  Add **-é, -aste, -ó, -amos, -asteis, -aron.**

  **repasar** [rreh-pah-SAHR] to review

| I reviewed | **yo repasé** | yoh rreh-pah-SEH |
| you reviewed | **tú repasaste** | too rreh-pah-SAHS-teh |
| he reviewed | **él repasó** | ehl rreh-pah-SOH |
| she reviewed | **ella repasó** | EH-yah rreh-pah-SOH |
| you reviewed | **Ud. repasó** | oos-TEHD rreh-pah-SOH |
| we reviewed | **nosotros repasamos** | noh-SOH-trohs rreh-pah-SAH-mohs |
| we reviewed | **nosotras repasamos** | noh-SOH-trahs rreh-pah-SAH-mohs |
| they reviewed | **ellos repasaron** | EH-yohs rreh-pah-SAH-rohn |
| they reviewed | **ellas repasaron** | EH-yahs rreh-pah-SAH-rohn |
| you (*plural*) reviewed | **Uds. repasaron** | oos-TEH-dehs rreh-pah-SAH-rohn |

- For verbs ending in **-er** or **-ir**

   Add **-í, -iste, -ió, -imos, -isteis, -ieron**.

   **toser** [toh-SEHR] to cough

| I coughed | **yo tosí** | yoh toh-SEE |
|---|---|---|
| you coughed | **tú tosiste** | too toh-SEES-teh |
| he coughed | **él tosió** | ehl toh-SYOH |
| she coughed | **ella tosió** | EH-yah toh-SYOH |
| you coughed | **Ud. tosió** | OOS-TEHD toh-SYOH |
| we coughed | **nosotros tosimos** | noh-SOH-trohs toh-SEE-mohs |
| we coughed | **nosotras tosimos** | noh-SOH-trahs toh-SEE-mohs |
| they coughed | **ellos tosieron** | EH-yohs toh-SYEH-rohn |
| they coughed | **ellas tosieron** | EH-yahs toh-SYEH-rohn |
| you (*plural*) coughed | **Uds. tosieron** | OOS-TEH-dehs toh-SYEH-rohn |

   **abrir** [ah-BREER] to open

| I opened | **yo abrí** | yoh ah-BREE |
|---|---|---|
| you opened | **tú abriste** | too ah-BREES-teh |
| he opened | **él abrió** | ehl ah-BRYOH |
| she opened | **ella abrió** | EH-yah ah-BRYOH |
| you opened | **Ud. abrió** | OOS-TEHD ah-BRYOH |
| we opened | **nosotros abrimos** | noh-SOH-trohs ah-BREE-mohs |
| we opened | **nosotras abrimos** | noh-SOH-trahs ah-BREE-mohs |
| they opened | **ellos abrieron** | EH-yohs ah-BRYEH-rohn |
| they opened | **ellas abrieron** | EH-yahs ah-BRYEH-rohn |
| you (*plural*) opened | **Uds. abrieron** | OOS-TEH-dehs ah-BRYEH-rohn |

You may find the following words and expressions useful when talking about the past.

| yesterday | **ayer** |
|---|---|
| | ah-YEHR |
| yesterday morning | **ayer por la mañana** |
| | ah-YEHR pohr lah mah-NYAH-nah |
| yesterday afternoon | **ayer por la tarde** |
| | ah-YEHR pohr lah TAHR-deh |
| last night | **anoche** |
| | ah-NOH-cheh |
| the day before yesterday | **anteayer** |
| | ahn-teh-ah-YEHR |
| the night before last | **anteanoche** |
| | ahn-teh-ah-NOH-cheh |

| last Tuesday | **el martes pasado** |
| | ehl MAHR-tehs pah-SAH-doh |
| last week | **la semana pasada** |
| | lah seh-MAH-nah pah-SAH-dah |
| last weekend | **el fin de semana pasado** |
| | ehl feen deh seh-MAH-nah pah-SAH-doh |
| last month | **el mes pasado** |
| | ehl mehs pah-SAH-doh |
| last summer | **el verano pasado** |
| | ehl beh-RAH-noh pah-SAH-doh |
| last year | **el año pasado** |
| | ehl AH-nyoh pah-SAH-doh |

## GRAMMAR · Reflexive Verbs II

Many of the verbs used to talk about accidents are reflexive verbs. You will recognize reflexive verbs by the **-se** which is attached to the infinitive. Some of the reflexive verbs that are most commonly used when talking about accidents are listed here.

| to break | **romperse** | rrohm-PEHR-seh |
| to burn | **quemarse** | keh-MAHR-seh |
| to cut | **cortarse** | kohr-TAHR-seh |
| to fall | **caerse** (*irreg.*) | kah-EHR-seh |
| to hit | **golpearse** | gohl-peh-AHR-seh |
| to sprain | **torcerse** | tohr-SEHR-seh |

Remember that reflexive verbs are conjugated like nonreflexive verbs except that the appropriate reflexive pronoun (**me** [meh], **te** [teh], **se** [seh], **nos** [nohs], **se** [seh]) must be placed immediately before the conjugated form of the reflexive verb. Affirmative commands formed with reflexive verbs are the only exception to this pattern. For a further explanation of reflexive verbs, see Chapter 3, pages 129–131.

## Injuries
### Las heridas

You will sometimes need to talk about injuries (**las heridas** [lahs eh-REE-dahs]) to specific parts of the body. The Spanish pattern for this is different from the English pattern with which you are familiar. English uses a nonreflexive verb and precedes the part of the body with a possessive adjective. Spanish uses a reflexive verb with the definite article before the named part of the body in the following pattern: reflexive verb + definite article + (*part of the body*).

| | |
|---|---|
| He broke his leg. | **Se rompió la pierna.**<br>seh rrohm-PYOH lah PYEHR-nah |
| She burned her hand. | **Se quemó la mano.**<br>seh keh-MOH lah MAH-noh |
| He cut his finger. | **Se cortó el dedo.**<br>seh kohr-TOH ehl DEH-doh |
| She hit her leg. | **Se golpeó la pierna.**<br>seh gohl-peh-OH lah PYEHR-nah |
| She sprained her ankle. | **Se torció el tobillo.**<br>seh tohr-SYOH ehl toh-BEE-yoh |

When using an adjective to describe the injury, you use a pattern with **tener** [teh-NEHR] as follows: **tener** + definite article + (*part of the body*) + adjective.

| | |
|---|---|
| He/She has a … (ankle). | **Tiene (el tobillo)….**<br>TYEH-neh (ehl toh-BEE-yoh) |
| broken | **roto**<br>RROH-toh |
| burned | **quemado**<br>keh-MAH-doh |
| infected | **infectado**<br>een-fehk-TAH-doh |
| swollen | **hinchado**<br>een-CHAH-doh |
| twisted | **torcido**<br>tohr-SEE-doh |
| He has a broken leg. | **Tiene la pierna rota.**<br>TYEH-neh lah PYEHR-nah RROH-tah |
| She has an infected foot. | **Tiene el pie infectado.**<br>TYEH-neh ehl pyeh een-fehk-TAH-doh |

Remember that for the feminine form of adjectives that end in **-o**, the **-o** changes to **-a**. When you have a plural adjective, add **-s**.

For a list of the parts of the body, see pages 237–238 in this chapter.

Other terms having to do with injuries that may be helpful to you are the following.

| | |
|---|---|
| He/She has … | **Tiene…**<br>TYEH-neh |
| a blister | **una ampolla**<br>oo-nah ahm-POH-yah |

| He/She has … | **Tiene…** |
|---|---|
| | TYEH-neh |
| a bruise | **un moretón** |
| | oon moh-reh-TOHN |
| a burn | **una quemadura** |
| | oo-nah keh-mah-DOO-rah |
| a cut | **una herida** |
| | oo-nah eh-REE-dah |
| a scratch/scrape | **un arañazo** |
| | oon ah-rah-NYAH-soh |
| a sprain | **una torcedura** |
| | oo-nah tohr-seh-DOO-rah |
| a wound | **una herida** |
| | oo-nah eh-REE-dah |
| He has a blister. | **Tiene una ampolla.** |
| | TYEH-neh oo-nah ahm-POH-yah |
| She has a burn. | **Tiene una quemadura.** |
| | TYEH-neh oo-nah keh-mah-DOO-rah |

For more on these and other types of emergencies that have to be dealt with right away, see pages 243–247 in this chapter.

## Practice 6-2

**A** *Complete the following sentences with the correct preterite form of the verb in parentheses.*

1. Antonio _____ (correr) en el parque.

2. ¿Qué le _____ (pasar) a Teresa?

3. Yo _____ (respirar) profundamente.

4. Tú no _____ (abrir) la boca.

5. Nosotros _____ (aprender) mucho.

6. Ellos _____ (salir) bien en el examen.

7. El maestro _____ (calificar) las composiciones.

8. Yo no _____ (asistir) a clase.

9. Ellos no _____ (comprender) nada.

10. Nosotros _____ (tomar) apuntes.

**B** Write the word or phrase that expresses each of the following in a past context.

MODELO    este año ___*el año pasado*___

1. hoy _____

2. esta tarde _____

3. esta noche _____

4. este verano _____

5. hoy por la mañana _____

6. este lunes _____

**C** Complete the following sentences by writing the correct form of the verb in parentheses in the first blank, then writing the Spanish equivalent of the English phrase in parentheses in the second blank.

1. Ellos _____ (toser) mucho _____
(the day before yesterday).

2. Ella _____ (visitar) al dentista _____
(last Friday).

3. La enfermera _____ (dar) información a los padres

_____ (last Tuesday).

4. Nosotros _____ (asistir) a la conferencia

_____ (the night before last).

5. Tú _____ (salir) de la escuela con Juan

_____ (yesterday).

## Contagious Illnesses

### Las enfermedades contagiosas

You may need to know about the following contagious illnesses (**las enfermedades contagiosas** [lahs ehn-fehr-meh-DAH-dehs kohn-tah-HYOH-sahs]).

| | |
|---|---|
| bronchitis | **la bronquitis** |
| | lah brohn-KEE-tees |
| chicken pox | **la varicela** |
| | lah bah-ree-SEH-lah |
| cold (common cold) | **el resfriado / el catarro** |
| | ehl rrehs-FRYAH-doh / ehl kah-TAH-rroh |

| | | |
|---|---|---|
| diphtheria | **la difteria** | |
| | lah deef-TEH-ryah | |
| flu | **la gripe** | |
| | lah GREE-peh | |
| hepatitis | **la hepatitis** | |
| | lah eh-pah-TEE-tees | |
| measles | **el sarampión** | |
| | ehl sah-rahm-PYOHN | |
| meningitis | **la meningitis** | |
| | lah meh-neen-HEE-tees | |
| mononucleosis | **la mononucleosis** | |
| | lah moh-noh-noo-kleh-OH-sees | |
| mumps | **las paperas** | |
| | lahs pah-PEH-rahs | |
| pneumonia | **la pulmonía** | |
| | lah pool-moh-NEE-ah | |
| rubella | **la rubéola** | |
| | lah rroo-BEH-oh-lah | |
| scarlet fever | **la escarlatina** | |
| | lah ehs-kahr-lah-TEE-nah | |
| tuberculosis | **la tuberculosis** | |
| | lah too-behr-koo-LOH-sees | |

## Verbs

| | | |
|---|---|---|
| to cough | **toser** | toh-SEHR |
| to faint | **desmayarse** | dehs-mah-YAHR-seh |
| to get better | **mejorarse** | meh-hoh-RAHR-seh |
| to get dizzy | **marearse** | mah-reh-AHR-seh |
| to get sick | **enfermarse** | ehn-fehr-MAHR-seh |
| to sneeze | **estornudar** | ehs-tohr-noo-DAHR |
| to stay in bed | **guardar cama** | gwahr-DAHR KAH-mah |
| to take care of yourself | **cuidarse** | kwee-DAHR-seh |
| to vomit | **vomitar** | boh-mee-TAHR |

To avoid several of the illnesses, get vaccinated!

**Para evitar varias de las enfermedades, ¡vacúnese!**

PAH-rah eh-bee-TAHR BAH-ryahs deh lahs ehn-fehr-meh-DAH-dehs, bah-KOO-neh-seh

# Parts of the Body

*Las partes del cuerpo*

| | | |
|---|---|---|
| ankle | **el tobillo** | ehl toh-BEE-yoh |
| arm | **el brazo** | ehl BRAH-soh |
| back | **la espalda** | lah ehs-PAHL-dah |
| blood | **la sangre** | lah SAHN-greh |
| brain | **el cerebro** | ehl seh-REH-broh |
| cheek | **la mejilla** | lah meh-HEE-yah |
| chest | **el pecho** | ehl PEH-choh |
| chin | **la barbilla** | lah bahr-BEE-yah |
| ear (inner) | **el oído** | ehl oh-EE-doh |
| ear (outer) | **la oreja** | lah oh-REH-hah |
| elbow | **el codo** | ehl KOH-doh |
| eye | **el ojo** | ehl OH-hoh |
| face | **la cara** | lah KAH-rah |
| finger | **el dedo** | ehl DEH-doh |
| foot | **el pie** | ehl pyeh |
| forehead | **la frente** | lah FREHN-teh |
| hair | **el pelo / el cabello** | ehl PEH-loh / ehl kah-BEH-yoh |
| hand | **la mano** | lah MAH-noh |
| head | **la cabeza** | lah kah-BEH-sah |
| heart | **el corazón** | ehl koh-rah-SOHN |
| hip | **la cadera** | lah kah-DEH-rah |
| knee | **la rodilla** | lah rroh-DEE-yah |
| leg | **la pierna** | lah PYEHR-nah |
| lip | **el labio** | ehl LAH-byoh |
| lung | **el pulmón** | ehl pool-MOHN |
| mouth | **la boca** | lah BOH-kah |
| nail | **la uña** | lah oo-nyah |
| neck | **el cuello** | ehl KWEH-yoh |
| nose | **la nariz** | lah nah-REES |
| shoulder | **el hombro** | ehl OHM-broh |
| skin | **la piel** | lah pyehl |
| stomach | **el estómago** | ehl ehs-TOH-mah-goh |

| thigh | **el muslo** | ehl MOOS-loh |
| throat | **la garganta** | lah gahr-GAHN-tah |
| toe | **el dedo del pie** | ehl DEH-doh dehl pyeh |
| tongue | **la lengua** | lah LEHN-gwah |
| tooth | **el diente** | ehl DYEHN-teh |
| waist | **la cintura** | lah seen-TOO-rah |
| wrist | **la muñeca** | lah moo-NYEH-kah |

## GRAMMAR · Talking About What Hurts or Aches

When a Spanish-speaking child talks about a part of the body that hurts, he or she is likely to use the verb **doler** [doh-LEHR], meaning "to hurt or ache," according to the following pattern: "my/his/her/our/their" + (part of the body) + "hurts" (**me/le/nos/les** [meh/leh/nohs/lehs] + **duele** [DWEH-leh] + definite article + (part of the body)).

| My (head) hurts. | **Me duele (la cabeza).** |
| | meh DWEH-leh (lah kah-BEH-sah) |
| His/Her (head) hurts. | **Le duele (la cabeza).** |
| | leh DWEH-leh (lah kah-BEH-sah) |
| Our (heads) hurt. | **Nos duele (la cabeza).** |
| | nohs DWEH-leh (lah kah-BEH-sah) |
| Their (heads) hurt. | **Les duele (la cabeza).** |
| | lehs DWEH-leh (lah kah-BEH-sah) |

Note that in Spanish, unlike English, when the subject is plural, you still use a singular noun for parts of the body. It is assumed that each person has only one—one "head" (**la cabeza** [lah kah-BEH-sah]) in the example above.

If you want to know what part of the body is hurting, ask the question "What hurts?" (**¿Qué te/le/les duele?** [keh teh/leh/lehs DWEH-leh]).

| What hurts (you [plural])? | **¿Qué les duele?** |
| | keh lehs DWEH-leh |
| Does your (stomach) hurt? | **¿Te duele (el estómago)?** |
| | teh DWEH-leh (ehl ehs-TOH-mah-goh) |

In a situation where the child may be too young or too sick to verbalize what he or she is feeling, but may be able to point to where it hurts, ask him/her *where* it hurts.

| Where does it hurt? | **¿Dónde te duele?** |
| | DOHN-deh teh DWEH-leh |

When more than one part of the body hurts, **duele** [DWEH-leh] changes to **duelen** [DWEH-lehn].

| | |
|---|---|
| Do your arms hurt? | **¿Te duelen los brazos?** |
| | teh DWEH-lehn lohs BRAH-sohs |
| No, my legs hurt. | **No, me duelen las piernas.** |
| | noh, meh DWEH-lehn lahs PYEHR-nahs |

## Practice 6-3

*Use the cue in parentheses to express who is hurting.*

1. _____ duele el brazo. (nosotros)

2. _____ duele la cabeza. (yo)

3. Juan, ¿_____ duele el muslo? (tú)

4. _____ duelen los dedos. (ella)

5. _____ duele la garganta. (ellos)

6. _____ duelen las rodillas. (él)

## Medical Equipment

### Los aparatos médicos

Minor accidents require only a Band-Aid® (**una curita**® / **una tirita**® [oo-nah koo-REE-tah / oo-nah tee-REE-tah]), but often something more is required. Here is a list of some common medical equipment (**los aparatos médicos** [lohs ah-pah-RAH-tohs MEH-dee-kohs]).

| | |
|---|---|
| bandage | **la venda** |
| | lah BEHN-dah |
| cane | **el bastón** |
| | ehl bahs-TOHN |
| cast | **el yeso** |
| | ehl YEH-soh |
| crutches | **las muletas** |
| | lahs moo-LEH-tahs |
| stitches | **los puntos** |
| | lohs POON-tohs |
| wheelchair | **la silla de ruedas** |
| | lah SEE-yah deh RRWEH-dahs |

## Verbs

| | |
|---|---|
| to bandage the wound | **vendar la herida**<br>behn-DAHR lah eh-REE-dah |
| to clean the wound | **limpiar la herida**<br>leem-PYAHR lah eh-REE-dah |
| to give a shot (injection) | **inyectar / ponerle una inyección**<br>een-yehk-TAHR / poh-NEHR-leh OO-nah<br>een-yehk-SYOHN |
| to put a cast on | **enyesar**<br>ehn-yeh-SAHR |
| to stitch (close with stitches) | **poner puntos**<br>poh-NEHR POON-tohs |
| to take (one's) blood pressure | **tomarle la presión arterial**<br>toh-MAHR-leh lah preh-SYOHN<br>ahr-teh-RYAHL |
| to take (one's) pulse | **tomarle el pulso**<br>toh-MAHR-leh ehl POOL-soh |
| to take (one's) temperature | **tomarle la temperatura**<br>toh-MAHR-leh lah tehm-peh-rah-TOO-rah |

For additional vocabulary having to do with students with special needs, see Chapter 7, pages 278–281.

# Communications from the Nurse's Office

## Los mensajes de la oficina del enfermero / de la enfermera

After the nurse examines a child, he/she may have to call the parent at home or at work. Here are some things that he/she may say in a message (**el mensaje** [ehl mehn-SAH-heh]).

| | |
|---|---|
| Your (*male*) child is sick. | **Su hijo está enfermo.**<br>soo EE-hoh ehs-TAH ehn-FEHR-moh |
| Your (*female*) child is sick. | **Su hija está enferma.**<br>soo EE-hah ehs-TAH ehn-FEHR-mah |
| He/She is … | **Está...**<br>ehs-TAH |
| bleeding | **sangrando**<br>sahn-GRAHN-doh |

| | |
|---|---|
| dehydrated | **deshidratado/deshidratada** |
| | dehs-ee-drah-TAH-doh/ |
| | dehs-ee-drah-TAH-dah |
| dizzy | **mareado/mareada** |
| | mah-reh-AH-doh/mah-reh-AH-dah |
| vomiting | **vomitando** |
| | boh-mee-TAHN-doh |
| wounded | **herido/herida** |
| | eh-REE-doh/eh-REE-dah |
| He/She has … | **Tiene...** |
| | TYEH-neh |
| a burn | **una quemadura** |
| | oo-nah keh-mah-DOO-rah |
| convulsions | **convulsiones** |
| | kohn-bool-SYOH-nehs |
| a rash | **una erupción** |
| | oo-nah eh-roop-SYOHN |
| sunstroke | **una insolación** |
| | oo-nah een-soh-lah-SYOHN |
| His/Her (stomach) hurts. | **Le duele (el estómago).** |
| | leh DWEH-leh (ehl ehs-TOH-mah-goh) |
| You have to pick him/her up immediately. | **Tiene que recogerlo/recogerla inmediatamente.** |
| | TYEH-neh keh rreh-koh-HEHR-loh/ |
| | rreh-koh-HEHR-lah |
| | een-meh-dyah-tah-MEHN-teh |
| You need to call the doctor. | **Necesita llamar al médico.** |
| | neh-seh-SEE-tah yah-MAHR ahl |
| | MEH-dee-koh |
| You need to take your child to the doctor. | **Necesita llevar a su hijo/hija al médico.** |
| | neh-seh-SEE-tah yeh-BAHR ah soo |
| | EE-hoh/EE-hah ahl MEH-dee-koh |
| You need to take your child to the pediatrician. | **Necesita llevar a su hijo/hija al pediatra.** |
| | neh-seh-SEE-tah yeh-BAHR ah soo |
| | EE-hoh/EE-hah ahl peh-DYAH-trah |
| You need to take your child to the hospital. | **Necesita llevar a su hijo/hija al hospital.** |
| | neh-seh-SEE-tah yeh-BAHR ah soo |
| | EE-hoh/EE-hah ahl ohs-pee-TAHL |

## Medications

*Las medicinas*

Some medications (**las medicinas** [lahs meh-dee-SEE-nahs]) that may be recommended by a doctor are the following.

| | |
|---|---|
| antacids | **los antiácidos** <br> lohs ahn-TYAH-see-dohs |
| antibiotics | **los antibióticos** <br> lohs ahn-tee-BYOH-tee-kohs |
| antihistamines | **los antihistamínicos** <br> lohs ahn-tees-tah-MEE-nee-kohs |
| antiseptic | **el antiséptico** <br> ehl ahn-tee-SEHP-tee-koh |
| aspirin | **la aspirina** <br> lah ahs-pee-REE-nah |
| cough syrup | **el jarabe para la tos** <br> ehl hah-RAH-beh PAH-rah lah tohs |
| cream | **la pomada** <br> lah poh-MAH-dah |
| iodine | **el yodo** <br> ehl YOH-doh |
| liniment | **el linimento** <br> ehl lee-nee-MEHN-toh |
| lotion | **la loción** <br> lah loh-SYOHN |
| penicillin | **la penicilina** <br> lah peh-nee-see-LEE-nah |
| powder | **el polvo** <br> ehl POHL-boh |
| tablets (lozenges) | **las pastillas** <br> lahs pahs-TEE-yahs |
| vitamins | **las vitaminas** <br> lahs bee-tah-MEE-nahs |

## In an Emergency

*En una emergencia*

It is impossible to know what on-site emergencies or disasters may occur while school is in session. Careful preparation and a plan of action are required in order to deal with the unforeseen as effectively as possible.

## Medical Emergencies

*Las emergencias médicas*

In certain situations, for example, if the child can't breathe (**no puede respirar** [noh PWEH-deh rrehs-pee-RAHR]), is choking or suffocating (**está asfixiándose** [ehs-TAH ahs-feek-SYAHN-doh-seh]), or is unconscious (**está sin conocimiento** [ehs-TAH seen koh-noh-see-MYEHN-toh]), the nurse would most likely call 9-1-1 (**nueve-uno-uno** [NWEH-beh OO-noh OO-noh]) before calling the parent. For more information about describing symptoms, see pages 226–228 in this chapter.

| | |
|---|---|
| Call 9-1-1. | **Llame al 9-1-1.** |
| | YAH-meh ahl NWEH-beh OO-noh OO-noh |
| I need an ambulance. | **Necesito una ambulancia.** |
| | neh-seh-SEE-toh OO-nah |
| | ahm-boo-LAHN-syah |

## Other Emergencies

*Otras emergencias*

While medical emergencies usually generate a call to 9-1-1, other types of emergencies may require a call to the fire department (**el cuerpo de bomberos** [ehl KWEHR-poh deh bohm-BEH-rohs]), the police department (**el cuerpo de policía** [ehl KWEHR-poh deh poh-lee-SEE-ah]), or another government agency.
   Some emergencies in this category might be the following.

| | |
|---|---|
| bomb scare | **la amenaza de bomba** |
| | lah ah-meh-NAH-sah deh BOHM-bah |
| chemical spill | **el derrame de sustancia química** |
| | ehl deh-RRAH-meh deh soos-TAHN-syah |
| | KEE-mee-kah |
| explosion | **la explosión / el estallido** |
| | lah ehs-PLOH-syohn / |
| | ehl ehs-tah-YEE-doh |
| gas leak | **el escape de gas** |
| | ehl ehs-KAH-peh deh gahs |

| | |
|---|---|
| riot | **el motín**<br>ehl moh-TEEN |
| robbery | **el robo**<br>ehl RROH-boh |
| shooting | **el tiroteo**<br>ehl tee-roh-TEH-oh |
| traffic accident | **el accidente de tráfico**<br>ehl ahk-see-DEHN-teh deh TRAH-fee-koh |

Here are some other useful words and expressions.

| | |
|---|---|
| Call the fire department. | **Llame a los bomberos.**<br>YAH-meh ah lohs bohm-BEH-rohs |
| fire | **el fuego / el incendio**<br>ehl FWEH-goh / ehl een-SEHN-dyoh |
| fire alarm | **la alarma de incendios**<br>lah ah-LAHR-mah deh een-SEHN-dyohs |
| fire door | **la puerta contra incendios**<br>lah PWEHR-tah KOHN-trah<br>een-SEHN-dyohs |
| fire drill | **el simulacro de incendio**<br>ehl see-moo-LAH-kroh deh<br>een-SEHN-dyoh |
| fire escape | **la escalera de emergencia**<br>lah ehs-kah-LEH-rah deh<br>eh-mehr-HEHN-syah |
| fire exit | **la salida de emergencia**<br>lah sah-LEE-dah deh<br>eh-mehr-HEHN-syah |
| fire extinguisher | **el extintor**<br>ehl ehs-teen-TOHR |
| firefighter | **el bombero**<br>ehl bohm-BEH-roh |
| flames | **las llamas**<br>lahs YAH-mahs |
| siren | **la sirena**<br>lah see-REH-nah |
| smoke | **el humo**<br>ehl oo-moh |
| smoke detector | **el detector de humo**<br>ehl deh-tehk-TOHR deh oo-moh |

| | |
|---|---|
| Call the police. | **Llame a la policía.**<br>YAH-meh ah lah poh-lee-SEE-ah |
| (in) police custody | **(bajo) custodia policial**<br>(BAH-hoh) koos-TOH-dyah<br>poh-lee-SYAHL |
| police record | **los antecedentes penales**<br>lohs ahn-teh-seh-DEHN-tehs<br>peh-NAH-lehs |
| police station | **la comisaría**<br>lah koh-mee-sah-REE-ah |
| policeman | **el policía**<br>ehl poh-lee-SEE-ah |
| policewoman | **la mujer policía**<br>lah moo-HEHR poh-lee-SEE-ah |

Safety (**la seguridad** [lah seh-goo-ree-DAHD]) is a major concern, and threats (**las amenazas** [lahs ah-meh-NAH-zahs]) must be taken seriously. A safe and orderly school usually includes its own security personnel (**el personal de seguridad** [ehl pehr-soh-NAHL deh seh-goo-ree-DAHD]).

You may also need the following key vocabulary.

| | |
|---|---|
| danger | **el peligro**<br>ehl peh-LEE-groh |
| evacuation | **la evacuación**<br>lah eh-bah-kwah-SYOHN |
| rescue | **el rescate**<br>ehl rrehs-KAH-teh |
| shelter | **el refugio**<br>ehl rreh-FOO-hyoh |
| threat | **la amenaza**<br>lah ah-meh-NAH-sah |
| warning | **la advertencia**<br>lah ahd-behr-TEHN-syah |

You may need to order the students to take certain actions in case of an emergency. Here are some phrases you should learn.

| | |
|---|---|
| Don't yell! | **¡No griten!**<br>noh GREE-tehn |
| Don't run! | **¡No corran!**<br>noh KOH-rrahn |
| Don't go near the window /<br>the door! | **¡No se acerquen a la ventana / la puerta!**<br>noh seh ah-SEHR-kehn ah lah<br>behn-TAH-nah / lah PWEHR-tah |

| | |
|---|---|
| Walk quietly! | **¡Caminen tranquilamente!**<br>kah-MEE-nehn trahn-kee-lah-MEHN-teh |
| Walk toward _____! | **¡Caminen hacia _____!**<br>kah-MEE-nehn AH-syah |
| Run toward _____! | **¡Corran hacia _____!**<br>KOH-rrahn AH-syah |
| Danger! | **¡Peligro!**<br>peh-LEE-groh |
| Fire! | **¡Fuego!**<br>FWEH-goh |
| Help! | **¡Socorro! / ¡Auxilio!**<br>soh-KOH-rroh / ah-ook-SEE-lyoh |
| Hurry up! | **¡Dense prisa!**<br>DEHN-seh PREE-sah |
| Listen! | **¡Escuchen!**<br>ehs-KOO-chehn |
| Look! | **¡Miren!**<br>MEE-rehn |
| Police! | **¡Policía!**<br>poh-lee-SEE-ah |
| Silence! | **¡Silencio!**<br>see-LEHN-syoh |
| Watch out! | **¡Cuidado!**<br>kwee-DAH-doh |
| Get under the desk! | **¡Pónganse debajo del pupitre!**<br>POHN-gahn-seh deh-BAH-hoh dehl<br>poo-PEE-treh |
| Cover your head! | **¡Cúbranse la cabeza!**<br>KOO-brahn-seh lah kah-BEH-sah |
| Cover your mouth! | **¡Cúbranse la boca!**<br>KOO-brahn-seh lah BOH-kah |

## Natural Disasters
### Los desastres naturales

Depending on the part of the country in which you live, the following natural disasters (**los desastres naturales** [lohs deh-SAHS-trehs nah-too-RAH-lehs]) may or may not be common occurrences.

| | |
|---|---|
| blackout | **el apagón**<br>ehl ah-pah-GOHN |
| earthquake | **el terremoto**<br>ehl teh-rreh-MOH-toh |

| | |
|---|---|
| epidemic | **la epidemia** |
| | lah eh-pee-DEH-myah |
| flood | **la inundación** |
| | lah ee-noon-dah-SYOHN |
| hailstorm | **la granizada** |
| | lah grah-nee-SAH-dah |
| hurricane | **el huracán** |
| | ehl oo-rah-KAHN |
| landslide | **el desprendimiento de tierra** |
| | ehl dehs-prehn-dee-MYEHN-toh deh TYEH-rrah |
| snowstorm | **la nevada** |
| | lah neh-BAH-dah |
| thunderstorm | **la tormenta** |
| | lah tohr-MEHN-tah |
| tornado | **el tornado** |
| | ehl tohr-NAH-doh |
| tsunami | **el maremoto** |
| | ehl mah-reh-MOH-toh |

## Practice 6-4

*Write what you would say in Spanish as a response to the following situations.*

1. There is an emergency in your school.

   _____

2. There is a fire in the science lab.

   _____

3. The students are yelling in the hallways.

   _____

4. There is a hole in the sidewalk.

   _____

5. You want the students to hurry.

   _____

6. You want all the students to get under their desks.

   _____

7. You want the students to walk quietly.

_____

8. Everyone must cover his or her head.

_____

## Summary Practice

*Express the following sentences in Spanish.*

1. You (**tú**) need to go to the nurse's office.

_____

2. Do you (**tú**) have a sore throat?

_____

3. She feels dizzy.

_____

4. What happened to her?

_____

5. He broke his foot.

_____

6. You (**tú**) have to stay in bed.

_____

7. Does your (**tú**) neck hurt?

_____

8. I have a toothache.

_____

9. There is smoke in the hallways.

_____

10. Cover (**Uds.**) your mouth!

_____

# In the Counselor's Office

*En la oficina del consejero*

Although counselors do different things in different schools, their work with students often begins with registration (**la matrícula** [lah mah-TREE-koo-lah]) and does not end until transfer (**la transferencia** [lah trahns-feh-REHN-syah]) or graduation (**la graduación** [lah grah-dwah-SYOHN]). In the following sections, you will find vocabulary and expressions that will prove useful in many of the situations in which a counselor (**el consejero / la consejera** [ehl kohn-seh-HEH-roh / lah kohn-seh-HEH-rah]) may be involved.

For information about enrolling students in school, see Chapter 1.

## Scheduling Classes

### Para establecer el horario de clases

Counselors sometimes advise students on which courses are best suited for them and which ones they should not take. The following phrases will help both the teacher and the counselor communicate about scheduling classes (**establecer el horario de clases** [ehs-tah-bleh-SEHR ehl oh-RAH-ryoh deh KLAH-sehs]).

| | |
|---|---|
| You can't take that class. | **No puedes tomar esa clase.**<br>noh PWEH-dehs toh-MAHR EH-sah KLAH-seh |
| It is too advanced. | **Es demasiado avanzada.**<br>ehs deh-mah-SYAH-doh ah-bahn-SAH-dah |
| It is too elementary. | **Es demasiado elemental.**<br>ehs deh-mah-SYAH-doh eh-leh-mehn-TAHL |
| You do not have the prerequisites. | **Tú no tienes los requisitos.**<br>too noh TYEH-nehs lohs rreh-kee-SEE-tohs |
| You already took that class. | **Ya tú tomaste esa clase.**<br>yah too toh-MAHS-teh EH-sah KLAH-seh |
| This class is at the same time as _____. | **Esta clase es a la misma hora que**<br>_____.<br>EHS-tah KLAH-seh ehs ah lah MEES-mah OH-rah keh |
| You already have a full program. | **Tú ya tienes un programa completo.**<br>too yah TYEH-nehs oon proh-GRAH-mah kohm-PLEH-toh |

If you need to discuss specific issues dealing with scheduling, such as the time a class meets, you will find some helpful information in Chapter 3.

## Bilingual Programs

*Los programas bilingües*

In many instances, students who come to this country not knowing English need to be placed in bilingual programs (**los programas bilingües** [lohs proh-GRAH-mahs bee-LEEN-gwehs]) or classes.

| | |
|---|---|
| Your child is going to participate in the bilingual program. | **Su hijo/hija va a participar en el programa bilingüe.**<br>soo EE-hoh/EE-hah bah ah pahr-tee-see-PAHR ehn ehl proh-GRAH-mah bee-LEEN-gweh |
| All the classes are in English and Spanish. | **Todas las clases son en inglés y en español.**<br>TOH-dahs lahs KLAH-sehs sohn ehn een-GLEHS ee ehn ehs-pah-NYOHL |
| The morning classes are in (English). | **Las clases de la mañana son en (inglés).**<br>lahs KLAH-sehs deh lah mah-NYAH-nah sohn ehn (een-GLEHS) |
| In the afternoon, / After lunch, the classes are in (Spanish). | **Por la tarde / Después del almuerzo las clases son en (español).**<br>pohr lah TAHR-deh / dehs-PWEHS dehl ahl-MWEHR-soh lahs KLAH-sehs sohn ehn (ehs-pah-NYOHL) |
| Your child is also going to attend the English as a Second Language classes. | **Su hijo/hija también va a asistir a clases de inglés como segunda lengua.**<br>soo EE-hoh/EE-hah tahm-BYEHN bah ah ah-sees-TEER ah KLAH-sehs deh een-GLEHS KOH-moh seh-GOON-dah LEHN-gwah |
| After (*number*) years, your child is going to attend all his/her classes in English. | **Después de (*number*) años, su hijo/hija va a asistir a todas las clases en inglés.**<br>dehs-PWEHS deh... AH-nyohs, soo EE-hoh/EE-hah bah ah ah-sees-TEER ah TOH-dahs lahs KLAH-sehs ehn een-GLEHS |
| Your child may feel more at ease in this program. | **Es posible que su hijo/hija se sienta más a gusto en este programa.**<br>ehs poh-SEE-bleh keh soo EE-hoh/EE-hah seh SYEHN-tah mahs ah GOOS-toh ehn EHS-teh proh-GRAH-mah |

## Emotional Problems and Feelings

*Los problemas emocionales y las emociones*

In many instances, it is the job of the counselor to deal with the students' emotional problems (**los problemas emocionales** [lohs proh-BLEH-mahs eh-moh-syoh-NAH-lehs]). Talking about emotional problems or feelings (**las emociones** [lahs eh-moh-SYOH-nehs]) is difficult for anyone. Here are some questions that may be useful in opening such a conversation.

| | |
|---|---|
| How do you feel? | **¿Cómo te sientes?**<br>KOH-moh teh SYEHN-tehs |
| What's wrong? | **¿Qué te pasa?**<br>keh teh PAH-sah |

Following is a list of some of the feelings that may come up.

| | |
|---|---|
| afraid | **asustado**<br>ah-soos-TAH-doh |
| angry | **enojado/enfadado**<br>eh-noh-HAH-doh/ehn-fah-DAH-doh |
| anxious | **ansioso**<br>ahn-SYOH-soh |
| ashamed | **avergonzado**<br>ah-behr-gohn-SAH-doh |
| bitter | **amargado**<br>ah-mahr-GAH-doh |
| depressed | **deprimido**<br>deh-pree-MEE-doh |
| embarrassed | **avergonzado**<br>ah-behr-gohn-SAH-doh |
| exhausted | **agotado**<br>ah-goh-TAH-doh |
| fed up | **harto**<br>AHR-toh |
| frustrated | **frustrado**<br>froos-TRAH-doh |
| furious | **furioso**<br>foo-RYOH-soh |
| insecure | **inseguro**<br>een-seh-GOO-roh |
| jealous | **celoso**<br>seh-LOH-soh |

| | |
|---|---|
| lost | **perdido** |
| | pehr-DEE-doh |
| nervous | **nervioso** |
| | nehr-BYOH-soh |
| resentful | **resentido** |
| | reh-sehn-TEE-doh |
| restless | **inquieto** |
| | een-KYEH-toh |
| sad | **triste** |
| | TREES-teh |
| sensitive | **sensible** |
| | sehn-SEE-bleh |
| tense | **tenso** |
| | TEHN-soh |
| tired | **cansado** |
| | kahn-SAH-doh |
| uncomfortable | **incómodo** |
| | een-KOH-moh-doh |
| unhappy | **descontento/infeliz** |
| | dehs-kohn-TEHN-toh/een-feh-LEES |
| worried | **preocupado** |
| | preh-oh-koo-PAH-doh |

Remember that when you are talking about how a person feels, you must use the verb **estar** [ehs-TAHR]. For more discussion on using the verb **estar** to express emotions or feelings, see Chapter 5, pages 203–204.

## Financial Problems
*Los problemas financieros*

Sometimes a student expresses feelings that are the consequence of financial problems (**los problemas financieros** [lohs proh-BLEH-mahs fee-nahn-SYEH-rohs]) at home. Depending on the circumstances, there are many programs to which parents can be referred, some of which are listed here.

| | |
|---|---|
| Salvation Army | **el Ejército de Salvación** |
| | ehl eh-HEHR-see-toh deh sahl-bah-SYOHN |
| Social Security office | **la Oficina de Seguro Social** |
| | lah oh-fee-SEE-nah deh seh-GOO-roh soh-SYAHL |
| Unemployment Office | **la Oficina de Desempleo** |
| | lah oh-fee-SEE-nah deh deh-sehm-PLEH-oh |

|   |   |
|---|---|
| Veteran's Administration office | **la Oficina de la Administración para Veteranos**<br>lah oh-fee-SEE-nah deh lah ahd-mee-nees-trah-SYOHN PAH-rah beh-teh-RAH-nohs |
| Welfare office | **la Oficina de Asistencia Social**<br>lah oh-fee-SEE-nah deh ah-sees-TEHN-syah soh-SYAHL |

## GRAMMAR · Adverbs

Many Spanish adverbs are formed from Spanish adjectives. To form adverbs in this way, you begin with the feminine singular form of the adjective and add -mente.

| ENGLISH ADJECTIVE | ENGLISH ADVERB | SPANISH ADJECTIVE MASCULINE | SPANISH ADJECTIVE FEMININE | SPANISH ADVERB |
|---|---|---|---|---|
| slow | slowly | lento | lenta | lentamente |
| intelligent | intelligently | inteligente | inteligente | inteligentemente |
| easy | easily | fácil | fácil | fácilmente |

|   |   |
|---|---|
| He/She reads slowly. | **Él/Ella lee lentamente.**<br>ehl/EH-yah leh-eh lehn-tah-MEHN-teh |
| Your son/daughter learns easily. | **Su hijo/hija aprende fácilmente.**<br>soo EE-hoh/EE-hah ah-PREHN-deh FAH-seel-MEHN-teh |

You have already learned to use **¿Cómo?** [KOH-moh], meaning "How?," to ask how someone is (**¿Cómo estás?** [KOH-moh ehs-TAHS]). **¿Cómo?** can also be used to find out how someone does something. Here are some examples.

|   |   |
|---|---|
| How does he/she act at home? | **¿Cómo actúa él/ella en casa?**<br>KOH-moh ahk-TOO-ah ehl/EH-yah ehn KAH-sah |
| He/She behaves very restlessly. | **Él/Ella se porta muy intranquilamente.**<br>ehl/EH-yah seh POHR-tah MOO-ee een-trahn-kee-lah-MEHN-teh |

The following list of adverbs will help you describe how your students do their work or how they do different activities in class.

| a little | **un poco** |
| | oon POH-koh |
| a lot | **mucho** |
| | MOO-choh |
| badly | **mal** |
| | mahl |
| better | **mejor** |
| | meh-HOHR |
| less | **menos** |
| | MEH-nohs |
| more | **más** |
| | mahs |
| quickly | **de prisa / rápidamente** |
| | deh PREE-sah / RRAH-pee-dah-MEHN-teh |
| slowly | **despacio** |
| | dehs-PAH-syoh |
| so-so | **regular** |
| | rreh-goo-LAHR |
| well | **bien** |
| | byehn |
| worse | **peor** |
| | peh-OHR |

The following adverbs can be used to express how often someone does something.

| frequently | **frecuentemente** |
| | freh-kwehn-teh-MEHN-teh |
| from time to time | **de vez en cuando** |
| | deh behs ehn KWAHN-doh |
| many times | **muchas veces** |
| | MOO-chahs BEH-sehs |
| once | **una vez** |
| | oo-nah behs |
| rarely | **rara vez** |
| | RRAH-rah behs |
| sometimes | **a veces** |
| | ah BEH-sehs |

| then | **entonces** |
| | ehn-TOHN-sehs |
| (four) times | **(cuatro) veces** |
| | (KWAH-troh) BEH-sehs |
| twice | **dos veces** |
| | dohs BEH-sehs |

## Practice 7-1

**A** *Complete the following sentences with the Spanish equivalent of the words in parentheses.*

1. Yo estoy muy _____ (*well*).

2. Salí _____ (*better*) en el examen de hoy.

3. Ahora tenemos _____ (*a lot*) trabajo.

4. Por favor, camina más _____ (*slowly*).

5. Juan, ayúdame _____ (*a little*).

6. Ahora se comporta _____ (*worse*).

**B** *Complete the following sentences with the Spanish equivalent of the words in parentheses.*

1. ¿Cuándo visitas a Hugo? Visito a Hugo _____ (*from time to time*).

2. ¿Vas al teatro frecuentemente? No, voy al teatro _____ (*rarely*).

3. ¿Cuántas veces llamas a tu padre? Yo llamo a mi padre

   _____ (*once*) al día.

4. ¿Asistes a los conciertos de rock? Sí, asisto a los conciertos

   _____ (*many times*).

5. ¿Haces los experimentos una vez? No, hago los experimentos

   _____ (*twice*).

6. ¿Viajas a otro estado regularmente? No, viajo a otro estado

   _____ (*sometimes*).

## Dealing with Personal Problems

*Para hacerles frente a los problemas personales*

Students often talk to counselors about personal problems that are bothering them. Because you may need to discuss some of these with your students, many of the issues that students have to face nowadays are listed below.

| | |
|---|---|
| abuse (emotional) | **el abuso mental**<br>ehl ah-BOO-soh mehn-TAHL |
| abuse (physical) | **el abuso físico**<br>ehl ah-BOO-soh FEE-see-koh |
| abuse (sexual) | **el abuso sexual**<br>ehl ah-BOO-soh sehk-SWAHL |
| alcoholism | **el alcoholismo**<br>ehl ahl-koh-LEES-moh |
| arson | **el incendio premeditado**<br>ehl een-SEHN-dyoh<br>preh-meh-dee-TAH-doh |
| attempted murder | **el intento de asesinato**<br>ehl een-TEHN-toh deh<br>ah-seh-see-NAH-toh |
| battery | **el maltrato**<br>ehl mahl-TRAH-toh |
| bullying | **la intimidación**<br>lah een-tee-mee-dah-SYOHN |
| child abuse | **el maltrato de niños**<br>ehl mahl-TRAH-toh deh NEE-nyohs |
| clothing style | **el estilo de ropa**<br>ehl ehs-TEE-loh deh RROH-pah |
| discrimination | **la discriminación**<br>lah dees-kree-mee-nah-SYOHN |
| domestic violence | **la violencia doméstica**<br>lah byoh-LEHN-syah doh-MEHS-tee-kah |
| drug abuse | **el abuso de drogas**<br>ehl ah-BOO-soh deh DROH-gahs |
| drug overdose | **la sobredosis (de drogas)**<br>lah soh-breh-DOH-sees (deh DROH-gahs) |
| emotional instability | **la falta de estabilidad emocional**<br>lah FAHL-tah deh ehs-tah-bee-lee-DAHD<br>eh-moh-syoh-NAHL |

| | |
|---|---|
| gambling | **las apuestas / el juego**<br>lahs ah-PWEHS-tahs / ehl HWEH-goh |
| gang | **la pandilla**<br>lah pahn-DEE-yah |
| harassment | **el acoso**<br>ehl ah-KOH-soh |
| homelessness | **el estar sin hogar/vivienda**<br>ehl ehs-TAHR seen oh-GAHR/<br>bee-BYEHN-dah |
| hunger | **el hambre**<br>ehl AHM-breh |
| incest | **el incesto**<br>ehl een-SEHS-toh |
| juvenile delinquency | **la delincuencia juvenil**<br>lah deh-leen-KWEHN-syah hoo-beh-NEEL |
| kidnapping | **el secuestro**<br>ehl seh-KWEHS-troh |
| manslaughter | **el homicidio involuntario**<br>ehl oh-mee-SEE-dyoh<br>een-boh-loon-TAH-ryoh |
| molestation | **el asalto sexual**<br>ehl ah-SAHL-toh sehk-SWAHL |
| murder | **el homicidio**<br>ehl oh-mee-SEE-dyoh |
| poverty | **la pobreza**<br>lah poh-BREH-sah |
| pregnancy (unwanted) | **el embarazo (no deseado)**<br>ehl ehm-bah-RAH-soh<br>(noh deh-seh-AH-doh) |
| racism | **el racismo**<br>ehl rrah-SEES-moh |
| rape | **la violación**<br>lah byoh-lah-SYOHN |
| runaway child | **el niño / la niña que huyó de casa**<br>ehl NEE-nyoh / lah NEE-nyah keh OO-YOH<br>deh KAH-sah |
| sexual harassment | **el acoso sexual**<br>ehl ah-KOH-soh sehk-SWAHL |
| sexual relations | **las relaciones sexuales**<br>lahs rreh-lah-SYOH-nehs sehk-SWAH-lehs |
| suicide | **el suicidio**<br>ehl swee-SEE-dyoh |

| theft | **el robo** |
| | ehl RROH-boh |
| threat | **la amenaza** |
| | lah ah-meh-NAH-sah |
| unemployment | **el desempleo** |
| | ehl deh-sehm-PLEH-oh |
| unwanted child | **el hijo no deseado** |
| | ehl EE-hoh noh deh-seh-AH-doh |
| | **la hija no deseada** |
| | lah EE-hah noh deh-seh-AH-dah |
| vandalism | **el vandalismo** |
| | ehl bahn-dah-LEES-moh |
| venereal disease | **la enfermedad venérea** |
| | lah ehn-fehr-meh-DAHD beh-NEH-reh-ah |
| violence | **la violencia** |
| | lah byoh-LEHN-syah |
| violent behavior | **el comportamiento violento** |
| | ehl kohm-pohr-tah-MYEHN-toh |
| | byoh-LEHN-toh |

## Advice

*Los consejos*

Here are some expressions that may be useful when giving advice (**los consejos** [lohs kohn-SEH-hohs]) to students.

| You should not … | **Tú no debes…** |
| | too noh DEH-behs |
| drink alcoholic beverages | **beber bebidas alcohólicas** |
| | beh-BEHR beh-BEE-dahs |
| | ahl-KOH-lee-kahs |
| get together with those students | **juntarte con esos estudiantes** |
| | hoon-TAHR-teh kohn EH-sohs |
| | ehs-too-DYAHN-tehs |
| smoke cigarettes | **fumar cigarrillos** |
| | foo-MAHR see-gah-RREE-yohs |
| smoke marijuana | **fumar marihuana** |
| | foo-MAHR mah-ree-WAH-nah |
| use drugs | **usar drogas** |
| | oo-SAHR DROH-gahs |

You can also use an impersonal expression + infinitive pattern.

| | |
|---|---|
| It is important not to ... | **Es importante no...** |
| | ehs eem-pohr-TAHN-teh noh |
| drink alcohol | **beber alcohol** |
| | beh-BEHR ahl-KOHL |
| drink and drive | **beber y conducir** |
| | beh-BEHR ee kohn-doo-SEER |

## GRAMMAR · Negative Sentences

Remember that to make a sentence negative in Spanish, you place **no** [noh] *before* the verb.

| | |
|---|---|
| I do not go to school on weekends. | **No voy a la escuela los fines de semana.** |
| | noh BOH-ee ah lah ehs-KWEH-lah lohs FEE-nehs deh seh-MAH-nah |

Other negative words that can be placed *before* the verb are the following.

| | |
|---|---|
| nothing | **nada** |
| | NAH-dah |
| no one, nobody | **nadie** |
| | NAH-dyeh |
| none, no one, no | **ninguno/ninguna** |
| | neen-GOO-noh/neen-GOO-nah |
| never | **nunca** |
| | NOON-kah |
| neither | **tampoco** |
| | tahm-POH-koh |

The negative words above can also be placed *after* the verb. However, this pattern requires that an additional negative word, usually **no** [noh], be placed *before* the verb. The meaning is exactly the same.

| | |
|---|---|
| Nobody does the homework. | **Nadie hace la tarea.** |
| | NAH-dyeh AH-seh lah tah-REH-ah |
| | **No hace la tarea nadie.** |
| | noh AH-seh lah tah-REH-ah NAH-dyeh |

The affirmative counterparts of these negative words are shown here.

| NEGATIVE | | AFFIRMATIVE | |
|---|---|---|---|
| nothing | **nada**<br>NAH-dah | something | **algo**<br>AHL-goh |
| no one, nobody | **nadie**<br>NAH-dyeh | someone,<br>anybody | **alguien**<br>AHL-gyehn |
| none, no one, no | **ninguno/ninguna**<br>neen-GOO-noh/<br>neen-GOO-nah | some, someone | **alguno/alguna**<br>ahl-GOO-noh/<br>ahl-GOO-nah |
| | | some, any | **algunos/algunas**<br>ahl-GOO-nohs/<br>ahl-GOO-nahs |
| never | **nunca**<br>NOON-kah | always | **siempre**<br>SYEHM-preh |
| neither | **tampoco**<br>tahm-POH-koh | also | **también**<br>tahm-BYEHN |

When used before a masculine singular noun, **ninguno** [neen-GOO-noh] changes to **ningún** [neen-GOON] and **alguno** [ahl-GOO-noh] changes to **algún** [ahl-GOON].

Compare the following pairs of sentences.

| I don't understand anything. | **No comprendo nada.**<br>noh kohm-PREHN-doh NAH-dah |
|---|---|
| I understand something. | **Comprendo algo.**<br>kohm-PREHN-doh AHL-goh |
| No one is going. | **Nadie va.**<br>NAH-dyeh bah |
| Someone is going. | **Alguien va.**<br>AHL-gyehn bah |
| I have no money. / I don't have any money. | **No tengo ningún dinero.**<br>noh TEHN-goh neen-GOON dee-NEH-roh |
| I have some money. | **Tengo algún dinero.**<br>TEHN-goh ahl-GOON dee-NEH-roh |
| We don't read any poems. | **No leemos ningún poema.**<br>noh leh-EH-mohs neen-GOON<br>poh-EH-mah |
| We read some poems. | **Leemos algunos poemas.**<br>leh-EH-mohs ahl-GOO-nohs poh-EH-mahs |

| I never arrive late. | **Nunca llego tarde.** |
| | NOON-kah YEH-goh TAHR-deh |

| I always arrive early. | **Siempre llego temprano.** |
| | SYEHM-preh YEH-goh tehm-PRAH-noh |

| I know how to sing also. | **Yo sé cantar también.** |
| | yoh seh kahn-TAHR tahm-BYEHN |

| I don't know how to sing either. | **Yo no sé cantar tampoco.** |
| | yoh noh seh kahn-TAHR tahm-POH-koh |

## Practice 7-2

**A** *Change the following sentences to negative sentences.*

1. Siempre estudio.

   _____

2. Nosotros comemos en la cafetería.

   _____

3. Alguien corre en el parque.

   _____

4. ¿Lees algunas novelas?

   _____

5. Ellos caminan en el parque también.

   _____

6. Alguien va a la fiesta.

   _____

**B** *Answer the following questions with as many negative words as possible.*

1. ¿Estás nervioso?

   _____

2. ¿Tienes mucho trabajo hoy?

   _____

3. ¿Visitas a tus tíos todos los días?

   _____

4. ¿Compras mucha ropa en la tienda?

   _____

5. ¿Comes el almuerzo en la escuela siempre?

_____

6. ¿Hay alguien en el pasillo?

_____

7. ¿Quieres beber algo?

_____

8. ¿Vas a la escuela los sábados también?

_____

## Disciplinary Action

### Las medidas de disciplina

You may have to inform students and their parents of disciplinary action (**las medidas de disciplina** [lahs meh-DEE-dahs deh dee-see-PLEE-nah]) taken by the school when their child breaks the school's rules.

| | |
|---|---|
| You need to come to school immediately and pick up your child. | **Ud. tiene que venir a la escuela inmediatamente y recoger a su hijo/hija.**<br>oohs-TEHD TYEH-neh keh beh-NEER ah lah ehs-KWEH-lah een-meh-dyah-tah-MEHN-teh ee rreh-koh-HEHR ah soo EE-hoh/EE-hah |
| Your (*male*) child is suspended for (*number*) days/weeks. | **Su hijo está suspendido de la escuela por (*number*) días/semanas.**<br>soo EE-hoh ehs-TAH soos-pehn-DEE-doh deh lah ehs-KWEH-lah pohr... DEE-ahs/seh-MAH-nahs |
| Your (*female*) child is suspended for (*number*) days/weeks. | **Su hija está suspendida de la escuela por (*number*) días/semanas.**<br>soo EE-hah ehs-TAH soos-pehn-DEE-dah deh lah ehs-KWEH-lah pohr... DEE-ahs/seh MAH-nahs |
| Your child cannot return to school for (*number*) days/weeks. | **Su hijo/hija no puede regresar a la escuela por (*number*) días/semanas.**<br>soo EE-hoh/EE-hah noh PWEH-deh rreh-greh-SAHR ah lah ehs-KWEH-lah pohr... DEE-ahs/seh-MAH-nahs |

| | |
|---|---|
| Your child has to spend all his/her free periods in the principal's office. | **Su hijo/hija tiene que pasar todos sus períodos libres en la oficina del director.**<br>soo EE-hoh/EE-hah TYEH-neh keh pah-SAHR TOH-dohs soos peh-REE-oh-dohs LEE-brehs ehn lah oh-fee-SEE-nah dehl dee-rehk-TOHR |
| Your child has to participate in an anger management program. | **Su hijo/hija tiene que asistir a un programa para el control de la cólera.**<br>soo EE-hoh/EE-hah TYEH-neh keh ah-sees-TEER ah oon proh-GRAH-mah PAH-rah ehl kohn-TROHL deh lah KOH-leh-rah |
| Your child has to attend a stop-smoking program. | **Su hijo/hija tiene que asistir a un programa para dejar de fumar.**<br>soo EE-hoh/EE-hah TYEH-neh keh ah-sees-TEER ah oon proh-GRAH-mah PAH-rah deh-HAHR deh foo-MAHR |
| Your child is not allowed to return to this school. | **Su hijo/hija no puede regresar a esta escuela.**<br>soo EE-hoh/EE-hah noh PWEH-deh rreh-greh-SAHR ah EHS-tah ehs-KWEH-lah |
| You must transfer your child to another school. | **Ud. tiene que trasladar a su hijo/hija a otra escuela.**<br>oos-TEHD TYEH-neh keh trahs-lah-DAHR ah soo EE-hoh/EE-hah ah OH-trah ehs-KWEH-lah |

Listed here are some of the programs available to help students deal with disciplinary problems.

| | |
|---|---|
| after school program | **el programa que ofrece diferentes actividades educacionales o recreativas después de las clases**<br>ehl proh-GRAH-mah keh oh-FREH-seh dee-feh-REHN-tehs ahk-tee-bee-DAH-dehs eh-doo-kah-syoh-NAH-lehs oh rreh-kreh-ah-TEE-bahs dehs-PWEHS deh lahs KLAH-sehs |
| anger management program | **el programa para controlar la cólera**<br>ehl proh-GRAH-mah PAH-rah kohn-troh-LAHR lah KOH-leh-rah |
| conflict resolution program | **el programa para resolver conflictos**<br>ehl proh-GRAH-mah PAH-rah rreh-sohl-BEHR kohn-FLEEK-tohs |

| | |
|---|---|
| counseling | **el asesoramiento**<br>ehl ah-seh-soh-rah-MYEHN-toh |
| peer mediation program | **el programa que usa a otros jóvenes como intermediarios en conflictos**<br>ehl proh-GRAH-mah keh oo-sah ah OH-trohs HOH-beh-nehs KOH-moh een-tehr-meh-DYAH-ryohs ehn kohn-FLEEK-tohs |

Other helpful information can be found in the section dealing with Rules of Behavior in Chapter 5, pages 192–193.

## After School Jobs

*Los trabajos después de las clases*

Although in some Spanish-speaking countries students work while they are attending school, you may need to explain to the student and to his/her parents what is involved in getting an after school job (**el trabajo después de las clases** [ehl trah-BAH-hoh dehs-PWEHS deh lahs KLAH-sehs]).

| | |
|---|---|
| Students can only work part-time. | **Los estudiantes sólo pueden trabajar a tiempo parcial.**<br>lohs ehs-too-DYAHN-tehs SOH-loh PWEH-dehn trah-bah-HAHR ah TYEHM-poh pahr-SYAHL |
| There are many opportunities in the neighborhood. | **Hay muchas oportunidades en el barrio.**<br>AH-ee MOO-chahs oh-pohr-too-nee-DAH-dehs ehn ehl BAH-rryoh |
| It is important that he/she keep up with his/her work/homework for school. | **Es importante que él/ella se mantenga al tanto de su trabajo/tarea para la escuela.**<br>ehs eem-pohr-TAHN-teh keh ehl/EH-yah seh mahn-TEHN-gah ahl TAHN-toh deh soo trah-BAH-hoh/tah-REH-ah PAH-rah lah ehs-KWEH-lah |

In the first set of examples that follow, the comments are addressed to the parents. A second set of examples provides the phrasing you will need if you are addressing the student.

| | |
|---|---|
| Your child needs … | **Su hijo/hija necesita…**<br>soo EE-hoh/EE-hah neh-seh-SEE-tah |
| to get a work permit | **obtener un permiso de trabajo**<br>ohb-teh-NEHR oon pehr-MEE-soh deh trah-BAH-hoh |

| Your child needs … | **Su hijo/hija necesita…** |
| --- | --- |
| | soo EE-hoh/EE-hah neh-seh-SEE-tah |
| to prepare a résumé | **preparar un resumen de su educación y su experiencia de trabajo** |
| | preh-pah-RAHR oon rreh-SOO-mehn deh soo eh-doo-kah-SYOHN ee soo ehs-peh-RYEHN-syah deh trah-BAH-hoh |
| to request references from one of his/her teachers | **pedir referencias de uno de sus maestros** |
| | peh-DEER rreh-feh-REHN-syahs deh oo-noh deh soos mah-EHS-trohs |
| to request an appointment | **pedir una cita** |
| | peh-DEER oo-nah SEE-tah |
| to request an interview | **pedir una entrevista** |
| | peh-DEER oo-nah ehn-treh-BEES-tah |
| to fill out a job application | **llenar una solicitud de empleo** |
| | yeh-NAHR oo-nah soh-lee-see-TOOD deh ehm-PLEH-oh |
| to have a driver's license | **tener una licencia de conducir** |
| | teh-NEHR oo-nah lee-SEHN-syah deh kohn-doo-SEER |
| to go through training | **pasar por un entrenamiento** |
| | pah-SAHR pohr oon ehn-treh-nah-MYEHN-toh |
| You need … | **Tú necesitas…** |
| | too neh-seh-SEE-tahs |
| to get a work permit | **obtener un permiso de trabajo** |
| | ohb-teh-NEHR oon pehr-MEE-soh deh trah-BAH-hoh |
| to prepare a résumé | **preparar un resumen de tu educación y tu experiencia de trabajo** |
| | preh-pah-RAHR oon rreh-SOO-mehn deh too eh-doo-kah-SYOHN ee too ehs-peh-RYEHN-syah deh trah-BAH-hoh |
| to request references from one of your teachers | **pedir referencias de uno de tus maestros** |
| | peh-DEER rreh-feh-REHN-syahs deh oo-noh deh toos mah-EHS-trohs |
| to request an appointment | **pedir una cita** |
| | peh-DEER oo-nah SEE-tah |
| to request an interview | **pedir una entrevista** |
| | peh-DEER oo-nah ehn-treh-BEES-tah |

| to fill out a job application | **llenar una solicitud de empleo** |
| | yeh-NAHR OO-nah soh-lee-see-TOOD |
| | deh ehm-PLEH-oh |
| to have a driver's license | **tener una licencia de conducir** |
| | teh-NEHR OO-nah lee-SEHN-syah deh |
| | kohn-doo-SEER |
| to go through training | **pasar por un entrenamiento** |
| | pah-SAHR pohr oon |
| | ehn-treh-nah-MYEHN-toh |

## Practice 7-3

*Complete the following sentences with the Spanish equivalent of the phrase in parentheses.*

1. Su hija _____ (*is suspended*) por tres días.

2. Ella necesita _____ (*to fill out a job application*).

3. Su hijo sólo puede trabajar _____ (*part-time*).

4. Todos los estudiantes participan en _____
(*an anger management program*).

5. Si quieres trabajar, tienes que _____
(*go through training*).

6. En la oficina puedes obtener _____
(*a work permit*).

7. Cuando vas a buscar un trabajo, tienes que estar preparada para

_____ (*an interview*).

8. Es necesario _____ (*to keep up
with your school work*).

## Career Plans

### Los planes para una carrera

Students often need guidance on the different career opportunities available to them. The following questions will help you open a conversation about career plans (**los planes para una carrera** [lohs PLAH-nehs PAH-rah oo-nah kah-RREH-rah]) with the student. There are many other questions you can ask to assess the student's interests; these are just a few to begin the dialogue.

| | |
|---|---|
| What would you like to do after finishing high school? | **¿Qué quisieras / te gustaría hacer después de terminar la escuela secundaria?**<br>keh kee-SYEH-rahs / teh goos-tah-REE-ah ah-SEHR dehs-PWEHS deh tehr-mee-NAHR lah ehs-KWEH-lah seh-koon-DAH-ryah |
| Is it more important for you to be happy or to make lots of money? | **¿Es más importante para ti ser feliz o ganar mucho dinero?**<br>ehs mahs eem-pohr-TAHN-teh PAH-rah tee sehr feh-LEES oh gah-NAHR MOO-choh dee-NEH-roh |

## Occupations and Professions
*Las ocupaciones y las profesiones*

The following is a list of some of the most common occupations and professions (**las ocupaciones y las profesiones** [lahs oh-koo-pah-SYOH-nehs ee lahs proh-feh-SYOH-nehs]) you may want to discuss with your students and their parents.

| | |
|---|---|
| accountant | **el contador / la contadora**<br>ehl kohn-tah-DOHR / lah kohn-tah-DOH-rah |
| actor | **el actor**<br>ehl ahk-TOHR |
| actress | **la actriz**<br>lah ahk-TREES |
| architect | **el arquitecto / la arquitecta**<br>ehl ahr-kee-TEHK-toh / lah ahr-kee-TEHK-tah |
| author | **el autor / la autora**<br>ehl ah-oo-TOHR / lah ah-oo-TOH-rah |
| businessman | **el hombre de negocios**<br>ehl OHM-breh deh neh-GOH-syohs |
| businesswoman | **la mujer de negocios**<br>lah moo-HEHR deh neh-GOH-syohs |
| carpenter | **el carpintero / la carpintera**<br>ehl kahr-peen-TEH-roh / lah kahr-peen-TEH-rah |
| cashier | **el cajero / la cajera**<br>ehl kah-HEH-roh / lah kah-HEH-rah |
| cook | **el cocinero / la cocinera**<br>ehl koh-see-NEH-roh / lah koh-see-NEH-rah |

| | |
|---|---|
| dentist | **el/la dentista** <br> ehl/lah dehn-TEES-tah |
| doctor | **el doctor / la doctora** <br> ehl dohk-TOHR / lah dohk-TOH-rah <br><br> **el médico / la médica** <br> ehl MEH-dee-koh / lah MEH-dee-kah |
| driver | **el conductor / la conductora** <br> ehl kohn-dook-TOHR / <br> lah kohn-dook-TOH-rah |
| engineer | **el ingeniero / la ingeniera** <br> ehl een-heh-NYEH-roh / <br> lah een-heh-NYEH-rah |
| firefighter | **el bombero / la bombera** <br> ehl bohm-BEH-roh / lah bohm-BEH-rah |
| flight attendant | **el/la asistente de vuelo** <br> ehl/lah ah-sees-TEHN-teh deh BWEH-loh |
| gardener | **el jardinero / la jardinera** <br> ehl hahr-dee-NEH-roh / <br> lah hahr-dee-NEH-rah |
| hairdresser | **el peluquero / la peluquera** <br> ehl peh-loo-KEH-roh / <br> lah peh-loo-KEH-rah |
| interpreter | **el/la intérprete** <br> ehl/lah een-TEHR-preh-teh |
| journalist | **el reportero / la reportera** <br> ehl rreh-pohr-TEH-roh / <br> lah rreh-pohr-TEH-rah |
| lawyer | **el abogado / la abogada** <br> ehl ah-boh-GAH-doh / <br> lah ah-boh-GAH-dah |
| mechanic | **el mecánico / la mecánica** <br> ehl meh-KAH-nee-koh / <br> lah meh-KAH-nee-kah |
| nurse | **el enfermero / la enfermera** <br> chl ehn-fehr-MEH-roh / <br> lah ehn-fehr-MEH-rah |
| painter | **el pintor / la pintora** <br> ehl peen-TOHR / lah peen-TOH-rah |
| photographer | **el fotógrafo / la fotógrafa** <br> ehl foh-TOH-grah-foh / <br> lah foh-TOH-grah-fah |
| plumber | **el plomero / la plomera** <br> ehl ploh-MEH-roh / lah ploh-MEH-rah |

| police officer | **el policía / la mujer policía** |
| | ehl poh-lee-SEE-ah / |
| | lah moo-HEHR poh-lee-SEE-ah |
| programmer | **el programador / la programadora** |
| | ehl proh-grah-mah-DOHR / |
| | lah proh-grah-mah-DOH-rah |
| salesperson | **el vendedor / la vendedora** |
| | ehl behn-deh-DOHR / |
| | lah behn-deh-DOH-rah |
| secretary | **el secretario / la secretaria** |
| | ehl seh-kreh-TAH-ryoh / |
| | lah seh-kreh-TAH-ryah |
| singer | **el/la cantante** |
| | ehl/lah kahn-TAHN-teh |
| surgeon | **el cirujano / la cirujana** |
| | ehl see-roo-HAH-noh / |
| | lah see-roo-HAH-nah |
| teacher | **el maestro / la maestra** |
| | ehl mah-EHS-troh / lah mah-EHS-trah |
| trainer | **el entrenador / la entrenadora** |
| | ehl ehn-treh-nah-DOHR / |
| | lah ehn-treh-nah-DOH-rah |
| writer | **el escritor / la escritora** |
| | ehl ehs-kree-TOHR / lah ehs-kree-TOH-rah |

The Army (**las fuerzas armadas** [lahs FWEHR-sahs ahr-MAH-dahs]), the Air Force (**las fuerzas aéreas** [lahs FWEHR-sahs ah-EH-reh-ahs]), and the Navy (**la marina de guerra** [lah mah-REE-nah deh GEH-rrah]) may also be viable options for your students. In most recruiting stations (**las oficinas de reclutamiento** [lahs oh-fee-SEE-nahs deh rreh-kloo-tah-MYEHN-toh]) they have Spanish-speaking personnel (**el personal hispanohablante** [ehl pehr-soh-NAHL ees-pah-noh-ah-BLAHN-teh]).

In Chapter 2, pages 66–68, you will find a list of professions and occupations found in the school setting.

## GRAMMAR · Demonstrative Adjectives

Demonstrative adjectives point out specific people and things. In Spanish, they precede the noun they are pointing out and agree with it in gender and number.

The demonstrative adjective "this" has four forms in Spanish.

- **este** [EHS-teh]          **este reportero** ("this journalist")
  (*masculine singular*)     EHS-teh rreh-pohr-TEH-roh

- **esta** [EHS-tah]
  (*feminine singular*)

  **esta reportera** ("this journalist")
  EHS-tah rreh-pohr-TEH-rah

- **estos** [EHS-tohs]
  (*masculine plural*)

  **estos reporteros** ("these journalists")
  EHS-tohs rreh-pohr-TEH-rohs

- **estas** [EHS-tahs]
  (*feminine plural*)

  **estas reporteras** ("these journalists")
  EHS-tahs rreh-pohr-TEH-rahs

This photographer is my favorite.

**Este fotógrafo es mi favorito.**
EHS-teh foh-TOH-grah-foh ehs mee
fah-boh-REE-toh

These secretaries are very hardworking.

**Estas secretarias son muy trabajadoras.**
EHS-tahs seh-kreh-TAH-ryahs sohn
MOO-ee trah-bah-hah-DOH-rahs

There are two words for the demonstrative adjective "that" in Spanish.

When referring to something or someone far from you, but near the person to whom you are speaking, use **ese** [EH-seh].

When referring to something or someone far from you, and also far from the person with whom you are speaking, use **aquel** [ah-KEHL].

**Ese** and **aquel** both have four forms.

- **ese** [EH-seh]
  (*masculine singular*)

  **ese arquitecto** ("that architect")
  EH-seh ahr-kee-TEHK-toh

- **esa** [EH-sah]
  (*feminine singular*)

  **esa arquitecta** ("that architect")
  EH-sah ahr-kee-TEHK-tah

- **esos** [EH-sohs]
  (*masculine plural*)

  **esos arquitectos** ("those architects")
  EH-sohs ahr-kee-TEHK-tohs

- **esas** [EH-sahs]
  (*feminine plural*)

  **esas arquitectas** ("those architects")
  EH-sahs ahr-kee-TEHK-tahs

- **aquel** [ah-KEHL]
  (*masculine singular*)

  **aquel ingeniero** ("that engineer")
  ah-KEHL een-heh-NYEH-roh

- **aquella** [ah-KEH-yah]
  (*feminine singular*)

  **aquella ingeniera** ("that engineer")
  ah-KEH-yah een-heh-NYEH-rah

- **aquellos** [ah-KEH-yohs]
  (*masculine plural*)

  **aquellos ingenieros** ("those engineers")
  ah-KEH-yohs een-heh-NYEH-rohs

- **aquellas** [ah-KEH-yahs]
  (*feminine plural*)

  **aquellas ingenieras** ("those engineers")
  ah-KEH-yahs een-heh-NYEH-rahs

That woman is an excellent dentist.

**Esa mujer es una dentista excelente.**
EH-sah moo-HEHR ehs OO-nah
dehn-TEES-tah ehk-seh-LEHN-teh

Those firefighters are very brave.

**Esos bomberos son muy valientes.**
EH-sohs bohm-BEH-rohs sohn MOO-ee bah-LYEHN-tehs

That mechanic is honest.

**Aquel mecánico es honesto.**
ah-KEHL meh-KAH-nee-koh ehs oh-NEHS-toh

## Practice 7-4

**A** *You are talking to one of your students about his/her interests. Using ¿Te gusta...?, ask him/her a question related to each of the following professions.*

MODELO     maestro   _¿Te gusta trabajar con niños?_

1. cocinero

   _____

2. actriz

   _____

3. fotógrafo

   _____

4. jardinera

   _____

5. mujer de negocios

   _____

**B** *Complete each sentence with the Spanish equivalent of the word in parentheses.*

1. _____ (This) libro es nuevo.

2. Quiero _____ (those—far from you and from the person you are talking to) mochilas.

3. _____ (This) cajera es muy eficiente.

4. _____ (That) chica es mi mejor amiga.

5. Me gustan mucho _____ (these) pantalones.

6. El libro es de _____ (that—far from you and from the person you are talking to) autor.

7. _____ (Those) mujeres son médicas.

8. _____ (Those) restaurantes son mexicanos.

## College Planning

*Los planes para la universidad*

Planning for college is a daunting experience for any student. It is even more daunting for students and parents who may not be familiar with the application process, admissions, and financial aid. There is an enormous amount of information that needs to be conveyed to the parent with regard to college planning (**los planes para la universidad** [lohs PLAH-nehs PAH-rah lah oo-nee-behr-see-DAHD]). We have included here some of the important issues you may need to relate to the parents, but this is not a complete list.

## Important Issues to Consider

*Algunos asuntos importantes que se deben considerar*

Finding out what the student and his/her parents are interested in with regard to college, as well as what options are available, are very important topics to explore. Here are a few questions that will allow you to start the dialogue. Since it is often the parents who come to talk with the counselor about their child's college plans, the questions are addressed to the parents. The verb form you need to use if you are addressing the student directly is in parentheses.

| | |
|---|---|
| Is your child (Are you) planning to attend a university? | **¿Piensa su hijo/hija (Piensas) asistir a una universidad?** <br> PYEHN-sah soo EE-hoh/EE-hah (PYEHN-sahs) ah-sees-TEER an oo-nah oo-nee-behr-see-DAHD |
| What university is he/she (are you) considering? | **¿Qué universidad está (estás) considerando?** <br> keh oo-nee-behr-see-DAHD ehs-TAH (ehs-TAHS) kohn-see-deh-RAHN-doh |
| Do you want your child (Do you want) to attend a university near your home? | **¿Quiere que su hijo/su hija asista (Quieres asistir) a una universidad cerca de casa?** <br> KYEH-reh keh soo EE-hoh/EE-hah ah-SEES-tah (KYEH-rehs ah oces-TEER) ah oo-nah oo-nee-behr-see-DAHD SEHR-kah deh KAH-sah |
| You can take a virtual tour of the university using your computer. | **Se puede hacer una visita virtual a la universidad usando la computadora.** <br> seh PWEH-deh ah-SEHR oo-nah bee-SEE-tah beer-TWAHL ah lah oo-nee-behr-see-DAHD oo-SAHN-doh lah kohm-poo-tah-DOH-rah |

| Many universities have programs to attract minorities. | **Muchas universidades tienen programas para atraer minorías.**<br>MOO-chahs oo-nee-behr-see-DAH-dehs TYEH-nehn proh-GRAH-mahs PAH-rah ah-trah-EHR mee-noh-REE-ahs |
|---|---|
| The requirements for admission vary at each university. | **Los requisitos para el ingreso varían en cada universidad.**<br>lohs rreh-kee-SEE-tohs PAH-rah ehl een-GREH-soh bah-REE-ahn ehn KAH-dah oo-nee-behr-see-DAHD |

## General Requirements
*Los requisitos generales*

Following is a list of words and phrases that will be helpful as you discuss many of the issues dealing with the general requirements (**los requisitos generales** [lohs rreh-kee-SEE-tohs heh-neh-RAH-lehs]) of college admissions.

| academic prize | **el premio académico**<br>ehl PREH-myoh ah-kah-DEH-mee-koh |
|---|---|
| admission exams | **los exámenes de ingreso**<br>lohs ehk-SAH-meh-nehs deh een-GREH-soh |
| application | **la solicitud**<br>lah soh-lee-see-TOOD |
| catalogue | **el catálogo**<br>ehl kah-TAH-loh-goh |
| deadline | **la fecha límite**<br>lah FEH-chah LEE-mee-teh |
| experience outside school | **la experiencia fuera de la escuela**<br>lah ehs-peh-RYEHN-syah FWEH-rah deh lah ehs-KWEH-lah |
| financial aid | **la ayuda financiera**<br>lah ah-YOO-dah fee-nahn-SYEH-rah |
| financial aid application | **la solicitud de ayuda financiera**<br>lah soh-lee-see-TOOD deh ah-YOO-dah fee-nahn-SYEH-rah |
| form | **el formulario**<br>ehl fohr-moo-LAH-ryoh |
| hobby | **el pasatiempo favorito**<br>ehl pah-sah-TYEHM-poh fah-boh-REE-toh |
| interview | **la entrevista**<br>lah ehn-treh-BEES-tah |

| | |
|---|---|
| letters of recommendation | **las cartas de recomendación**<br>lahs KAHR-tahs deh<br>rreh-koh-mehn-dah-SYOHN |
| personal essay | **el ensayo personal**<br>ehl ehn-SAH-yoh pehr-soh-NAHL |
| success | **el éxito**<br>ehl EHK-see-toh |
| summer jobs | **los trabajos de verano**<br>lohs trah-BAH-hohs deh beh-RAH-noh |
| transcript | **la relación de notas**<br>lah rreh-lah-SYOHN deh NOH-tahs |
| volunteer work | **el trabajo voluntario**<br>ehl trah-BAH-hoh boh-loon-TAH-ryoh |

## Standardized Testing
### *Las pruebas uniformes*

Most universities require students to take standardized tests so that the institution has an assessment of the student that is independent of the student's high school testing.

| | |
|---|---|
| A standardized test is a test administered according to standardized procedures that assesses a student's aptitude compared to a standard. | **Una prueba uniforme es una prueba que se administra bajo procedimientos uniformes y que asesora la capacidad de un estudiante comparándola con una norma.**<br>OO-nah PRWEH-bah oo-nee-FOHR-meh ehs OO-nah PRWEH-bah keh seh ahd-mee-NEES-trah BAH-hoh proh-seh-dee-MYEHN-tohs oo-nee-FOHR-mehs ee keh ah-seh-SOH-rah lah kah-pah-see-DAHD deh oon ehs-too-DYAHN-teh kohm-pah-RAHN-doh-lah kohn oo-nah NOHR-mah |

It is typical for colleges and universities to require students to take the SAT exams. These exams do not exist in the Spanish-speaking world, so you may have to explain what they are.

| | |
|---|---|
| SAT test (Scholastic Aptitude Test) | **el examen de SAT / de aptitud escolar**<br>ehl ehk-SAH-mehn deh ehs EH-ee tee / deh ahp-tee-TOOD ehs-koh-LAHR |

| | |
|---|---|
| The Scholastic Aptitude Test is a test used to predict the degree of success in college. | **El examen de aptitud escolar es un examen que se usa para predecir el grado de éxito en la universidad.** |
| | ehl ehk-SAH-mehn deh ahp-tee-TOOD ehs-koh-LAHR ehs oon ehk-SAH-mehn keh seh oo-sah PAH-rah preh-deh-SEER ehl GRAH-doh deh EHK-see-toh ehn lah oo-nee-behr-see-DAHD |
| There are also SAT tests on specific subjects. | **También hay exámenes de SAT (de aptitud) en asignaturas específicas.** |
| | tahm-BYEHN AH-ee ehk-SAH-meh-nehs deh ehs EH-ee tee (deh ahp-tee-TOOD) ehn ah-seeg-nah-TOO-rahs ehs-peh-SEE-fee-kahs |
| To take the exam, one needs to register by (date). | **Para hacer el examen tiene que matricularse para el (date).** |
| | PAH-rah ah-SEHR ehl ehk-SAH-mehn TYEH-neh keh mah-tree-koo-LAHR-seh PAH-rah ehl |
| The maximum score a student can receive is (number). | **La nota más alta que un estudiante puede recibir es (number).** |
| | lah NOH-tah mahs AHL-tah keh oon ehs-too-DYAHN-teh PWEH-deh rreh-see-BEER ehs |
| (number) is a very good score. | **(number) es una nota muy buena.** |
| | ehs oo-nah NOH-tah MOO-ee BWEH-nah |
| (number) is a low score. | **(number) es una nota baja.** |
| | ehs oo-nah NOH-tah BAH-hah |
| Your child should take the test again. | **Su hijo/hija debe hacer el examen de nuevo.** |
| | SOO EE-hoh/EE-hah DEH-beh ah-SEHR ehl ehk-SAH-mehn deh NWEH-boh |
| There are places that offer courses to prepare oneself for the test. | **Hay lugares que ofrecen cursos para prepararse para el examen.** |
| | AH-ee loo-GAH-rehs keh oh-FREH-sehn KOOR-sohs PAH-rah preh-pah-RAHR-seh PAH-rah ehl ehk-SAH-mehn |

Students can also take advanced courses while still in high school. The Advanced Placement courses and exams, sometimes called AP courses and exams, will also need to be explained.

| | |
|---|---|
| The AP courses are advanced courses in a number of subjects. | **Los cursos de AP son cursos avanzados en varias asignaturas.**<br>lohs KOOR-sohs deh EH-ee pee sohn KOOR-sohs ah-bahn-SAH-dohs ehn BAH-ryahs ah-seeg-nah-TOO-rahs |
| The courses are very demanding. | **Los cursos son muy exigentes.**<br>lohs KOOR-sohs sohn MOO-ee ehk-see-HEHN-tehs |
| Universities like applicants who have taken these courses. | **A las universidades les gustan los candidatos que han tomado estos cursos.**<br>ah lahs oo-nee-behr-see-DAH-dehs lehs GOOS-tahn lohs kahn-dee-DAH-tohs keh ahn toh-MAH-doh EHS-tohs KOOR-sohs |
| Some universities will give credit to students who do well on an AP exam. | **Algunas universidades les dan crédito a los estudiantes que salen bien en un examen de AP.**<br>ahl-GOO-nahs oo-nee-behr-see-DAH-dehs lehs dahn KREH-dee-toh ah lohs ehs-too-DYAHN-tehs keh SAH-lehn byehn ehn oon ehk-SAH-mehn deh EH-ee pee |

# Paying for College
*Para pagar por la universidad*

Parents are generally very concerned about how to pay for their child's college education (**pagar por la universidad** [pah-GAHR pohr lah oo-nee-behr-see-DAHD]). You can reassure them that there are good possibilities for financial aid.

| | |
|---|---|
| How do you plan to pay for college? | **¿Cómo piensan Uds. pagar por los estudios?**<br>KOH-moh PYEHN-sahn oos-TEH-dehs pah-GAHR pohr lohs ehs-TOO-dyohs |
| Do you know the different organizations that offer scholarships? | **¿Conoce Ud. las diferentes organizaciones que ofrecen becas?**<br>koh-NOH-seh oos-TEHD lahs dee-feh-REHN-tehs ohr-gah-nee-sah-SYOH-nehs keh oh-FREH-sehn BEH-kahs |
| Often the unions offer scholarships. | **Muchas veces los sindicatos ofrecen becas.**<br>MOO-chahs BEH-sehs lohs seen-dee-KAH-tohs oh-FREH-sehn BEH-kahs |
| The government offers grants and loans. | **El gobierno ofrece becas y préstamos.**<br>ehl goh-BYEHR-noh oh-FREH-seh BEH-kahs ee PREHS-tah-mohs |

| Financial aid depends on your income and your need. | **La ayuda financiera depende de sus ingresos y de su necesidad.** lah ah-YOO-dah fee-nahn-SYEH-rah deh-PEHN-deh deh soos een-GREH-sohs ee deh soo neh-seh-see-DAHD |
|---|---|

## GRAMMAR · Talking About What Just Happened

When talking about something that just happened, such as something that you just did, you use the present tense of the verb **acabar de** [ah-kah-BAHR deh] + an infinitive.

| He has just taken the test. | **Él acaba de hacer el examen.** ehl ah-KAH-bah deh ah-SEHR ehl ehk-SAH-mehn |
|---|---|
| They have just started their studies. | **Ellos acaban de empezar sus estudios.** EH-yohs ah-KAH-bahn deh ehm-peh-SAHR soos ehs-TOO-dyohs |

## Practice 7-5

*Complete the following sentences with the Spanish equivalent of the phrase in parentheses.*

1. _____ (*We have just*) recibir una beca.

2. _____ (*He has just*) pedir una solicitud para la universidad.

3. _____ (*She has just*) tener una entrevista.

4. _____ (*They have just*) hacer el examen de SAT.

5. _____ (*I have just*) recibir una nota excelente.

## Students with Special Needs

*Los estudiantes con necesidades especiales*

The counselor, together with the school nurse, is usually the person in school who is most familiar with students who have special needs (**los estudiantes con necesidades especiales** [lohs ehs-too-DYAHN-tehs kohn neh-seh-see-DAH-dehs ehs-peh-SYAH-lehs]). The counselor helps to inform the teachers and, together with the teachers and the family, helps to accommodate the student in order to make it possible for him/her to achieve his/her full potential. Students with special needs may suffer from a variety of different illnesses and birth defects, including the following.

| | |
|---|---|
| AIDS | **el SIDA**<br>ehl SEE-dah |
| asthma | **el asma**<br>ehl AHS-mah |
| attention deficit disorder | **el desorden deficitario de la atención**<br>ehl dehs-OHR-dehn deh-fee-see-TAH-ryoh deh ah-tehn-SYOHN |
| autism | **el autismo / el trastorno generalizado del desarrollo**<br>ehl ah-oo-TEES-moh / ehl trahs-TOHR-noh heh-neh-rah-lee-SAH-doh dehl deh-sah-RROH-yoh |
| blindness | **la ceguera**<br>lah seh-GEH-rah |
| cancer | **el cáncer**<br>ehl KAHN-sehr |
| cerebral palsy | **la parálisis cerebral**<br>lah pah-RAH-lee-sees seh-reh-BRAHL |
| diabetes | **la diabetes**<br>lah dyah-BEH-tehs |
| Down's syndrome | **el síndrome de Down**<br>ehl SEEN-droh-meh deh DAH-oon |
| dyslexia | **la dislexia**<br>lah dees-LEHK-syah |
| emotional problems | **los problemas emocionales**<br>lohs proh-BLEH-mahs eh-moh-syoh-NAH-lehs |
| epilepsy | **la epilepsia**<br>lah eh-pee-LEHP-syah |
| fainting spells | **los desmayos**<br>lohs dehs-MAH-yohs |
| hearing problems | **la sordera / la pérdida de capacidad auditiva**<br>lah sohr-DEH-rah / lah PEHR-dee-dah deh kah-pah-see-DAHD ah-oo-dee-TEE-bah |
| high blood pressure | **la presión (arterial) alta**<br>lah preh-SYOHN (ahr-teh-RYAHL) AHL-tah |
| infectious disease | **la enfermedad infecciosa**<br>lah ehn-fehr-meh-DAHD een-fehk-SYOH-sah |

| | |
|---|---|
| learning disability | **la discapacidad de aprendizaje**<br>lah dees-kah-pah-see-DAHD deh<br>ah-prehn-dee-SAH-heh |
| leukemia | **la leucemia**<br>lah leh-oo-SEH-myah |
| low blood pressure | **la presión (arterial) baja**<br>lah preh-SYOHN (ahr-teh-RYAHL) BAH-hah |
| mental retardation | **el retraso mental**<br>ehl rreh-TRAH-soh mehn-TAHL |
| migraine | **la jaqueca**<br>lah hah-KEH-kah |
| multiple sclerosis | **la esclerosis múltiple**<br>lah ehs-kleh-ROH-sees MOOL-tee-pleh |
| muscular dystrophy | **la distrofia muscular**<br>lah dees-TROH-fyah moos-koo-LAHR |
| obesity | **la obesidad**<br>lah oh-beh-see-DAHD |
| paralysis | **la parálisis**<br>lah pah-RAH-lee-sees |
| rheumatism | **el reumatismo**<br>ehl rreh-oo-mah-TEES-moh |
| speaking problems | **los trastornos del habla y el lenguaje**<br>lohs trahs-TOHR-nohs dehl AH-blah<br>ee ehl lehn-GWAH-heh |
| spina bifida | **la espina bífida**<br>lah ehs-PEE-nah BEE-fee-dah |
| visual impediments | **los impedimentos visuales**<br>lohs eem-peh-dee-MEHN-tohs<br>bee-SWAH-lehs |

## Special Needs
### Las necesidades especiales

When talking to parents about any special need (**la necesidad especial** [lah neh-seh-see-DAHD ehs-peh-SYAHL]) that the child might have, you will need to find out what extra accommodations or attention he/she might need during the school day.

| | |
|---|---|
| Does your child need ...? | **¿Necesita su hijo/hija...?**<br>neh-seh-SEE-tah soo EE-hoh/EE-hah |
| to take medicines regularly | **tomar medicinas regularmente**<br>toh-MAHR meh-dee-SEE-nahs<br>rreh-goo-lahr-MEHN-teh |

| | |
|---|---|
| to sit in the front of the class | **sentarse al frente de la clase**<br>sehn-TAHR-seh ahl FREHN-teh deh lah KLAH-seh |
| to go to the bathroom frequently | **ir al baño frecuentemente**<br>eer ahl BAH-nyoh freh-kwehn-teh-MEHN-teh |
| to use a hearing aid | **usar un audífono / aparato de oído**<br>OO-SAHR oon ah-oo-DEE-foh-noh / ah-pah-RAH-toh deh oh-EE-doh |
| to use a wheelchair | **usar una silla de ruedas**<br>OO-SAHR OO-nah SEE-yah deh RRWEH-dahs |
| more time for tests | **más tiempo para los exámenes**<br>mahs TYEHM-poh PAH-rah lohs ehk-SAH-meh-nehs |

## Learning Disability
*La discapacidad de aprendizaje*

If a child shows a number of problems with learning, then the parents and teacher will need to consider the possibility that the child has a learning disability (**la discapacidad de aprendizaje** [lah dees-kah-pah-see-DAHD deh ah-prehn-dee-SAH-heh]). Indications of such problems that you may want to share with the parents are the following.

| | |
|---|---|
| Your child … | **Su hijo/hija...**<br>soo EE-hoh/EE-hah |
| has trouble connecting letters to their sound | **tiene problemas en relacionar las letras con su sonido**<br>TYEH-neh proh-BLEH-mahs ehn rreh-lah-syoh-NAHR lahs LEH-trahs kohn soo soh-NEE-doh |
| does not understand what he/she reads | **no comprende lo que él/ella lee**<br>noh kohm-PREHN-deh loh keh ehl/EH-yah LEH-eh |
| has a great deal of trouble with spelling | **tiene gran dificultad con el deletreo**<br>TYEH-neh grahn dee-fee-kool-TAHD kohn ehl deh-leh-TREH-oh |
| confuses math symbols | **confunde los signos de matemáticas**<br>kohn-FOON-deh lohs SEEG-nohs deh mah-teh-MAH-tee-kahs |
| misreads numbers | **interpreta mal los números**<br>een-tehr-PREH-tah mahl lohs NOO-meh-rohs |

If a child has unexpected problems learning to read, write, listen, speak, or do math, then you may want to suggest that the child be evaluated to see if he or she has a learning disability.

| | |
|---|---|
| Your child needs to be evaluated to see if he/she has a learning disability. | **Su hijo/hija debe pasar una evaluación para determinar si él/ella tiene una discapacidad de aprendizaje.** |
| | soo EE-hoh/EE-hah DEH-beh pah-SAHR oo-nah eh-bah-lwah-SYOHN PAH-rah deh-tehr-mee-NAHR see ehl/EH-yah TYEH-neh oo-nah dees-kah-pah-see-DAHD deh ah-prehn-dee-SAH-heh |

Although the information is not in Spanish, the National Center for Learning Disabilities is a good place for parents to start learning about this topic. Its Web address is **www.ncld.org.** In addition, several governmental agencies have information in Spanish.

## Homeschooling

*La escuela en casa*

Some parents may not be familiar with the concept of homeschooling (**la escuela en casa** [lah ehs-KWEH-lah ehn KAH-sah]). The following phrases will help you explain it to them.

| | |
|---|---|
| When your child cannot come to school for a long period of time, he/she can receive instruction at home. | **Cuando su hijo/hija no puede venir a la escuela por un período largo de tiempo, él/ella puede recibir instrucción en casa.** |
| | KWAHN-doh soo EE-hoh/EE-hah noh PWEH-deh beh-NEER ah lah ehs-KWEH-lah pohr oon peh-REE-oh-doh LAHR-goh deh TYEHM-poh, ehl/EH-yah PWEH-deh rreh-see-BEER eens-trook-SYOHN ehn KAH-sah |
| The state can provide an instructor free of charge. | **El estado puede proveer un instructor / una instructora gratis.** |
| | ehl ehs-TAH-doh PWEH-deh proh-beh-EHR oon eens-trook-TOHR / oo-nah eens-trook-TOH-rah GRAH-tees |

| | |
|---|---|
| Your child can take all the tests at home, too. | **Su hijo/hija puede hacer los exámenes en casa también.**<br>soo EE-hoh/EE-hah PWEH-deh ah-SEHR lohs ehk-SAH-meh-nehs ehn KAH-sah tahm-BYEHN |
| If your child receives instruction at home, he/she is not going to lose the year. | **Si su hijo/hija recibe instrucción en casa no va a perder el año.**<br>see soo EE-hoh/EE-hah rreh-SEE-beh eens-trook-SYOHN ehn KAH-sah noh bah ah pehr-DEHR ehl AH-nyoh |

## Summer School

### *La escuela de verano*

For some students, summer school (**la escuela de verano** [lah ehs-KWEH-lah deh beh-RAH-noh]) is a necessity. Parents need to understand what it entails.

| | |
|---|---|
| Students need to go to summer school when they fail a course. | **Los estudiantes tienen que ir a la escuela de verano cuando suspenden una asignatura.**<br>lohs ehs-too-DYAHN-tehs TYEH-nehn keh eer ah lah ehs-KWEH-lah deh beh-RAH-noh KWAHN-doh soos-PEHN-dehn oo-nah ah-seeg-nah-TOO-rah |
| Your child needs to take (*number*) courses in summer school. | **Su hijo/hija necesita tomar (*number*) cursos en la escuela de verano.**<br>soo EE-hoh/EE-hah neh-seh-SEE-tah toh-MAHR… KOOR-sohs ehn lah ehs-KWEH-lah deh beh-RAH-noh |
| Summer school lasts (*number*) weeks. | **La escuela de verano dura (*number*) semanas.**<br>lah ehs-KWEH-lah deh beh-RAH-noh DOO-rah… seh-MAH-nahs |
| If he/she passes summer school, he/she can go on to the next grade. | **Si él/ella aprueba los cursos de la escuela de verano, puede avanzar al próximo grado.**<br>see ehl/EH-yah ah-PRWEH-bah lohs KOOR-sohs deh lah ehs-KWEH-lah deh beh-RAH-noh, PWEH-deh ah-bahn-SAHR ahl PROHK-see-moh GRAH-doh |

| | |
|---|---|
| He/She needs to pass/take that course to graduate. | **Él/Ella necesita aprobar/tomar ese curso para graduarse.**<br>ehl/EH-yah neh-seh-SEE-tah ah-proh-BAHR/toh-MAHR EH-seh KOOR-soh PAH-rah grah-DWAHR-seh |

## General Education Diploma
*El diploma de educación general*

The General Education Diploma (**el diploma de educación general** [ehl dee-PLOH-mah deh eh-doo-kah-SYOHN heh-neh-RAHL]), also known as the GED [yee ee dee], could be an alternative for those students who cannot complete their high school education in a regular school. This concept may be new to some parents.

| | |
|---|---|
| Your child can study and take the GED exam. | **Su hijo/hija puede estudiar y hacer el examen de GED.**<br>soo EE-hoh/EE-hah PWEH-deh ehs-too-DYAHR ee ah-SEHR ehl ehk-SAH-mehn deh yee ee dee |
| If your child passes the GED exam, he/she will receive the General Education Diploma / the GED. | **Si su hijo/hija aprueba el examen de GED, él/ella va a recibir el diploma de educación general / el GED.**<br>see soo EE-hoh/EE-hah ah-PRWEH-bah ehl ehk-SAH-men deh yee ee dee, ehl/EH-yah bah ah rreh-see-BEER ehl dee-PLOH-mah deh eh-doo-kah-SYOHN heh-neh-RAHL / ehl yee ee dee |
| The GED diploma is considered equal to a high school diploma. | **El diploma de GED se considera equivalente a un diploma de escuela secundaria.**<br>ehl dee-PLOH-mah deh yee ee dee seh kohn-see-DEH-rah eh-kee-bah-LEHN-teh ah oon dee-PLOH-mah de ehs-KWEH-lah seh-koon-DAH-ryah |

## Practice 7-6

*Write a complete sentence in Spanish to explain the following phrases.*

1. summer school

_____

2. GED exam

   _____

3. learning disability

   _____

4. visual impediments

   _____

5. hearing aid

   _____

6. attention deficit disorder

   _____

## Graduation

### *La graduación*

In some schools it is the responsibility of the counselor to handle matters related to graduation (**la graduación** [lah grah-dwah-SYOHN]). Following is a list of many of the terms related to the graduation ceremony and other elements typical of American schools.

| | |
|---|---|
| cap and gown | **el birrete y la toga que llevan los estudiantes durante la ceremonia de graduación**<br>ehl bee-RREH-teh ee lah TOH-gah keh YEH-bahn lohs ehs-too-DYAHN-tehs doo-RAHN-teh lah seh-reh-MOH-nyah deh grah-dwah-SYOHN |
| class photos | **las fotos de la clase de su hijo/hija**<br>lahs FOH-tohs deh lah KLAH-seh deh soo EE-hoh/EE-hah |
| class ring | **el anillo de la clase (un anillo que simboliza la graduación de una escuela en particular)**<br>ehl ah-NEE-yoh deh lah KLAH-seh (oon ah-NEE-yoh keh seem-boh-LEE-sah lah grah-dwah-SYOHN deh oo-nah ehs-KWEH-lah ehn pahr-tee-koo-LAHR) |
| commencement exercises | **la ceremonia de graduación**<br>lah seh-reh-MOH-nyah deh grah-dwah-SYOHN |

| | |
|---|---|
| diploma | **el diploma** <br> ehl dee-PLOH-mah |
| graduation fees | **el dinero que se usa para pagar por varias actividades de graduación** <br> ehl dee-NEH-roh keh seh oo-sah PAH-rah pah-GAHR pohr BAH-ryahs ahk-tee-bee-DAH-dehs deh grah-dwah-SYOHN |
| graduation speech | **el discurso de graduación** <br> ehl dees-KOOR-soh deh grah-dwah-SYOHN |
| homecoming | **el regreso a la escuela de estudiantes que se han graduado en años anteriores** <br> ehl rreh-GREH-soh ah lah ehs-KWEH-lah deh ehs-too-DYAHN-tehs keh seh ahn grah-DWAH-doh ehn AH-nyohs ahn-teh-RYOH-rehs |
| prom | **la fiesta donde los estudiantes celebran su graduación** <br> lah FYEHS-tah DOHN-deh lohs ehs-too-DYAHN-tehs seh-LEH-brahn soo grah-dwah-SYOHN |
| valedictorian | **el estudiante que da la oración de despedida a los estudiantes que se gradúan** <br> ehl ehs-too-DYAHN-teh keh dah lah oh-rah-SYOHN deh dehs-peh-DEE-dah ah lohs ehs-too-DYAHN-tehs keh seh grah-DOO-ahn |
| yearbook | **el anuario (un libro con fotos y recuerdos de los años en la escuela)** <br> ehl ah-NWAH-ryoh (oon LEE-broh kohn FOH-tohs ee rreh-KWEHR-dohs deh lohs AH-nyohs ehn lah ehs-KWEH-lah) |

## GRAMMAR · Summary: *ser* and *estar*

The verb "to be" can be translated two ways in Spanish: **ser** [sehr] and **estar** [ehs-TAHR]. These two Spanish verbs are not interchangeable. Each one is used in very specific situations.

The verb **ser** is used in the following ways.

- To find out or state the identity of people, places, and things

     What is he/she/it?          **¿Qué es?** <br>
                                      keh ehs

It's a diploma.　　　　　　　　　**Es un diploma.**
　　　　　　　　　　　　　　　　ehs oon dee-PLOH-mah

Who is he/she/it?　　　　　　　**¿Quién es?**
　　　　　　　　　　　　　　　　kyehn ehs

It is the dance teacher.　　　　　**Es el maestro de baile.**
　　　　　　　　　　　　　　　　ehs ehl mah-EHS-troh deh BAH-ee-leh

- To find out or state ownership

Whose is it?　　　　　　　　　　**¿De quién es?**
　　　　　　　　　　　　　　　　deh kyehn ehs

It is my classmate's.　　　　　　**Es de mi compañero de clase.**
　　　　　　　　　　　　　　　　ehs deh mee kohm-pah-NYEH-roh deh
　　　　　　　　　　　　　　　　KLAH-seh

- To find out or state the origin of someone or something

Where is he/she/it from?　　　　**¿De dónde es?**
　　　　　　　　　　　　　　　　deh DOHN-deh ehs

He/She/It is from Venezuela.　　**Es de Venezuela.**
　　　　　　　　　　　　　　　　ehs deh beh-neh-SWEH-lah

- To find out or state the nationality of someone or something

What nationality is he/she/it?　　**¿De qué nacionalidad es?**
　　　　　　　　　　　　　　　　deh keh nah-syoh-nah-lee-DAHD ehs

He/She/It is Peruvian.　　　　　**Es peruano/peruana.**
　　　　　　　　　　　　　　　　ehs peh-RWAH-noh/peh-RWAH-nah

- To find out or state of what material something is made

What is it made of?　　　　　　**¿De qué es?**
　　　　　　　　　　　　　　　　deh keh ehs

It's made of silver.　　　　　　**Es de plata.**
　　　　　　　　　　　　　　　　ehs deh PLAH-tah

- To find out or state the characteristics of someone or something

What is he/she/it like?　　　　　**¿Cómo es?**
　　　　　　　　　　　　　　　　KOH-moh ehs

It's very exciting.　　　　　　　**Es muy emocionante.**
　　　　　　　　　　　　　　　　ehs MOO-ee eh-moh-syoh-NAHN-teh

For a list of adjectives that can be used with the verb **ser**, see Chapter 5, pages 217–218.

The verb **estar** is used in the following ways.

- To find out or state where someone or something is located

| | |
|---|---|
| Where is he/she/it? | **¿Dónde está?** |
| | DOHN-deh ehs-TAH |
| He/She/It is in the counselor's office. | **Está en la oficina del consejero.** |
| | ehs-TAH ehn lah oh-fee-SEE-nah dehl kohn-seh-HEH-roh |

- To find out or state the physical or emotional condition of a person or thing

| | |
|---|---|
| How are they? | **¿Cómo están?** |
| | KOH-moh ehs-TAHN |
| They are tired. | **Están cansados.** |
| | ehs-TAHN kahn-SAH-dohs |
| How's lunch today? | **¿Cómo está el almuerzo hoy?** |
| | KOH-moh ehs-TAH ehl ahl-MWEHR-soh OH-ee |
| It's delicious. | **Está delicioso.** |
| | ehs-TAH deh-lee-SYOH-soh |

For a list of adjectives that can be used with the verb **estar**, see Chapter 5, pages 203–204 and also pages 252–253 in this chapter.

## Summary Practice

**A** *Match the words on the left with their meaning on the right.*

1. _____ una vez               a. *clothing*
2. _____ el secuestro          b. *gang*
3. _____ el robo               c. *neither*
4. _____ a veces               d. *someone*
5. _____ la amenaza            e. *kidnapping*
6. _____ tampoco               f. *unemployment*
7. _____ la fecha límite       g. *sometimes*
8. _____ la pandilla           h. *theft*
9. _____ el desempleo          i. *threat*
10. _____ la jaqueca           j. *once*
11. _____ alguien              k. *deadline*
12. _____ la ropa              l. *migraine*

**B** *Express the following sentences in Spanish.*

1. That class is too advanced and you do not have the prerequisites.

   _____

2. The bilingual program is a transitional program.

   _____

3. Your child has to go to summer school.

   _____

4. Your child misreads the words when she reads.

   _____

5. The students should not smoke in the schoolyard.

   _____

**C** *Use the verb* **estar** *and one of the adjectives from the list below to express how each person is feeling. There are more adjectives than you need, and there may be more than one possible answer.*

cansado       perdido
inquieto      preocupado
frustrado     incómodo
asustado

1. Juan tiene miedo. Él _____.

2. Gilberto no sabe donde ir. Él _____.

3. Nosotros trabajamos mucho hoy. Nosotros _____.

4. María, tú no estudiaste para el examen. Tú _____.

5. Ellas no comprenden el problema. Ellas _____.

**D** *Complete the following sentences with the correct form of* **ser** *or* **estar***.*

1. Yo acabo de hacer un examen, _____ nervioso.

2. Y tú, ¿de dónde _____?

3. Los bomberos _____ muy valientes.

4. Ellos _____ de Honduras.

5. María y Marco _____ en la oficina del enfermero.

6. La graduación _____ muy emocionante.

7. Ese hombre _____ el director de la escuela.

8. ¿Dónde _____ el gimnasio?

# Appendix

## VERB CONJUGATION CHARTS

### Regular Verbs

| | | ENDINGS | | | | |
|---|---|---|---|---|---|---|
| | STEM | FIRST-PERSON SING. | SECOND-PERSON SING. | THIRD-PERSON SING. | FIRST-PERSON PLURAL | THIRD-PERSON PLURAL |

#### -ar Verbs

**hablar** *to speak*

| | | | | | | |
|---|---|---|---|---|---|---|
| PRESENT | habl- | o | as | a | amos | an |
| PRETERITE | habl- | é | aste | ó | amos | aron |
| PRES. SUBJUNCTIVE | habl- | e | es | e | emos | en |
| COMMAND | habl- | | a | e | | en |

#### -er Verbs

**comer** *to eat*

| | | | | | | |
|---|---|---|---|---|---|---|
| PRESENT | com- | o | es | e | emos | en |
| PRETERITE | com- | í | iste | ió | imos | ieron |
| PRES. SUBJUNCTIVE | com- | a | as | a | amos | an |
| COMMAND | com- | | e | a | | an |

#### -ir Verbs

**vivir** *to live*

| | | | | | | |
|---|---|---|---|---|---|---|
| PRESENT | viv- | o | es | e | imos | en |
| PRETERITE | viv- | í | iste | ió | imos | ieron |
| PRES. SUBJUNCTIVE | viv- | a | as | a | amos | an |
| COMMAND | viv- | | e | a | | an |

## Verbs with Stem Changes

### *e > ie (-ar* and *-er* Verbs)

| INFINITIVE | **cerrar** *to close* |
|---|---|
| PRESENT | cierro, cierras, cierra, cerramos, cierran |
| PRES. SUBJUNCTIVE | cierre, cierres, cierre, cerremos, cierren |

| INFINITIVE | **perder** *to lose* |
|---|---|
| PRESENT | pierdo, pierdes, pierde, perdemos, pierden |
| PRES. SUBJUNCTIVE | pierda, pierdas, pierda, perdamos, pierdan |

Also atender, comenzar, despertar(se), empezar, entender, negar, pensar, recomendar, sentar(se)

### *e > ie, e > i (-ir* Verbs)

| INFINITIVE | **sentir** *to feel* |
|---|---|
| PRESENT | siento, sientes, siente, sentimos, sienten |
| PRETERITE | sentí, sentiste, sintió, sentimos, sintieron |
| PRES. SUBJUNCTIVE | sienta, sientas, sienta, sintamos, sientan |

Also herir, mentir, preferir, requerir

### *e > i (-ir* Verbs)

| INFINITIVE | **pedir** *to request* |
|---|---|
| PRESENT | pido, pides, pide, pedimos, piden |
| PRETERITE | pedí, pediste, pidió, pedimos, pidieron |
| PRES. SUBJUNCTIVE | pida, pidas, pida, pidamos, pidan |

Also conseguir, corregir, desvestir(se), repetir, seguir, servir, vestir(se)

| INFINITIVE | **reír** *to laugh* |
|---|---|
| PRESENT | río, ríes, ríe, reímos, ríen |
| PRETERITE | reí, reíste, rió, reímos, rieron |
| PRES. SUBJUNCTIVE | ría, rías, ría, riamos, rían |

Also reírse, sonreír(se)

## o > ue (-ar and -er Verbs)

| | |
|---|---|
| INFINITIVE | **contar** to count, tell |
| PRESENT | cuento, cuentas, cuenta, contamos, cuentan |
| PRES. SUBJUNCTIVE | cuente, cuentes, cuente, contemos, cuenten |
| INFINITIVE | **volver** to return |
| PRESENT | vuelvo, vuelves, vuelve, volvemos, vuelven |
| PRES. SUBJUNCTIVE | vuelva, vuelvas, vuelva, volvamos, vuelvan |

Also  acostar(se), almorzar, aprobar, costar, demostrar,
devolver, doler, encontrar, morder, mostrar, probar(se),
recordar, soñar

## o > ue, o > u (-ir Verbs)

| | |
|---|---|
| INFINITIVE | **dormir** to sleep |
| PRESENT | duermo, duermes, duerme, dormimos, duermen |
| PRETERITE | dormí, dormiste, durmió, dormimos, durmieron |
| PRES. SUBJUNCTIVE | duerma, duermas, duerma, durmamos, duerman |

Also  dormirse, morir

## u > ue (-ar Verbs)

| | |
|---|---|
| INFINITIVE | **jugar** to play |
| PRESENT | juego, juegas, juega, jugamos, juegan |
| PRES. SUBJUNCTIVE | juegue, juegues, juegue, juguemos, jueguen |

## Irregular Verbs

**caer** to fall

| | |
|---|---|
| PRESENT | caigo, caes, cae, caemos, caen |
| PRETERITE | caí, caíste, cayó, caímos, cayeron |
| PRES. SUBJUNCTIVE | caiga, caigas, caiga, caigamos, caigan |

Also  caerse

**coger** to catch

| | |
|---|---|
| PRESENT | cojo, coges, coge, cogemos, cogen |
| PRES. SUBJUNCTIVE | coja, cojas, coja, cojamos, cojan |

Also  recoger

## conducir *to drive*

| | |
|---|---|
| PRESENT | conduzco, conduces, conduce, conducimos, conducen |
| PRETERITE | conduje, condujiste, condujo, condujimos, condujeron |
| PRES. SUBJUNCTIVE | conduzca, conduzcas, conduzca, conduzcamos, conduzcan |

*Also* traducir

## conocer *to know, be acquainted with*

| | |
|---|---|
| PRESENT | conozco, conoces, conoce, conocemos, conocen |
| PRES. SUBJUNCTIVE | conozca, conozcas, conozca, conozcamos, conozcan |

*Also* desobedecer, establecer, lucir, obedecer

## construir *to build*

| | |
|---|---|
| PRESENT | construyo, construyes, construye, construimos, construyen |
| PRETERITE | construí, construiste, construyó, construimos, construyeron |
| PRES. SUBJUNCTIVE | construya, construyas, construya, construyamos, construyan |

## continuar *to continue*

| | |
|---|---|
| PRESENT | continúo, continúas, continúa, continuamos, continúan |
| PRES. SUBJUNCTIVE | continúe, continúes, continúe, continuemos, continúen |

## dar *to give*

| | |
|---|---|
| PRESENT | doy, das, da, damos, dan |
| PRETERITE | di, diste, dio, dimos, dieron |
| PRES. SUBJUNCTIVE | dé, des, dé, demos, den |

## decir *to say*

| | |
|---|---|
| PRESENT | digo, dices, dice, decimos, dicen |
| PRETERITE | dije, dijiste, dijo, dijimos, dijeron |
| PRES. SUBJUNCTIVE | diga, digas, diga, digamos, digan |
| tú COMMAND | di |

## estar *to be*

| | |
|---|---|
| PRESENT | estoy, estás, está, estamos, están |
| PRETERITE | estuve, estuviste, estuvo, estuvimos, estuvieron |
| PRES. SUBJUNCTIVE | esté, estés, esté, estemos, estén |

**hacer** *to do, make*

| | |
|---|---|
| PRESENT | hago, haces, hace, hacemos, hacen |
| PRETERITE | hice, hiciste, hizo, hicimos, hicieron |
| PRES. SUBJUNCTIVE | haga, hagas, haga, hagamos, hagan |
| tú COMMAND | haz |

**ir** *to go*

| | |
|---|---|
| PRESENT | voy, vas, va, vamos, van |
| PRETERITE | fui, fuiste, fue, fuimos, fueron |
| PRES. SUBJUNCTIVE | vaya, vayas, vaya, vayamos, vayan |
| tú COMMAND | ve |

**leer** *to read*

| | |
|---|---|
| PRETERITE | leí, leíste, leyó, leímos, leyeron |

*Also* creer

**oír** *to hear*

| | |
|---|---|
| PRESENT | oigo, oyes, oye, oímos, oyen |
| PRETERITE | oí, oíste, oyó, oímos, oyeron |
| PRES. SUBJUNCTIVE | oiga, oigas, oiga, oigamos, oigan |

**poder** *to be able, can*

| | |
|---|---|
| PRESENT | puedo, puedes, puede, podemos, pueden |
| PRETERITE | pude, pudiste, pudo, pudimos, pudieron |
| PRES. SUBJUNCTIVE | pueda, puedas, pueda, podamos, puedan |

**poner** *to put, place*

| | |
|---|---|
| PRESENT | pongo, pones, pone, ponemos, ponen |
| PRETERITE | puse, pusiste, puso, pusimos, pusieron |
| PRES. SUBJUNCTIVE | ponga, pongas, ponga, pongamos, pongan |
| tú COMMAND | pon |

*Also* ponerse

**querer** *to want*

| | |
|---|---|
| PRESENT | quiero, quieres, quiere, queremos, quieren |
| PRETERITE | quise, quisiste, quiso, quisimos, quisieron |
| PRES. SUBJUNCTIVE | quiera, quieras, quiera, queramos, quieran |

**saber** *to know (facts)*

| | |
|---|---|
| PRESENT | sé, sabes, sabe, sabemos, saben |
| PRETERITE | supe, supiste, supo, supimos, supieron |
| PRES. SUBJUNCTIVE | sepa, sepas, sepa, sepamos, sepan |

**salir** *to leave*

| | |
|---|---|
| PRESENT | salgo, sales, sale, salimos, salen |
| PRES. SUBJUNCTIVE | salga, salgas, salga, salgamos, salgan |
| tú COMMAND | sal |

**ser** *to be*

| | |
|---|---|
| PRESENT | soy, eres, es, somos, son |
| PRETERITE | fui, fuiste, fue, fuimos, fueron |
| PRES. SUBJUNCTIVE | sea, seas, sea, seamos, sean |
| tú COMMAND | sé |

**tener** *to have*

| | |
|---|---|
| PRESENT | tengo, tienes, tiene, tenemos, tienen |
| PRETERITE | tuve, tuviste, tuvo, tuvimos, tuvieron |
| PRES. SUBJUNCTIVE | tenga, tengas, tenga, tengamos, tengan |
| tú COMMAND | ten |

*Also* obtener

**traer** *to bring*

| | |
|---|---|
| PRESENT | traigo, traes, trae, traemos, traen |
| PRETERITE | traje, trajiste, trajo, trajimos, trajeron |
| PRES. SUBJUNCTIVE | traiga, traigas, traiga, traigamos, traigan |

**venir** *to come*

| | |
|---|---|
| PRESENT | vengo, vienes, viene, venimos, vienen |
| PRETERITE | vine, viniste, vino, vinimos, vinieron |
| PRES. SUBJUNCTIVE | venga, vengas, venga, vengamos, vengan |
| tú COMMAND | ven |

**ver** *to see*

| | |
|---|---|
| PRESENT | veo, ves, ve, vemos, ven |
| PRETERITE | vi, viste, vio, vimos, vieron |
| PRES. SUBJUNCTIVE | vea, veas, vea, veamos, vean |

## Answer Key

### Introduction
#### Practice I-1
1. Este es el señor / Esta es la señora / la señorita (*student teacher's last name*). / Quisiera presentarle al señor / a la señora / a la señorita (*student teacher's last name*).
2. Mucho gusto. / Es un placer conocerlo.
3. Buenas noches. / Hasta pronto.
4. Soy el señor / la señora / la señorita (*your last name*).
5. Hasta el lunes.
6. Hasta la semana próxima.
7. ¿Cómo estás? / ¿Cómo te va? / ¿Qué tal?
8. Regular. / Así, así, gracias.
9. Estoy bien, gracias. ¿Y tú?
10. ¡Que te vaya bien!

#### Practice I-2
**A**
1. nosotros/nosotras
2. él/ella/Ud.
3. ellos/ellas/Uds.
4. tú
5. yo
6. ellos/ellas/Uds.

**B**
1. comprenden, comprendo, comprendemos
2. recibes, reciben, recibe
3. termino, termina, terminamos

**C**
1. they understand, I understand, we understand
2. you receive, you receive, she receives
3. I finish, you finish, we finish

**D**
1. I write a novel. / I do write a novel. / I am writing a novel.
2. Do you study very little? / Are you studying very little?
3. We are running in the park tomorrow. / We'll run in the park tomorrow.

#### Practice I-3
**A**
1. cierran
2. volvemos
3. vistes
4. sirvo
5. dormimos
6. piensa
7. encuentran
8. juega
9. pedimos
10. comienzo

**B**
1. cierras
2. duermen
3. servimos
4. repite
5. entiendo
6. devolvemos
7. cuesta
8. comenzamos
9. Juegan
10. vuelvo

## Practice I-4

**A**
1. camine, caminen
2. lea, lean
3. vaya, vayan
4. asista, asistan
5. dé, den
6. sepa, sepan
7. esté, estén
8. escuche, escuchen
9. sea, sean
10. beba, beban
11. traduzca, traduzcan
12. traiga, traigan

**B** Put **no** before the commands in Exercise A. The verb does not change.

**C**
1. Camine
2. Sean
3. Dé
4. Vayan
5. Asista
6. Escuchen
7. Lean
8. Borre
9. Corra
10. Estén

**D**
1. No camine
2. No sean
3. No dé
4. No vayan
5. No asista
6. No escuchen
7. No lean
8. No borre
9. No corra
10. No estén

## Practice I-5

1. Haz
2. Sal
3. Sé
4. Pon
5. Ven
6. Di
7. Ve

## Practice I-6

**A**
1. escucha, no escuches
2. sal, no salgas
3. haz, no hagas
4. escribe, no escribas
5. sé, no seas
6. come, no comas
7. pon, no pongas
8. ve, no vayas

**B**
1. Come
2. Habla
3. corras
4. Ven
5. escuches
6. Copia
7. Aprende
8. Trae
9. borres
10. abras
11. Repite
12. estés

## Practice I-7

**A**
1. (Tú) hablas español, ¿verdad?
2. ¿Asisten (Uds.) a la clase de física?
3. ¿(Ellos) corren en el parque?
4. ¿(Nosotros) terminamos la tarea?
5. ¿(Ella) no aprende mucho en la clase?

**B**  1. Sí, hablo español. / No, no hablo español.
2. No, no asistimos a la clase de física. / Sí, asistimos a la clase de física.
3. Sí, ellos corren en el parque. / No, ellos no corren en el parque.
4. Sí, Uds. terminan la tarea. / Sí, nosotros terminamos la tarea. /
No, Uds. no terminan la tarea. / No, nosotros no terminamos la tarea.
5. No, no aprende mucho en la clase. / Sí, aprende mucho en clase.

## Practice I-8

**A**

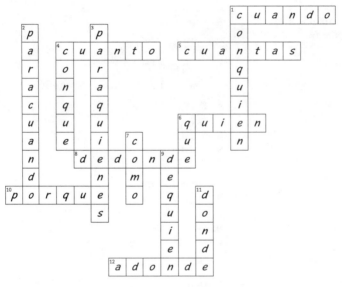

**B**  1. Quiénes
2. Qué
3. Por qué
4. Dónde
5. De dónde
6. Cuánto
7. Quién
8. Cuándo
9. Cómo
10. Con quiénes

## Summary Practice

1. Este es el señor / Esta es la señora / Esta es la señorita (*principal's last name*).
2. ¡Qué le vaya bien!
3. Hasta la semana próxima.
4. Firme, por favor.
5. Escribe en la pizarra.
6. No corras en los pasillos.
7. ¿Dónde está el señor Smith?
8. ¿De quién es el libro?

# Chapter 1

## Practice 1-1

1. | t | e | n | e | m | o | s | | f | r | í | o |

2. | t | i | e | n | e | n | | s | u | e | ñ | o |

3. | t | e | n | g | o | | s | u | e | r | t | e |

4. | t | i | e | n | e | s | | p | r | i | s | a |

5. | t | i | e | n | e | | h | a | m | b | r | e |

6. | t | e | n | e | m | o | s | | s | e | d |

7. | t | e | n | g | o | | m | i | e | d | o |

8. | t | i | e | n | e | | d | i | e | z | | a | ñ | o | s |

## Practice 1-2

1. ¿Cuántos años tiene el niño / la niña / (*name of student*)?
2. ¿Cuál es su dirección?
3. ¿Tiene el niño / la niña hermanos?
4. ¿Cuál es la fecha de nacimiento del niño / de la niña?
5. ¿Quién está a cargo del niño / de la niña?
6. ¿Cuál es el número de teléfono del trabajo?

## Practice 1-3

**A**

```
T B H E R M A N A S T R A X V
M A V G O R M G N O V I O W P
L Z E V O L E U B A E V F S A
W Y E R M O D O N I R D A P D
S E U V D D V T A U D S U O R
U R N F F A A Q A O A B V M A
E N F M I U P M J H M J Z C S
G O T L A C K M I I D M E E T
R T A T H D A U O R H G S T R
A P T I D I R N H C P L P N O
R G X Y Y I Q I A L R W O E S
T W W L B J Y C N M L L S I Q
B V J E J E O B H A R Q A R R
A D A J I H A A L D U E M A K
D L X T C U Y K C W D K H P B
```

**B**

1. tío
2. cuñada
3. abuela
4. sobrino
5. hijo
6. prima
7. nieta
8. novia

## Practice 1-4

**A**

```
T O D O P A N A M E Ñ O S S O
M D O M I N I C A N A O S A M
O C E T L A M E T A U G E R I
O C A N O S E W D K A G Q N P
N F A N A I B M O L O C C A E
A R S C E E M W X D R X C Z R
L F O N A C I X E M X I H A U
O X F H B W N K N W D Y I N A
Z X F Q X Q R P V L H R L I N
E V O N A I R O T A U C E T O
N Z V V T Z G H E K L M N N S
E A O Y H C U B A N O X A E N
V X K Q B E P Y L W G D D G Y
H P B J R B E B D L T O K R B
P U E R T O R R I Q U E Ñ A P
```

*TODOS   SOMOS   AMERICANOS*

**B**

| A | B | C | D | E | F | G | H | I | J | K | L | M | N | O | P | Q | R | S | T | U | V | W | X | Y | Z |
|---|---|---|---|---|---|---|---|---|---|---|---|---|---|---|---|---|---|---|---|---|---|---|---|---|---|
| N |   |   | L | R | E |   |   |   | Y | O | T | S |   |   |   |   | D |   |   |   | I | A | U |   |   |

¿*DE   DONDE   ERES*?  *SOY   DE   LOS*
 R F   R J A R F   F E F L    L J I   R F   D J L

*ESTADOS   UNIDOS* .
F L K W R J L   X A V R J L

**C**
1. ¿De dónde es (Ud.)?
2. ¿Eres (tú) de Colombia?
3. ¿De qué nacionalidad es (él)?
4. (Nosotras) somos españolas.
5. (Yo) soy de Nicaragua.

## Practice 1-5

**A**
1. la chica mexicana
2. los papeles blancos
3. los estudiantes inteligentes
4. la doctora guatemalteca
5. las pizarras grandes
6. el hombre cubano

**B**
1. las chicas mexicanas
2. el papel blanco
3. el estudiante inteligente
4. las doctoras guatemaltecas
5. la pizarra grande
6. los hombres cubanos

## Practice 1-6

**A**
1. ¿Tiene Ud. <u>otros ingresos</u>?
2. ¿Tiene problemas con <u>el oído</u>?
3. ¿Está tomando su hijo <u>alguna medicina</u>?
4. En caso de emergencia, ¿<u>a quién debemos llamar</u>?
5. ¿Tiene Ud. <u>seguro médico</u>?

6. Para comprobar su dirección, <u>Ud. puede traer</u> la licencia de conducir.
7. Necesita traer <u>el reporte de todas las vacunas</u>.

**B**

| l | a | v | i | s | t | a |

| l | a | e | n | f | e | r | m | e | d | a | d |

| e | l | p | o | l | v | o |

| l | o | s | m | a | r | i | s | c | o | s |

| l | a | h | i | e | r | b | a |

| e | l | p | e | s | o |

| l | a | m | o | r | d | e | d | u | r | a | d | e | a | b | e | j | a | s |

¿ <u>T</u> <u>i</u> <u>e</u> <u>n</u> <u>e</u>  <u>s</u> <u>u</u>  <u>h</u> <u>i</u> <u>j</u> <u>o</u>  <u>a</u> <u>l</u> g u n <u>a</u>  <u>a</u> <u>l</u> <u>e</u> <u>r</u> g <u>i</u> <u>a</u> ?
  1 2 3 4 5  6 7  8 9 10 11  12 13    14  15 16 17 18  19 20

## Practice 1-7

**A**

```
L Y X Z B P J C U I G X F Q X
F S C S W J O I C I F I D E V
U A C E R A A E B N K Y P R N
L A W E I E C V E A N S A E K
N R R I M T T M E J U B W W T
T D N A D L K N I N A V D M J
E A V O S Y S J E E I I G G J
D U I A J C Y V A U H D G G E
E C T X K E A S D N R S A V L
F D R U C H L C N W I B W U L
D S I J D U N L I G P U D N A
C U N O C Z H B A E S H Q G C
K J A B K C M N J C L I Y S X
A N A Z N A M J C C Y O U N E
H O Q C I M G O W M K Y S D T
```

**B**

**C**   1. Esperen la luz verde.
2. Suban al autobús.
3. No empujen.
4. Caminen, no corran.
5. No griten.

## Practice 1-8

1. Juan, (tú) tienes que cruzar la calle.
2. Nosotros tenemos que esperar la luz verde.
3. Ellos tienen que llegar a tiempo a la parada.
4. Ella tiene que ir hasta la esquina.
5. Yo tengo que doblar a la derecha.

## Summary Practice

1. ¿Tiene su hijo/hija alguna condición que requiere atención especial?
2. ¿Cuántas personas viven en su casa?
3. (Yo) tengo mucha prisa.
4. ¿Cuántos años tiene (ella)?
5. La oficina está a dos cuadras.
6. ¿De dónde es (usted)?
7. (Usted) tiene que seguir derecho.
8. ¿Cómo llega su hija a la escuela?
9. Ud. tiene que esperar la llegada del autobús en la parada indicada.
10. Estoy perdido/perdida.
11. Espere la señal del chofer antes de cruzar.

# Chapter 2

## Practice 2-1

1. el bibliotecario / la bibliotecaria
2. el guardián / la guardiana
3. el/la conserje
4. el traductor / la traductora
5. la persona encargada de ayudar a los niños a cruzar la calle
6. el/la recepcionista
7. el/la guardia de seguridad
8. el cocinero / la cocinera
9. el entrenador / la entrenadora
10. el conductor / la conductora de autobús

## Practice 2-2

1. Es una calculadora.
2. Es un lápiz.
3. Es una mochila.
4. Son unas tijeras.
5. Es un cuaderno.
6. Son cinco libros.

## Practice 2-3

**A**

| e | l | c | u | a | r | t | o | d | e | b | a | ñ | o |

| l | a | s | a | l | a | d | e | m | a | e | s | t | r | o | s |

| e | l | s | ó | t | a | n | o |

| e | l | s | a | l | ó | n | d | e | c | l | a | s | e | s |

| l | a | b | i | b | l | i | o | t | e | c | a |

| e | l | a | u | d | i | t | o | r | i | o |

| e | l | c | u | a | r | t | o | d | e | c | o | r | r | e | o |

| e | l | g | i | m | n | a | s | i | o |

| e | l | v | e | s | t | u | a | r | i | o |

| l | a | o | f | i | c | i | n | a | d | e | l | c | o | n | s | e | j | e | r | o |

<u>l o s</u>  <u>c u a r t o s</u>  <u>d e</u>  <u>l a</u>  <u>e s c u e l a</u>
1 2 3   4 5 6 7 8 9 10  11 12  13 14  15 16 17 18 19 20 21

**B**

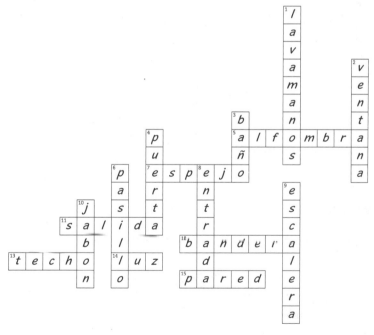

**C**
1. Está en el sótano.
2. Están allí.
3. Están en el cajón.
4. Está enfrente del auditorio / salón de actos.
5. Está al lado de la impresora.
6. Está en el rincón.
7. Están en la pared.
8. Está al lado del enfermero / de la enfermera.
9. Está enfrente de los pupitres.
10. Están detrás de la copiadora.

**D**
1. gymnasium
2. water fountains
3. paper towels
4. principal's office
5. stapler
6. trash can
7. posters
8. counselor
9. desk
10. bookcases

## Practice 2-4

1. el boletín
2. la taquilla
3. la butaca
4. la multa
5. el recreo
6. la tarea
7. el periódico
8. el examen / la prueba
9. el horario
10. la nota

## Practice 2-5

**A**
1. la carne
2. la sopa
3. el maíz
4. el arroz
5. traer
6. el pescado
7. la naranja
8. el pollo
9. limpiar
10. jamón

**B**
1. Sí, me gusta beber té. / No, no me gusta beber té.
2. Sí, le gustan las fresas. / No, no le gustan las fresas.
3. Sí, les gusta comer en la cafetería. / No, no les gusta comer en la cafetería.
4. Sí, me gustan los postres. / No, no me gustan los postres.
5. Sí, le gusta el melocotón. / No, no le gusta el melocotón.

**C** ¿Qué les gusta?

## Summary Practice

*Answers will vary.*
1. ¿Quiénes son Uds.? / ¿Quiénes son los estudiantes en el pasillo?
2. ¿Te gusta compartir el/tu almuerzo?
3. ¿Hay ensalada (para el almuerzo)?
4. ¿Dónde está el cuarto de baño para damas?
5. ¿Cuál es el postre?
6. ¿No les gusta traer el almuerzo de casa?
7. ¿Dónde está el sacapuntas?
8. ¿Qué son esos papeles?
9. ¿Está la oficina del director / de la directora a la derecha de la entrada?
10. ¿Hay una luz en el estacionamiento?

# Chapter 3

## Practice 3-1

**A**  1. el quince de septiembre de mil novecientos noventa
2. el veinte y cinco de octubre del dos mil uno
3. el primero de julio del dos mil seis
4. el treinta y uno de enero de mil novecientos ochenta y cuatro

**B**  lunes, miércoles, viernes, domingo

**C**  1. Son las nueve y diez de la mañana.
2. Es (el) mediodía.
3. Son las tres menos veinte y cinco de la tarde.
4. Son las cinco de la tarde.
5. Es (la) medianoche.
6. Son las siete y media de la noche.
7. Son las once y cuarto de la mañana.

**D**  1. todos los días
2. a principios de
3. ahora mismo
4. a partir de
5. a mediados de

**E**  1. ¿Qué hora es?
2. ¿Cuál es la fecha de hoy? / ¿A cómo estamos hoy?
3. ¿Cuándo es?
4. ¿A qué hora es la clase de español?

## Practice 3-2

1. ¿Qué tiempo hizo ayer?
2. Hace frío y está nublado.
3. Hace mal tiempo.
4. Va a hacer buen tiempo mañana.
5. Está nevando.

## Practice 3-3

**A**  *Answers will vary.*
1. pantalones cortos / una camiseta / una blusa de algodón
2. un suéter / un sombrero
3. una gabardina / un impermeable
4. un abrigo / una bufanda / guantes
5. una chaqueta / pantalones largos

**B**  1. (La camiseta) es de Juan.
2. (Los calcetines) son de Alberto y Pedro.
3. (La falda) es de Graciela.
4. (Los calzoncillos) son de David.
5. (Las chaquetas) son de Diego y Tina.

**C**  1. Mi, azul
2. Nuestros, negros
3. Su, amarilla
4. Tus, blancos
5. Sus, rojos

## Practice 3-4

1. Sí, sé deletrear en español. / No, no sé deletrear en español.
2. Sí, traigo un sacapuntas a la escuela. / No, no traigo un sacapuntas a la escuela.
3. Salgo de la escuela a la(s) (*number*).
4. Sí, conozco a todos los estudiantes. / No, no conozco a todos los estudiantes.
5. Sí, doy mucha tarea. / No, no doy mucha tarea.
6. Sí, hago mucho trabajo en la escuela. / No, no hago mucho trabajo en la escuela.

## Practice 3-5

**A**

| d | u | é | r | m | e | t | e |

| n | o | l | l | o | r | e | s |

| l | e | v | á | n | t | a | t | e |

| n | o | p | e | l | e | e | s |

| n | o | c | o | r | r | a | s |

| n | o | t | e | p | o | r | t | e | s | m | a | l |

| a | c | u | é | s | t | a | t | e |

| p | ó | r | t | a | t | e | b | i | e | n |

**B**
1. me
2. se
3. nos
4. te
5. se

**C**
1. lo
2. las
3. te
4. la
5. los

**D**
1. a
2. X
3. X
4. a
5. X
6. a

## Summary Practice

1. ¿Conoces al director / a la directora?
2. ¿Cuándo es la reunión? / ¿A qué hora es la reunión?
3. ¿Qué tiempo va a hacer mañana?
4. Está lloviendo.
5. Mi bufanda es blanca y negra.
6. ¿De quién es el abrigo?
7. El vestido está de moda.
8. ¿De qué color es la camisa?
9. Escríbelo en la pizarra.
10. No las pongas en tu mochila.
11. Guarden los juguetes.
12. Pórtense bien.

# Chapter 4

## Practice 4-1

1. conozco
2. sabemos
3. saben
4. Conoces
5. sabe
6. sé
7. conocen
8. conoce

## Practice 4-2

**A**  *Answers will vary. Possible answers:* una subasta, un concurso, una fiesta, un baile, una rifa, un sorteo, una función.

**B**
1. el museo
2. el parque zoológico / la granja / el acuario
3. el parque de atracciones
4. el ayuntamiento
5. la casa de bomberos
6. la biblioteca

**C**  *Answers will vary. Possible answers:*
1. Los padres tienen que firmar la carta.
2. Uds. tienen que traer el almuerzo.
3. Avíseme si Ud. está dispuesto a acompañarnos.

**D**
1. Toma a tu / Tomen a su compañero de la mano.
2. Súbete/Súbanse al autobús.
3. Ponte/Pónganse en fila.

# Chapter 5

## Practice 5-1

*Answers will vary.*
1. Es aconsejable traer una nota de tu/su padre.
2. Es mejor llamar a un compañero de clase.
3. Es necesario prestar atención.
4. Es bueno hacer la tarea todos los días.
5. Hay que estudiar regularmente.

## Practice 5-2

1. Podemos
2. puedes
3. pueden
4. puede
5. puedo
6. pueden

## Practice 5-3

*Answers will vary.*
1. No, (ellos) no pueden pelear en el patio. Se prohíbe pelear en la escuela.
2. No, (yo) no puedo llegar tarde. Se prohíbe llegar tarde a la escuela.
3. No, (tú) no puedes comer fuera de la cafetería. Se prohíbe comer fuera de la cafetería en la escuela.
4. No, (ella) no puede salir sin permiso. Se prohíbe salir de la escuela sin permiso.
5. No, (Uds.) no pueden / (nosotros) no podemos jugar en los pasillos. Se prohíbe jugar en los pasillos de la escuela.

## Practice 5-4

**A**
1. (Tú) tienes que estudiar ahora.
2. (Uds.) tienen que / (Nosotros) tenemos que asistir a clases de repaso.
3. (Yo) tengo que trabajar con un profesor / una profesora particular.
4. (Ellos) tienen que quedarse en la escuela después de las clases.

**B**
1. Nosotros vamos a estudiar en la biblioteca más tarde.
2. Ellos van a asistir a las clases de repaso mañana por la tarde.
3. Tú vas a hacer el examen la semana próxima.
4. Yo voy a hacer la tarea mañana por la mañana.
5. Ud. va a llamar al director pasado mañana.

**C**
1. peleas, vas
2. asistimos, vamos
3. usa, va
4. salen, va
5. hablo, van

## Practice 5-5

1. cansado
2. ansiosos/furiosos
3. sorprendidos
4. avergonzado/avergonzada / ansioso/ansiosa
5. aburridos
6. ocupada/furiosa
7. sorprendido/sorprendida / avergonzado/avergonzada / ansioso/ansiosa / furioso/furiosa

## Practice 5-6

**A**
1. vengan
2. leas
3. coman
4. entregues
5. sea
6. sepan
7. hable
8. repasemos

**B**
1. estudies temprano
2. vengan a tiempo
3. estudies en la biblioteca
4. no vayan al parque hoy
5. sepa cuando (tú) estás / (Ud.) está ausente / (Uds.) están ausentes
6. coman en los pasillos
7. participe más en clase
8. hable con Ud. / contigo
9. copien la tarea de otro estudiante
10. salgas bien en el examen

## Summary Practice

1. Al regresar a la escuela, su hijo/hija tiene que traer una nota firmada por Ud.
2. Es importante prestar atención.
3. Para salir bien, (tú) tienes que hacer preguntas cuando no comprendes.
4. Se prohíbe gritar en los pasillos.
5. Tienes que hacer el examen otra vez.
6. Uds. van a tener un examen la semana próxima / que viene.
7. Si se porta mal, (ella) no puede participar en los deportes.
8. ¡Qué tarea más/tan estupenda!

9. (Yo) espero que / Ojalá que estudies mucho.
10. Es importante que (él) duerma por lo menos ocho horas cada noche.

# Chapter 6

## Practice 6-1

```
U N M N L O S M A R E O S S E
Z Q R K S Z X X L O P C G H B
N G K D E A L G E R A L A L K
L H A D L A P S E A L C J A U
É L J O R S I I Y R C T D F T
R A D D E L D O L O R Z Y L W
B F N A L A T O S P P B D E G
E K U T L C E L H I P O L M U
I B M O Y A T N A G R A G A L
F O U G D Y E Z F K S D L Q P
A N L A N G L I B E D S N Q Y
L N Q C D E O D I O L E A K R
A D X R B V S O J O I P S O L
W D K K L A E R U P C I O N J
I L X O X P O X L R Z F K S W
```

## Practice 6-2

**A**
1. corrió
2. pasó
3. respiré
4. abriste
5. aprendimos
6. salieron
7. calificó
8. asistí
9. comprendieron
10. tomamos

**B**
1. ayer
2. ayer por la tarde
3. anoche
4. el verano pasado
5. ayer por la mañana
6. el lunes pasado

**C**
1. tosieron, anteayer
2. visitó, el viernes pasado
3. dio, el martes pasado
4. asistimos, anteanoche
5. saliste, ayer

## Practice 6-3

1. Nos
2. Me
3. te
4. Le
5. Les
6. Le

## Practice 6-4

1. ¡Socorro!
2. ¡Fuego!
3. ¡No griten!
4. ¡Cuidado!
5. ¡Dense prisa!
6. ¡Pónganse debajo del pupitre!
7. ¡Caminen tranquilamente!
8. ¡Cúbranse la cabeza!

### Summary Practice

1. Tienes que ir a la oficina del enfermero / de la enfermera.
2. ¿Tienes dolor de garganta?
3. Se siente / Está mareada.
4. ¿Qué le pasó?
5. Él se rompió el pie.
6. Tienes que guardar cama.
7. ¿Te duele el cuello?
8. Tengo dolor de muelas.
9. Hay humo en los pasillos.
10. ¡Cúbranse la boca!

## Chapter 7

### Practice 7-1

**A**
1. bien
2. mejor
3. mucho
4. despacio
5. un poco
6. peor

**B**
1. de vez en cuando
2. rara vez
3. una vez
4. muchas veces
5. dos veces
6. a veces

### Practice 7-2

**A**
1. Nunca estudio. / No estudio nunca.
2. Nosotros no comemos en la cafetería.
3. Nadie corre en el parque.
4. ¿No lees ninguna novela?
5. Ellos no caminan en el parque tampoco.
6. Nadie va a la fiesta.

**B**
1. No, no estoy nervioso nunca.
2. No, no tengo ningún trabajo nunca.
3. No, no visito a mis tíos nunca.
4. No, no compro ninguna ropa en la tienda nunca.
5. No, no como el almuerzo en la escuela nunca.
6. No, no hay nadie en el pasillo nunca.
7. No, no quiero beber nada nunca.
8. No, no voy a la escuela los sábados tampoco.

### Practice 7-3

1. está suspendida
2. llenar una solicitud de empleo
3. a tiempo parcial
4. un programa para controlar la cólera
5. pasar por un entrenamiento
6. un permiso de trabajo
7. una entrevista
8. mantenerte al tanto de tu trabajo / tus tareas para la escuela

## Practice 7-4

**A**  *Answers will vary.*

1. ¿Te gusta cocinar?
2. ¿Te gusta actuar?
3. ¿Te gusta sacar fotos?
4. ¿Te gusta trabajar al aire libre?
5. ¿Te gusta trabajar con computadoras?

**B**

| | |
|---|---|
| 1. Este | 5. estos |
| 2. aquellas | 6. aquel |
| 3. Esta | 7. Esas |
| 4. Esa | 8. Esos |

## Practice 7-5

1. Acabamos de
2. (Él) acaba de
3. (Ella) acaba de
4. (Ellos) acaban de
5. (Yo) acabo de

## Practice 7-6

*Answers will vary.*

1. Los estudiantes tienen que ir a la escuela de verano cuando suspenden una asignatura. Si el estudiante aprueba los cursos de la escuela de verano, puede avanzar al próximo grado.
2. El examen de GED incluye escritura, lectura, estudios sociales, ciencia y matemáticas. Si un estudiante aprueba el examen de GED, él/ella va a recibir un diploma equivalente a un diploma de escuela secundaria.
3. Si un estudiante tiene mucha dificultad para aprender a leer, escribir, escuchar, hablar o con las matemáticas, es posible que tenga una discapacidad de aprendizaje.
4. Un impedimento visual no permite que un estudiante vea todo lo que necesita ver y puede impedir que aprenda.
5. Un audífono / aparato de oído ayuda a las personas que no oyen bien a oír mejor.
6. Cuando un estudiante no puede estar sentado, enfocar su atención en el trabajo ni controlar sus impulsos es posible que tenga un desorden deficitario de la atención.

## Summary Practice

**A**

| | |
|---|---|
| 1. j | 7. k |
| 2. e | 8. b |
| 3. h | 9. f |
| 4. g | 10. l |
| 5. i | 11. d |
| 6. c | 12. a |

**B**

1. Esa clase es demasiado avanzada y tú no tienes los requisitos.
2. El programa bilingüe es un programa de transición.
3. Su hijo/hija tiene que asistir a la escuela de verano.
4. Su hijo/hija interpreta mal las palabras cuando lee.
5. Los estudiantes no deben fumar en el patio de la escuela.

**C**  1. está inquieto / está asustado
2. está perdido / está frustrado
3. estamos cansados
4. estás asustada / estás inquieta / estás preocupada
5. están frustradas / están perdidas

**D**  1. estoy
2. eres
3. son
4. son
5. están
6. es
7. es
8. está

# English–Spanish Glossary

## A

**a/an** un/una [oon/oo-nah]

**a little** un poco [oon POH-koh]

**a lot** mucho [MOO-choh]

**able, to be** poder (ue) (*irreg.*) [poh-DEHR]

**about the middle of** a mediados de
[ah meh-DYAH-dohs deh]

**absent** ausente [ah-oo-SEHN-teh]

**abuse (physical)** el abuso físico
[ehl ah-BOO-soh FEE-see-koh]

**abuse (sexual)** el abuso sexual
[ehl ah-BOO-soh sehk-SWAHL]

**academic prize** el premio académico
[ehl PREH-myoh ah-kah-DEH-mee-koh]

**accident** el accidente
[ehl ahk-see-DEHN-teh]

**accountant** el contador/la contadora
[ehl kohn-tah-DOHR/
lah kohn-tah-DOH-rah]

**acne** el acné [ehl ahk-NEH]

**acquainted with, to be** conocer (*irreg.*)
[koh-noh-SEHR]

**actor** el actor [ehl ahk-TOHR]

**actress** la actriz [lah ahk-TREES]

**address** la dirección
[lah dee-rehk-SYOHN]

**administrator** el administrador/
la administradora
[ehl ahd-mee-nees-trah-DOHR/
lah ahd-mee-nees-trah-DOH-rah]

**admission exam** el examen de ingreso
[ehl ehk-SAH-mehn deh een-GREH-soh]

**advanced** avanzado [ah-bahn-SAH-doh]

**advice** el consejo [ehl kohn-SEH-hoh]

**afraid** asustado [ah-soos-TAH-doh]

**afraid, to be** tener (*irreg.*) miedo
[teh-NEHR MYEH-doh]

**afterwards** después [dehs-PWEHS]

**aide** el/la asistente
[ehl/lah ah-sees-TEHN-teh]

**AIDS** el SIDA [ehl SEE-dah]

**air conditioning** el aire acondicionado
[ehl AH-ee-reh
ah-kohn-dee-syoh-NAH-doh]

**Air Force** las fuerzas aéreas
[lahs FWEHR-sahs ah-EH-reh-ahs]

**aisle** el pasillo [ehl pah-SEE-yoh]

**alcoholic** alcohólico [ahl-KOH-lee-koh]

**alcoholism** el alcoholismo
[ehl ahl-koh-LEES-moh]

**allergy** la alergia [lah ah-LEHR-hyah]

**alley** el callejón [ehl kah-yeh-HOHN]

**alphabet** el abecedario
[ehl ah-beh-seh-DAH-ryoh];
el alfabeto [ehl ahl-fah-BEH-toh]

**already** ya [yah]

**also** también [tahm-BYEHN]

**always** siempre [SYEHM-preh]

**anger management program**
el programa para controlar la cólera
[ehl proh-GRAH-mah PAH-rah
kohn-troh-LAHR lah KOH-leh-rah]

**angry** enfadado [ehn-fah-DAH-doh];
enojado [eh-noh-HAH-doh]

**animal** el animal [ehl ah-nee-MAHL]

**ankle** el tobillo [ehl toh-BEE-yoh]

**announce, to** anunciar [ah-noon-SYAHR]

**announcer (radio/TV)** el locutor/
la locutora [ehl loh-koo-TOHR/
lah loh-koo-TOH-rah]

**another** otro [OH-troh]

**answer** la respuesta
[lah rrehs-PWEHS-tah]

**antacid** el antiácido
[ehl ahn-TYAH-see-doh]

**antibiotic** el antibiótico
[ehl ahn-tee-BYOH-tee-koh]

**antihistamine** el antihistamínico
[ehl ahn-tees-tah-MEE-nee-koh]

**antiseptic** el antiséptico
[ehl ahn-tee-SEHP-tee-koh]

**anxious** ansioso [ahn-SYOH-soh]

**anybody** alguien [AHL-gyehn]

**applaud, to** aplaudir [ah-plah-oo-DEER]

**application** la solicitud
[lah soh-lee-see-TOOD]

**appointment** la cita [lah SEE-tah]

**April** abril [ah-BREEL]

**apron** el delantal [ehl deh-lahn-TAHL]

**architect** el arquitecto / la arquitecta
[ehl ahr-kee-TEHK-toh /
lah ahr-kee-TEHK-tah]

**argue, to** discutir [dees-koo-TEER]

**arm** el brazo [ehl BRAH-soh]

**Army** las fuerzas armadas
[lahs FWEHR-sahs ahr-MAH-dahs];
el ejército [ehl eh-HEHR-see-toh]

**around** alrededor [ahl-rreh-deh-DOHR]

**arrive, to** llegar [yeh-GAHR]

**arson** el incendio premeditado [ehl
een-SEHN-dyoh preh-meh-dee-TAH-doh]

**art** el arte [ehl AHR-teh]

**artistic** artístico [ahr-TEES-tee-koh]

**ashamed** avergonzado
[ah-behr-gohn-SAH-doh]

**ask, to** preguntar [preh-goon-TAHR]

**ask for, to** pedir (i) [peh-DEER]

**ask for permission, to** pedir (i) permiso
[peh-DEER pehr-MEE-soh]

**aspirin** la aspirina [lah ahs-pee-REE-nah]

**assistant principal (vice-principal)**
el/la asistente al director / a la directora
[ehl/lah ah-sees-TEHN-teh ahl
dee-rehk-TOHR / ah lah dee-rehk-TOH-rah]

**assure, to** asegurar [ah-seh-goo-RAHR]

**asthma** el asma [ehl AHS-mah]

**astronaut** el/la astronauta
[ehl/lah ahs-troh-NAH-oo-tah]

**at once** en seguida [ehn seh-GEE-dah]

**at the beginning of** a principios de
[ah preen-SEE-pyohs deh]

**at the end of** a fines de [ah FEE-nehs deh]

**athletic** atlético [ah-TLEH-tee-koh]

**attempted murder** el intento de
asesinato [ehl een-TEHN-toh deh
ah-seh-see-NAH-toh]

**attend, to** asistir [ah-sees-TEER]

**attendance** la asistencia
[lah ah-sees-TEHN-syah]

**attention deficit disorder** el desorden
deficitario de la atención
[ehl dehs-OHR-dehn deh-fee-see-TAH-ryoh
deh lah ah-tehn-SYOHN]

**auditorium** el auditorio
[ehl ah-oo-dee-TOH-ryoh];
el salón / la sala de actos
[ehl sah-LOHN / lah SAH-lah deh AHK-tohs]

**August** agosto [ah-GOHS-toh]

**aunt** la tía [lah TEE-ah]

**author** el autor / la autora
[ehl ah-oo-TOHR / lah ah-oo-TOH-rah]

**autism** el autismo [ehl ah-oo-TEES-moh];
el trastorno generalizado del desarrollo
[ehl trahs-TOHR-noh heh-neh-rah-lee-
SAH-doh dehl deh-sah-RROH-yoh]

**autumn** el otoño [ehl oh-TOH-nyoh]

**avenue** la avenida [lah ah-beh-NEE-dah]

# B

**back** la espalda [lah ehs-PAHL-dah]

**backache** el dolor de espalda
[ehl doh-LOHR deh ehs-PAHL-dah]

**backpack** la mochila [lah moh-CHEE-lah]

**bacon** el tocino [ehl toh-SEE-noh]

**bad grades, to get** sacar malas notas
[sah-KAHR MAH-lahs NOH-tahs]

**badly** mal [mahl]

**bag** la bolsa [lah BOHL-sah]

**baker** el panadero / la panadera
[ehl pah-nah-DEH-roh /
lah pah-nah-DEH-rah]

**ball** la pelota [lah peh-LOH-tah]; el balón
[ehl bah-LOHN]

**balloon** el globo [ehl GLOH-boh]

**ballpoint pen** el bolígrafo
[ehl boh-LEE-grah-foh]

**banana** el plátano [ehl PLAH-tah-noh]

**bandage** la venda [lah BEHN-dah]

**bandage, to** vendar [behn-DAHR]

**Band-Aid®** la curita® / la tirita®
[lah koo-REE-tah / lah tee-REE-tah]

**barber** el barbero [ehl bahr-BEH-roh]

**basement** el sótano [ehl SOH-tah-noh]

**bathing suit** el traje de baño
[ehl TRAH-heh deh BAH-nyoh]

**bathroom** el cuarto de baño
[ehl KWAHR-toh deh BAH-nyoh]

**bathroom (boy's/girl's)** el baño (para
niños/niñas) [ehl BAH-nyoh (PAH-rah
NEE-nyohs/NEE-nyahs)]

**battery** la batería [lah bah-teh-REE-ah]

**battery (physical)** el maltrato
[ehl mahl-TRAH-toh]

**be, to** estar (*irreg.*) [ehs-TAHR]; ser (*irreg.*)
[sehr]

**bean** el frijol [ehl free-HOHL]

**beard** la barba [lah BAHR-bah]

**bed** la cama [lah KAH-mah]

**before** antes [AHN-tehs]

**begin, to** comenzar (ie) [koh-mehn-
SAHR]; empezar (ie) [ehm-peh-SAHR]

**beginning** el principio
[ehl preen-SEE-pyoh]

**behave oneself, to** portarse bien
[pohr-TAHR-seh byehn]

**behavior** el comportamiento
[ehl kohm-pohr-tah-MYEHN-toh]

**behind** detrás de [deh-TRAHS deh]

**bell (electric)** el timbre [ehl TEEM-breh]

**bell (hand)** la campana
[lah kahm-PAH-nah]

**belt** el cinturón [ehl seen-too-ROHN]

**bench** el banco [ehl BAHN-koh]

**better** mejor [meh-HOHR]

**better, to get** mejorarse
[meh-hoh-RAHR-seh]

**bicycle** la bicicleta
[lah bee-see-KLEH-tah]

**birth** el nacimiento
[ehl nah-see-MYEHN-toh]

**bite, to** morder (ue) [mohr-DEHR]

**bitter** amargado [ah-mahr-GAH-doh]

**black** negro [NEH-groh]

**blackout** el apagón [ehl ah-pah-GOHN]

**bleed, to** sangrar [sahn-GRAHR]

**blindness** la ceguera [lah seh-GEH-rah]

**blister** la ampolla [lah ahm-POH-yah]

**block (city)** la cuadra [lah KWAH-drah]

**blocks (wooden)** los bloques (de madera)
[lohs BLOH-kehs (deh mah-DEH-rah)]

**blood** la sangre [lah SAHN-greh]

**blood pressure (high/low)** la presión
arterial (alta/baja) [lah preh-SYOHN
ahr-teh-RYAHL (AHL-tah/BAH-hah)]

**blouse** la blusa [lah BLOO-sah]

**blue** azul [ah-SOOL]

**board member** el miembro de la junta
directiva [ehl MYEHM-broh deh lah
HOON-tah dee-rehk-TEE-bah]

**body** el cuerpo [ehl KWEHR-poh]

**boiler** la caldera [lah kahl-DEH-rah]

**bomb explosion** el estallido de una
bomba [ehl ehs-tah-YEE-doh deh oo-nah
BOHM-bah]

**bomb scare** la amenaza de bomba
[lah ah-meh-NAH-sah deh BOHM-bah]

**book** el libro [ehl LEE-broh]

**bookcase** la estantería
[lah ehs-tahn-teh-REE-ah]

**bored** aburrido [ah-boo-RREE-doh]

**borrow, to** pedir (i) prestado
[peh-DEER prehs-TAH-doh]

**both** ambos [AHM-bohs]

**bottle** la botella [lah boh-TEH-yah]

**boulevard** el paseo [ehl pah-SEH-oh]

**bounce (ball), to** hacer (*irreg.*) rebotar
(la pelota) [ah-SEHR rreh-boh-TAHR
(lah peh-LOH-tah)]

**box** la caja [lah KAH-hah]

**box office** la taquilla [lah tah-KEE-yah]

**boy** el niño [ehl NEE-nyoh]

**boyfriend** el novio [ehl NOH-byoh]

**bra** el sostén [ehl sohs-TEHN]

**brace** el corrector [ehl koh-rrehk-TOHR]

**brain** el cerebro [ehl seh-REH-broh]

**bread** el pan [ehl pahn]

**break, to** romper [rrohm-PEHR];
romperse [rrohm-PEHR-seh]

**breakfast** el desayuno
[ehl deh-sah-YOO-noh]

**breathe, to** respirar [rrehs-pee-RAHR]

**breathless** sin respiración
[seen rrehs-pee-rah-SYOHN]

**bridge** el puente [ehl PWEHN-teh]

**briefs** los calzoncillos
[lohs kahl-sohn-SEE-yohs]

**bring, to** traer (*irreg.*) [trah-EHR]

**broccoli** el brécol [ehl BREH-kohl]

**broken** roto [RROH-toh]

**bronchitis** la bronquitis
[lah brohn-KEE-tees]

**broom** la escoba [lah ehs-KOH-bah]

**brother** el hermano [ehl ehr-MAH-noh]

**brother-in-law** el cuñado
[ehl koo-NYAH-doh]

**brown** marrón [mah-RROHN]

**bruise** el moretón [ehl moh-reh-TOHN]

**brush (artist's)** el pincel [ehl peen-SEHL]

**brush one's hair, to** cepillarse el pelo
[seh-pee-YAHR-seh ehl PEH-loh]

**brush one's teeth, to** cepillarse los
dientes
[seh-pee-YAHR-seh lohs DYEHN-tehs]

**bucket** el balde [ehl BAHL-deh];
el cubo [ehl KOO-boh]

**building** el edificio [ehl eh-dee-FEE-syoh]

**building site** el solar [ehl soh-LAHR]

**bullying** la intimidación
[lah een-tee-mee-dah-SYOHN]

**burn** la quemadura
[lah keh-mah-DOO-rah]

**burn, to** quemar [keh-MAHR]

**burn up, to** quemarse [keh-MAHR-seh]

**burned** quemado [keh-MAH-doh]

**bus** el autobús [ehl ah-oo-toh-BOOS]

**bus stop** la parada de autobuses
[lah pah-RAH-dah deh ah-oo-toh-BOO-sehs]

**businessman** el hombre de negocios
[ehl OHM-breh deh neh-GOH-syohs]

**businesswoman** la mujer de negocios
[lah moo-HEHR deh neh-GOH-syohs]

**busy** ocupado [oh-koo-PAH-doh]

**butcher** el carnicero / la carnicera [ehl
kahr-nee-SEH-roh / lah kahr-nee-SEH-rah]

**butter** la mantequilla
[lah mahn-teh-KEE-yah]

**button** el botón [ehl boh-TOHN]

**button up, to** abrocharse
[ah-broh-CHAHR-seh]

## C

**cafeteria** la cafetería
[lah kah-feh-teh-REE-ah]

**cake** el bizcocho [ehl bees-KOH-choh]

**calculator** la calculadora
[lah kahl-koo-lah-DOH-rah]

**calendar** el calendario
[ehl kah-lehn-DAH-ryoh]

**call, to** llamar [yah-MAHR]

**calm** tranquilo [trahn-KEE-loh]

**calm down, to** tranquilizarse
[trahn-kee-lee-SAHR-seh]

**cancer** el cáncer [ehl KAHN-sehr]

**candle** la vela [lah BEH-lah]

**cane** el bastón [ehl bahs-TOHN]

**cap** la gorra [lah GOH-rrah]

**cards (playing)** las cartas
[lahs KAHR-tahs]

**career** la carrera [lah kah-RREH-rah]

**careful** cuidadoso [kwee-dah-DOH-soh]

**carpenter** el carpintero / la carpintera
[ehl kahr-peen-TEH-roh /
lah kahr-peen-TEH-rah]

**carpet** la alfombra [lah ahl-FOHM-brah]

**carrot** la zanahoria
[lah sah-nah-OH-ryah]

**cart (small)** el carretón
[ehl kah-rreh-TOHN]

**cashier** el cajero / la cajera
[ehl kah-HEH-roh / lah kah-HEH-rah]

**catalogue** el catálogo
[ehl kah-TAH-loh-goh]

**ceiling** el techo [ehl TEH-choh]

**cell phone** el celular [ehl seh-loo-LAHR]

**cereal** el cereal [ehl seh-reh-AHL]

**cerebral palsy** la parálisis cerebral
[lah pah-RAH-lee-sees seh-reh-BRAHL]

**chair** la silla [lah SEE-yah]

**chairperson (of the _____ department)**
el jefe / la jefa (de la cátedra de _____)
[ehl HEH-feh / lah HEH-fah
(deh lah KAH-teh-drah deh)]

**chalk** la tiza [lah TEE-sah]

**chalkboard** la pizarra [lah pee-SAH-rrah]

**chapter** el capítulo [ehl kah-PEE-too-loh]

**character** el personaje
[ehl pehr-soh-NAH-heh]

**checkers** las damas [lahs DAH-mahs]

**cheek** la mejilla [lah meh-HEE-yah]

**cheese** el queso [ehl KEH-soh]

**chess** el ajedrez [ehl ah-heh-DREHS]

**chest** el pecho [ehl PEH-choh]

**chew, to** masticar [mahs-tee-KAHR]

**chicken** el pollo [ehl POH-yoh]

**chicken pox** la varicela
[lah bah-ree-SEH-lah]

**child** el niño / la niña
[ehl NEE-nyoh / lah NEE-nyah]

**child abuse** el maltrato de niños
[ehl mahl-TRAH-toh deh NEE-nyohs]

**chills** los escalofríos
[lohs ehs-kah-loh-FREE-ohs]

**chin** la barbilla [lah bahr-BEE-yah]

**Christmas** la Navidad
[lah nah-bee-DAHD]

**city** la ciudad [lah see-oo-DAHD]

**classroom** el aula [ehl AH-oo-lah];
el salón de clases
[ehl sah-LOHN deh KLAH-sehs]

**clean** limpio [LEEM-pyoh]

**clean, to** limpiar [leem-PYAHR]

**clear (weather)** despejado
[dehs-peh-HAH-doh]

**clerk** el/la dependiente
[ehl/lah deh-pehn-DYEHN-teh]

**climb, to** subir [soo-BEER]

**clinic** la clínica [lah KLEE-nee-kah]

**clock** el reloj [ehl rreh-LOH]

**close, to** cerrar (ie) [seh-RRAHR]

**closet** el armario [ehl ahr-MAH-ryoh]

**clothing** la ropa [lah RROH-pah]

**clothing style** el estilo de ropa
[ehl ehs-TEE-loh deh RROH-pah]

**cloudy** nublado [noo-BLAH-doh]

**coach (sports)** el entrenador / la entrenadora [ehl ehn-treh-nah-DOHR / lah ehn-treh-nah-DOH-rah]

**coat** el abrigo [ehl ah-BREE-goh]; el sobretodo [ehl soh-breh-TOH-doh]

**coffee** el café [ehl kah-FEH]

**cold** frío [FREE-oh]

**cold (common cold)** el catarro [ehl kah-TAH-rroh]; el resfriado [ehl rrehs-FRYAH-doh]

**cold, to be/feel** tener (*irreg.*) frío [teh-NEHR FREE-oh]

**colic** el cólico [ehl KOH-lee-koh]

**color** el color [ehl koh-LOHR]

**color, to** colorear [koh-loh-reh-AHR]

**coloring book** el libro de colorear [ehl LEE-broh deh koh-loh-reh-AHR]

**Columbus Day** el día de la Raza [ehl DEE-ah deh lah RRAH-sah]

**come, to** venir (*irreg.*) [beh-NEER]

**comfortable** cómodo [KOH-moh-doh]

**compass** el compás [ehl kohm-PAHS]

**computer** la computadora [lah kohm-poo-tah-DOH-rah]

**computer lab** el laboratorio de computadoras [ehl lah-boh-rah-TOH-ryoh deh kohm-poo-tah-DOH-rahs]

**concentrate, to** concentrarse [kohn-sehn-TRAHR-seh]

**conflict resolution program** el programa para resolver conflictos [ehl proh-GRAH-mah PAH-rah rreh-sohl-BEHR kohn-FLEEK-tohs]

**constipation** el estreñimiento [ehl ehs-treh-nyee-MYEHN-toh]

**consultant** el consultor / la consultora [ehl kohn-sool-TOHR / lah kohn-sool-TOH-rah]; el asesor / la asesora [ehl ah-seh-SOHR / lah ah-seh-SOH-rah]

**contagious** contagioso [kohn-tah-HYOH-soh]

**cook** el cocinero / la cocinera [ehl koh-see-NEH-roh / lah koh-see-NEH-rah]

**cookie** la galletita [lah gah-yeh-TEE-tah]

**cool** fresco [FREHS-koh]

**cooperate, to** cooperar [koh-oh-peh-RAHR]

**copy, to** copiar [koh-PYAHR]

**copy machine** la copiadora [lah koh-pyah-DOH-rah]

**copy machine ink** la tinta de copiar [lah TEEN-tah deh koh-PYAHR]

**copy machine room** el cuarto de la copiadora [ehl KWAHR-toh deh lah koh-pyah-DOH-rah]

**corn** el maíz [ehl mah-EES]

**corner (inside)** el rincón [ehl rreen-KOHN]

**corner (outside)** la esquina [lah ehs-KEE-nah]

**correspondence** la correspondencia [lah koh-rrehs-pohn-DEHN-syah]

**cost, to** costar (ue) [kohs-TAHR]

**costume** el disfraz [ehl dees-FRAHS]

**cotton** el algodón [ehl ahl-goh-DOHN]

**cough** la tos [lah tohs]

**cough, to** toser [toh-SEHR]

**cough syrup** el jarabe para la tos [ehl hah-RAH-beh PAH-rah lah tohs]

**counseling** el asesoramiento [ehl ah-seh-soh-rah-MYEHN-toh]

**counseling office** la oficina del consejero / de la consejera [lah oh-fee-SEE-nah dehl kohn-seh-HEH-roh / deh lah kohn-seh-HEH-rah]

**counselor (advisor)** el consejero / la consejera [ehl kohn-seh-HEH-roh / lah kohn-seh-HEH-rah]

**count, to** contar (ue) [kohn-TAHR]

**counter** el mostrador [ehl mohs-trah-DOHR]

**country** el país [ehl pah-EES]

**cousin** el primo / la prima [ehl PREE-moh / lah PREE-mah]

**cramp** el calambre [ehl kah-LAHM-breh]

**crayons** los lápices para pintar [lohs LAH-pee-sehs PAH-rah peen-TAHR]

**cream (ointment)** la pomada [lah poh-MAH-dah]

**cream cheese** el queso crema [ehl KEH-soh KREH-mah]

**creative** creativo [kreh-ah-TEE-boh]

**cross, to** cruzar [kroo-SAHR]

**crossing guard** la persona encargada de ayudar a los niños a cruzar la calle [lah pehr-SOH-nah ehn-kahr-GAH-dah deh ah-yoo-DAHR ah lohs NEE-nyohs ah kroo-SAHR lah KAH-yeh]

**crutches** las muletas [lahs moo-LEH-tahs]

**cry, to** llorar [yoh-RAHR]

**cucumber** el pepino [ehl peh-PEE-noh]

**curb** el contén [ehl kohn-TEHN]

**curriculum**  el plan de estudio
[ehl plahn deh ehs-TOO-dyoh]

**curse, to**  decir (*irreg.*) malas palabras
[deh-SEER MAH-lahs pah-LAH-brahs]

**curse words**  las malas palabras
[lahs MAH-lahs pah-LAH-brahs]

**curtain**  el telón  [ehl teh-LOHN]

**custodian**  el guardián / la guardiana
[ehl gwahr-DYAHN / lah gwahr-DYAH-nah]

**cut, to**  cortar(se)  [kohr-TAHR(seh)]

## D

**dad(dy)**  el papá  [ehl pah-PAH]

**daily**  a diario  [ah DYAH-ryoh];
diariamente  [dyah-ryah-MEHN-teh]

**danger**  el peligro  [ehl peh-LEE-groh]

**date (appointment)**  la cita  [lah SEE-tah]

**date (on calendar)**  la fecha
[lah FEH-chah]

**daughter**  la hija  [lah EE-hah]

**daughter-in-law**  la nuera  [lah NWEH-rah]

**day**  el día  [ehl DEE-ah]

**day after tomorrow**  pasado mañana
[pah-SAH-doh mah-NYAH-nah]

**day before yesterday**  anteayer
[ahn-teh-ah-YEHR]

**deadline**  la fecha límite  [lah FEH-chah
LEE-mee-teh]

**December**  diciembre  [dee-SYEHM-breh]

**deeply**  profundamente
[proh-foon-dah-MEHN-teh]

**defibrillator**  el desfibrilador
[ehl dehs-fee-bree-lah-DOHR]

**dehydrated**  deshidratado
[dehs-ee-drah-TAH-doh]

**demanding**  exigente  [ehk-see-HEHN-teh]

**denim**  la mezclilla  [lah mehs-KLEE-yah]

**depressed**  deprimido
[deh-pree-MEE-doh]

**desk**  el escritorio  [ehl ehs-kree-TOH-ryoh]

**desk (student)**  el pupitre
[ehl poo-PEE-treh]

**dessert**  el postre  [ehl POHS-treh]

**detention room**  el aula de castigo
[ehl AH-oo-lah deh kahs-TEE-goh]

**development**  el desarrollo
[ehl dehs-ah-RROH-yoh]

**diabetes**  la diabetes  [lah dyah-BEH-tehs]

**diarrhea**  la diarrea  [lah dyah-RREH-ah]

**dictionary**  el diccionario
[ehl deek-syoh-NAH-ryoh]

**die, to**  morir (ue)  [moh-REER]

**dinner**  la cena  [lah SEH-nah]

**diphtheria**  la difteria  [lah deef-TEH-ryah]

**discrimination**  la discriminación
[lah dees-kree-mee-nah-SYOHN]

**disobey, to**  desobedecer (*irreg.*)
[dehs-oh-beh-deh-SEHR]

**disrespectful, to be**  faltar el respeto
[fahl-TAHR ehl rrehs-PEH-toh]

**dizziness**  el mareo  [ehl mah-REH-oh]

**dizzy**  mareado  [mah-reh-AH-doh]

**dizzy, to get**  marearse
[mah-reh-AHR-seh]

**do, to**  hacer (*irreg.*)  [ah-SEHR]

**doctor**  el doctor / la doctora
[ehl dohk-TOHR / lah dohk-TOH-rah];
el médico / la médica
[ehl MEH-dee-koh / lah MEH-dee-kah]

**doctor's office**  la consulta del médico /
de la médica  [lah kohn-SOOL-tah dehl
MEH-dee-koh / deh lah MEH-dee-kah]

**doll**  la muñeca  [lah moo-NYEH-kah]

**domestic violence**  la violencia doméstica
[lah byoh-LEHN-syah doh-MEHS-tee-kah]

**door**  la puerta  [lah PWEHR-tah]

**down the street**  calle abajo
[KAH-yeh ah-BAH-hoh]

**Down's syndrome**  el síndrome de Down
[ehl SEEN-droh-meh deh DAH-oon]

**downpour**  el aguacero
[ehl ah-gwah-SEH-roh]

**draw, to**  dibujar  [dee-boo-HAHR]

**drawer**  el cajón  [ehl kah-HOHN]

**dress**  el vestido  [ehl behs-TEE-doh]

**dress, to**  vestir (i)  [behs-TEER]

**dressed, to get**  vestirse (i)
[behs-TEER-seh]

**dressy**  vistoso  [bees-TOH-soh]

**drink**  la bebida  [lah beh-BEE-dah]

**drink, to**  beber  [beh-BEHR]

**driver**  el chofer  [ehl choh-FEHR];
el conductor / la conductora
[ehl kohn-dook-TOHR /
lah kohn-dook-TOH-rah]

**driver's license**  la licencia de conducir
[lah lee-SEHN-syah deh kohn-doo-SEER]

**driveway**  la entrada (para carros)
[lah ehn-TRAH-dah (PAH-rah KAH-rrohs)]

**drizzle, to**  lloviznar  [yoh-bees-NAHR]

**drug abuse**  el abuso de drogas
[ehl ah-BOO-soh deh DROH-gahs]

**drug overdose**  la sobredosis (de drogas)
[lah soh-breh-DOH-sees (deh DROH-gahs)]

**dry your hands, to** secarse las manos
[seh-KAHR-seh lahs MAH-nohs]

**dust** el polvo [ehl POHL-boh]

**dust, to** sacudir [sah-koo-DEER]

**dust rag** el trapo [ehl TRAH-poh]

**dustpan** el recogedor de basura
[ehl rreh-koh-heh-DOHR deh bah-SOO-rah]

**dyslexia** la dislexia [lah dees-LEHK-syah]

# E

**each** cada [KAH-dah]

**each day** cada día [KAH-dah DEE-ah]

**ear** la oreja [lah oh-REH-hah]

**earache** el dolor de oído
[ehl doh-LOHR deh oh-EE-doh]

**early** temprano [tehm-PRAH-noh]

**earthquake** el terremoto
[ehl teh-rreh-MOH-toh]

**earwax** la cerilla [lah seh-REE-yah]

**Easter** la Pascua de Resurrección
[lah PAHS-kwah deh rreh-soo-rrehk-SYOHN]

**easy** fácil [FAH-seel]

**eat, to** comer [koh-MEHR]

**eat breakfast, to** desayunar
[deh-sah-yoo-NAHR]

**eat dinner, to** cenar [seh-NAHR]

**eat lunch, to** almorzar (ue)
[ahl-mohr-SAHR]

**egg** el huevo [ehl WEH-boh]

**elbow** el codo [ehl KOH-doh]

**electrician** el/la electricista
[ehl/lah eh-lehk-tree-SEES-tah]

**electronic organizer** el organizador
electrónico [ehl ohr-gah-nee-sah-DOHR
eh-lehk-TROH-nee-koh]

**elegant** elegante [eh-leh-GAHN-teh]

**elementary school** la escuela primaria
[lah ehs-KWEH-lah pree-MAH-ryah]

**elevator** el ascensor [ehl ah-sehn-SOHR]

**e-mail** el correo electrónico
[ehl koh-RREH-oh eh-lehk-TROH-nee-koh]

**embarrassed** avergonzado
[ah-behr-gohn-SAH-doh]

**emergency room** la sala de emergencia
[lah SAH-lah deh eh-mehr-HEHN-syah]

**emotional abuse** el abuso mental
[ehl ah-BOO-soh mehn-TAHL]

**emotional instability** la falta de
estabilidad emocional [lah FAHL-tah deh
ehs-tah-bee-lee-DAHD eh-moh-syoh-NAHL]

**emotional problems** los problemas
emocionales [lohs proh-BLEH-mahs
eh-moh-syoh-NAH-lehs]

**encourage, to** animar [ah-nee-MAHR]

**end** el fin [ehl feen]

**engineer** el ingeniero / la ingeniera
[ehl een-heh-NYEH-roh /
lah een-heh-NYEH-rah]

**enroll, to** matricular
[mah-tree-koo-LAHR]

**entrance** la entrada [lah ehn-TRAH-dah]

**envelope** el sobre [ehl SOH-breh]

**epidemic** la epidemia
[lah eh-pee-DEH-myah]

**epilepsy** la epilepsia
[lah eh-pee-LEHP-syah]

**erase, to** borrar [boh-RRAHR]

**eraser (chalkboard)** el borrador
(de pizarra)
[ehl boh-rrah-DOHR (deh pee-SAH-rrah)]

**eraser (rubber)** la goma de borrar
[lah GOH-mah deh boh-RRAHR]

**escalator** la escalera mecánica
[lah ehs-kah-LEH-rah meh-KAH-nee-kah]

**essay** el ensayo [ehl ehn-SAH-yoh]

**establish, to** establecer (*irreg.*)
[ehs-tah-bleh-SEHR]

**evacuation** la evacuación
[lah eh-bah-kwah-SYOHN]

**evaluate, to** evaluar [eh-bah-LWAHR]

**evening** la noche [lah NOH-cheh]

**every day** todos los días
[TOH-dohs lohs DEE-ahs]

**exam** la prueba [lah PRWEH-bah];
el examen [ehl ehk-SAH-mehn]

**examination (medical)**
el reconocimiento
[ehl rreh-koh-noh-see-MYEHN-toh]

**exhale, to** exhalar [ehk-sah-LAHR]

**exhausted** agotado [ah-goh-TAH-doh]

**exit** la salida [lah sah-LEE-dah]

**expensive** caro [KAH-roh]

**experience** la experiencia
[lah ehs-peh-RYEHN-syah]

**explosion** el estallido
[ehl ehs-tah-YEE-doh];
la explosión [lah ehs-ploh-SYOHN]

**extract a tooth, to** sacar una muela
[sah-KAHR OO-nah MWEH-lah]

**eye** el ojo [ehl OH-hoh]

**eye doctor** el/la oculista
[ehl/lah oh-koo-LEES-tah]

**eyebrow**   la ceja   [lah SEH-hah]

**eyeglasses**   los anteojos
[lohs ahn-teh-OH-hohs]

**F**

**face**   la cara   [lah KAH-rah]

**facing**   frente a   [FREHN-teh ah]

**fail (an exam), to**   suspender
[soos-pehn-DEHR]

**fainting spell**   el desmayo
[ehl dehs-MAH-yoh]

**fall, to**   caerse (*irreg.*)   [kah-EHR-seh]

**fall asleep, to**   dormirse (ue)
[dohr-MEER-seh]

**family**   la familia   [lah fah-MEE-lyah]

**far away**   lejos   [LEH-hohs]

**fast**   rápido   [RRAH-pee-doh]

**father**   el padre   [ehl PAH-dreh]

**father-in-law**   el suegro   [ehl SWEH-groh]

**fax, to**   mandar por fax
[mahn-DAHR pohr fahks]

**fax machine**   el telefax
[ehl teh-leh-FAHKS]

**February**   febrero   [feh-BREH-roh]

**fed up**   harto   [AHR-toh]

**fence**   la cerca   [lah SEHR-kah]

**fever**   la fiebre   [lah FYEH-breh]

**fight, to**   pelear   [peh-leh-AHR]

**file**   el archivo   [ehl ahr-CHEE-boh]

**file, to**   archivar   [ahr-chee-BAHR]

**file cabinet**   el fichero   [ehl fee-CHEH-roh]

**file folder**   la carpeta   [lah kahr-PEH-tah]

**fill out, to**   llenar   [yeh-NAHR]

**filling (tooth)**   el empaste
[ehl ehm-PAHS-teh]

**financial aid**   la ayuda financiera
[lah ah-YOO-dah fee-nahn-SYEH-rah]

**find, to**   encontrar (ue)   [ehn-kohn-TRAHR]

**fine**   la multa   [lah MOOL-tah]

**finger**   el dedo   [ehl DEH-doh]

**fire**   el fuego   [ehl FWEH-goh];
el incendio   [ehl een-SEHN-dyoh]

**fire alarm**   la alarma de incendios
[lah ah-LAHR-mah deh een-SEHN-dyohs]

**fire door**   la puerta contra incendios
[lah PWEHR-tah KOHN-trah
een-SEHN-dyohs]

**fire drill**   el simulacro de incendio
[ehl see-moo-LAH-kroh deh
een-SEHN-dyoh]

**fire escape**   la escalera de emergencia
[lah ehs-kah-LEH-rah deh
eh-mehr-HEHN-syah]

**fire exit**   la salida de emergencia
[lah sah-LEE-dah deh eh-mehr-HEHN-syah]

**fire extinguisher**   el extintor
[ehl ehs-teen-TOHR]

**firefighter**   el bombero / la bombera
[ehl bohm-BEH-roh / lah bohm-BEH-rah]

**first aid kit**   la caja de primeros auxilios
[lah KAH-hah deh pree-MEH-rohs
ah-ook-SEE-lyohs]

**fish (alive)**   el pez   [ehl PEHS]

**fish (on a plate)**   el pescado
[ehl pehs-KAH-doh]

**fix, to**   arreglar   [ah-rreh-GLAHR]

**flag**   la bandera   [lah bahn-DEH-rah]

**flame**   la llama   [lah YAH-mah]

**flannel**   la franela   [lah frah-NEH-lah]

**flashlight**   la linterna   [lah leen-TEHR-nah]

**flight attendant**   el/la asistente de vuelo
[ehl/lah ah-sees-TEHN-teh deh BWEH-loh]

**flood**   la inundación
[lah ee-noon-dah-SYOHN]

**floor (ground, surface, flooring)**   el suelo
[ehl SWEH-loh]

**floor (story)**   el piso   [ehl PEE-soh]

**flu**   la gripe   [lah GREE-peh]

**flush (the toilet), to**   descargar
[dehs-kahr-GAHR]

**fog**   la neblina   [lah neh-BLEE-nah]

**fold, to**   doblar   [doh-BLAHR]

**food**   el alimento   [ehl ah-lee-MEHN-toh];
la comida   [lah koh-MEE-dah]

**foodstuff**   los comestibles
[lohs koh-mehs-TEE-blehs]

**foot**   el pie   [ehl pyeh]

**for what**   para qué   [PAH-rah keh]

**for when**   para cuándo
[PAH-rah KWAHN-doh]

**for whom**   para quién / para quiénes
[PAH-rah kyehn / PAH-rah KYEH-nehs]

**forbid, to**   prohibir   [proh-ee-BEER]

**forehead**   la frente   [lah FREHN-teh]

**form**   el formulario
[ehl fohr-moo-LAH-ryoh]

**fountain**   la fuente   [lah FWEHN-teh]

**fraud**   el fraude   [ehl FRAH-oo-deh]

**frequently**   frecuentemente
[freh-kwehn-teh-MEHN-teh]

**Friday**   el viernes   [ehl BYEHR-nehs]

**from time to time** de vez en cuando
[deh behs ehn KWAHN-doh]

**from where** de dónde [deh DOHN-deh]

**front of, in** enfrente de
[ehn-FREHN-teh deh]

**fruit** la fruta [lah FROO-tah]

**frustrated** frustrado [froos-TRAH-doh]

**furious** furioso [foo-RYOH-soh]

# G

**gang** la pandilla [lah pahn-DEE-yah]

**gardener** el jardinero / la jardinera
[ehl hahr-dee-NEH-roh /
lah hahr-dee-NEH-rah]

**garlic** el ajo [ehl AH-hoh]

**garment** la prenda de vestir
[lah PREHN-dah deh behs-TEER]

**gas leak** el escape de gas
[ehl ehs-KAH-peh deh gahs]

**gate** la verja [lah BEHR-hah]

**get, to** obtener (*irreg.*) [ohb-teh-NEHR]

**get off, to** bajar de [bah-HAHR deh]

**get on, to** subir a [soo-BEER ah]

**get up, to** levantarse
[leh-bahn-TAHR-seh]

**girl** la niña [lah NEE-nyah]

**girlfriend** la novia [lah NOH-byah]

**give, to** dar (*irreg.*) [dahr]

**give a shot (injection), to** inyectar
[een-yehk-TAHR];
ponerle (*irreg.*) una inyección
[poh-NEHR-leh oo-nah een-yehk-SYOHN]

**give advice, to** aconsejar
[ah-kohn-seh-HAHR]

**give back, to** devolver (ue)
[deh-bohl-BEHR]

**glove** el guante [ehl GWAHN-teh]

**glue** la cola [lah KOH-lah]

**go, to** ir (*irreg.*) [eer]

**go down, to** bajar [bah-HAHR]

**go out, to** salir (*irreg.*) [sah-LEER]

**go to (a place), to** ir (*irreg.*) a (+ *place*)
[eer ah]

**go to bed, to** acostarse (ue)
[ah-kohs-TAHR-seh]

**go to sleep, to** dormirse (ue)
[dohr-MEER-seh]

**go up, to** subir [soo-BEER]

**goddaughter** la ahijada
[lah ah-ee-HAH-dah]

**godfather** el compadre [ehl kohm-PAH-
dreh]; el padrino [ehl pah-DREE-noh]

**godmother** la comadre [lah koh-MAH-
dreh]; la madrina [lah mah-DREE-nah]

**godson** el ahijado [ehl ah-ee-HAH-doh]

**good grades, to get** sacar buenas notas
[sah-KAHR BWEH-nahs NOH-tahs]

**good-bye** adiós [ah-DYOHS]

**grab, to** agarrar [ah-gah-RRAHR]

**grade (level)** el grado [ehl GRAH-doh]

**grade (mark)** la nota [lah NOH-tah]

**grade, to** calificar [kah-lee-fee-KAHR]

**graduation** la graduación
[lah grah-dwah-SYOHN]

**granddaughter** la nieta [lah NYEH-tah]

**grandfather** el abuelo [ehl ah-BWEH-loh]

**grandmother** la abuela
[lah ah-BWEH-lah]

**grandson** el nieto [ehl NYEH-toh]

**grape** la uva [lah OO-bah]

**grass** la hierba [lah YEHR-bah]

**grateful** agradecido
[ah-grah-deh-SEE-doh]

**gray** gris [grees]

**green** verde [BEHR-deh]

**green pea** el guisante [ehl gee-SAHN-teh]

**guide dog** el perro guía
[ehl PEH-rroh GEE-ah]

**gymnasium** el gimnasio
[ehl heem-NAH-syoh]

# H

**hail** el granizo [ehl grah-NEE-soh]

**hailstorm** la granizada
[lah grah-nee-SAH-dah]

**hair** el cabello [ehl kah-BEH-yoh];
el pelo [ehl PEH-loh]

**hairdresser** el peluquero / la peluquera
[ehl peh-loo-KEH-roh /
lah peh-loo-KEH-rah]

**Halloween** la Víspera de Todos los Santos
[lah BEES-peh-rah deh TOH-dohs lohs
SAHN-tohs]

**hallway** el pasillo [ehl pah-SEE-yoh]

**ham** el jamón [ehl hah-MOHN]

**hamburger** la hamburguesa
[lah ahm-boor-GEH-sah]

**hand** la mano [lah MAH-noh]

**handkerchief** el pañuelo
[ehl pah-NYWEH-loh]

**handwriting** la caligrafía
[lah kah-lee-grah-FEE-ah];
la escritura [lah ehs-kree-TOO-rah]

**Hanukkah**   la Fiesta de las Luces
[lah FYEHS-tah deh lahs LOO-sehs]

**happy**   contento [kohn-TEHN-toh]

**harassment**   el acoso [ehl ah-KOH-soh]

**hardworking**   trabajador/trabajadora
[trah-bah-hah-DOHR/
trah-bah-hah-DOH-rah]

**hat**   el sombrero [ehl sohm-BREH-roh]

**have, to**   tener (*irreg.*) [teh-NEHR]

**head**   la cabeza [lah kah-BEH-sah]

**headache**   el dolor de cabeza
[ehl doh-LOHR deh kah-BEH-sah]

**headmaster/headmistress**   el director /
la directora   [ehl dee-rehk-TOHR /
lah dee-rehk-TOH-rah]

**headscarf**   el pañuelo
[ehl pah-NYWEH-loh]

**health**   la salud [lah sah-LOOD]

**healthy**   saludable [sah-loo-DAH-bleh]

**hear, to**   oír (*irreg.*) [oh-EER]

**hearing aid**   el audífono
[ehl ah-oo-DEE-foh-noh];
el aparato de oído
[ehl ah-pah-RAH-toh deh oh-EE-doh]

**hearing problems**   la sordera
[lah sohr-DEH-rah];
la pérdida de capacidad auditiva
[lah PEHR-dee-dah deh kah-pah-see-DAHD
ah-oo-dee-TEE-bah]

**heart**   el corazón [ehl koh-rah-SOHN]

**heart attack**   el ataque cardíaco
[ehl ah-TAH-keh kahr-DEE-ah-koh]

**heat (weather, warmth)**   el calor
[ehl kah-LOHR]

**heat(ing)**   la calefacción
[lah kah-leh-fahk-SYOHN]

**height**   la estatura
[lah ehs-tah-TOO-rah]

**hello**   hola [OH-lah]

**help**   el auxilio [ehl ah-ook-SEE-lyoh];
el socorro [ehl soh-KOH-rroh]

**hepatitis**   la hepatitis
[lah eh-pah-TEE-tees]

**her**   su [soo]

**here**   aquí [ah-KEE]

**hiccup(s)**   el hipo [ehl EE-poh]

**high school**   la escuela secundaria
[lah ehs-KWEH-lah seh-koon-DAH-ryah]

**highlighter**   el marcador
[ehl mahr-kah-DOHR]

**hip**   la cadera [lah kah-DEH-rah]

**his**   su [soo]

**hit, to**   golpear [gohl-peh-AHR];
pegar [peh-GAHR]

**hobby**   el pasatiempo favorito
[ehl pah-sah-TYEHM-poh fah-boh-REE-toh]

**holiday**   el día feriado
[ehl DEE-ah feh-RYAH-doh]

**home**   el hogar [ehl oh-GAHR]

**homeless, to be**   estar (*irreg.*) sin hogar/
vivienda [ehs-TAHR seen oh-GAHR/
bee-BYEHN-dah]

**homelessness**   la falta de hogar/vivienda
[lah FAHL-tah deh oh-GAHR/
bee-BYEHN-dah]

**homework**   la tarea [lah tah-REH-ah]

**honest**   honesto [oh-NEHS-toh]

**hope, to**   esperar [ehs-peh-RAHR]

**hot dog**   el perro caliente
[ehl PEH-rroh kah-LYEHN-teh]

**house**   la casa [lah KAH-sah]

**how**   cómo [KOH-moh]

**how many**   cuántos/cuántas
[KWAHN-tohs/KWAHN-tahs]

**how much**   cuánto/cuánta
[KWAHN-toh/KWAHN-tah]

**hunger**   el hambre [ehl AHM-breh]

**hungry, to be**   tener (*irreg.*) hambre
[teh-NEHR AHM-breh]

**hurricane**   el huracán [ehl oo-rah-KAHN]

**hurry, to be in a**   tener (*irreg.*) prisa
[teh-NEHR PREE-sah]

**hurry up, to**   darse (*irreg.*) prisa
[DAHR-seh PREE-sah]

**hurt, to**   doler (ue) [doh-LEHR]

**husband**   el esposo [ehl ehs-POH-soh]

# I

**I**   yo [yoh]

**illness**   la enfermedad
[lah ehn-fehr-meh-DAHD]

**immediately**   inmediatamente
[een-meh-dyah-tah-MEHN-teh]

**improve, to**   mejorarse
[meh-hoh-RAHR-seh]

**in the middle of**   a mediados de
[ah meh-DYAH-dohs deh]

**incest**   el incesto [ehl een-SEHS-toh]

**income**   el ingreso [ehl een-GREH-soh]

**independent**   independiente
[een-deh-pehn-DYEHN-teh]

**indigestion**   la indigestión
[lah een-dee-hehs-TYOHN]

**inexpensive**   barato [bah-RAH-toh]

**infected** infectado [een-fehk-TAH-doh]

**infection** la infección
[lah een-fehk-SYOHN]

**infectious disease** la enfermedad
infecciosa [lah ehn-fehr-meh-DAHD
een-fehk-SYOH-sah]

**inhale, to** inhalar [ee-nah-LAHR]

**ink** la tinta [lah TEEN-tah]

**ink jet printer** la impresora de chorro
de tinta [lah eem-preh-SOH-rah deh
CHOH-rroh deh TEEN-tah]

**inner ear (hearing)** el oído
[ehl oh-EE-doh]

**inquisitive** curioso [koo-RYOH-soh]

**insect bite** la picadura
[lah pee-kah-DOO-rah]

**insecure** inseguro [een-seh-GOO-roh]

**inside** adentro [ah-DEHN-troh]

**inside of** dentro de [DEHN-troh deh]

**instructor** el instructor / la instructora
[ehl eens-trook-TOHR /
lah eens-trook-TOH-rah]

**insurance** el seguro [ehl seh-GOO-roh]

**intelligent** inteligente
[een-teh-lee-HEHN-teh]

**interpreter** el/la intérprete
[ehl/lah een-TEHR-preh-teh]

**intersection** la bocacalle
[lah boh-kah-KAH-yeh]

**interview** la entrevista
[lah ehn-treh-BEES-tah]

**iodine** el yodo [ehl YOH-doh]

**itch** la picazón [lah pee-kah-SOHN]

## J

**jacket** el saco [ehl SAH-koh]; la chaqueta
[lah chah-KEH-tah]

**janitor** el/la conserje
[ehl/lah kohn-SEHR-heh]

**January** enero [eh-NEH-roh]

**jealous** celoso [seh-LOH-soh]

**jeans** los blue jeans [lohs bloo yeens];
los vaqueros [lohs bah-KEH-rohs]

**job application** la solicitud de empleo
[lah soh-lee-see-TOOD deh ehm-PLEH-oh]

**journalist** el reportero / la reportera
[ehl rreh-pohr-TEH-roh /
lah rreh-pohr-TEH-rah]

**juice** el jugo [ehl HOO-goh]

**July** julio [HOO-lyoh]

**jump, to** saltar [sahl-TAHR]

**jump rope** la cuerda de saltar
[lah KWEHR-dah deh sahl-TAHR]

**June** junio [HOO-nyoh]

**juvenile delinquency** la delincuencia
juvenil
[lah deh-leen-KWEHN-syah hoo-beh-NEEL]

## K

**keep silent, to** guardar silencio
[gwahr-DAHR see-LEHN-syoh]

**kick, to** dar (*irreg.*) patadas
[dahr pah-TAH-dahs];
patear [pah-teh-AHR]

**kidnapping** el secuestro
[ehl seh-KWEHS-troh]

**kindergarten** el jardín de infancia
[ehl hahr-DEEN deh een-FAHN-syah];
el kinder [ehl KEEN-dehr]

**kite** la cometa [lah koh-MEH-tah]

**knee** la rodilla [lah rroh-DEE-yah]

**know (facts), to** saber (*irreg.*) [sah-BEHR]

**know (person, place), to** conocer (*irreg.*)
[koh-noh-SEHR]

## L

**Labor Day** el día del Trabajador
[ehl DEE-ah dehl trah-bah-hah-DOHR]

**labor union** el sindicato
[ehl seen-dee-KAH-toh]

**laboratory** el laboratorio
[ehl lah-boh-rah-TOH-ryoh]

**landslide** el desprendimiento de tierra
[ehl dehs-prehn-dee-MYEHN-toh deh
TYEH-rrah]

**language** el lenguaje
[ehl lehn-GWAH-heh]

**last, to** durar [doo-RAHR]

**last night** anoche [ah-NOH-cheh]

**late** atrasado [ah-trah-SAH-doh]

**later** luego [LWEH-goh]; más tarde
[mahs TAHR-deh]

**laugh, to** reír(se) (*irreg.*) [rreh-EER(seh)]

**lawyer** el abogado / la abogada
[ehl ah-boh-GAH-doh /
lah ah-boh-GAH-dah]

**lead** el plomo [ehl PLOH-moh]

**learn, to** aprender [ah-prehn-DEHR]

**learning disability** la discapacidad de
aprendizaje [lah dees-kah-pah-see-DAHD
deh ah-prehn-dee-SAH-heh]

**leather** el cuero [ehl KWEH-roh]

**leave, to** salir (*irreg.*) [sah-LEER]

**left** izquierda [ees-KYEHR-dah]

**leg** pierna [lah PYEHR-nah]

**lemonade** la limonada [lah lee-moh-NAH-dah]

**less (fewer)** menos [MEH-nohs]

**lesson** la lección [lah lehk-SYOHN]

**letter** la carta [lah KAHR-tah]

**letter of recommendation** la carta de recomendación [lah KAHR-tah deh rreh-koh-mehn-dah-SYOHN]

**lettuce** la lechuga [lah leh-CHOO-gah]

**leukemia** la leucemia [lah leh-oo-SEH-myah]

**librarian** el bibliotecario / la bibliotecaria [ehl bee-blyoh-teh-KAH-ryoh / lah bee-blyoh-teh-KAH-ryah]

**library** la biblioteca [lah bee-blyoh-TEH-kah]

**library card** la tarjeta de biblioteca [lah tahr-HEH-tah deh bee-blyoh-TEH-kah]

**lice** los piojos [lohs PYOH-hohs]

**lie down, to** acostarse (ue) [ah-kohs-TAHR-seh]

**light** la luz [lah loos]

**lighting** las luces [lahs LOO-sehs]

**lightning** el relámpago [ehl rreh-LAHM-pah-goh]

**like, to** gustar [goos-TAHR]

**liniment** el linimento [ehl lee-nee-MEHN-toh]

**lip** el labio [ehl LAH-byoh]

**listen, to** escuchar [ehs-koo-CHAHR]

**little (not much)** poco [POH-koh]

**loan** el préstamo [ehl PREHS-tah-moh]

**lobby** el vestíbulo [ehl behs-TEE-boo-loh]

**lock** el candado [ehl kahn-DAH-doh]

**locker** el cajón con llave [ehl kah-HOHN kohn YAH-beh]

**locker room** el vestuario [ehl behs-TWAH-ryoh]

**long** largo [LAHR-goh]

**look bad, to** lucir (irreg.) mal [loo-SEER mahl]

**look for, to** buscar [boos-KAHR]

**look good, to** lucir (irreg.) bien [loo-SEER byehn]

**lose, to** perder (ie) [pehr-DEHR]

**lost** perdido [pehr-DEE-doh]

**lotion** la loción [lah loh-SYOHN]

**loudspeaker** el altavoz [ehl ahl-tah-BOHS]

**lucky, to be** tener (irreg.) suerte [teh-NEHR SWEHR-teh]

**lunch** el almuerzo [ehl ahl-MWEHR-soh]

**lung** el pulmón [ehl pool-MOHN]

## M

**magazine** la revista [lah rreh-BEES-tah]

**mail room** el cuarto de correo [ehl KWAHR-toh deh koh-RREH-oh]

**make, to** hacer (irreg.) [ah-SEHR]

**make an appointment, to** hacer (irreg.) una cita [ah-SEHR OO-nah SEE-tah]

**make better, to** mejorar [meh-hoh-RAHR]

**make fun, to** burlarse [boor-LAHR-seh]

**man** el hombre [ehl OHM-breh]

**mandatory** obligatorio [oh-blee-gah-TOH-ryoh]

**manslaughter** el homicidio involuntario [ehl oh-mee-SEE-dyoh een-boh-loon-TAH-ryoh]

**many times** muchas veces [MOO-chahs BEH-sehs]

**marble (toy)** la canica [lah kah-NEE-kah]

**March** marzo [MAHR-soh]

**margarine** la margarina [lah mahr-gah-REE-nah]

**marvelous** maravilloso [mah-rah-bee-YOH-soh]

**match** el fósforo [ehl FOHS-foh-roh]

**match (game)** el partido [ehl pahr-TEE-doh]

**match, to** hacer (irreg.) juego con [ah-SEHR HWEH-goh kohn]

**mathematics** las matemáticas [lahs mah-teh-MAH-tee-kahs]

**May** mayo [MAH-yoh]

**measles** el sarampión [ehl sah-rahm-PYOHN]

**meat** la carne [lah KAHR-neh]

**mechanic** el mecánico / la mecánica [ehl meh-KAH-nee-koh / lah meh-KAH-nee-kah]

**medicine** la medicina [lah meh-dee-SEE-nah]

**medicine (drug)** el medicamento [ehl meh-dee-kah-MEHN-toh]

**meeting** la reunión [lah rreh-oo-NYOHN]

**melon** el melón [ehl meh-LOHN]

**meningitis** la meningitis [lah meh-neen-HEE-tees]

**menstrual period**
la regla  [lah RREH-glah];
el período  [ehl peh-REE-oh-doh]

**mental retardation**  el retraso mental
[ehl rreh-TRAH-soh mehn-TAHL]

**merry-go-round**  el tiovivo
[ehl tee-oh-BEE-boh]

**microphone**  el micrófono
[ehl mee-KROH-foh-noh]

**middle (center)**  el medio  [ehl MEH-dyoh]

**middle (half)**  medio  [MEH-dyoh]

**migraine**  la jaqueca  [lah hah-KEH-kah]

**milk**  la leche  [lah LEH-cheh]

**mineral water**  el agua mineral
[ehl AH-gwah mee-neh-RAHL]

**minus (sign)**  menos  [MEH-nohs]

**mirror**  el espejo  [ehl ehs-PEH-hoh]

**misbehave, to**  portarse mal
[pohr-TAHR-seh mahl]

**Miss**  la señorita  [lah seh-nyoh-REE-tah]

**modeling clay**  la plasticina
[lah plahs-tee-SEE-nah]

**molestation**  el asalto sexual
[ehl ah-SAHL-toh sehk-SWAHL]

**Monday**  el lunes  [ehl LOO-nehs]

**money**  el dinero  [ehl dee-NEH-roh]

**mononucleosis**  la mononucleosis
[lah moh-noh-noo-kleh-OH-sees]

**month**  el mes  [ehl mehs]

**mop**  el trapeador  [ehl trah-peh-ah-DOHR]

**mop, to**  trapear  [trah-peh-AHR]

**more**  más  [mahs]

**morning**  la mañana  [lah mah-NYAH-nah]

**mother**  la madre  [lah MAH-dreh]

**mother-in-law**  la suegra  [lah SWEH-grah]

**moustache**  el bigote  [ehl bee-GOH-teh]

**mouth**  la boca  [lah BOH-kah]

**Mr./mister/sir**  el señor  [chl seh-NYOHR]

**Mrs./madam**  la señora
[lah seh-NYOH-rah]

**mucus**  la flema  [lah FLEH-mah]

**multiple sclerosis**  la esclerosis múltiple
[lah ehs-kleh-ROH-sees MOOL-tee-pleh]

**mumps**  las paperas  [lahs pah-PEH-rahs]

**murder**  el homicidio
[ehl oh-mee-SEE-dyoh]

**muscular dystrophy**  la distrofia
muscular  [lah dees-TROH-fyah
moos-koo-LAHR]

**music**  la música  [lah MOO-see-kah]

**my**  mi  [mee]

## N

**nail**  la uña  [lah OO-nyah]

**nap**  la siesta  [lah SYEHS-tah]

**nap, to**  dormir (ue) la siesta
[dohr-MEER lah SYEHS-tah]

**nausea**  la náusea  [lah NAH-oo-seh-ah]

**nauseous**  mareado  [mah-reh-AH-doh]

**Navy**  la marina de guerra
[lah mah-REE-nah deh GEH-rrah]

**navy blue**  azul marino
[ah-SOOL mah-REE-noh]

**nearby**  cerca  [SEHR-kah]

**neck**  el cuello  [ehl KWEH-yoh]

**neighborhood**  el barrio  [ehl BAH-rryoh]

**neither**  tampoco  [tahm-POH-koh]

**nephew**  el sobrino  [ehl soh-BREE-noh]

**nervous**  nervioso  [nehr-BYOH-soh]

**never**  nunca  [NOON-kah]

**New Year's Day**  el día de Año Nuevo
[ehl DEE-ah deh AH-nyoh NWEH-boh]

**newspaper**  el periódico
[ehl peh-RYOH-dee-koh]

**next**  próximo  [PROHK-see-moh]

**next to**  al lado de  [ahl LAH-doh deh]

**niece**  la sobrina  [lah soh-BREE-nah]

**night**  la noche  [lah NOH-cheh]

**night before last**  anteanoche
[ahn-teh-ah-NOH-cheh]

**no**  no  [noh]

**no one**  nadie  [NAH-dyeh];
ninguno/ninguna
[neen-GOO-noh/neen-GOO-nah]

**nobody**  nadie  [NAH-dyeh];
ninguno/ninguna
[neen-GOO-noh/neen-GOO-nah]

**none**  ninguno/ninguna
[neen-GOO-noh/neen-GOO-nah]

**noon**  el mediodía
[ehl meh-dyoh-DEE-ah]

**nose**  la nariz  [lah nah-REES]

**not yet**  todavía no  [toh-dah-BEE-ah noh]

**notebook**  el cuaderno
[ehl kwah-DEHR-noh]

**nothing**  nada  [NAH-dah]

**November**  noviembre
[noh-BYEHM-breh]

**now**  ahora  [ah-OH-rah]

**nurse**  el enfermero / la enfermera
[ehl ehn-fehr-MEH-roh /
lah ehn-fehr-MEH-rah]

**nurse's office** la oficina del enfermero /
de la enfermera [lah oh-fee-SEE-nah
dehl ehn-fehr-MEH-roh /
deh lah ehn-fehr-MEH-rah]

**nursery** la guardería
[lah gwahr-deh-REE-ah]

## O

**oatmeal** la avena [lah ah-BEH-nah]

**obedient** obediente [oh-beh-DYEHN-teh]

**obesity** la obesidad
[lah oh-beh-see-DAHD]

**obey, to** obedecer (*irreg.*)
[oh-beh-deh-SEHR]

**obscene phone call** la llamada
telefónica indecente/obscena
[lah yah-MAH-dah teh-leh-FOH-nee-kah
een-deh-SEHN-teh/ohb-SEH-nah]

**obtain, to** obtener (*irreg.*) [ohb-teh-NEHR]

**occupation** la profesión
[lah proh-feh-SYOHN]

**October** octubre [ohk-TOO-breh]

**often** a menudo [ah meh-NOO-doh]

**omelet** la tortilla [lah tohr-TEE-yah]

**once** una vez [oo-nah behs]

**one** un/uno/una [oon/oo-noh/oo-nah]

**one-way street** la calle de dirección
única [lah KAH-yeh deh dee-rehk-SYOHN
oo-nee-kah]

**onion** la cebolla [lah seh-BOH-yah]

**open, to** abrir [ah-BREER]

**orange (color)** anaranjado
[ah-nah-rahn-HAH-doh]

**orange (fruit)** la naranja
[lah nah-RAHN-hah]

**organized** organizado
[ohr-gah-nee-SAH-doh]

**orthodontist** el/la ortodontista
[ehl/lah ohr-toh-dohn-TEES-tah]

**our** nuestro [NWEHS-troh]

**outdoors** al aire libre
[ahl AH-ee-reh LEE-breh]

**outside** afuera [ah-FWEH-rah]

**outside of** fuera de [FWEH-rah deh]

**over there** allá [ah-YAH]

**overalls** el overol [ehl oh-beh-ROHL]

**overhead projector** el retroproyector
[ehl rreh-troh-proh-yehk-TOHR]

## P

**page** la página [lah PAH-hee-nah]

**paint, to** pintar [peen-TAHR]

**painter** el pintor / la pintora
[ehl peen-TOHR / lah peen-TOH-rah]

**painting** el cuadro [ehl KWAH-droh];
la pintura [lah peen-TOO-rah]

**pajamas** la piyama
[lah pee-YAH-mah]

**panties** las bragas
[lahs BRAH-gahs]

**pants** los pantalones
[lohs pahn-tah-LOH-nehs]

**pantyhose** las pantimedias
[lahs pahn-tee-MEH-dyahs];
los pantis [lohs PAHN-tees]

**paper** el papel [ehl pah-PEHL]

**paper (colored)** el papel (de colores)
[ehl pah-PEHL (deh koh-LOH-rehs)]

**paper clip** el sujetapapeles
[ehl soo-heh-tah-pah-PEH-lehs]

**paper towel** la toalla de papel
[lah toh-AH-yah deh pah-PEHL]

**paralysis** la parálisis
[lah pah-RAH-lee-sees]

**parents** los padres
[lohs PAH-drehs]

**park** el parque [ehl PAHR-keh]

**parking lot** el estacionamiento
[ehl ehs-tah-syoh-nah-MYEHN-toh]

**part-time** a tiempo parcial
[ah TYEHM-poh pahr-SYAHL]

**pass (permission)** el pase [ehl PAH-seh];
el permiso [ehl pehr-MEE-soh]

**pass (a class), to** aprobar (ue)
[ah-proh-BAHR]

**Passover** la Pascua (de los judíos)
[lah PAHS-kwah (deh lohs hoo-DEE-ohs)]

**paste, to** pegar [peh-GAHR]

**pay, to** pagar [pah-GAHR]

**pay attention, to** prestar atención
[prehs-TAHR ah-tehn-SYOHN]

**pay the fine, to** pagar la multa
[pah-GAHR lah MOOL-tah]

**peach** el melocotón
[ehl meh-loh-koh-TOHN]

**peanut** el cacahuete
[ehl kah-kah-WEH-teh];
el maní [ehl mah-NEE]

**pear** la pera [lah PEH-rah]

**pedestrian crossing** el paso de peatones
[ehl PAH-soh deh peh-ah-TOH-nehs]

**peer mediation program** el programa
que usa a otros jóvenes como
intermediarios en conflictos
[ehl proh-GRAH-mah keh OO-sah ah
OH-trohs HOH-beh-nehs KOH-moh
een-tehr-meh-DYAH-ryohs ehn
kohn-FLEEK-tohs]

**pen** la pluma [lah PLOO-mah]

**pencil** el lápiz [ehl LAH-pees]

**pencil sharpener** el sacapuntas
[ehl sah-kah-POON-tahs]

**penicillin** la penicilina
[lah peh-nee-see-LEE-nah]

**people** la gente [lah HEHN-teh];
las personas [lahs pehr-SOH-nahs]

**pepper** la pimienta [lah pee-MYEHN-tah]

**pet** el animal doméstico
[ehl ah-nee-MAHL doh-MEHS-tee-koh]

**photocopy, to** fotocopiar
[foh-toh-koh-PYAHR]

**photographer** el fotógrafo / la fotógrafa
[ehl foh-TOH-grah-foh /
lah foh-TOH-grah-fah]

**physical education** la educación física
[lah eh-doo-kah-SYOHN FEE-see-kah]

**pick up, to** recoger (*irreg.*)
[rreh-koh-HEHR]

**picture** el cuadro [ehl KWAH-droh];
la pintura [lah peen-TOO-rah]

**pineapple** la piña [lah PEE-nyah]

**pink** rosado [rroh-SAH-doh]

**place, to** poner (*irreg.*) [poh-NEHR]

**play, to** jugar (ue) [hoo-GAHR]

**play (a game), to** jugar (ue) a (+ *game*)
[hoo-GAHR ah]

**play (a musical instrument), to** tocar
[toh-KAHR]

**play "dress up," to** jugar (ue) a
disfrazarse
[hoo-GAHR ah dees-frah-SAHR-seh]

**play hide-and-seek, to** jugar (ue) al
escondite
[hoo-GAHR ahl ehs-kohn-DEE-teh]

**play "house," to** jugar (ue) a la casita
[hoo-GAHR ah lah kah-SEE-tah]

**playground** el patio de recreo
[ehl PAH-tyoh deh rreh-KREH-oh]

**plumber** el plomero / la plomera
[ehl ploh-MEH-roh / lah ploh-MEH-rah]

**pneumonia** la pulmonía
[lah pool-moh-NEE-ah]

**pocket** el bolsillo [ehl bohl-SEE-yoh]

**pocketbook** el bolso [ehl BOHL-soh]

**poisoning** el envenenamiento
[ehl ehn-beh-neh-nah-MYEHN-toh]

**police** la policía [lah poh-lee-SEE-ah]

**police custody** la custodia policial
[lah koos-TOH-dyah poh-lee-SYAHL]

**police force** el cuerpo de policía
[ehl KWEHR-poh deh poh-lee-SEE-ah]

**police officer** el policía / la mujer policía
[ehl poh-lee-SEE-ah /
lah moo-HEHR poh-lee-SEE-ah]

**police record** los antecedentes penales
[lohs ahn-teh-seh-DEHN-tehs
peh-NAH-lehs]

**police station** la comisaría
[lah koh-mee-sah-REE-ah]

**polyester** el poliéster
[ehl poh-LYEHS-tehr]

**poster** el cartel [ehl kahr-TEHL]

**potato** la papa [lah PAH-pah];
la patata [lah pah-TAH-tah]

**poverty** la pobreza [lah poh-BREH-sah]

**powder** el polvo [ehl POHL-boh]

**pregnancy (unwanted)** el embarazo
(no deseado) [ehl ehm-bah-RAH-soh
(noh deh-seh-AH-doh)]

**President's Day** el día de los Presidentes
[ehl DEE-ah deh lohs preh-see-DEHN-tehs]

**pretty** bonito [boh-NEE-toh]; lindo
[LEEN-doh]

**principal** el director / la directora
[ehl dee-rehk-TOHR /
lah dee-rehk-TOH-rah]

**print, to** imprimir [eem-pree-MEER]

**print (write in block letters), to** escribir
en letra de molde [ehs-kree-BEER ehn
LEH-trah deh MOHL-deh]

**printer** la impresora
[lah eem-preh-SOH-rah]

**problem** el problema
[ehl proh-BLEH-mah]

**programmer** el programador /
la programadora
[ehl proh-grah-mah-DOHR /
lah proh-grah-mah-DOH-rah]

**prohibit, to** prohibir [proh-ee-BEER]

**pronunciation** la pronunciación
[lah proh-noon-syah-SYOHN]

**proud** orgulloso [ohr-goo-YOH-soh]

**psychologist** el psicólogo / la psicóloga
[ehl see-KOH-loh-goh /
lah see-KOH-loh-gah]

**pull, to** jalar [hah-LAHR]; tirar de
[tee-RAHR deh]

**punctual** puntual [poon-TWAHL]

**puppet** el títere [ehl TEE-teh-reh]

**purple** morado [moh-RAH-doh]

**purse** el monedero
[ehl moh-neh-DEH-roh];
el portamonedas
[ehl pohr-tah-moh-NEH-dahs]

**push, to** empujar [ehm-poo-HAHR]

**put, to** poner (*irreg.*) [poh-NEHR]

**put a cast on, to** enyesar [ehn-yeh-SAHR]

**put away, to** guardar [gwahr-DAHR]

**put on, to** ponerse (*irreg.*) [poh-NEHR-seh]

**put puzzles together, to** armar
rompecabezas
[ahr-MAHR rrohm-peh-kah-BEH-sahs]

**puzzle (jigsaw)** el rompecabezas
[ehl rrohm-peh-kah-BEH-sahs]

## Q

**quarter (one-fourth part)** un cuarto
[oon KWAHR-toh]

**question** la pregunta
[lah preh-GOON-tah]

**quickly** de prisa [deh PREE-sah];
rápidamente [RRAH-pee-dah-MEHN-teh]

## R

**racism** el racismo [ehl rrah-SEES-moh]

**radio (battery-powered)** el radio
(de baterías)
[ehl RRAH-dyoh (deh bah-teh-REE-ahs)]

**railroad crossing** el cruce de ferrocarril
[ehl KROO-seh deh feh-rroh-kah-RREEL]

**railroad track** la vía de ferrocarril
[lah BEE-ah deh feh-rroh-kah-RREEL]

**rain** la lluvia [lah YOO-byah]

**rain, to** llover (ue) [yoh-BEHR]

**raincoat** el impermeable
[ehl eem-pehr-meh-AH-bleh];
la gabardina [lah gah-bahr-DEE-nah]

**rainy** lluvioso [yoo-BYOH-soh]

**Ramadan** Ramadán [rrah-mah-DAHN]

**rape** la violación [lah byoh-lah-SYOHN]

**rarely** rara vez [RRAH-rah behs]

**rash** la erupción [lah eh-roop-SYOHN]

**read, to** leer (*irreg.*) [leh-EHR]

**reading** la lectura [lah lehk-TOO-rah]

**receive, to** recibir [rreh-see-BEER]

**receptionist** el/la recepcionista
[ehl/lah rreh-sehp-syoh-NEES-tah]

**recess** el recreo [ehl rreh-KREH-oh]

**recommend, to** recomendar (ie)
[rreh-koh-mehn-DAHR]

**recruiting station** la oficina de
reclutamiento [lah oh-fee-SEE-nah deh
rreh-kloo-tah-MYEHN-toh]

**red** rojo [RROH-hoh]

**reference** la referencia
[lah rreh-feh-REHN-syah]

**registration** la matrícula
[lah mah-TREE-koo-lah]

**relative** el/la pariente
[ehl/lah pah-RYEHN-teh]

**relax, to** relajarse [rreh-lah-HAHR-seh]

**relaxed** relajado [rreh-lah-HAH-doh]

**remember, to** recordar (ue)
[rreh-kohr-DAHR]

**repeat, to** repetir (i) [rreh-peh-TEER]

**report** el informe [ehl een-FOHR-meh]

**report card** el boletín
[ehl boh-leh-TEEN]

**request, to** pedir (i) [peh-DEER]

**require, to** requerir (ie) [rreh-keh-REER]

**requirement** el requisito
[ehl rreh-kee-SEE-toh]

**rescue** el rescate [ehl rrehs-KAH-teh]

**research, to** investigar
[een-behs-tee-GAHR]

**resentful** resentido [rreh-sehn-TEE-doh]

**respectful** respetuoso
[rrehs-peh-TWOH-soh]

**rest, to** descansar [dehs-kahn-SAHR]

**restless** inquieto [een-KYEH-toh]

**return (give back), to** devolver (ue)
[deh-bohl-BEHR]

**return (go back), to** regresar
[rreh-greh-SAHR]; volver (ue) [bohl-BEHR]

**return date** la fecha de devolución
[lah FEH-chah deh deh-boh-loo-SYOHN]

**review, to** repasar [rreh-pah-SAHR]

**rheumatism** el reumatismo
[ehl rreh-oo-mah-TEES-moh]

**rice** el arroz [ehl ah-RROHS]

**ride, to** montar [mohn-TAHR]

**right now** ahora mismo
[ah-OH-rah MEES-moh]

**right of way sign** la señal de preferencia
[lah seh-NYAHL deh preh-feh-REHN-syah]

**riot** el motín [ehl moh-TEEN]

**roll** el panecillo [ehl pah-neh-SEE-yoh]

**roof** el techo [ehl TEH-choh]

**room** el cuarto [ehl KWAHR-toh]

**Rosh Hashanah** el día de Año Nuevo Judío [ehl DEE-ah deh AH-nyoh NWEH-boh hoo-DEE-oh]

**row** la fila [lah FEE-lah]

**rubella** la rubéola [lah rroo-BEH-oh-lah]

**rug** la alfombra [lah ahl-FOHM-brah]

**rule** la regla [lah RREH-glah]

**ruler (instrument)** la regla [lah RREH-glah]

**run, to** correr [koh-RREHR]

**runaway child** el niño / la niña que huyó de casa [ehl NEE-nyoh / lah NEE-nyah keh oo-YOH deh KAH-sah]

**S**

**sad** triste [TREES-teh]

**salad** la ensalada [lah ehn-sah-LAH-dah]

**salesperson** el vendedor / la vendedora [ehl behn-deh-DOHR / lah behn-deh-DOH-rah]

**salt** la sal [lah sahl]

**same** mismo [MEES-moh]

**sandbox** el cajón de arena [ehl kah-HOHN deh ah-REH-nah]

**sandwich** el emparedado [ehl ehm-pah-reh-DAH-doh]; el sándwich [ehl SAHND-weech]

**Saturday** el sábado [ehl SAH-bah-doh]

**sausage** la salchicha [lah sahl-CHEE-chah]

**scarf** la bufanda [lah boo-FAHN-dah]

**scarlet fever** la escarlatina [lah ehs-kahr-lah-TEE-nah]

**schedule** el horario [ehl oh-RAH-ryoh]

**scholarship** la beca [lah BEH-kah]

**school** la escuela [lah ehs-KWEH-lah]

**school crossing** el cruce escolar [ehl KROO-seh ehs-koh-LAHR]

**school supplies** los materiales para la clase [lohs mah-teh-RYAH-lehs PAH-rah lah KLAH-seh]

**school year** el año escolar [ehl AH-nyoh ehs-koh-LAHR]

**science** la ciencia [lah SYEHN-syah]

**scissors (plastic)** las tijeras (de plástico) [lahs tee-HEH-rahs (deh PLAHS-tee-koh)]

**scratch (scrape)** el arañazo [ehl ah-rah-NYAH-soh]

**season (of the year)** la estación [lah ehs-tah-SYOHN]

**seat (theater)** la butaca [lah boo-TAH-kah]

**secretary** el secretario / la secretaria [ehl seh-kreh-TAH-ryoh / lah seh-kreh-TAH-ryah]

**security guard** el/la guardia de seguridad [ehl/lah GWAHR-dyah deh seh-goo-ree-DAHD]

**security personnel** el personal de seguridad [ehl pehr-soh-NAHL deh seh-goo-ree-DAHD]

**see, to** ver (*irreg.*) [behr]

**seesaw** el subibaja [ehl soo-bee-BAH-hah]

**seizure** la convulsión [lah kohn-bool-SYOHN]

**semester** el semestre [ehl seh-MEHS-treh]

**sensitive** sensible [sehn-SEE-bleh]

**sentence** la oración [lah oh-rah-SYOHN]

**September** septiembre [sehp-TYEHM-breh]

**serve, to** servir (i) [sehr-BEER]

**several** varios [BAH-ryohs]

**sexual harassment** el acoso sexual [ehl ah-KOH-soh sehk-SWAHL]

**sexual relations** las relaciones sexuales [lahs rreh-lah-SYOH-nehs sehk-SWAH-lehs]

**shake, to** sacudir [sah-koo-DEER]

**share, to** compartir [kohm-pahr-TEER]

**sheet of paper** la hoja de papel [lah OH-hah deh pah-PEHL]

**shelf** el estante [ehl ehs-TAHN-teh]

**shellfish** el marisco [ehl mah-REES-koh]

**shelter** el refugio [ehl rreh-FOO-hyoh]

**shirt** la camisa [lah kah-MEE-sah]

**shoemaker** el zapatero / la zapatera [ehl sah-pah-TEH-roh / lah sah-pah-TEH-rah]

**shooting** el tiroteo [ehl tee-roh-TEH-oh]

**short** corto [KOHR-toh]

**shorts** los pantalones cortos [lohs pahn-tah-LOH-nehs KOHR-tohs]

**shoulder** el hombro [ehl OHM-broh]

**shout, to** gritar [gree-TAHR]

**show, to** demostrar (ue) [deh-mohs-TRAHR]; mostrar (ue) [mohs-TRAHR]

**sick** enfermo [ehn-FEHR-moh]

**sick, to get** enfermarse [ehn-fehr-MAHR-seh]

**sidewalk** la acera [lah ah-SEH-rah]

**sign (notice)** el letrero [ehl leh-TREH-roh]

**sign (road)** la señal [lah seh-NYAHL]

**sign, to** firmar [feer-MAHR]

**signal**   la señal   [lah seh-NYAHL]

**singer**   el/la cantante
[ehl/lah kahn-TAHN-teh]

**sink**   el lavamanos
[ehl lah-bah-MAH-nohs]

**siren**   la sirena   [lah see-REH-nah]

**sister**   la hermana   [lah ehr-MAH-nah]

**sister-in-law**   la cuñada
[lah koo-NYAH-dah]

**sit (down), to**   sentarse (ie)
[sehn-TAHR-seh]

**skates**   los patines   [lohs pah-TEE-nehs]

**skim milk**   la leche desnatada
[lah LEH-cheh dehs-nah-TAH-dah]

**skin**   la piel   [lah pyehl]

**skirt**   la falda   [lah FAHL-dah]

**skyscraper**   el rascacielos
[ehl rrahs-kah-SYEH-lohs]

**sled**   el trineo   [ehl tree-NEH-oh]

**sleep, to**   dormir (ue)   [dohr-MEER]

**sleepy, to be**   tener (irreg.) sueño
[teh-NEHR SWEH-nyoh]

**sleeve**   la manga   [lah MAHN-gah]

**slide**   el tobogán   [ehl toh-boh-GAHN]

**slowly**   despacio   [dehs-PAH-syoh]

**smoke**   el humo   [ehl OO-moh]

**smoke, to**   fumar   [foo-MAHR]

**smoke detector**   el detector de humo
[ehl deh-tehk-TOHR deh OO-moh]

**snack**   la merienda   [lah meh-RYEHN-dah]

**snake**   la culebra   [lah koo-LEH-brah]

**sneeze, to**   estornudar
[ehs-tohr-noo-DAHR]

**snow**   la nieve   [lah NYEH-beh]

**snow, to**   nevar (ie)   [neh-BAHR]

**snowstorm**   la nevada   [lah neh-BAH-dah]

**soap**   el jabón   [ehl hah-BOHN]

**social studies**   los estudios sociales
[lohs ehs-TOO-dyohs soh-SYAH-lehs]

**socks**   los calcetines
[lohs kahl-seh-TEE-nehs]

**soft drink**   el refresco
[ehl rreh-FREHS-koh]

**some**   alguno   [ahl-GOO-noh]

**somebody**   alguien   [AHL-gyehn]

**someone**   alguien   [AHL-gyehn]

**something**   algo   [AHL-goh]

**sometimes**   a veces   [ah BEH-sehs]

**son**   el hijo   [ehl EE-hoh]

**son-in-law**   el yerno   [ehl YEHR-noh]

**soon**   pronto   [PROHN-toh]

**sore throat**   el dolor de garganta
[ehl doh-LOHR deh gahr-GAHN-tah]

**so-so**   regular   [rreh-goo-LAHR]

**sound**   el sonido   [ehl soh-NEE-doh]

**soup**   la sopa   [lah SOH-pah]

**spaghetti**   los espaguetis
[lohs ehs-pah-GEH-tees]

**speaking problems**   los trastornos
del habla y el lenguaje
[lohs trahs-TOHR-nohs dehl AH-blah
ee ehl lehn-GWAH-heh]

**spell, to**   deletrear   [deh-leh-treh-AHR]

**spelling**   la ortografía
[lah ohr-toh-grah-FEE-ah];
el deletreo   [ehl deh-leh-TREH-oh]

**spelling book**   el abecedario
[ehl ah-beh-seh-DAH-ryoh]

**spina bifida**   la espina bífida
[lah ehs-PEE-nah BEE-fee-dah]

**spinach**   la espinaca
[lah ehs-pee-NAH-kah]

**spit, to**   escupir   [ehs-koo-PEER]

**sponge**   la esponja   [lah ehs-POHN-hah]

**sport**   el deporte   [ehl deh-POHR-teh]

**sprain**   la torcedura
[lah tohr-seh-DOO-rah]

**spring (season)**   la primavera
[lah pree-mah-BEH-rah]

**square (city)**   la plaza   [lah PLAH-sah]

**staff room**   la sala de maestros
[lah SAH-lah deh mah-EHS-trohs]

**stage**   el escenario   [ehl eh-seh-NAH-ryoh]

**staircase**   la escalera
[lah ehs-kah-LEH-rah]

**stamp**   el sello   [ehl SEH-yoh]

**standardized test**   la prueba uniforme
[lah PRWEH-bah oo-nee-FOHR-meh]

**staple**   la grapa   [lah GRAH-pah]

**staple, to**   sujetar con grapas
[soo-heh-TAHR kohn GRAH-pahs]

**stapler**   la grapadora
[lah grah-pah-DOH-rah]

**starting from ____ on**   a partir de
[ah pahr-TEER deh]

**station**   la estación   [lah ehs-tah-SYOHN]

**statue**   la estatua   [lah ehs-TAH-twah]

**stay in bed, to**   guardar cama
[gwahr-DAHR KAH-mah]

**stepbrother**   el hermanastro
[ehl ehr-mah-NAHS-troh]

**stepdaughter**   la hijastra
[lah ee-HAHS-trah]

**stepfather** el padrastro
[ehl pah-DRAHS-troh]

**stepmother** la madrastra
[lah mah-DRAHS-trah]

**stepsister** la hermanastra
[lah ehr-mah-NAHS-trah]

**stepson** el hijastro [ehl ee-HAHS-troh]

**sting** la mordedura
[lah mohr-deh-DOO-rah]

**stitch** el punto [ehl POON-toh]

**stockings (hose)** las medias
[lahs MEH-dyahs]

**stomach** el estómago
[ehl ehs-TOH-mah-goh]

**stomachache** el dolor de estómago
[ehl doh-LOHR deh ehs-TOH-mah-goh]

**stop** la parada [lah pah-RAH-dah]

**stop sign** la señal de parar
[lah seh-NYAHL deh pah-RAHR]

**store window** la vitrina
[lah bee-TREE-nah]

**story** el cuento [ehl KWEHN-toh]

**straight** derecho [deh-REH-choh]

**stranger** desconocido
[dehs-koh-noh-SEE-doh]

**strawberry** la fresa [lah FREH-sah]

**street** la calle [lah KAH-yeh]

**streetlight** el farol [ehl fah-ROHL]

**strike** la huelga [lah WEHL-gah]

**strong** fuerte [FWEHR-teh]

**student** el/la estudiante
[ehl/lah ehs-too-DYAHN-teh];
el alumno / la alumna
[ehl ah-LOOM-noh / lah ah-LOOM-nah]

**studious** aplicado [ah-plee-KAH-doh];
estudioso [ehs-too-DYOH-soh]

**study, to** estudiar [ehs-too-DYAHR]

**stuffed animal** el animal de peluche
[ehl ah-nee-MAHL deh peh-LOO-cheh]

**style, to be in** estar (*irreg.*) de moda
[ehs-TAHR deh MOH-dah]

**style, to be out of** estar (*irreg.*) pasado
de moda
[ehs-TAHR pah-SAH-doh deh MOH-dah]

**subject (school)** la asignatura
[lah ah-seeg-nah-TOO-rah];
la materia [lah mah-TEH-ryah]

**subscription** la suscripción
[lah soos-kreep-SYOHN]

**subway station** la estación de metro
[lah ehs-tah-SYOHN deh MEH-troh]

**success** el éxito [ehl EHK-see-toh]

**successful, to be** tener (*irreg.*) éxito
[teh-NEHR EHK-see-toh]

**suicide** el suicidio [ehl swee-SEE-dyoh]

**suit** el traje [ehl TRAH-heh]

**summary** el resumen
[ehl rreh-SOO-mehn]

**summer** el verano [ehl beh-RAH-noh]

**sun** el sol [ehl sohl]

**Sunday** el domingo
[ehl doh-MEEN-goh]

**sunny** soleado [soh-leh-AH-doh]

**superintendent** el/la superintendente
[ehl/lah soo-pehr-een-tehn-DEHN-teh]

**supervisor** el supervisor / la supervisora
[ehl soo-pehr-bee-SOHR /
lah soo-pehr-bee-SOH-rah]

**surgeon** el cirujano / la cirujana
[ehl see-roo-HAH-noh /
lah see-roo-HAH-nah]

**surprised** sorprendido
[sohr-prehn-DEE-doh]

**suspenders** los tirantes
[lohs tee-RAHN-tehs]

**swallow, to** tragar [trah-GAHR]

**sweater** el suéter [ehl SWEH-tehr]

**sweatshirt** la sudadera
[lah soo-dah-DEH-rah]

**sweep, to** barrer [bah-RREHR]

**swimming pool** la piscina
[lah pee-SEE-nah]

**swing** el columpio [ehl koh-LOOM-pyoh]

**swollen** hinchado [een-CHAH-doh]

## T

**table** la mesa [lah MEH-sah]

**table game** el juego de mesa
[ehl HWEH-goh deh MEH-sah]

**tablet (lozenge)** la pastilla
[lah pahs-TEE-yah]

**take care of yourself, to** cuidarse
[kwee-DAHR-seh]

**take notes, to** hacer (*irreg.*) apuntes
[ah-SEHR ah-POON-tehs]

**take off, to** quitarse [kee-TAHR-seh]

**take (one's) blood pressure, to** tomarle
la presión arterial [toh-MAHR-leh
lah preh-SYOHN ahr-teh-RYAHL]

**take (one's) pulse, to** tomarle el pulso
[toh-MAHR-leh ehl POOL-soh]

**take (one's) temperature, to** tomarle
la temperatura [toh-MAHR-leh
lah tehm-peh-rah-TOO-rah]

**take pictures, to**   sacar fotos
  [sah-KAHR FOH-tohs]

**tea**   el té  [ehl teh]

**teacher**   el maestro / la maestra
  [ehl mah-EHS-troh / lah mah-EHS-trah]

**teacher's aide**   el/la asistente de
  maestro / de maestra
  [ehl/lah ah-sees-TEHN-teh deh
  mah-EHS-troh / deh mah-EHS-trah]

**tee shirt**   la camiseta
  [lah kah-mee-SEH-tah]

**telephone**   el teléfono
  [ehl teh-LEH-foh-noh]

**tell, to**   contar (ue)  [kohn-TAHR];
  decir (irreg.)  [deh-SEER]

**tell stories, to**   contar (ue) cuentos
  [kohn-TAHR KWEHN-tohs]

**tense**   tenso  [TEHN-soh]

**test**   la prueba  [lah PRWEH-bah];
  el examen  [ehl ehk-SAH-mehn]

**tetanus**   el tétano  [ehl TEH-tah-noh]

**Thanksgiving**   el día de Acción de Gracias
  [ehl DEE-ah deh ahk-SYOHN deh
  GRAH-syahs]

**that**   aquel/aquella  [ah-KEHL/ah-KEH-yah];
  ese/esa  [EH-seh/EH-sah]

**the**   el/la  [ehl/lah]

**theft**   el robo  [ehl RROH-boh]

**their**   su  [soo]

**theme**   el tema  [ehl TEH-mah]

**then**   entonces  [ehn-TOHN-sehs]

**therapist**   el/la terapista
  [ehl/lah teh-rah-PEES-tah]

**there**   allí  [ah-YEE]

**there is / there are**   hay  [AH-ee]

**thermometer**   el termómetro
  [ehl tehr-MOH-meh-troh]

**these**   estos/estas  [EHS-tohs/EHS-tahs]

**thigh**   el muslo  [ehl MOOS-loh]

**think, to**   pensar (ie)  [pehn-SAHR]

**thirsty, to be**   tener (irreg.) sed
  [teh-NEHR sehd]

**this**   este/esta  [EHS-teh/EHS-tah]

**those**   aquellos/aquellas
  [ah-KEH-yohs/ah-KEH-yahs];
  esos/esas  [EH-sohs/EH-sahs]

**threat**   la amenaza
  [lah ah-meh-NAH-sah]

**throat**   la garganta  [lah gahr-GAHN-tah]

**throw, to**   lanzar  [lahn-SAHR];
  tirar  [tee-RAHR]

**throw away, to**   botar  [boh-TAHR];
  tirar  [tee-RAHR]

**thunder**   el trueno  [ehl TRWEH-noh]

**thunderstorm**   la tormenta
  [lah tohr-MEHN-tah]

**Thursday**   el jueves  [ehl HWEH-behs]

**tie**   la corbata  [lah kohr-BAH-tah]

**tie, to**   amarrar  [ah-mah-RRAHR]

**tie one's shoes, to**   abrocharse los
  zapatos
  [ah-broh-CHAHR-seh lohs sah-PAH-tohs]

**tights**   los leotardos
  [lohs leh-oh-TAHR-dohs]

**time**   el tiempo  [ehl TYEHM-poh]

**time (clock)**   la hora  [lah OH-rah]

**time, on**   a tiempo  [ah TYEHM-poh]

**tired**   cansado  [kahn-SAH-doh]

**title**   el título  [ehl TEE-too-loh]

**toast**   el pan tostado
  [ehl pahn tohs-TAH-doh]

**today**   hoy  [OH-ee]

**toe**   el dedo del pie
  [ehl DEH-doh dehl pyeh]

**together, to get**   juntarse  [hoon-TAHR-seh]

**toilet**   el servicio  [ehl sehr-BEE-syoh]

**toilet paper**   el papel higiénico
  [ehl pah-PEHL ee-HYEH-nee-koh]

**tomato**   el tomate  [ehl toh-MAH-teh]

**tomorrow**   mañana  [mah-NYAH-nah]

**tomorrow afternoon**   mañana por la
  tarde
  [mah-NYAH-nah pohr lah TAHR-deh]

**tomorrow morning**   mañana por la
  mañana
  [mah-NYAH-nah pohr lah mah-NYAH-nah]

**tomorrow night**   mañana por la noche
  [mah-NYAH-nah pohr lah NOH-cheh]

**tongue**   la lengua  [lah LEHN-gwah]

**tonight**   esta noche  [EHS-tah NOH-cheh]

**too (much)**   demasiado
  [deh-mah-SYAH-doh]

**tooth**   el diente  [ehl DYEHN-teh]

**toothache**   el dolor de muelas
  [ehl doh-LOHR deh MWEH-lahs]

**top (spinning)**   el trompo
  [ehl TROHM-poh]

**tornado**   el tornado  [ehl tohr-NAH-doh]

**toward**   hacia  [AH-syah]

**towel**   la toalla  [lah toh-AH-yah]

**town**   el pueblo  [ehl PWEH-bloh]

**toy**   el juguete  [ehl hoo-GEH-teh]

**traffic**  el tránsito  [ehl TRAHN-see-toh]

**traffic accident**  el accidente de tráfico
[ehl ahk-see-DEHN-teh deh TRAH-fee-koh]

**traffic light**  el semáforo
[ehl seh-MAH-foh-roh]

**train**  el tren  [ehl trehn]

**trainer**  el entrenador / la entrenadora
[ehl ehn-treh-nah-DOHR /
lah ehn-treh-nah-DOH-rah]

**training**  el entrenamiento
[ehl ehn-treh-nah-MYEHN-toh]

**transcript**  la relación de notas
[lah rreh-lah-SYOHN deh NOH-tahs]

**transfer**  la transferencia
[lah trahns-feh-REHN-syah]

**transfer, to**  trasladar(se)
[trahs-lah-dahr(seh)]

**translate, to**  traducir (*irreg.*)
[trah-doo-SEER]

**translator**  el traductor / la traductora
[ehl trah-dook-TOHR /
lah trah-dook-TOH-rah]

**transportation**  el transporte
[ehl trahns-POHR-teh]

**trash can**  el cubo de basura
[ehl KOO-boh deh bah-SOO-rah];
el basurero  [ehl bah-soo-REH-roh]

**tricycle**  el triciclo  [ehl tree-SEE-kloh]

**truck**  el camión  [ehl kah-MYOHN]

**true**  la verdad  [lah behr-DAHD]

**try on, to**  probarse (ue)  [proh-BAHR-seh]

**tsunami**  el maremoto
[ehl mah-reh-MOH-toh]

**tuberculosis**  la tuberculosis
[lah too-behr-koo-LOH-sees]

**Tuesday**  el martes  [ehl MAHR-tehs]

**tunnel**  el túnel  [ehl TOO-nehl]

**turn in, to**  entregar  [ehn-treh-GAHR]

**twice**  dos veces  [dohs BEH-sehs]

**twisted**  torcido  [tohr-SEE-doh]

**two-way street**  la calle de doble sentido
[lah KAH-yeh deh DOH-bleh sehn-TEE-doh]

## U

**ugly**  feo  [FEH-oh]

**uncle**  el tío  [ehl TEE-oh]

**uncomfortable**  incómodo
[een-KOH-moh-doh]

**under**  debajo (de)  [deh-BAH-hoh (deh)]

**understand, to**  comprender
[kohm-prehn-DEHR];
entender (ie)  [ehn-tehn-DEHR]

**undress, to**  desvestirse (i)
[dehs-behs-TEER-seh]

**unemployment**  el desempleo
[ehl deh-sehm-PLEH-oh]

**unhappy**  descontento
[dehs-kohn-TEHN-toh];
infeliz  [een-feh-LEES]

**uniform**  el uniforme
[ehl oo-nee-FOHR-meh]

**until**  hasta  [AHS-tah]

**unwanted**  no deseado
[noh deh-seh-AH-doh]

**upstairs**  arriba  [ah-RREE-bah]

**urinal**  el orinal  [ehl oh-ree-NAHL]

## V

**vacation**  las vacaciones
[lahs bah-kah-SYOH-nehs]

**vaccinated, to get**  vacunarse
[bah-koo-NAHR-seh]

**vaccination**  la vacuna  [lah bah-KOO-nah]

**Valentine's Day**  el día de los
Enamorados  [ehl DEE-ah deh lohs
eh-nah-moh-RAH-dohs]

**vandalism**  el vandalismo
[ehl bahn-dah-LEES-moh]

**vegetables**  los vegetales
[lohs beh-heh-TAH-lehs]

**venereal disease**  la enfermedad venérea
[lah ehn-fehr-meh-DAHD beh-NEH-reh-ah]

**violence**  la violencia
[lah byoh-LEHN-syah]

**violent**  violento  [byoh-LEHN-toh]

**violet**  morado  [moh-RAH-doh]

**visual impediments**  los impedimentos
visuales  [lohs eem-peh-dee-MEHN-tohs
bee-SWAH-lehs]

**vitamin**  la vitamina
[lah bee-tah-MEE-nah]

**voice**  la voz  [lah bohs]

**volume (book)**  el tomo  [ehl TOH-moh]

**volunteer**  el voluntario / la voluntaria
[ehl boh-loon-TAH-ryoh /
lah boh-loon-TAH-ryah]

**vomit, to**  vomitar  [boh-mee-TAHR]

## W

**waist**  la cintura  [lah seen-TOO-rah]

**wait for, to**  esperar  [ehs-peh-RAHR]

**wake up, to**  despertarse (ie)
[dehs-pehr-TAHR-seh]

**walk, to**  caminar  [kah-mee-NAHR]

**wall**   la pared   [lah pah-REHD]

**wallet**   la billetera   [lah bee-yeh-TEH-rah];
la cartera   [lah kahr-TEH-rah]

**want, to**   querer (ie) (*irreg.*)   [keh-REHR]

**warning**   la advertencia
[lah ahd-behr-TEHN-syah]

**wash, to**   lavar   [lah-BAHR]

**wash (a part of one's body), to**   lavarse
(+ *part of body*)   [lah-BAHR-seh]

**wash up, to**   lavarse   [lah-BAHR-seh]

**wastepaper basket**   la papelera
[lah pah-peh-LEH-rah]

**watch, to**   mirar   [mee-RAHR]

**water**   el agua   [ehl AH-gwah]

**water fountain**   la fuente de agua potable
[lah FWEHN-teh deh AH-gwah
poh-TAH-bleh]

**watermelon**   la sandía   [lah sahn-DEE-ah]

**weak**   débil   [DEH-beel]

**wear, to**   llevar   [yeh-BAHR]

**weather**   el tiempo   [ehl TYEHM-poh]

**weather forecast**   el pronóstico del
tiempo
[ehl proh-NOHS-tee-koh dehl TYEHM-poh]

**Wednesday**   el miércoles
[ehl MYEHR-koh-lehs]

**week**   la semana   [lah seh-MAH-nah]

**weight**   el peso   [ehl PEH-soh]

**welfare**   la asistencia social
[lah ah-sees-TEHN-syah soh-SYAHL]

**well**   bien   [byehn]

**what**   qué   [keh]

**wheelchair**   la silla de ruedas
[lah SEE-yah deh RRWEH-dahs]

**when**   cuándo   [KWAHN-doh]

**where**   dónde   [DOHN-deh]

**where (to)**   adónde   [ah-DOHN-deh]

**which**   cuál   [kwahl]

**white**   blanco   [BLAHN-koh]

**who**   quién/quiénes   [kyehn/KYEH-nehs]

**whooping cough**   la tos ferina
[lah tohs feh-REE-nah]

**whose**   de quién / de quiénes
[deh kyehn / deh KYEH-nehs]

**why**   por qué   [pohr keh]

**wife**   la esposa   [lah ehs-POH-sah]

**wind**   el viento   [ehl BYEHN-toh]

**window**   la ventana   [lah behn-TAH-nah]

**window shade/blind**   la persiana
[lah pehr-SYAH-nah]

**winter**   el invierno   [ehl een-BYEHR-noh]

**wish, to**   desear   [deh-seh-AHR]

**with me**   conmigo   [kohn-MEE-goh]

**with what**   con qué   [kohn keh]

**with whom**   con quién / con quiénes
[kohn kyehn / kohn KYEH-nehs]

**with you** (*familiar*)   contigo
[kohn-TEE-goh]

**woman**   la mujer   [lah moo-HEHR]

**wool**   la lana   [lah LAH-nah]

**word**   la palabra   [lah pah-LAH-brah]

**work**   el trabajo   [ehl trah-BAH-hoh]

**worried**   preocupado
[preh-oh-koo-PAH-doh]

**worry, to**   preocuparse
[preh-oh-koo-PAHR-seh]

**worse**   peor   [peh-OHR]

**wound (cut)**   la herida   [lah eh-REE-dah]

**wound, to**   herir (ie)   [eh-REER]

**write, to**   escribir   [ehs-kree-BEER]

**write in longhand, to**   escribir a mano
[ehs-kree-BEER ah MAH-noh];
escribir en cursiva
[ehs-kree-BEER ehn koor-SEE-bah]

**writer**   el escritor / la escritora
[ehl ehs-kree-TOHR /
lah ehs-kree-TOH-rah]

## Y

**year**   el año   [ehl AH-nyoh]

**yell, to**   gritar   [gree-TAHR]

**yellow**   amarillo   [ah-mah-REE-yoh]

**yesterday**   ayer   [ah-YEHR]

**yesterday afternoon**   ayer por la tarde
[ah-YEHR pohr lah TAHR-deh]

**yesterday morning**   ayer por la mañana
[ah-YEHR pohr lah mah-NYAH-nah]

**yogurt**   el yogurt   [ehl yoh-GOOR]

**your** (*familiar*)   tu   [too]

**your** (*formal*)   su   [soo]